NEW EXILES

SOUL AWAKENING

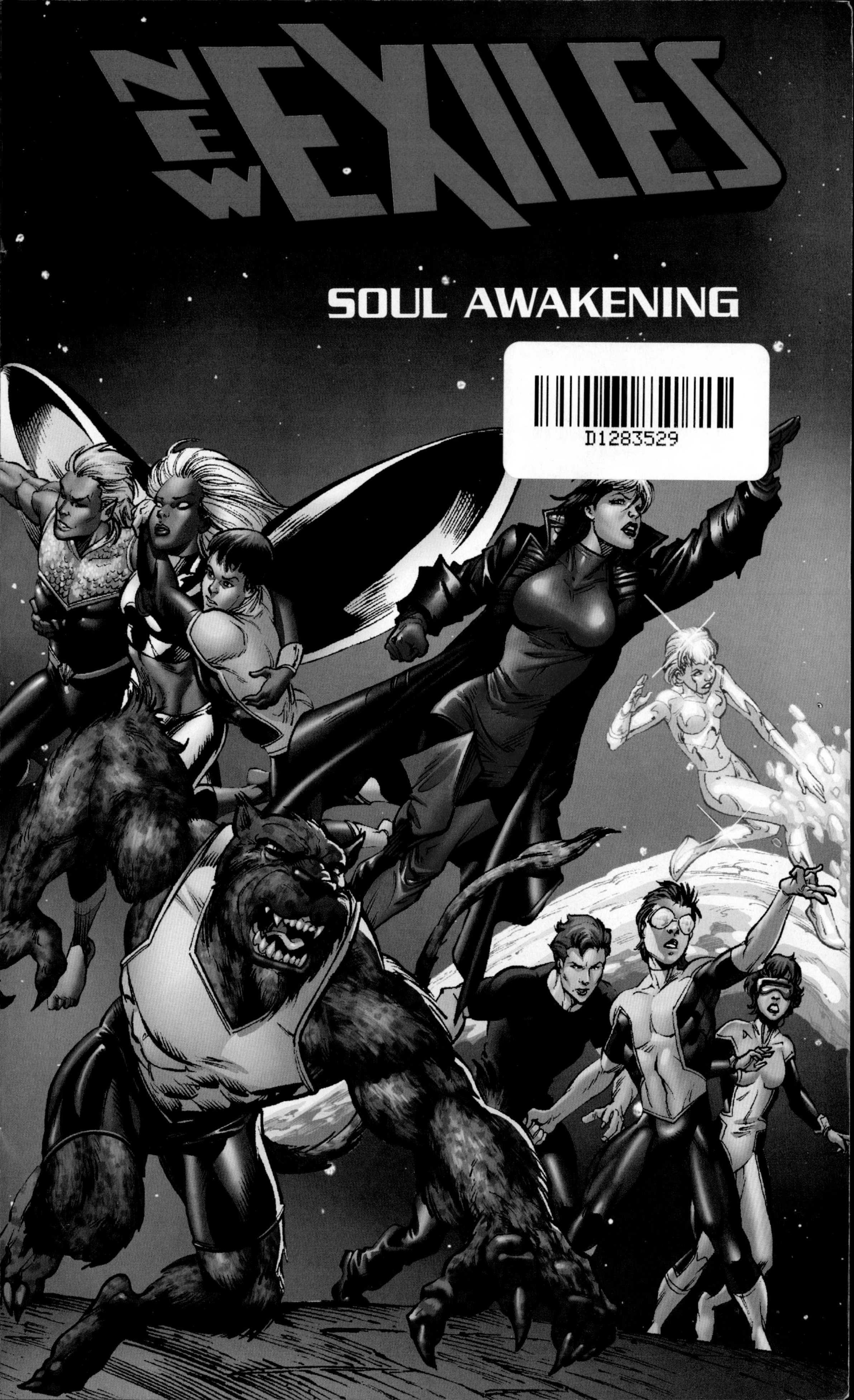

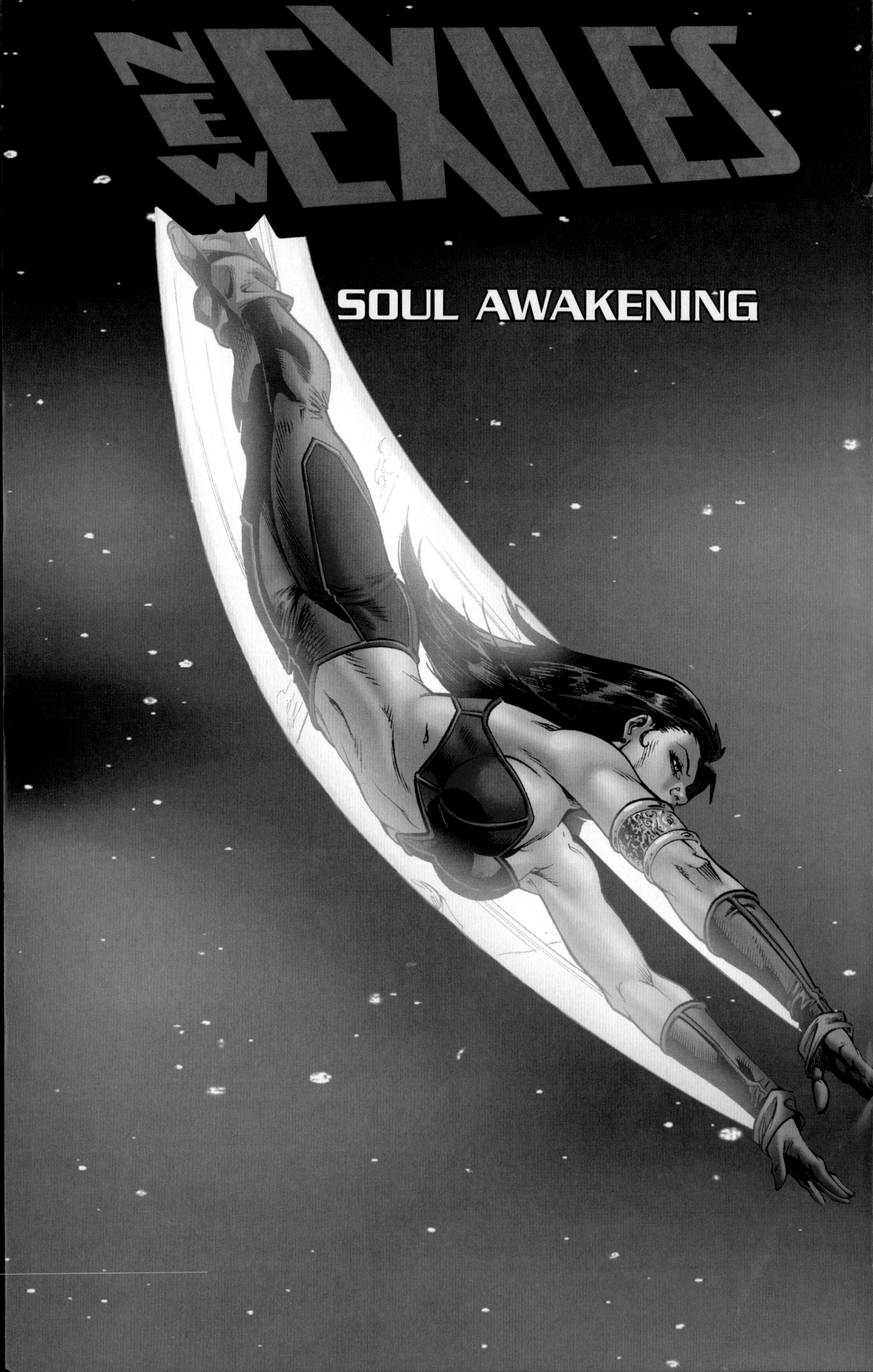
NEW EXILES
SOUL AWAKENING

CHRIS CLAREMONT

TOM GRUMMETT &
PACO DIAZ LUQUE (ISSUES #11-12)

INKERS
TOM GRUMMETT,
VICENTE CIFUENTES &
NORBERTO FERNANDEZ

COLORIST
WILFREDO QUINTANA

LETTERERS
TOM ORZECHOWSKI &
SIMON BOWLAND (ISSUE #11)

COVERS
MICHAEL GOLDEN; ALAN DAVIS,
MARK FARMER & GURU eFX;
AND ALEX GARNER

ASSISTANT EDITOR
JORDAN D. WHITE

EDITOR
MARK PANICCIA

SPECIAL THANKS TO STEPHEN MARCHAND

COLLECTION CREDITS

COLLECTION EDITOR
CORY LEVINE

ASSISTANT EDITOR
JOHN DENNING

EDITORIAL ASSISTANT
ALEX STARBUCK

EDITORS, SPECIAL PROJECTS
JENNIFER GRÜNWALD &
MARK D. BEAZLEY

SENIOR EDITOR, SPECIAL PROJECTS
JEFF YOUNGQUIST

SENIOR VICE PRESIDENT OF SALES
DAVID GABRIEL

PRODUCTION:
JERRON QUALITY COLOR

EDITOR IN CHIEF
JOE QUESADA

PUBLISHER
DAN BUCKLEY

Some heroes protect cities. Some, countries. Some, worlds. But who's looking out for the entire Omniverse? One band of heroes has left the lives and worlds of their births behind, each for their own reasons, and shouldered the weight of all possible universes. From their base in the Crystal Palace, they see the biggest possible picture, and go wherever they are needed. They are...THE NEW EXILES!

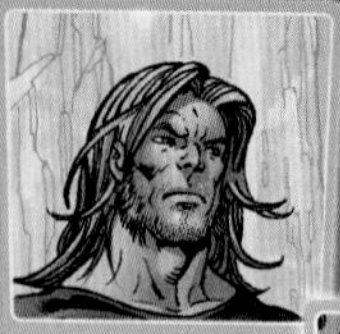

SABRETOOTH
Earth-295

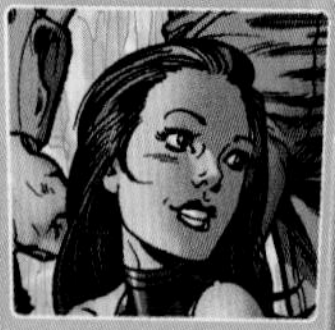

CAT
Unknown Earth

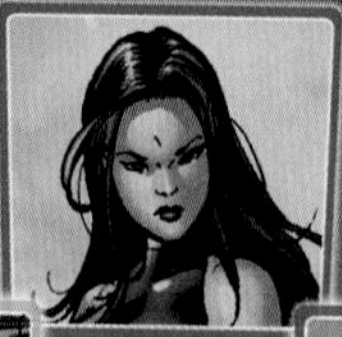

PSYLOCKE
Earth-616

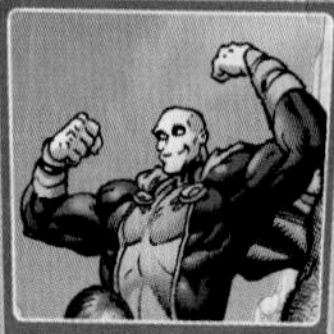

MORPH
Earth-1081

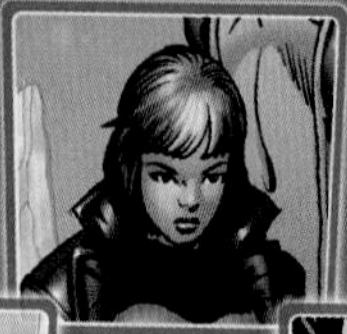

ROGUE
Earth-1009

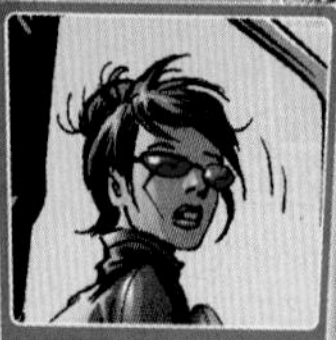

SAGE
Earth-616

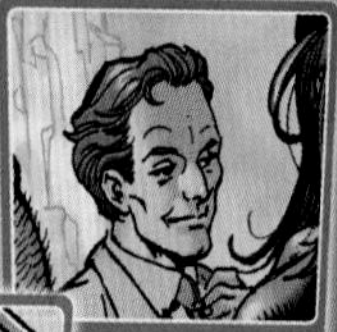

MYSTIQ
Earth-797

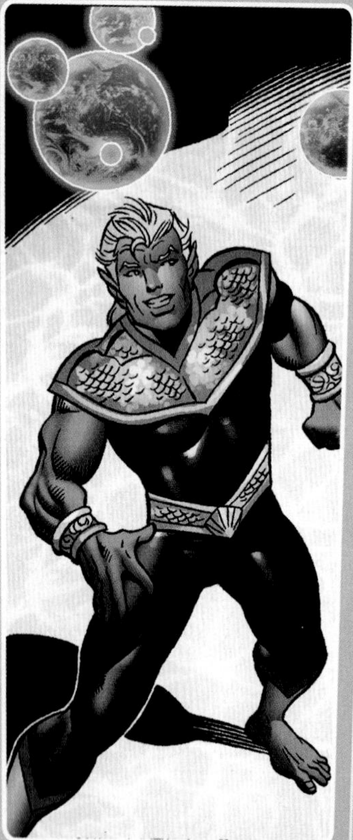

The New Exiles have finally all returned to the Crystal Palace after being split between two alternate worlds.

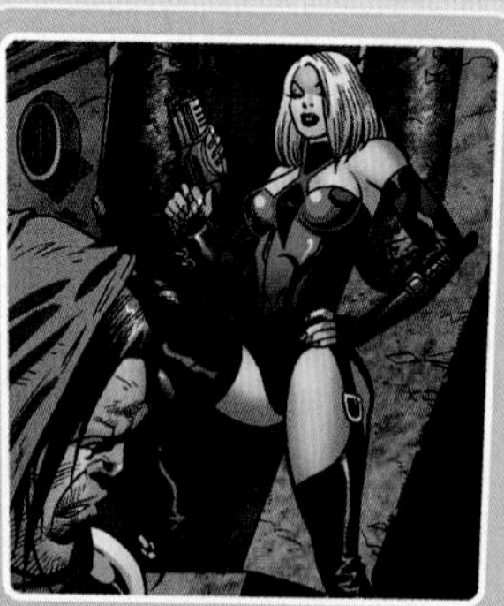

Meanwhile, another Omniversal traveler, this one a Sue Storm who was head of her dimension's Hydra, has been dimension-hopping, recruiting for a team of her own.

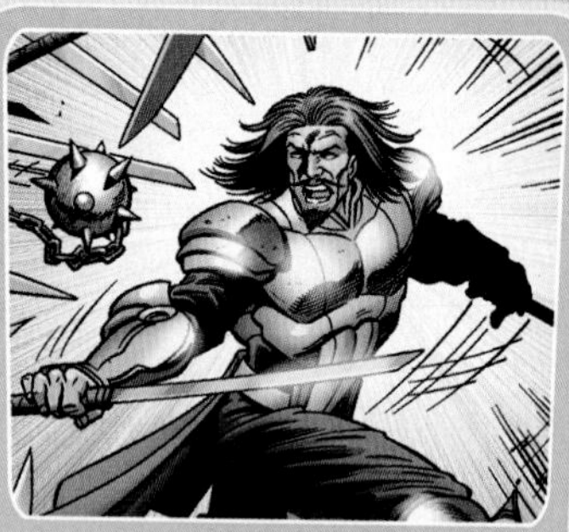

Among her allies is man called Slaymaster. Psylocke had a history with his Earth-616 counterpart, but this alternate version has taken their rivalry personal.

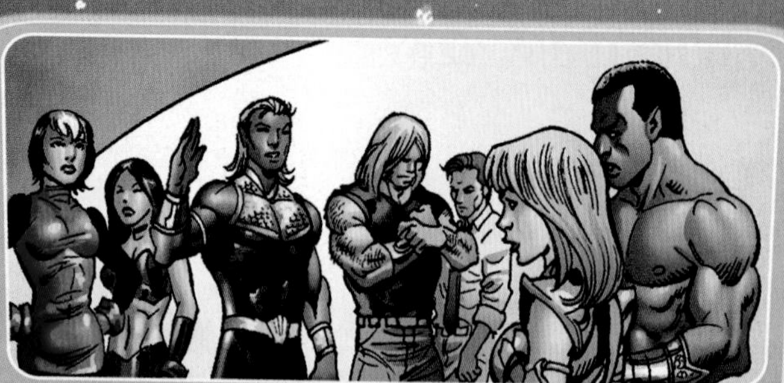

Now, joined by their newest member, Gambit (in his world, the son of Namor and another Sue Storm), the Exiles continue their goal of protecting the Omniverse, going on their second official mission as a team.

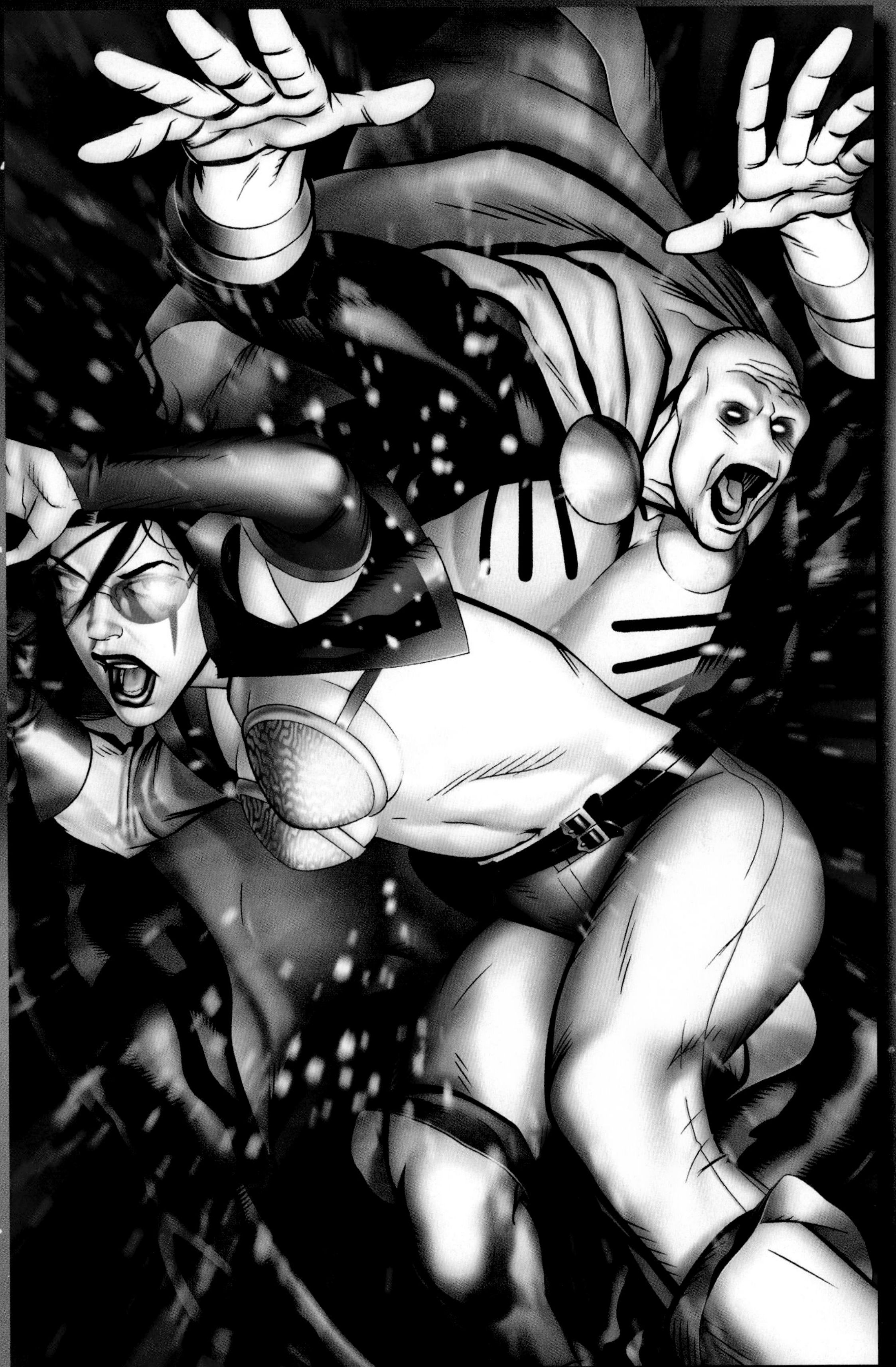

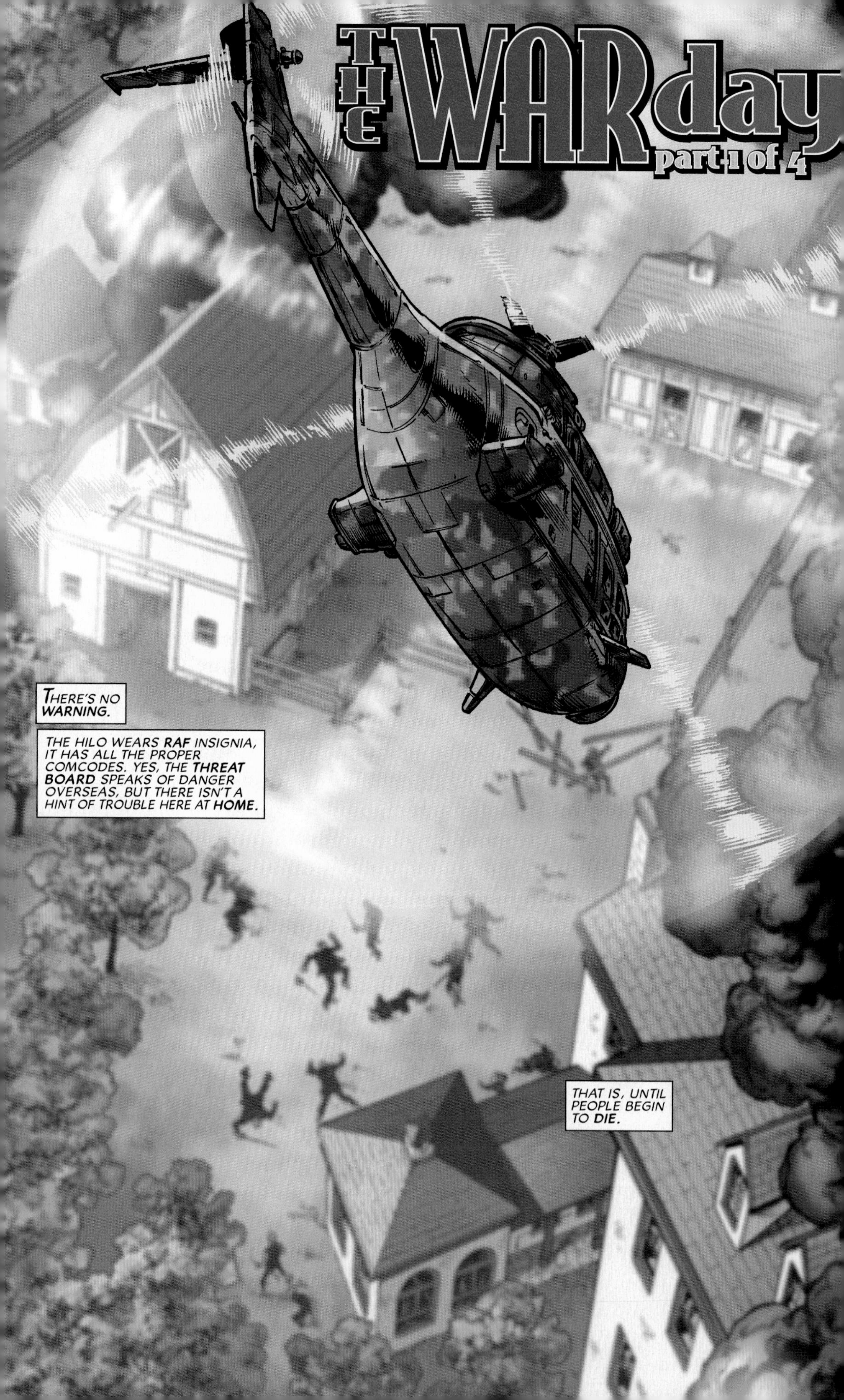
THE WARday
part 1 of 4
THERE'S NO WARNING.
THE HILO WEARS RAF INSIGNIA, IT HAS ALL THE PROPER COMCODES. YES, THE THREAT BOARD SPEAKS OF DANGER OVERSEAS, BUT THERE ISN'T A HINT OF TROUBLE HERE AT HOME.
THAT IS, UNTIL PEOPLE BEGIN TO DIE.

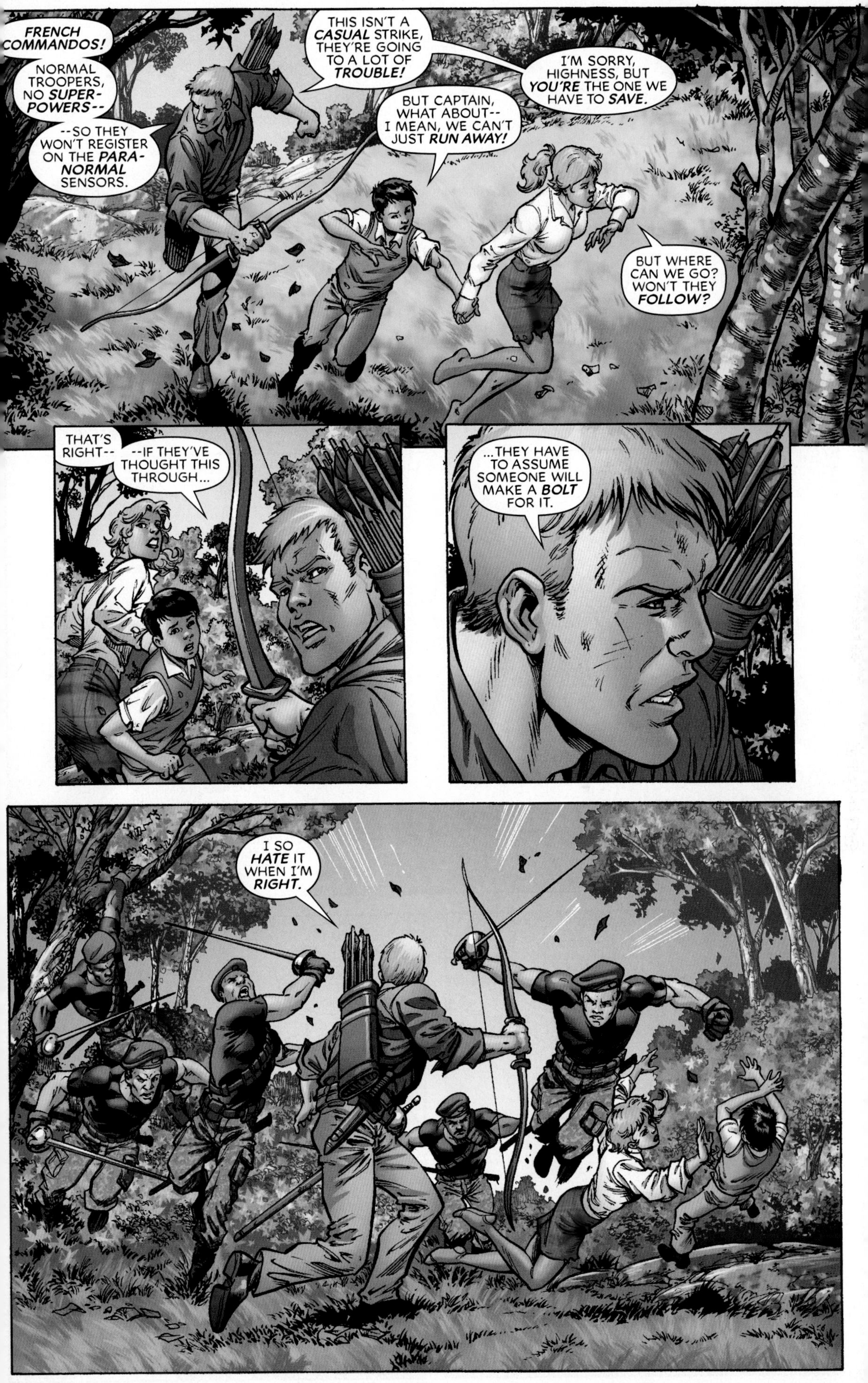
FRENCH COMMANDOS!
NORMAL TROOPERS, NO SUPER-POWERS--
--SO THEY WON'T REGISTER ON THE PARA-NORMAL SENSORS.
THIS ISN'T A CASUAL STRIKE, THEY'RE GOING TO A LOT OF TROUBLE!
I'M SORRY, HIGHNESS, BUT YOU'RE THE ONE WE HAVE TO SAVE.
BUT CAPTAIN, WHAT ABOUT-- I MEAN, WE CAN'T JUST RUN AWAY!
BUT WHERE CAN WE GO? WON'T THEY FOLLOW?
THAT'S RIGHT--
--IF THEY'VE THOUGHT THIS THROUGH...
...THEY HAVE TO ASSUME SOMEONE WILL MAKE A BOLT FOR IT.
I SO HATE IT WHEN I'M RIGHT.

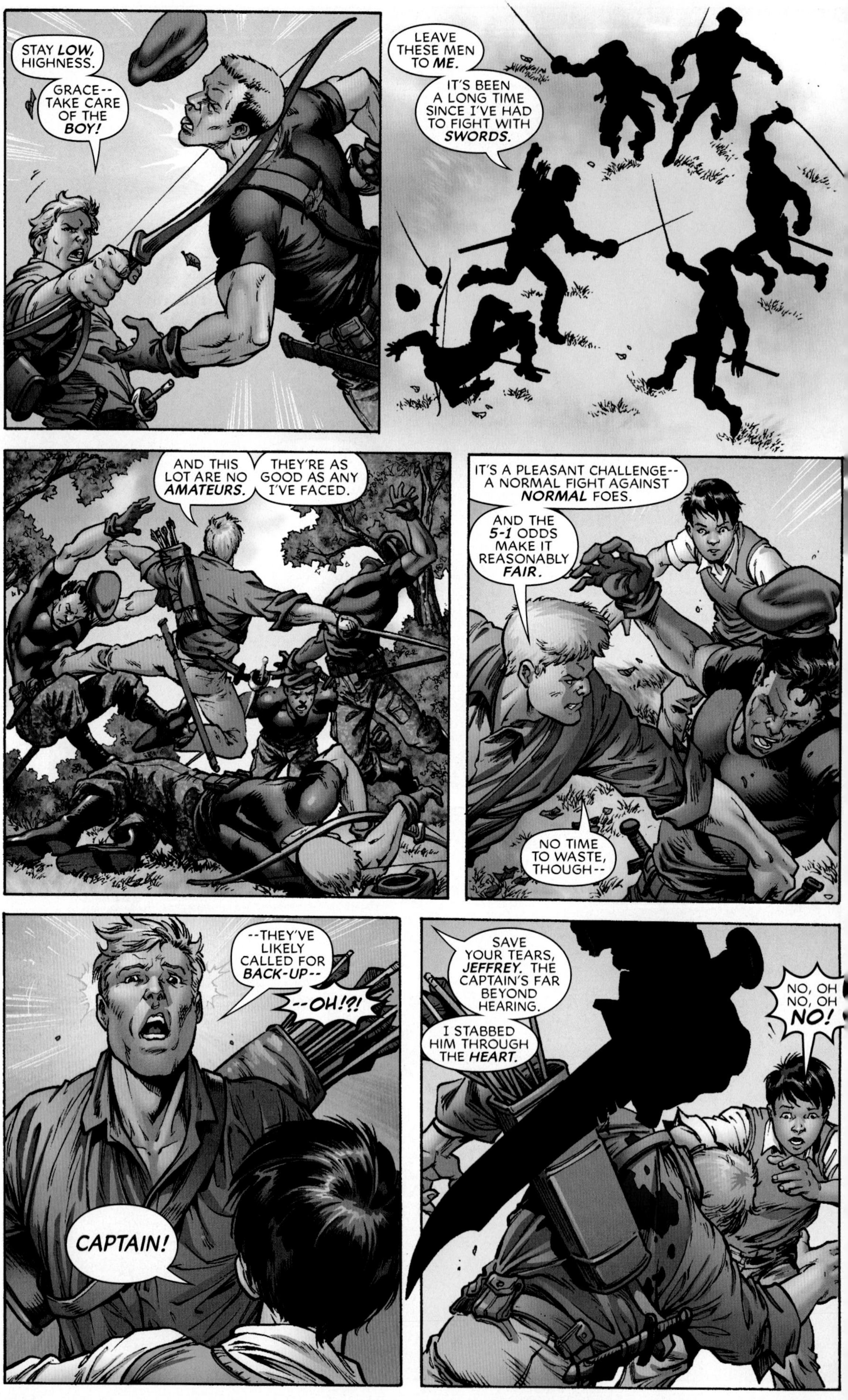

STAY LOW, HIGHNESS.
GRACE--TAKE CARE OF THE BOY!
LEAVE THESE MEN TO ME.
IT'S BEEN A LONG TIME SINCE I'VE HAD TO FIGHT WITH SWORDS.
AND THIS LOT ARE NO AMATEURS.
THEY'RE AS GOOD AS ANY I'VE FACED.
IT'S A PLEASANT CHALLENGE--A NORMAL FIGHT AGAINST NORMAL FOES.
AND THE 5-1 ODDS MAKE IT REASONABLY FAIR.
NO TIME TO WASTE, THOUGH--
--THEY'VE LIKELY CALLED FOR BACK-UP--
--OH!?!
CAPTAIN!
SAVE YOUR TEARS, JEFFREY. THE CAPTAIN'S FAR BEYOND HEARING.
I STABBED HIM THROUGH THE HEART.
NO, OH NO, OH NO!

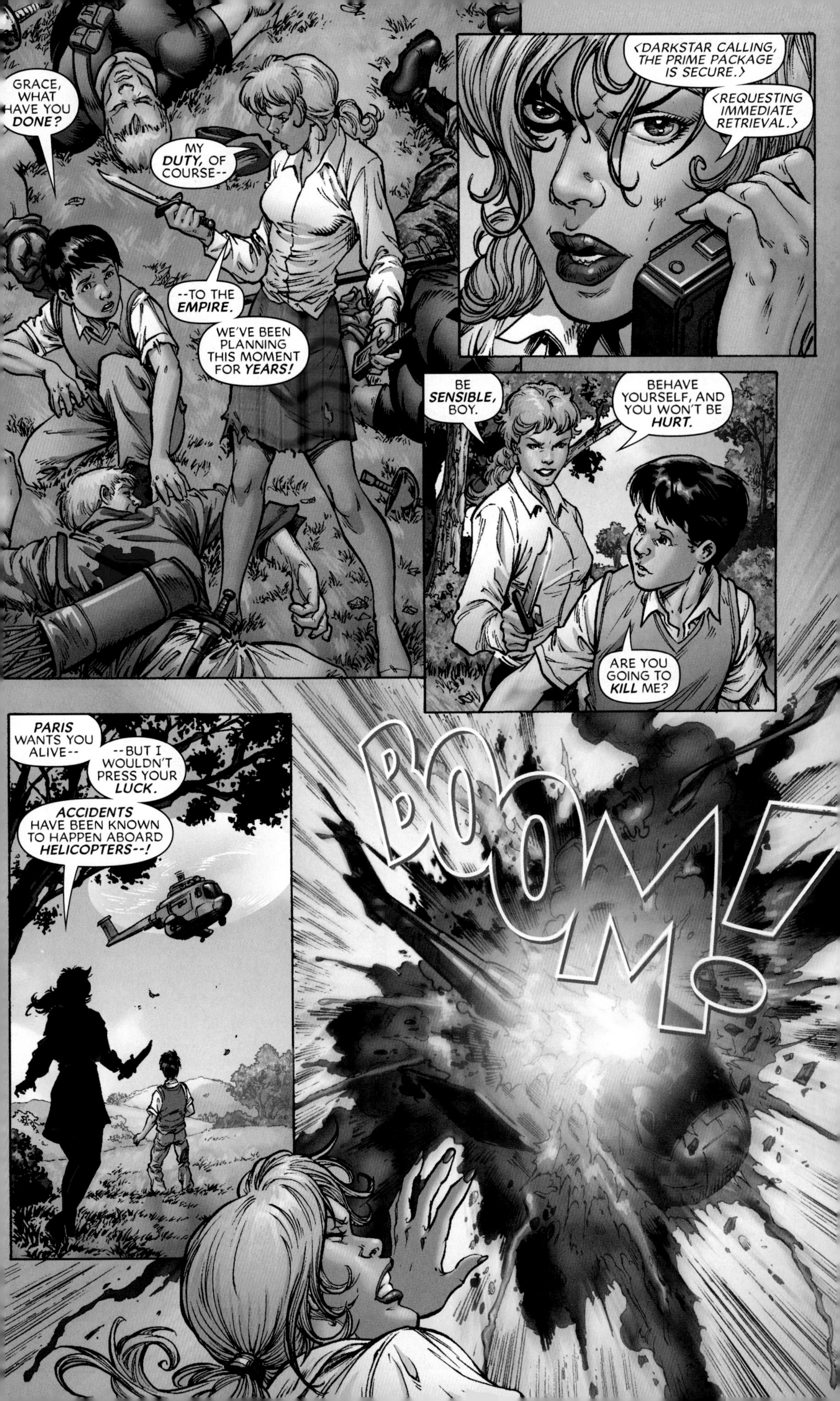
GRACE, WHAT HAVE YOU DONE?
MY DUTY, OF COURSE--
--TO THE EMPIRE.
WE'VE BEEN PLANNING THIS MOMENT FOR YEARS!
<DARKSTAR CALLING, THE PRIME PACKAGE IS SECURE.>
<REQUESTING IMMEDIATE RETRIEVAL.>
BE SENSIBLE, BOY.
BEHAVE YOURSELF, AND YOU WON'T BE HURT.
ARE YOU GOING TO KILL ME?
PARIS WANTS YOU ALIVE--
--BUT I WOULDN'T PRESS YOUR LUCK.
ACCIDENTS HAVE BEEN KNOWN TO HAPPEN ABOARD HELICOPTERS--!
BOOOM!

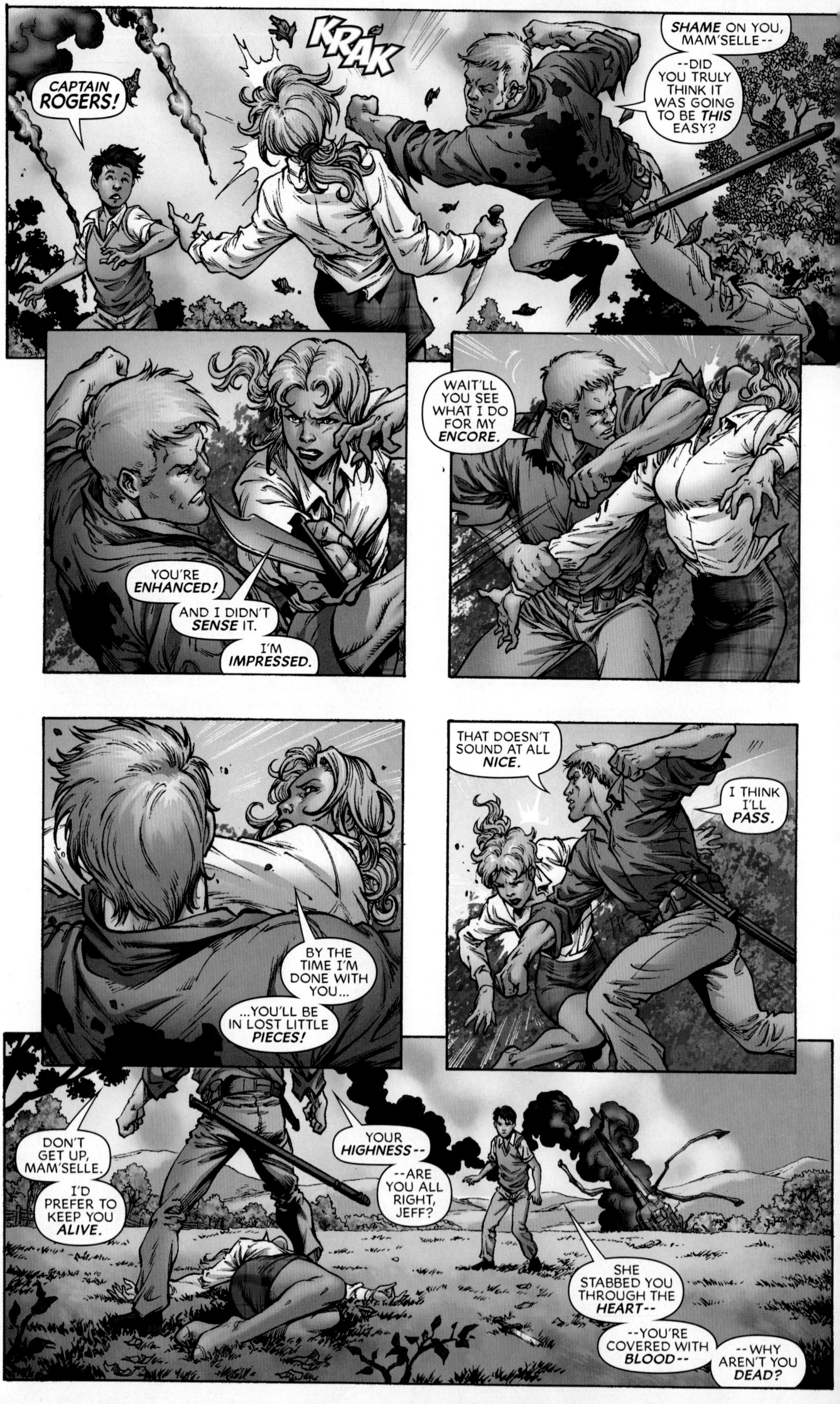
CAPTAIN ROGERS!
KRAK
SHAME ON YOU, MAM'SELLE--
--DID YOU TRULY THINK IT WAS GOING TO BE THIS EASY?
YOU'RE ENHANCED!
AND I DIDN'T SENSE IT.
I'M IMPRESSED.
WAIT'LL YOU SEE WHAT I DO FOR MY ENCORE.
BY THE TIME I'M DONE WITH YOU...
...YOU'LL BE IN LOST LITTLE PIECES!
THAT DOESN'T SOUND AT ALL NICE.
I THINK I'LL PASS.
DON'T GET UP, MAM'SELLE.
I'D PREFER TO KEEP YOU ALIVE.
YOUR HIGHNESS--
--ARE YOU ALL RIGHT, JEFF?
SHE STABBED YOU THROUGH THE HEART--
--YOU'RE COVERED WITH BLOOD--
--WHY AREN'T YOU DEAD?

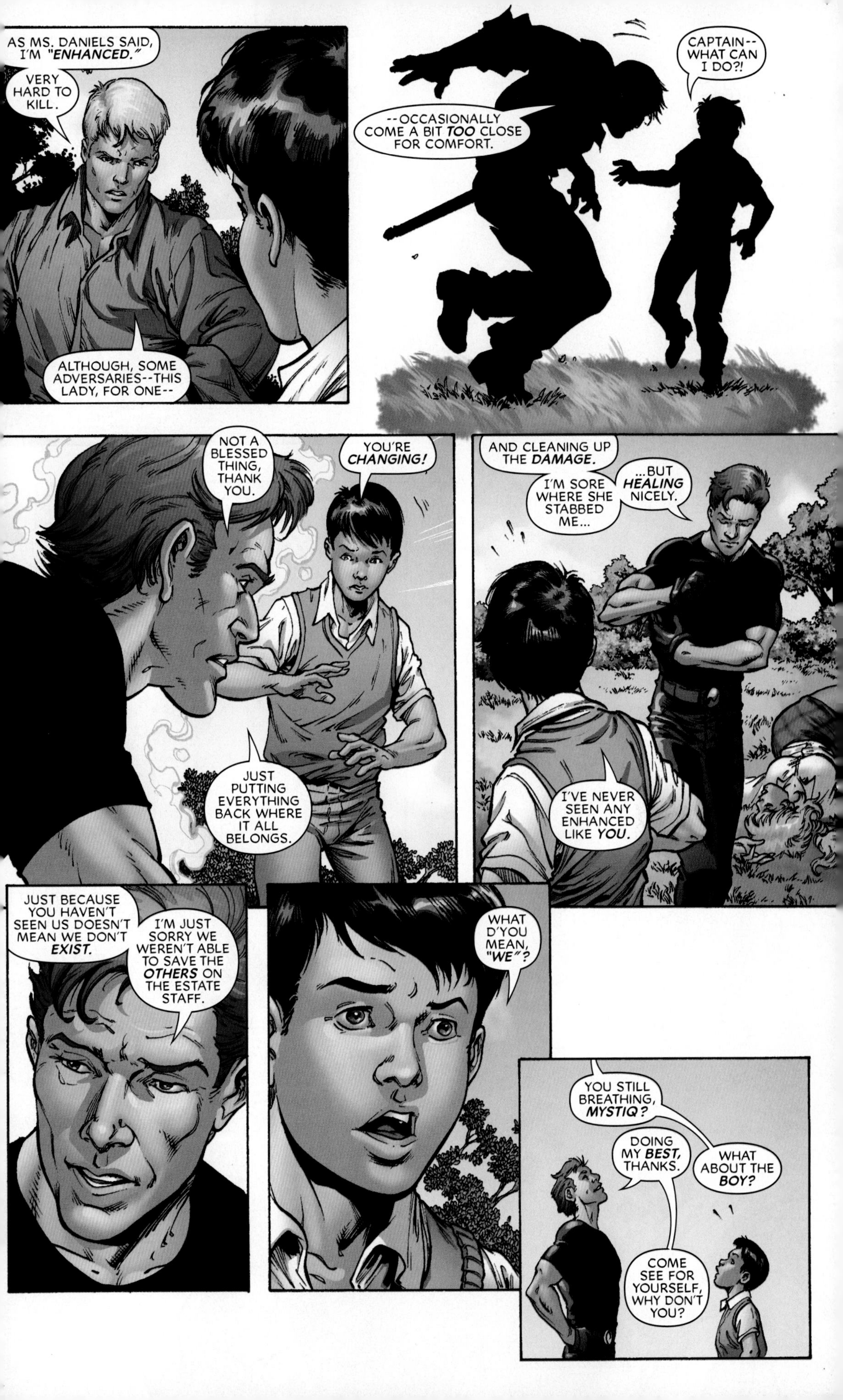

AS MS. DANIELS SAID, I'M "ENHANCED."
VERY HARD TO KILL.
ALTHOUGH, SOME ADVERSARIES--THIS LADY, FOR ONE--
--OCCASIONALLY COME A BIT TOO CLOSE FOR COMFORT.
CAPTAIN-- WHAT CAN I DO?!
NOT A BLESSED THING, THANK YOU.
YOU'RE CHANGING!
JUST PUTTING EVERYTHING BACK WHERE IT ALL BELONGS.
AND CLEANING UP THE DAMAGE.
I'M SORE WHERE SHE STABBED ME...
...BUT HEALING NICELY.
I'VE NEVER SEEN ANY ENHANCED LIKE YOU.
JUST BECAUSE YOU HAVEN'T SEEN US DOESN'T MEAN WE DON'T EXIST.
I'M JUST SORRY WE WEREN'T ABLE TO SAVE THE OTHERS ON THE ESTATE STAFF.
WHAT D'YOU MEAN, "WE"?
YOU STILL BREATHING, MYSTIQ?
DOING MY BEST, THANKS.
WHAT ABOUT THE BOY?
COME SEE FOR YOURSELF, WHY DON'T YOU?

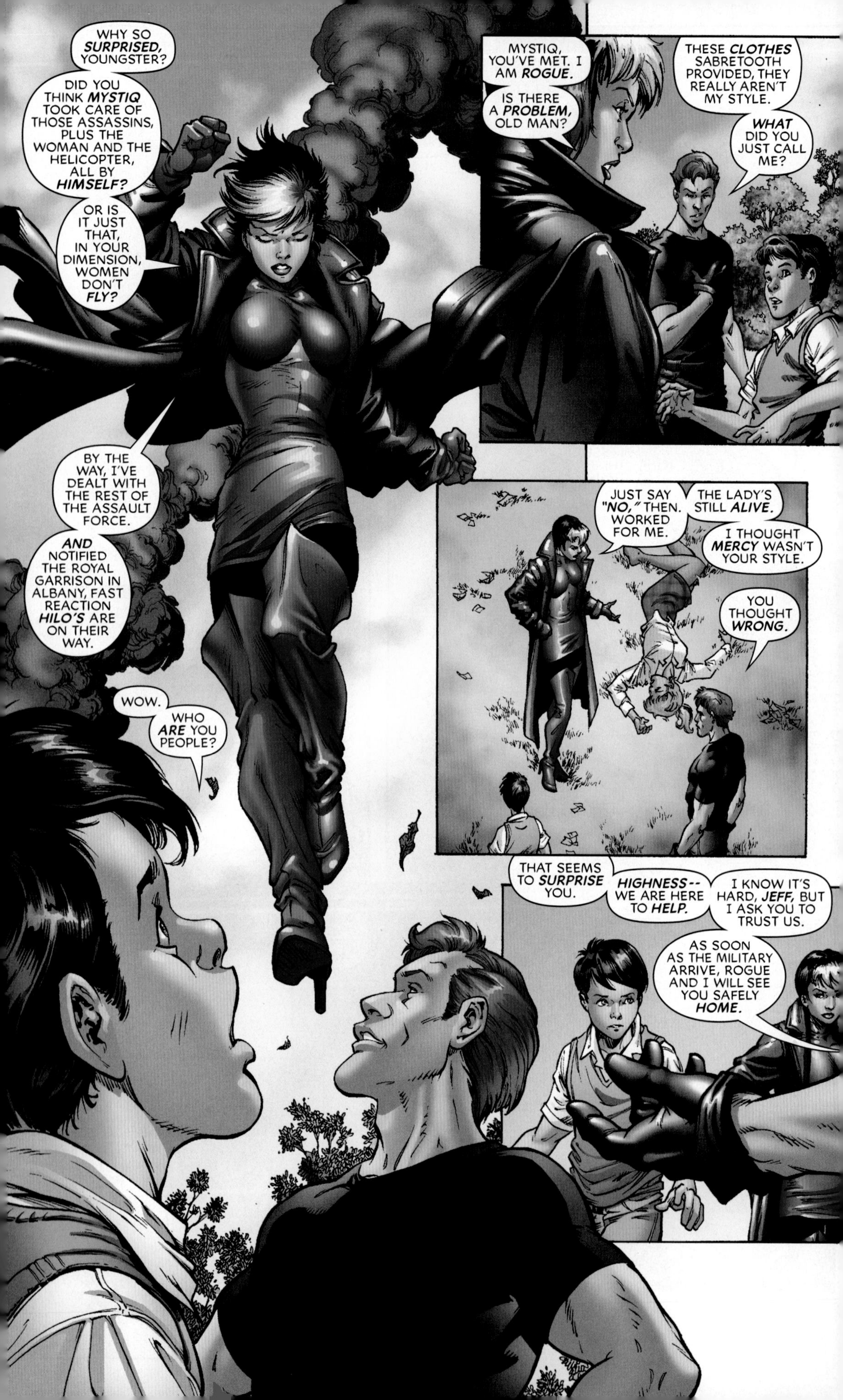
WHY SO SURPRISED, YOUNGSTER?
DID YOU THINK MYSTIQ TOOK CARE OF THOSE ASSASSINS, PLUS THE WOMAN AND THE HELICOPTER, ALL BY HIMSELF?
OR IS IT JUST THAT, IN YOUR DIMENSION, WOMEN DON'T FLY?
BY THE WAY, I'VE DEALT WITH THE REST OF THE ASSAULT FORCE.
AND NOTIFIED THE ROYAL GARRISON IN ALBANY, FAST REACTION HILO'S ARE ON THEIR WAY.
WOW.
WHO ARE YOU PEOPLE?
MYSTIQ, YOU'VE MET. I AM ROGUE.
IS THERE A PROBLEM, OLD MAN?
THESE CLOTHES SABRETOOTH PROVIDED, THEY REALLY AREN'T MY STYLE.
WHAT DID YOU JUST CALL ME?
JUST SAY "NO," THEN. WORKED FOR ME.
THE LADY'S STILL ALIVE.
I THOUGHT MERCY WASN'T YOUR STYLE.
YOU THOUGHT WRONG.
THAT SEEMS TO SURPRISE YOU.
HIGHNESS-- WE ARE HERE TO HELP.
I KNOW IT'S HARD, JEFF, BUT I ASK YOU TO TRUST US.
AS SOON AS THE MILITARY ARRIVE, ROGUE AND I WILL SEE YOU SAFELY HOME.

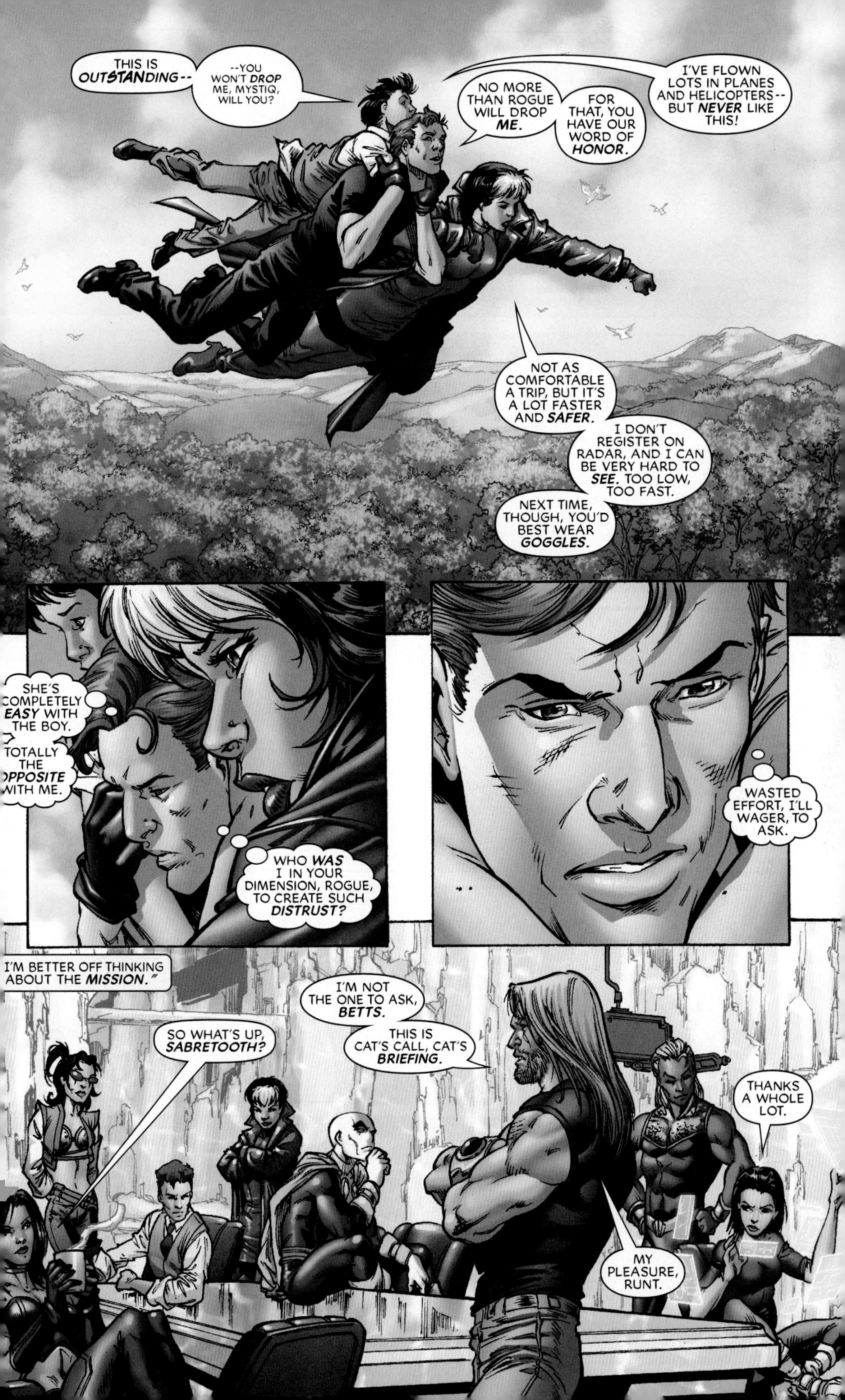
THIS IS OUTSTANDING--
--YOU WON'T DROP ME, MYSTIQ, WILL YOU?
NO MORE THAN ROGUE WILL DROP ME.
FOR THAT, YOU HAVE OUR WORD OF HONOR.
I'VE FLOWN LOTS IN PLANES AND HELICOPTERS--BUT NEVER LIKE THIS!
NOT AS COMFORTABLE A TRIP, BUT IT'S A LOT FASTER AND SAFER.
I DON'T REGISTER ON RADAR, AND I CAN BE VERY HARD TO SEE. TOO LOW, TOO FAST.
NEXT TIME, THOUGH, YOU'D BEST WEAR GOGGLES.
SHE'S COMPLETELY EASY WITH THE BOY.
TOTALLY THE OPPOSITE WITH ME.
WHO WAS I IN YOUR DIMENSION, ROGUE, TO CREATE SUCH DISTRUST?
WASTED EFFORT, I'LL WAGER, TO ASK.
I'M BETTER OFF THINKING ABOUT THE MISSION."
SO WHAT'S UP, SABRETOOTH?
I'M NOT THE ONE TO ASK, BETTS.
THIS IS CAT'S CALL, CAT'S BRIEFING.
THANKS A WHOLE LOT.
MY PLEASURE, RUNT.

SO START **TALKIN'.**

OKAY--SO I'VE BEEN TRYING TO COLLATE ALL THE DATA IN THE PALACE **MAINFRAMES.**

IS THAT EVEN **POSSIBLE,** CAT? I MEAN, AREN'T YOU DEALING WITH FUNCTIONAL **INFINITY?**

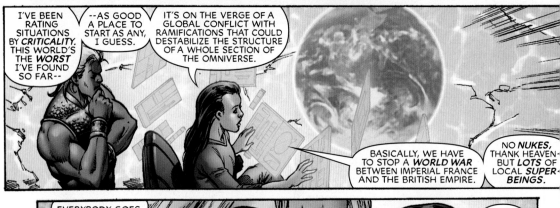

WELL, **DUH!**

BUT Y'KNOW, **MORPH,** WE GOTTA START SOMEWHERE.

THING IS, EVEN AT THE **"BEGINNER"** LEVEL I'VE ESTABLISHED, I'M PICKING UP EDDIES AND STRAINS OF RAY **CHAOS** SCATTERING THROUGH EXISTENCE.

GUYS, THIS IS SERIOUS **TROUBLE.**

I'VE BEEN RATING SITUATIONS BY **CRITICALITY.** THIS WORLD'S THE **WORST** I'VE FOUND SO FAR--

--AS GOOD A PLACE TO START AS ANY, I GUESS.

IT'S ON THE VERGE OF A **GLOBAL** CONFLICT WITH RAMIFICATIONS THAT COULD DESTABILIZE THE STRUCTURE OF A WHOLE SECTION OF THE OMNIVERSE.

BASICALLY, WE HAVE TO STOP A **WORLD WAR** BETWEEN IMPERIAL FRANCE AND THE BRITISH EMPIRE.

NO **NUKES,** THANK HEAVEN-- BUT **LOTS** OF LOCAL **SUPER-BEINGS.**

EVERYBODY GOES, **BETSY** LEADS.

CAT AN' I STAY BEHIND TO MIND THE STORE.

WHAT?!

YOU GOT A **PROBLEM?**

YOU JUST CAUGHT ME BY SURPRISE, IS ALL.

THAT WAS THE IDEA.

SO PROVE TO ME HOW **BRILLIANT** I AM AND SAVE THAT WORLD.

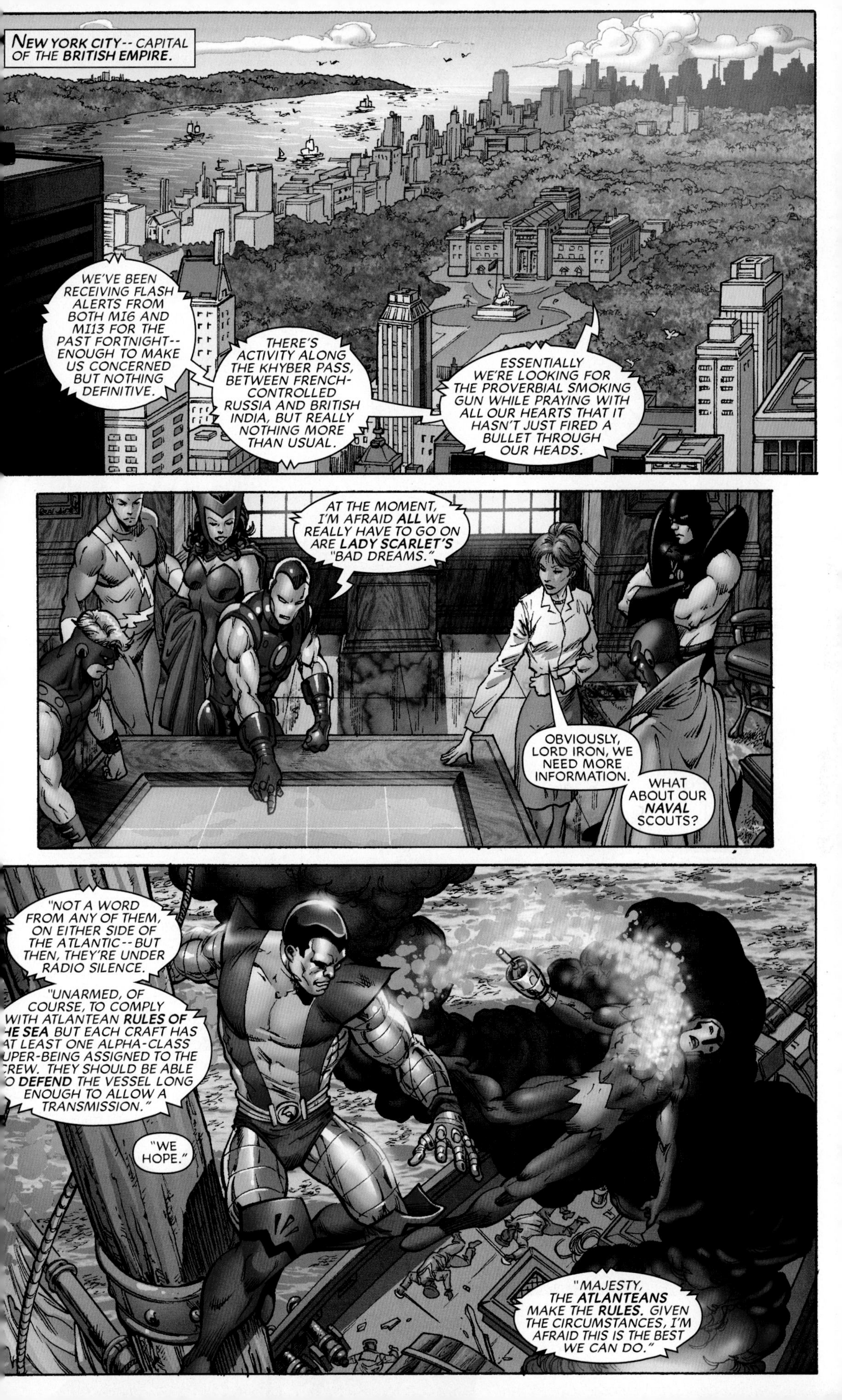
NEW YORK CITY-- CAPITAL OF THE BRITISH EMPIRE.
WE'VE BEEN RECEIVING FLASH ALERTS FROM BOTH MI6 AND MI13 FOR THE PAST FORTNIGHT-- ENOUGH TO MAKE US CONCERNED BUT NOTHING DEFINITIVE.
THERE'S ACTIVITY ALONG THE KHYBER PASS, BETWEEN FRENCH-CONTROLLED RUSSIA AND BRITISH INDIA, BUT REALLY NOTHING MORE THAN USUAL.
ESSENTIALLY WE'RE LOOKING FOR THE PROVERBIAL SMOKING GUN WHILE PRAYING WITH ALL OUR HEARTS THAT IT HASN'T JUST FIRED A BULLET THROUGH OUR HEADS.
AT THE MOMENT, I'M AFRAID ALL WE REALLY HAVE TO GO ON ARE LADY SCARLET'S "BAD DREAMS."
OBVIOUSLY, LORD IRON, WE NEED MORE INFORMATION.
WHAT ABOUT OUR NAVAL SCOUTS?
"NOT A WORD FROM ANY OF THEM, ON EITHER SIDE OF THE ATLANTIC-- BUT THEN, THEY'RE UNDER RADIO SILENCE.
"UNARMED, OF COURSE, TO COMPLY WITH ATLANTEAN RULES OF THE SEA BUT EACH CRAFT HAS AT LEAST ONE ALPHA-CLASS SUPER-BEING ASSIGNED TO THE CREW. THEY SHOULD BE ABLE TO DEFEND THE VESSEL LONG ENOUGH TO ALLOW A TRANSMISSION."
"WE HOPE."
"MAJESTY, THE ATLANTEANS MAKE THE RULES. GIVEN THE CIRCUMSTANCES, I'M AFRAID THIS IS THE BEST WE CAN DO."

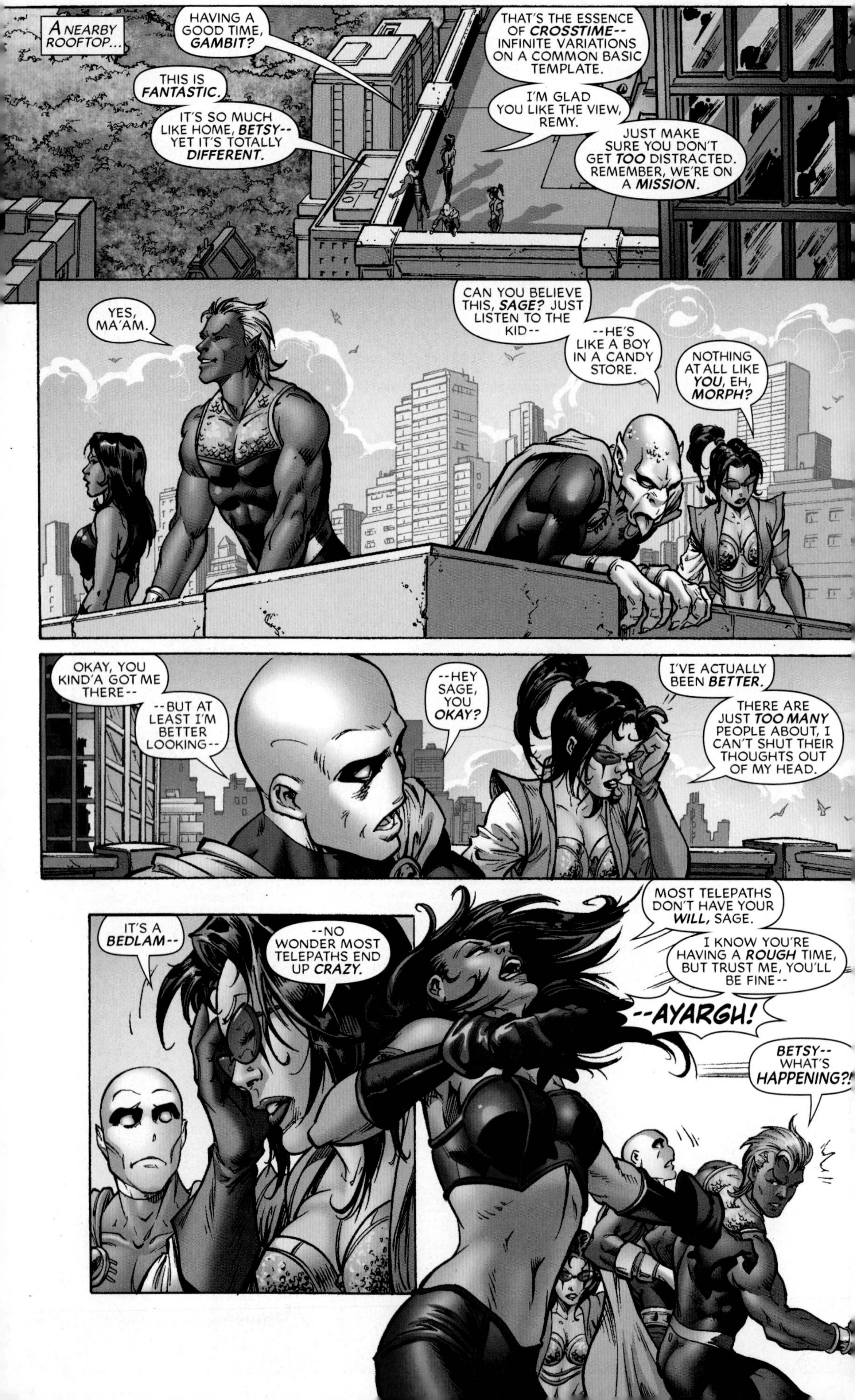
A NEARBY ROOFTOP...
HAVING A GOOD TIME, GAMBIT?
THIS IS FANTASTIC.
IT'S SO MUCH LIKE HOME, BETSY-- YET IT'S TOTALLY DIFFERENT.
THAT'S THE ESSENCE OF CROSSTIME-- INFINITE VARIATIONS ON A COMMON BASIC TEMPLATE.
I'M GLAD YOU LIKE THE VIEW, REMY.
JUST MAKE SURE YOU DON'T GET TOO DISTRACTED. REMEMBER, WE'RE ON A MISSION.
YES, MA'AM.
CAN YOU BELIEVE THIS, SAGE? JUST LISTEN TO THE KID--
--HE'S LIKE A BOY IN A CANDY STORE.
NOTHING AT ALL LIKE YOU, EH, MORPH?
OKAY, YOU KIND'A GOT ME THERE--
--BUT AT LEAST I'M BETTER LOOKING--
--HEY SAGE, YOU OKAY?
I'VE ACTUALLY BEEN BETTER.
THERE ARE JUST TOO MANY PEOPLE ABOUT, I CAN'T SHUT THEIR THOUGHTS OUT OF MY HEAD.
IT'S A BEDLAM--
--NO WONDER MOST TELEPATHS END UP CRAZY.
MOST TELEPATHS DON'T HAVE YOUR WILL, SAGE.
I KNOW YOU'RE HAVING A ROUGH TIME, BUT TRUST ME, YOU'LL BE FINE--
--AYARGH!
BETSY-- WHAT'S HAPPENING?!

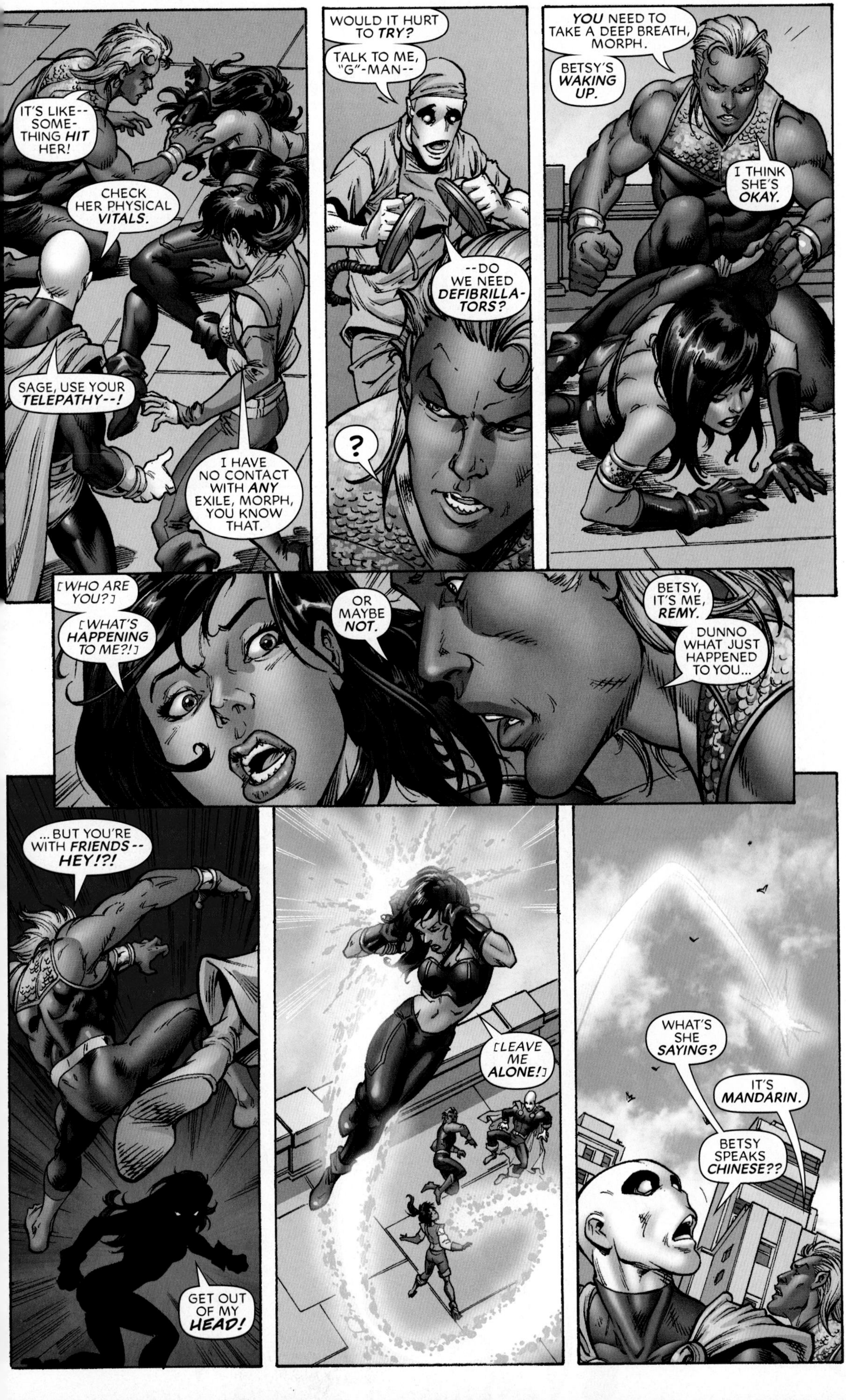
IT'S LIKE--SOME-THING HIT HER!
CHECK HER PHYSICAL VITALS.
SAGE, USE YOUR TELEPATHY--!
I HAVE NO CONTACT WITH ANY EXILE, MORPH, YOU KNOW THAT.
WOULD IT HURT TO TRY?
TALK TO ME, "G"-MAN--
--DO WE NEED DEFIBRILLA-TORS?
?
YOU NEED TO TAKE A DEEP BREATH, MORPH.
BETSY'S WAKING UP.
I THINK SHE'S OKAY.
[WHO ARE YOU?]
[WHAT'S HAPPENING TO ME?!]
OR MAYBE NOT.
BETSY, IT'S ME, REMY.
DUNNO WHAT JUST HAPPENED TO YOU...
...BUT YOU'RE WITH FRIENDS--HEY!?!
GET OUT OF MY HEAD!
[LEAVE ME ALONE!]
WHAT'S SHE SAYING?
IT'S MANDARIN.
BETSY SPEAKS CHINESE??

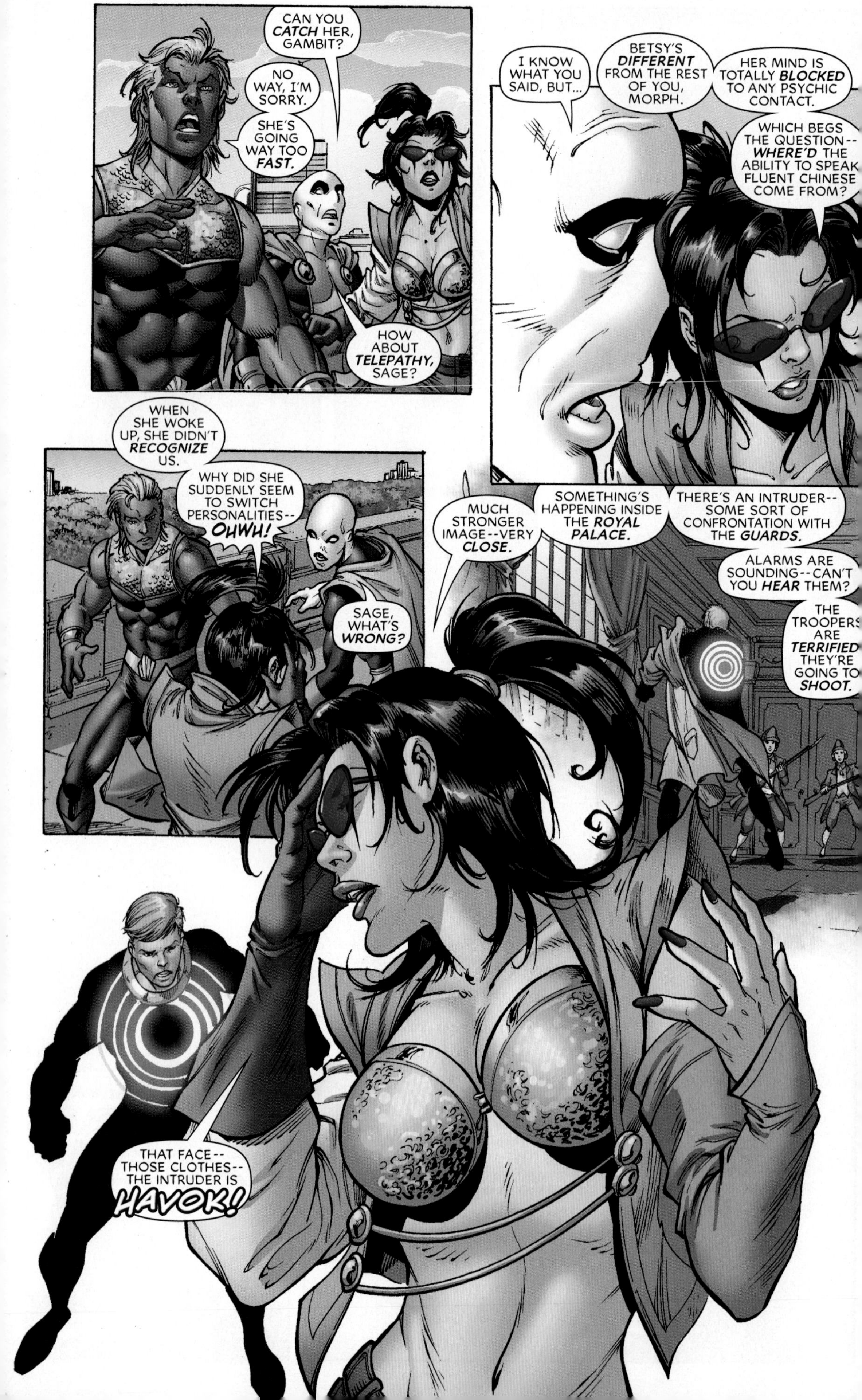
CAN YOU CATCH HER, GAMBIT?
NO WAY, I'M SORRY.
SHE'S GOING WAY TOO FAST.
HOW ABOUT TELEPATHY, SAGE?
I KNOW WHAT YOU SAID, BUT...
BETSY'S DIFFERENT FROM THE REST OF YOU, MORPH.
HER MIND IS TOTALLY BLOCKED TO ANY PSYCHIC CONTACT.
WHICH BEGS THE QUESTION--WHERE'D THE ABILITY TO SPEAK FLUENT CHINESE COME FROM?
WHEN SHE WOKE UP, SHE DIDN'T RECOGNIZE US.
WHY DID SHE SUDDENLY SEEM TO SWITCH PERSONALITIES--
OHWH!
SAGE, WHAT'S WRONG?
MUCH STRONGER IMAGE--VERY CLOSE.
SOMETHING'S HAPPENING INSIDE THE ROYAL PALACE.
THERE'S AN INTRUDER--SOME SORT OF CONFRONTATION WITH THE GUARDS.
ALARMS ARE SOUNDING--CAN'T YOU HEAR THEM?
THE TROOPERS ARE TERRIFIED THEY'RE GOING TO SHOOT.
THAT FACE--THOSE CLOTHES--THE INTRUDER IS HAVOK!

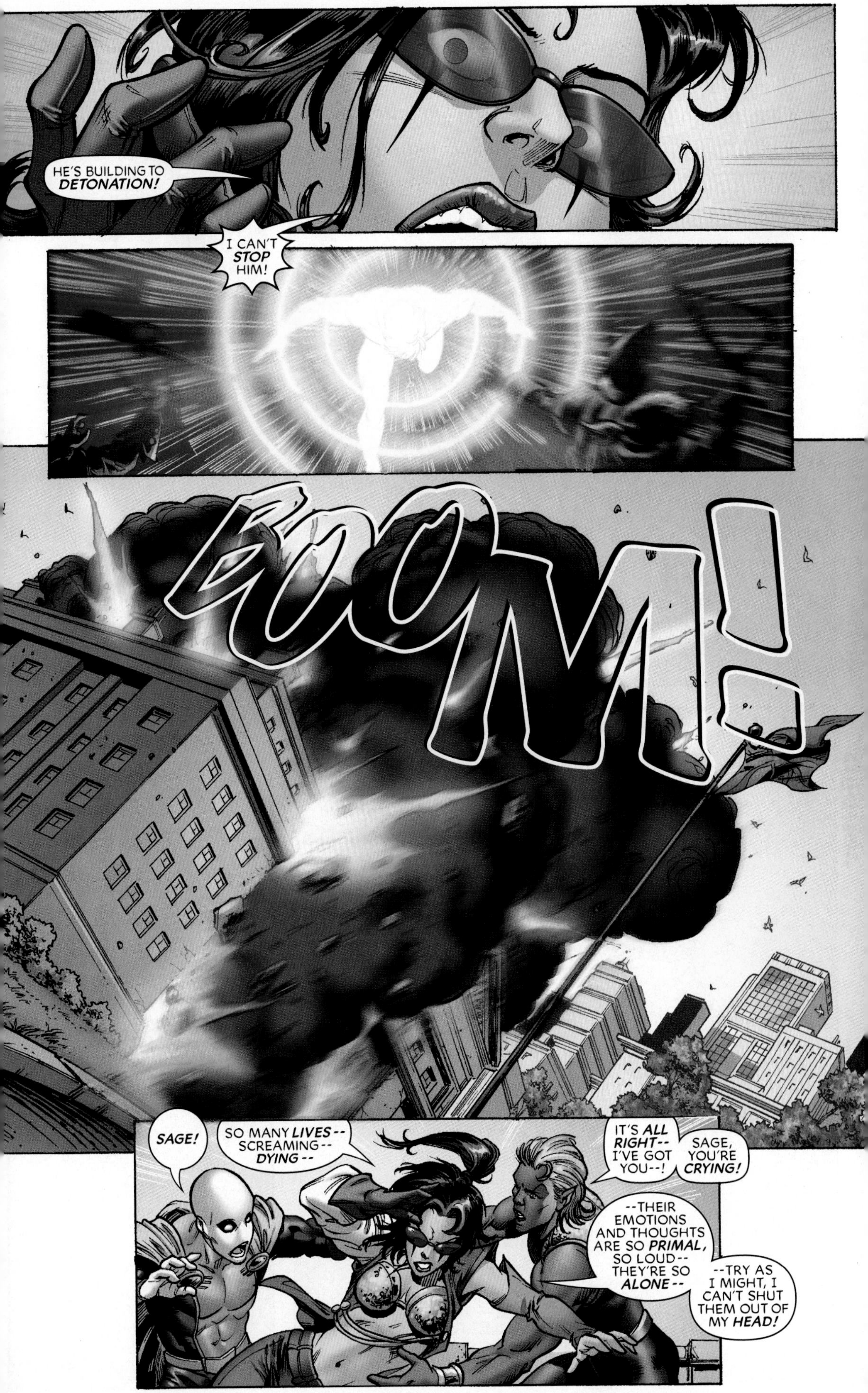

HE'S BUILDING TO DETONATION!
I CAN'T STOP HIM!
BOOM!
SAGE!
SO MANY LIVES-- SCREAMING-- DYING--
IT'S ALL RIGHT-- I'VE GOT YOU--!
SAGE, YOU'RE CRYING!
--THEIR EMOTIONS AND THOUGHTS ARE SO PRIMAL, SO LOUD-- THEY'RE SO ALONE--
--TRY AS I MIGHT, I CAN'T SHUT THEM OUT OF MY HEAD!

ARE YOU *OKAY?*

NO. I WANT TO *SCREAM.*

I'M SORRY TO ASK THIS, SAGE--BUT WE NEED YOU TO SCAN FOR *SURVIVORS.*

SUCK IT UP, GIRL, WE REALLY NEED YOUR *HELP!*

I'M--

--TRYING!

GO *EASY* ON HER, MORPH. SHE'S *HURTING!*

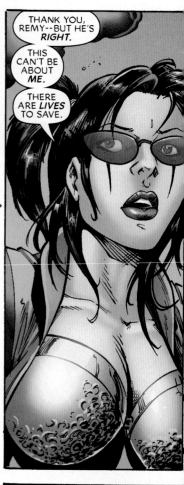

THANK YOU, REMY--BUT HE'S *RIGHT.*

THIS CAN'T BE ABOUT *ME.*

THERE ARE *LIVES* TO SAVE.

I'M LINKING WITH *EMS.* THEY'RE SETTING UP A *TRIAGE* CENTER IN THE MALL.

I'VE FOUND THE *QUEEN!*

TAKE IT EASY, MA'AM.

LORD IRON TOOK THE FULL FORCE OF THE BLAST TO PROTECT ME.

MY *HEROES*-- HOW ARE THEY?

I'M *SORRY,* YOUR MAJESTY.

IT DOESN'T LOOK *GOOD.*

SAGE, CAN YOU *INHIBIT* THE QUEEN'S *PAIN* RECEPTORS? THAT'LL MAKE THINGS *EASIER* FOR HER.

DONE, REMY.

HE'S VERY GOOD AT THIS, IN TERMS OF BOTH MANNER AND MOVES.

WHAT'S *THAT?!*

MORPH-- *TROUBLE!*

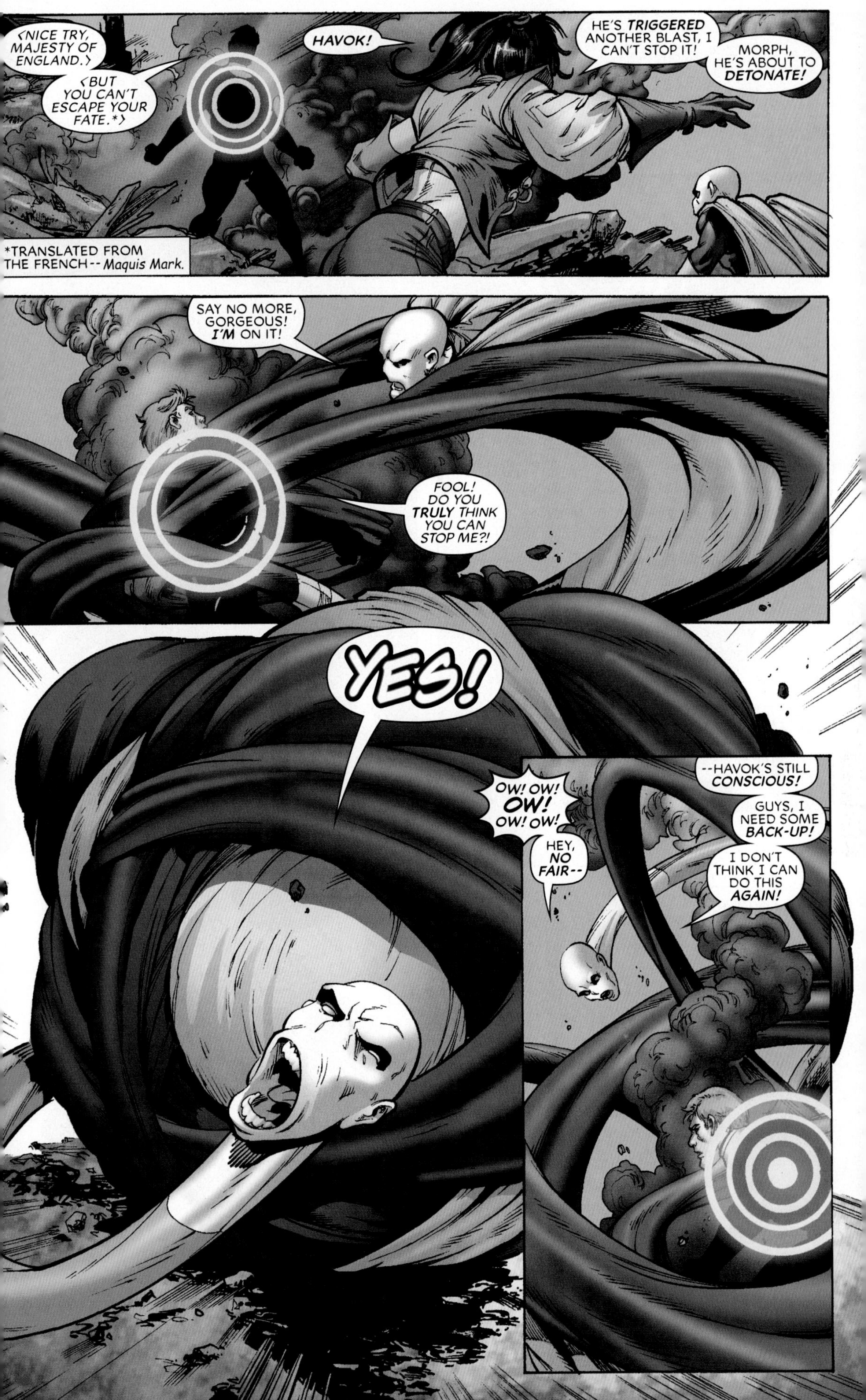
<NICE TRY, MAJESTY OF ENGLAND.>
<BUT YOU CAN'T ESCAPE YOUR FATE.*>
HAVOK!
HE'S TRIGGERED ANOTHER BLAST, I CAN'T STOP IT!
MORPH, HE'S ABOUT TO DETONATE!
*TRANSLATED FROM THE FRENCH -- Maquis Mark.
SAY NO MORE, GORGEOUS! I'M ON IT!
FOOL! DO YOU TRULY THINK YOU CAN STOP ME?!
YES!
OW! OW! OW! OW! OW!
HEY, NO FAIR--
--HAVOK'S STILL CONSCIOUS!
GUYS, I NEED SOME BACK-UP!
I DON'T THINK I CAN DO THIS AGAIN!

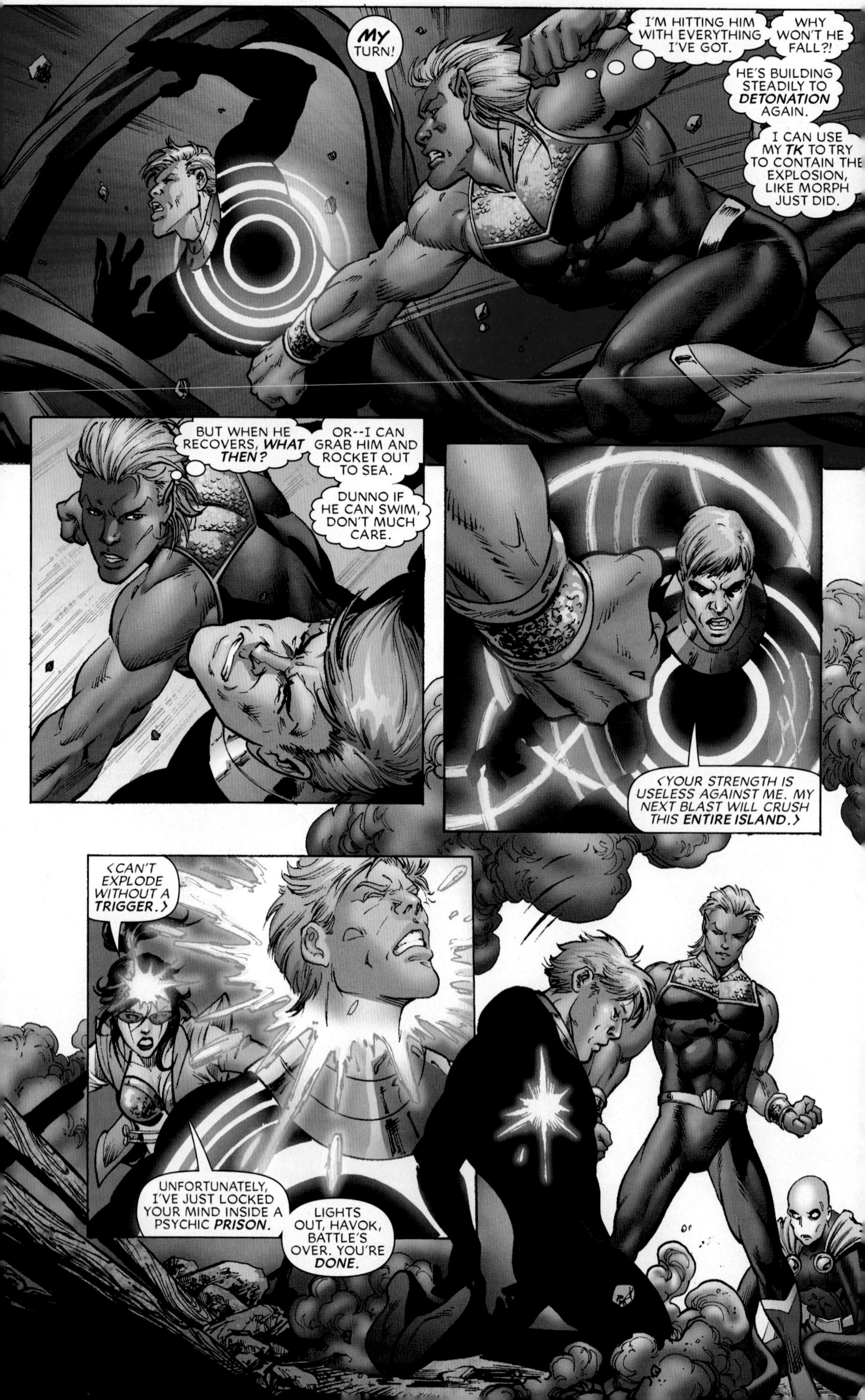
MY TURN!
I'M HITTING HIM WITH EVERYTHING I'VE GOT.
WHY WON'T HE FALL?!
HE'S BUILDING STEADILY TO DETONATION AGAIN.
I CAN USE MY TK TO TRY TO CONTAIN THE EXPLOSION, LIKE MORPH JUST DID.
BUT WHEN HE RECOVERS, WHAT THEN?
OR--I CAN GRAB HIM AND ROCKET OUT TO SEA.
DUNNO IF HE CAN SWIM, DON'T MUCH CARE.
<YOUR STRENGTH IS USELESS AGAINST ME. MY NEXT BLAST WILL CRUSH THIS ENTIRE ISLAND.>
<CAN'T EXPLODE WITHOUT A TRIGGER.>
UNFORTUNATELY, I'VE JUST LOCKED YOUR MIND INSIDE A PSYCHIC PRISON.
LIGHTS OUT, HAVOK, BATTLE'S OVER. YOU'RE DONE.

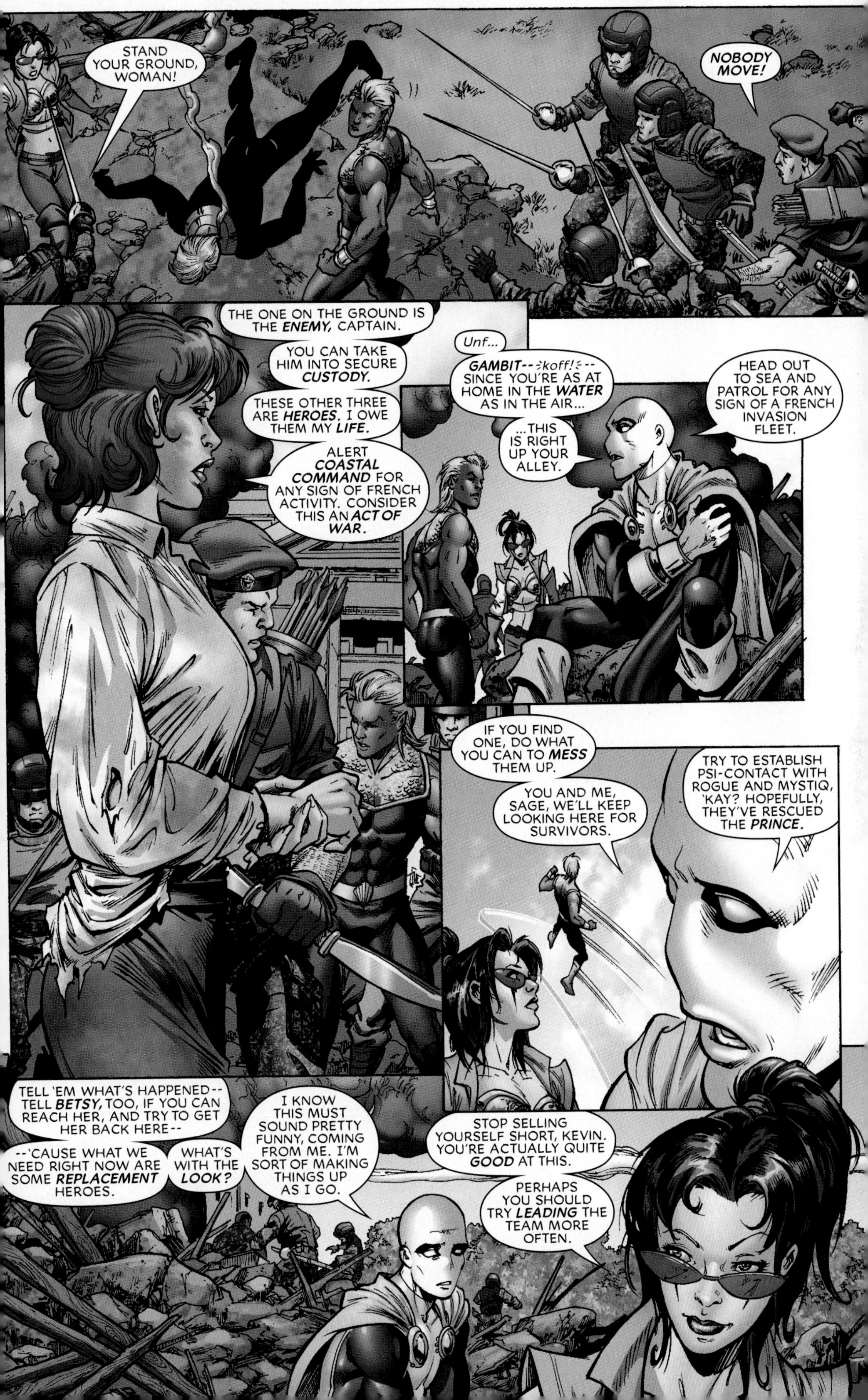
STAND YOUR GROUND, WOMAN!
NOBODY MOVE!
THE ONE ON THE GROUND IS THE ENEMY, CAPTAIN.
YOU CAN TAKE HIM INTO SECURE CUSTODY.
THESE OTHER THREE ARE HEROES. I OWE THEM MY LIFE.
ALERT COASTAL COMMAND FOR ANY SIGN OF FRENCH ACTIVITY. CONSIDER THIS AN ACT OF WAR.
Unf...
GAMBIT-- koff! -- SINCE YOU'RE AS AT HOME IN THE WATER AS IN THE AIR...
...THIS IS RIGHT UP YOUR ALLEY.
HEAD OUT TO SEA AND PATROL FOR ANY SIGN OF A FRENCH INVASION FLEET.
IF YOU FIND ONE, DO WHAT YOU CAN TO MESS THEM UP.
YOU AND ME, SAGE, WE'LL KEEP LOOKING HERE FOR SURVIVORS.
TRY TO ESTABLISH PSI-CONTACT WITH ROGUE AND MYSTIQ, 'KAY? HOPEFULLY, THEY'VE RESCUED THE PRINCE.
TELL 'EM WHAT'S HAPPENED-- TELL BETSY, TOO, IF YOU CAN REACH HER, AND TRY TO GET HER BACK HERE--
--'CAUSE WHAT WE NEED RIGHT NOW ARE SOME REPLACEMENT HEROES.
WHAT'S WITH THE LOOK?
I KNOW THIS MUST SOUND PRETTY FUNNY, COMING FROM ME. I'M SORT OF MAKING THINGS UP AS I GO.
STOP SELLING YOURSELF SHORT, KEVIN. YOU'RE ACTUALLY QUITE GOOD AT THIS.
PERHAPS YOU SHOULD TRY LEADING THE TEAM MORE OFTEN.

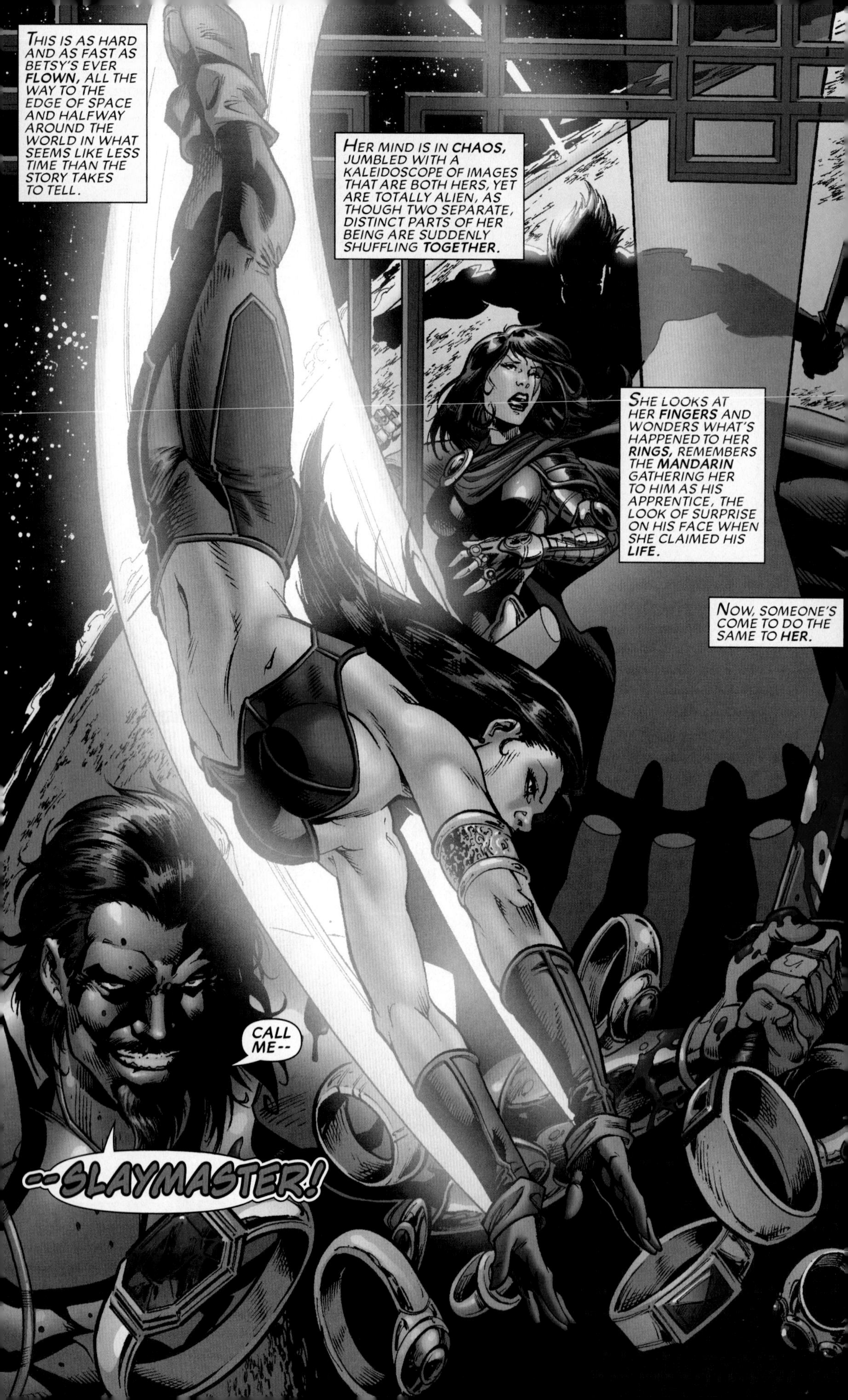

THIS IS AS HARD AND AS FAST AS BETSY'S EVER FLOWN, ALL THE WAY TO THE EDGE OF SPACE AND HALFWAY AROUND THE WORLD IN WHAT SEEMS LIKE LESS TIME THAN THE STORY TAKES TO TELL.
HER MIND IS IN CHAOS, JUMBLED WITH A KALEIDOSCOPE OF IMAGES THAT ARE BOTH HERS, YET ARE TOTALLY ALIEN, AS THOUGH TWO SEPARATE, DISTINCT PARTS OF HER BEING ARE SUDDENLY SHUFFLING TOGETHER.
SHE LOOKS AT HER FINGERS AND WONDERS WHAT'S HAPPENED TO HER RINGS, REMEMBERS THE MANDARIN GATHERING HER TO HIM AS HIS APPRENTICE, THE LOOK OF SURPRISE ON HIS FACE WHEN SHE CLAIMED HIS LIFE.
NOW, SOMEONE'S COME TO DO THE SAME TO HER.
CALL ME--
--SLAYMASTER!

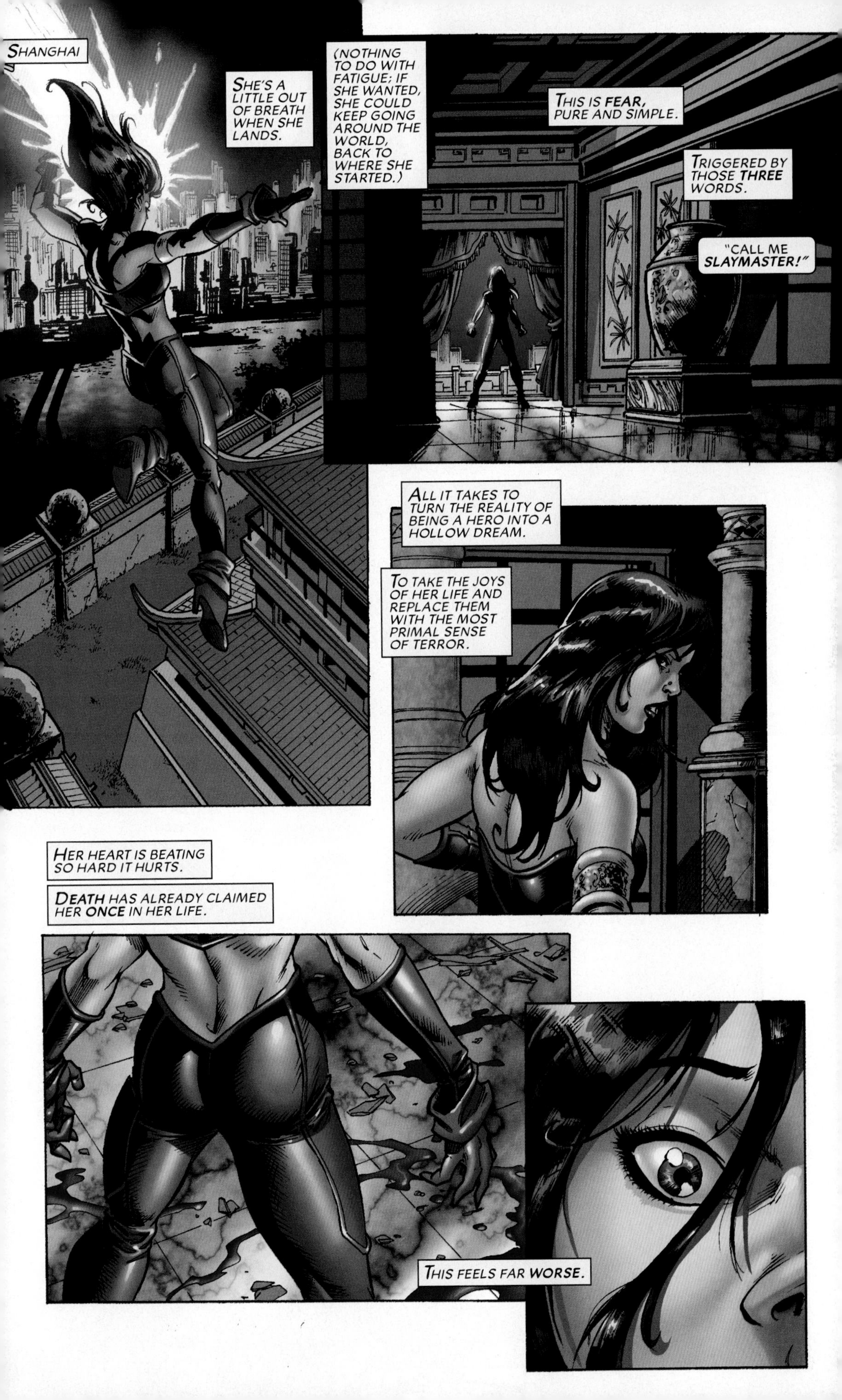
SHANGHAI
SHE'S A LITTLE OUT OF BREATH WHEN SHE LANDS.
(NOTHING TO DO WITH FATIGUE; IF SHE WANTED, SHE COULD KEEP GOING AROUND THE WORLD, BACK TO WHERE SHE STARTED.)
THIS IS FEAR, PURE AND SIMPLE.
TRIGGERED BY THOSE THREE WORDS.
"CALL ME SLAYMASTER!"
ALL IT TAKES TO TURN THE REALITY OF BEING A HERO INTO A HOLLOW DREAM.
TO TAKE THE JOYS OF HER LIFE AND REPLACE THEM WITH THE MOST PRIMAL SENSE OF TERROR.
HER HEART IS BEATING SO HARD IT HURTS.
DEATH HAS ALREADY CLAIMED HER ONCE IN HER LIFE.
THIS FEELS FAR WORSE.

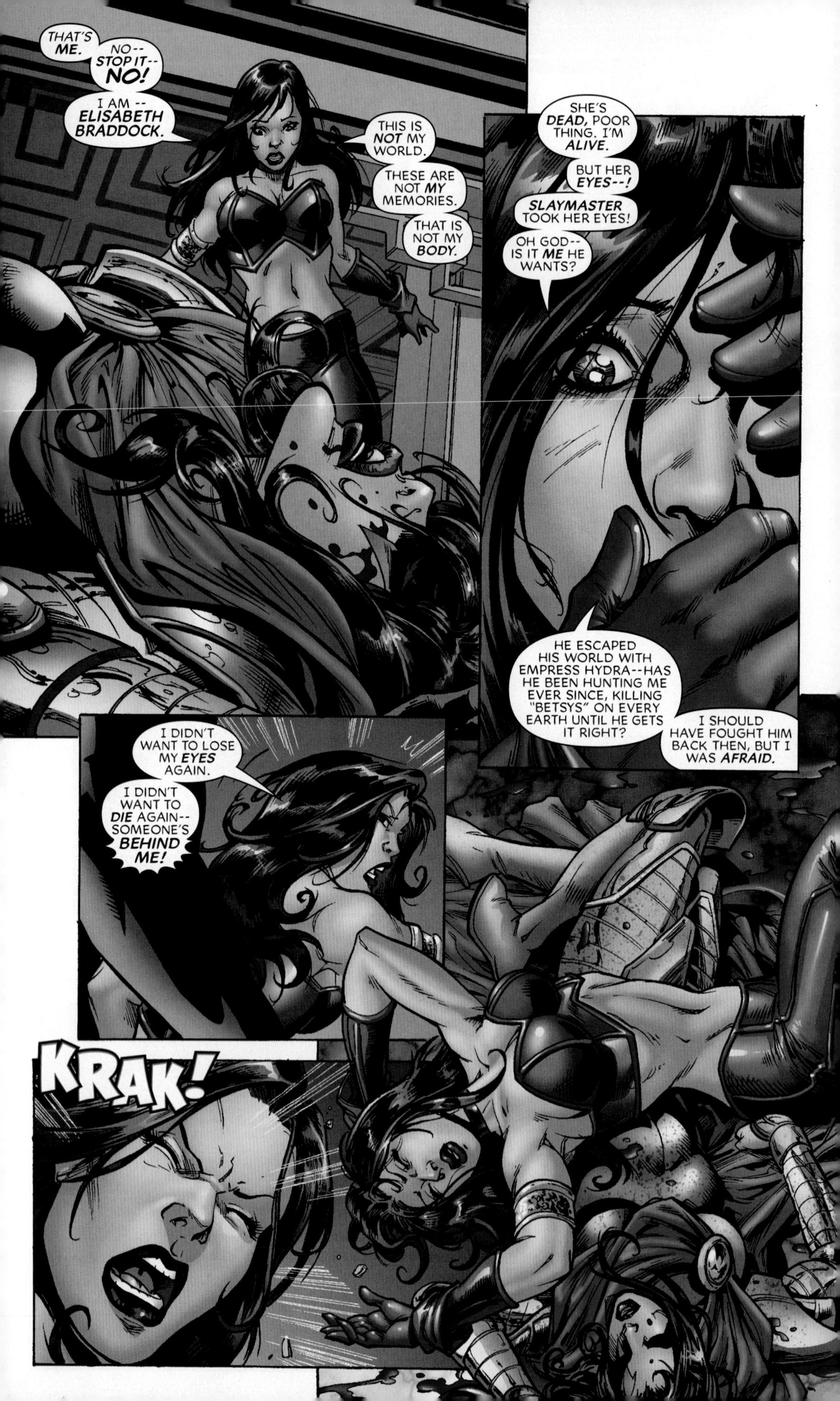

THAT'S ME.
NO-- STOP IT-- NO!
I AM -- ELISABETH BRADDOCK.
THIS IS NOT MY WORLD.
THESE ARE NOT MY MEMORIES.
THAT IS NOT MY BODY.
SHE'S DEAD, POOR THING. I'M ALIVE.
BUT HER EYES--!
SLAYMASTER TOOK HER EYES!
OH GOD-- IS IT ME HE WANTS?
HE ESCAPED HIS WORLD WITH EMPRESS HYDRA--HAS HE BEEN HUNTING ME EVER SINCE, KILLING "BETSYS" ON EVERY EARTH UNTIL HE GETS IT RIGHT?
I SHOULD HAVE FOUGHT HIM BACK THEN, BUT I WAS AFRAID.
I DIDN'T WANT TO LOSE MY EYES AGAIN.
I DIDN'T WANT TO DIE AGAIN-- SOMEONE'S BEHIND ME!
KRAK!

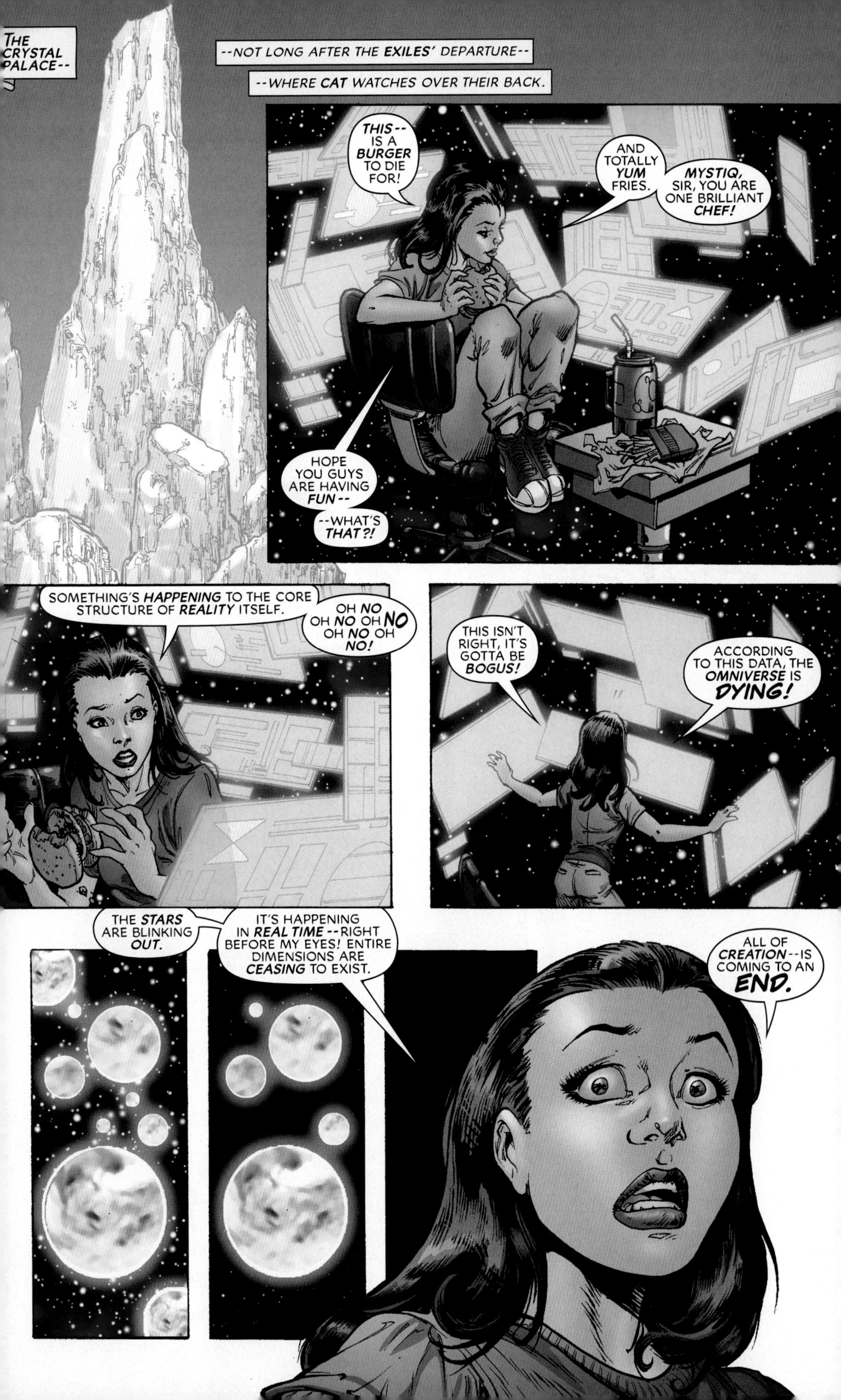

THE CRYSTAL PALACE--
--NOT LONG AFTER THE EXILES' DEPARTURE--
--WHERE CAT WATCHES OVER THEIR BACK.
THIS-- IS A BURGER TO DIE FOR!
AND TOTALLY YUM FRIES.
MYSTIQ, SIR, YOU ARE ONE BRILLIANT CHEF!
HOPE YOU GUYS ARE HAVING FUN--
--WHAT'S THAT?!
SOMETHING'S HAPPENING TO THE CORE STRUCTURE OF REALITY ITSELF.
OH NO OH NO OH NO OH NO OH NO!
THIS ISN'T RIGHT, IT'S GOTTA BE BOGUS!
ACCORDING TO THIS DATA, THE OMNIVERSE IS DYING!
THE STARS ARE BLINKING OUT.
IT'S HAPPENING IN REAL TIME--RIGHT BEFORE MY EYES! ENTIRE DIMENSIONS ARE CEASING TO EXIST.
ALL OF CREATION--IS COMING TO AN END.

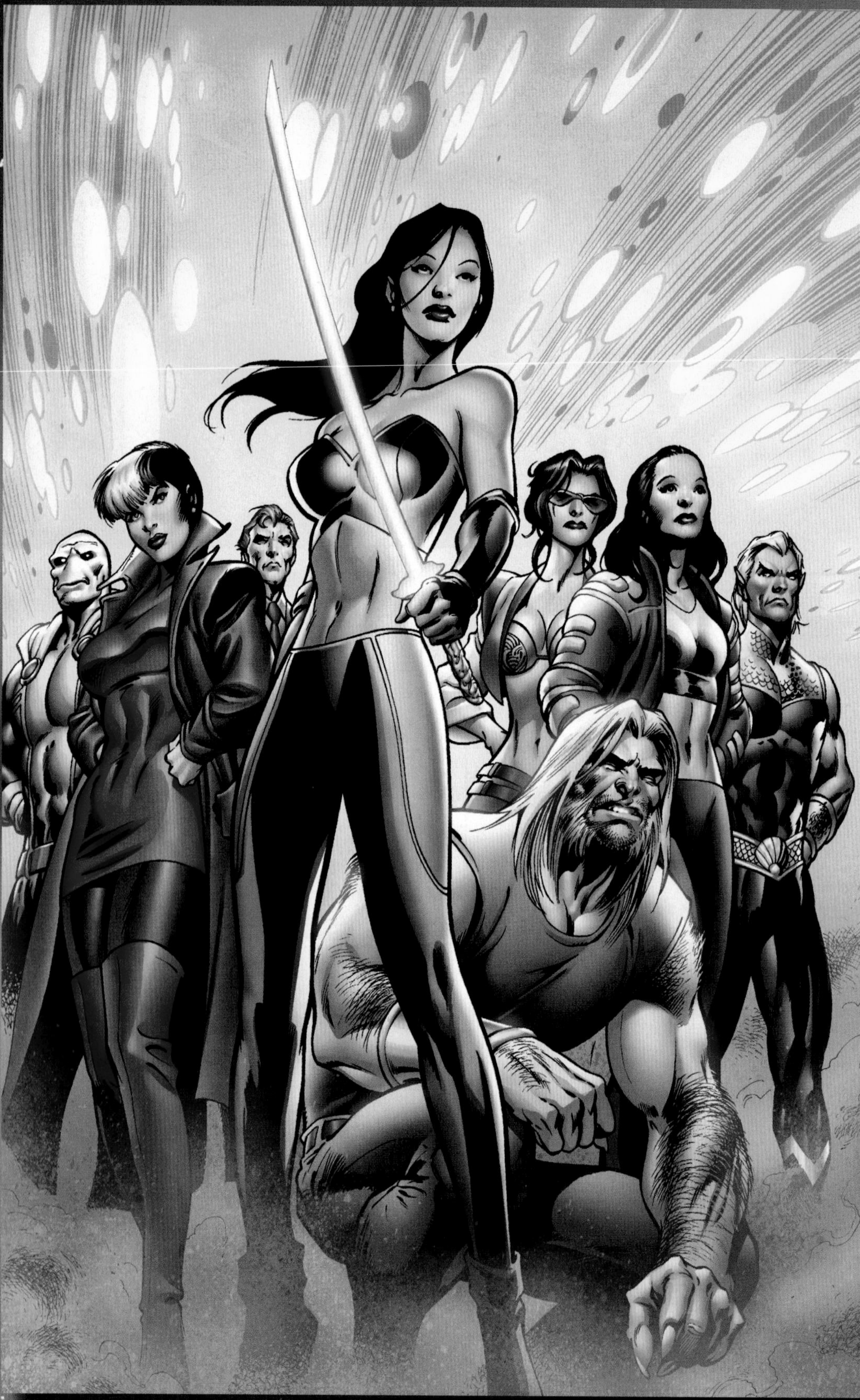

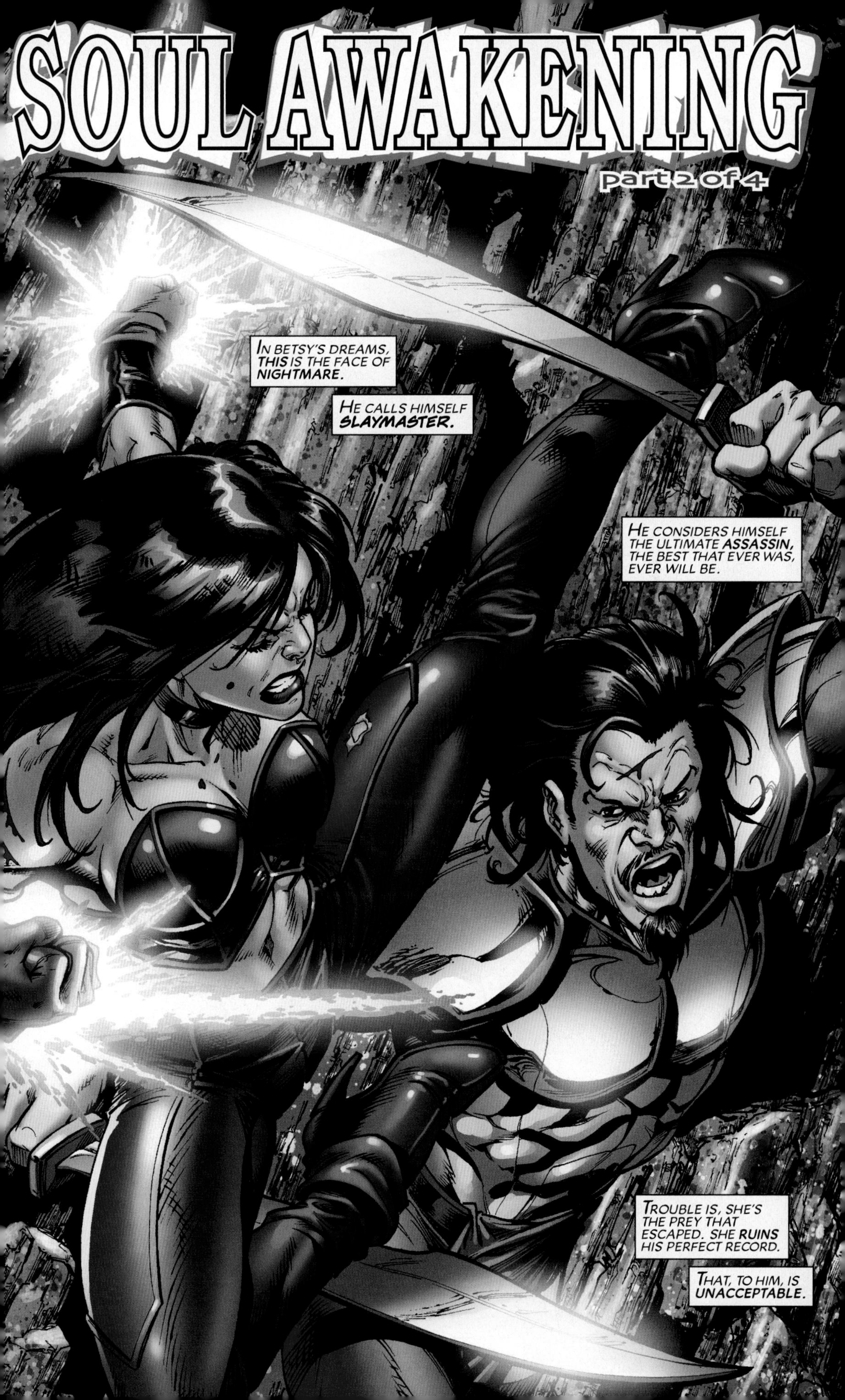
SOUL AWAKENING
part 2 of 4
IN BETSY'S DREAMS, THIS IS THE FACE OF NIGHTMARE.
HE CALLS HIMSELF SLAYMASTER.
HE CONSIDERS HIMSELF THE ULTIMATE ASSASSIN, THE BEST THAT EVER WAS, EVER WILL BE.
TROUBLE IS, SHE'S THE PREY THAT ESCAPED. SHE RUINS HIS PERFECT RECORD.
THAT, TO HIM, IS UNACCEPTABLE.

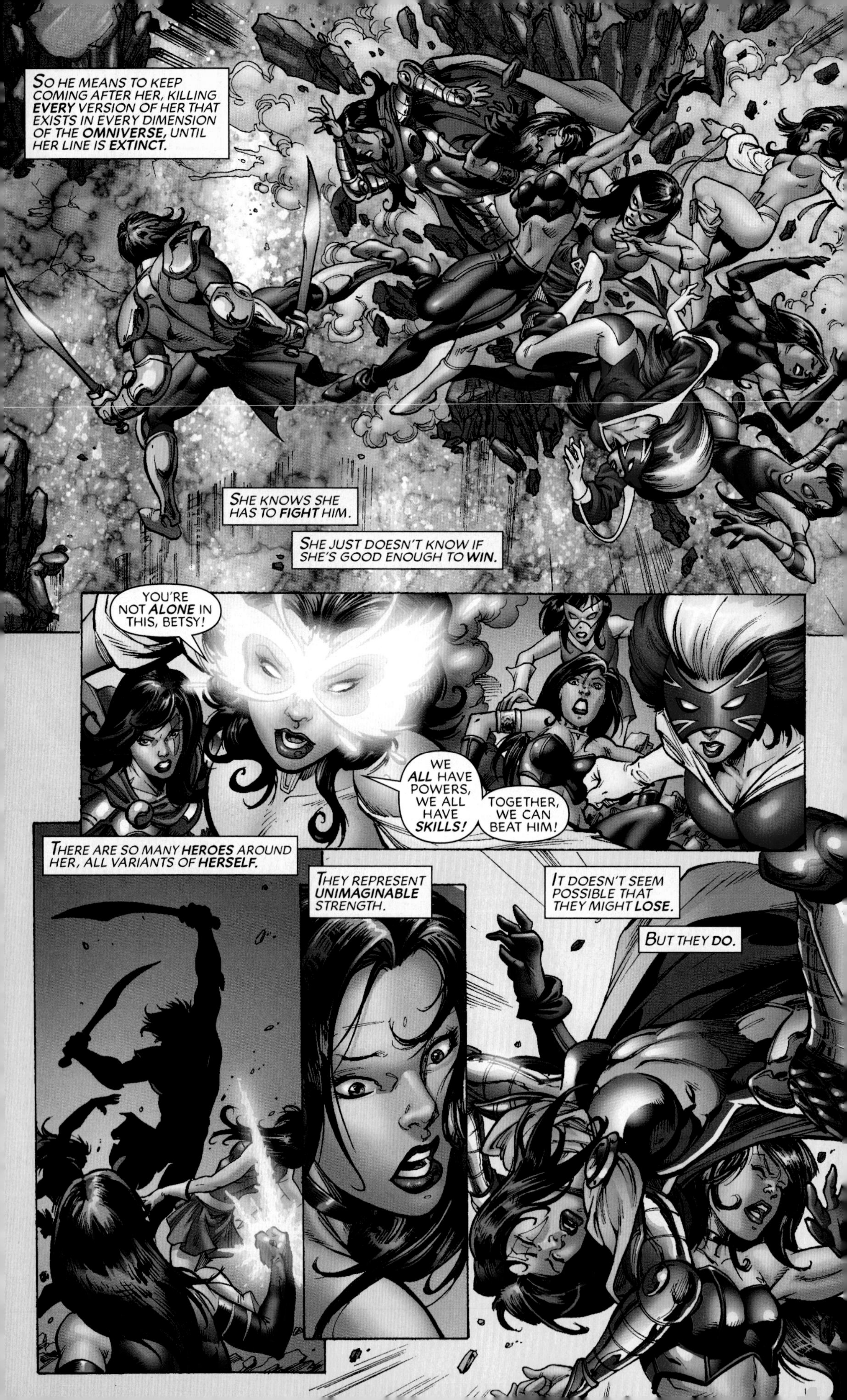
So he means to keep coming after her, killing **every** version of her that exists in every dimension of the **omniverse,** until her line is **extinct.**
She knows she has to **fight** him.
She just doesn't know if she's good enough to **win.**
YOU'RE NOT **ALONE** IN THIS, BETSY!
WE **ALL** HAVE POWERS, WE ALL HAVE **SKILLS!**
TOGETHER, WE CAN BEAT HIM!
There are so many **heroes** around her, all variants of **herself.**
They represent **unimaginable** strength.
It doesn't seem possible that they might **lose.**
But they **do.**

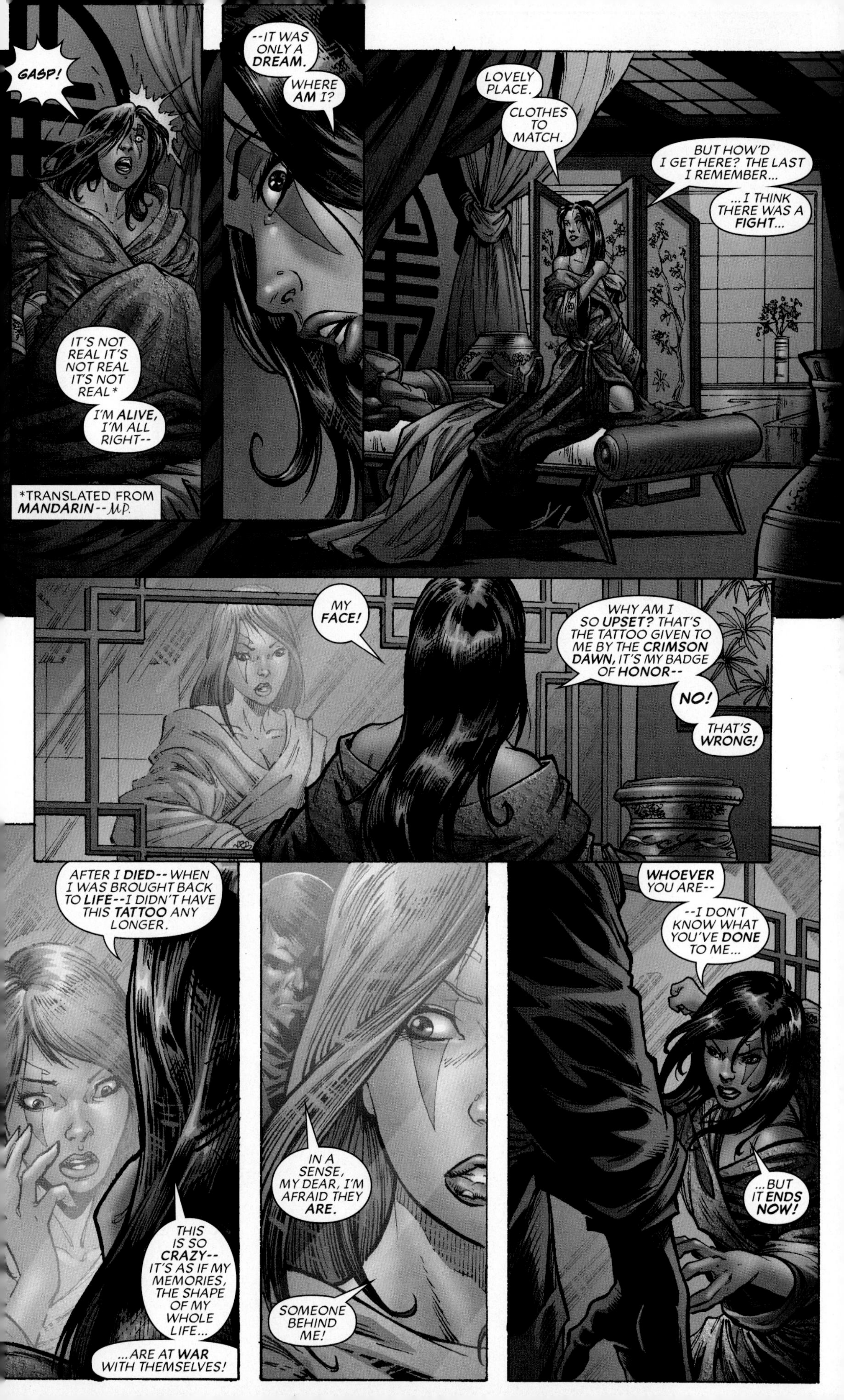
GASP!
IT'S NOT REAL IT'S NOT REAL IT'S NOT REAL*
I'M ALIVE, I'M ALL RIGHT--
*TRANSLATED FROM MANDARIN--M.P.
--IT WAS ONLY A DREAM.
WHERE AM I?
LOVELY PLACE.
CLOTHES TO MATCH.
BUT HOW'D I GET HERE? THE LAST I REMEMBER...
...I THINK THERE WAS A FIGHT...
MY FACE!
WHY AM I SO UPSET? THAT'S THE TATTOO GIVEN TO ME BY THE CRIMSON DAWN, IT'S MY BADGE OF HONOR--
NO!
THAT'S WRONG!
AFTER I DIED--WHEN I WAS BROUGHT BACK TO LIFE--I DIDN'T HAVE THIS TATTOO ANY LONGER.
THIS IS SO CRAZY--IT'S AS IF MY MEMORIES, THE SHAPE OF MY WHOLE LIFE...
...ARE AT WAR WITH THEMSELVES!
IN A SENSE, MY DEAR, I'M AFRAID THEY ARE.
SOMEONE BEHIND ME!
WHOEVER YOU ARE--
--I DON'T KNOW WHAT YOU'VE DONE TO ME...
...BUT IT ENDS NOW!

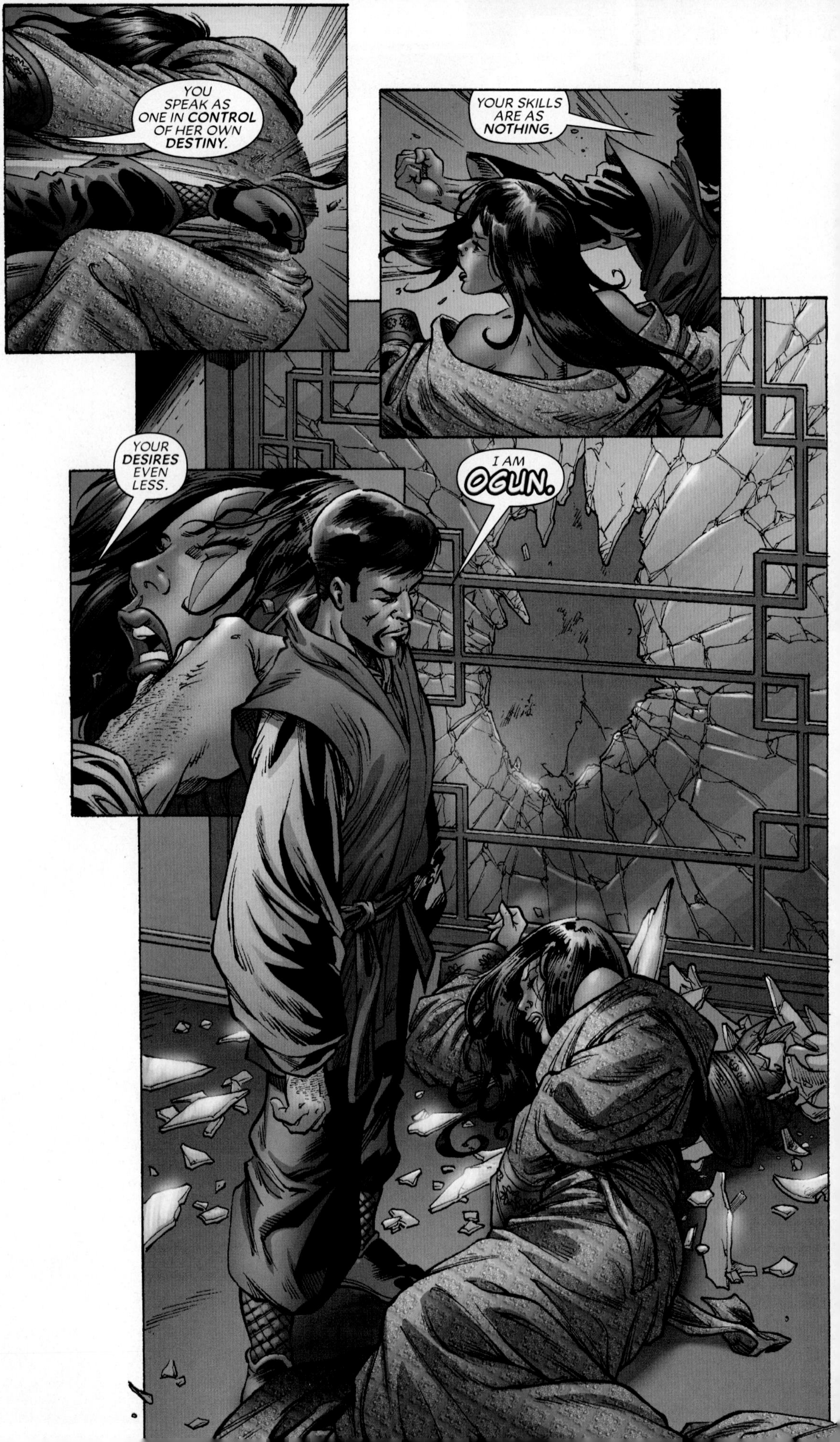
YOU SPEAK AS ONE IN CONTROL OF HER OWN DESTINY.
YOUR SKILLS ARE AS NOTHING.
YOUR DESIRES EVEN LESS.
I AM OGUN.

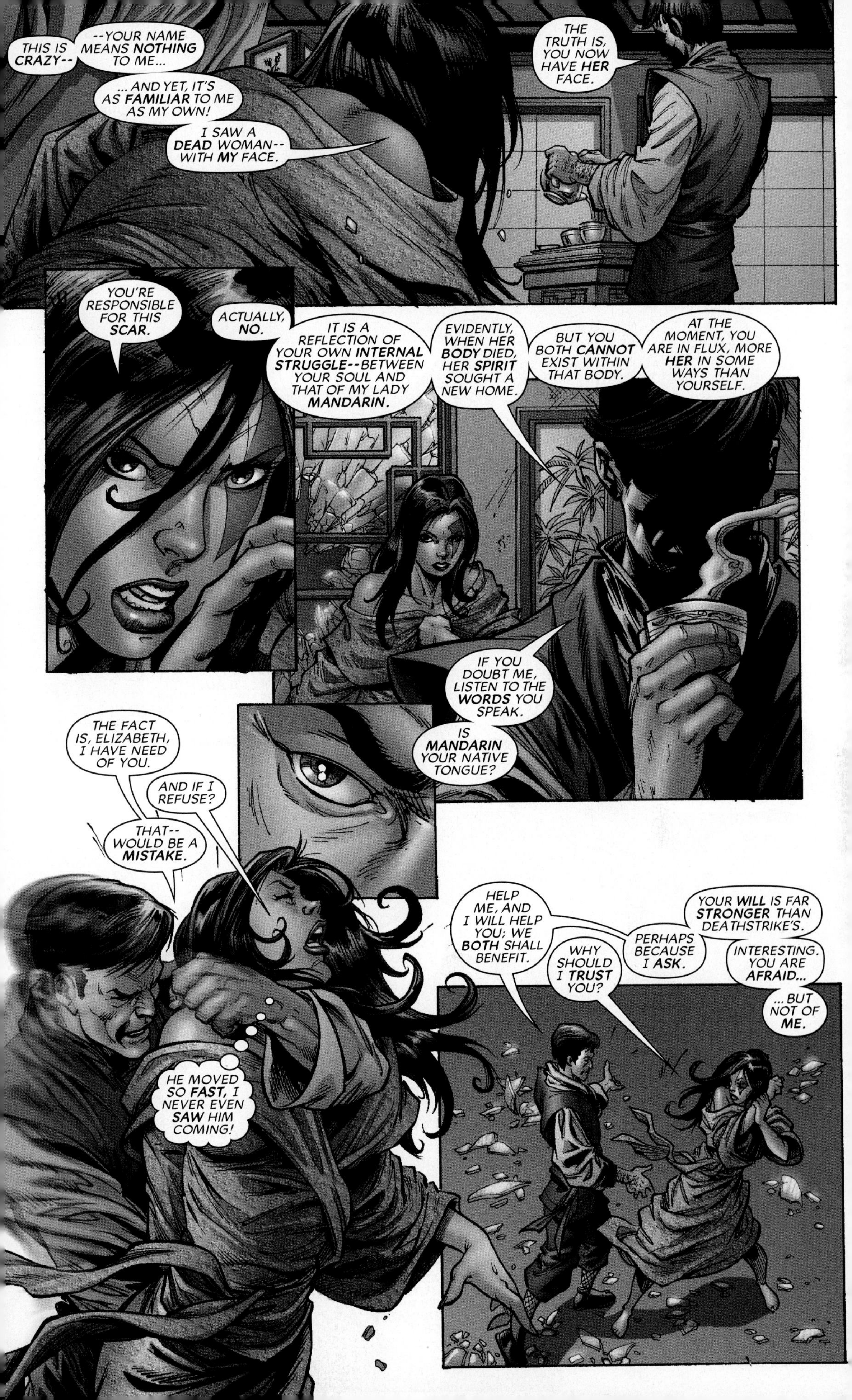
THIS IS CRAZY--
--YOUR NAME MEANS NOTHING TO ME...
...AND YET, IT'S AS FAMILIAR TO ME AS MY OWN!
I SAW A DEAD WOMAN--WITH MY FACE.
THE TRUTH IS, YOU NOW HAVE HER FACE.
YOU'RE RESPONSIBLE FOR THIS SCAR.
ACTUALLY, NO.
IT IS A REFLECTION OF YOUR OWN INTERNAL STRUGGLE--BETWEEN YOUR SOUL AND THAT OF MY LADY MANDARIN.
EVIDENTLY, WHEN HER BODY DIED, HER SPIRIT SOUGHT A NEW HOME.
BUT YOU BOTH CANNOT EXIST WITHIN THAT BODY.
AT THE MOMENT, YOU ARE IN FLUX, MORE HER IN SOME WAYS THAN YOURSELF.
IF YOU DOUBT ME, LISTEN TO THE WORDS YOU SPEAK.
IS MANDARIN YOUR NATIVE TONGUE?
THE FACT IS, ELIZABETH, I HAVE NEED OF YOU.
AND IF I REFUSE?
THAT--WOULD BE A MISTAKE.
HE MOVED SO FAST, I NEVER EVEN SAW HIM COMING!
HELP ME, AND I WILL HELP YOU; WE BOTH SHALL BENEFIT.
WHY SHOULD I TRUST YOU?
PERHAPS BECAUSE I ASK.
YOUR WILL IS FAR STRONGER THAN DEATHSTRIKE'S.
INTERESTING. YOU ARE AFRAID...
...BUT NOT OF ME.

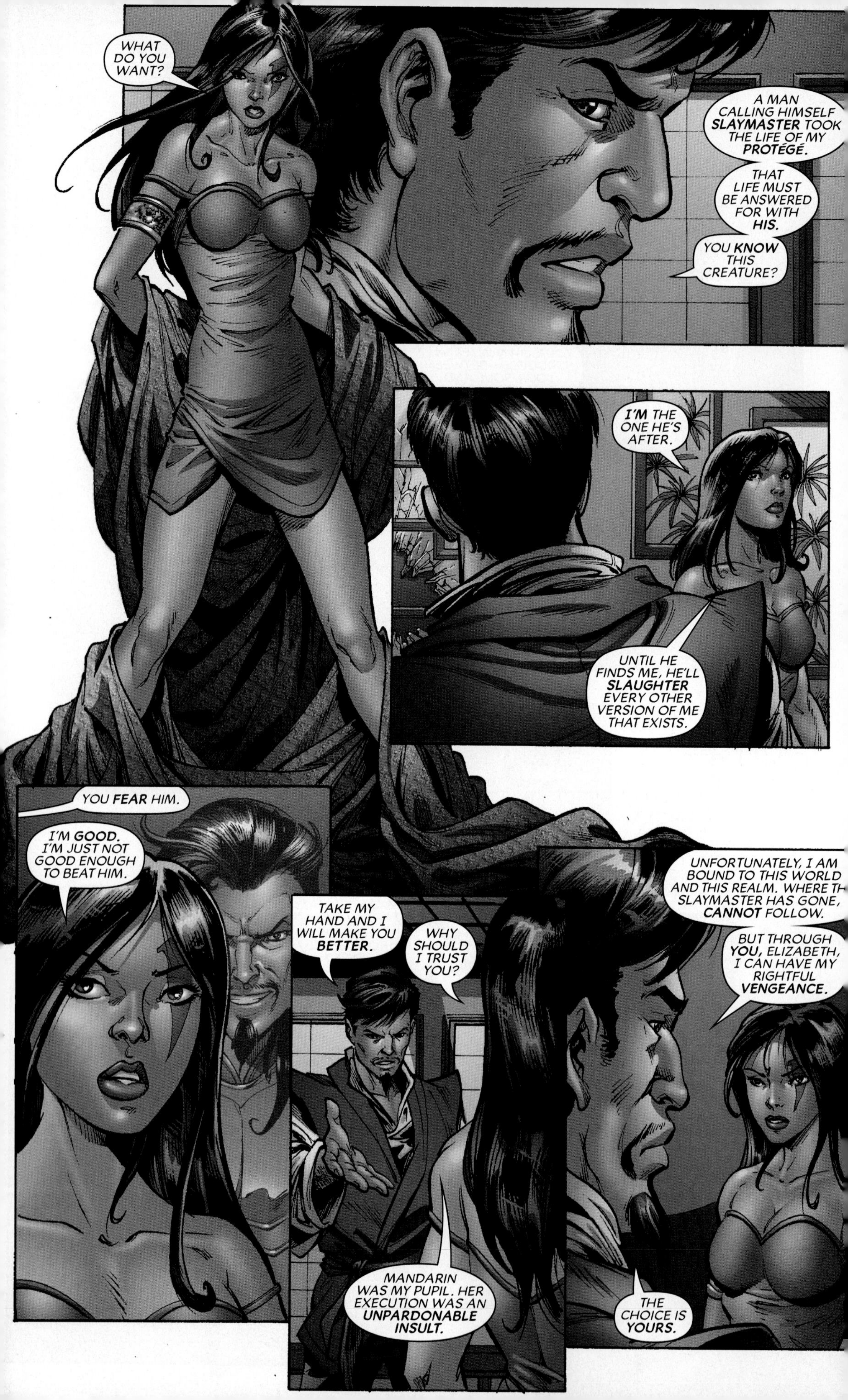
WHAT DO YOU WANT?
A MAN CALLING HIMSELF SLAYMASTER TOOK THE LIFE OF MY PROTÉGÉ.
THAT LIFE MUST BE ANSWERED FOR WITH HIS.
YOU KNOW THIS CREATURE?
I'M THE ONE HE'S AFTER.
UNTIL HE FINDS ME, HE'LL SLAUGHTER EVERY OTHER VERSION OF ME THAT EXISTS.
YOU FEAR HIM.
I'M GOOD. I'M JUST NOT GOOD ENOUGH TO BEAT HIM.
TAKE MY HAND AND I WILL MAKE YOU BETTER.
WHY SHOULD I TRUST YOU?
MANDARIN WAS MY PUPIL. HER EXECUTION WAS AN UNPARDONABLE INSULT.
UNFORTUNATELY, I AM BOUND TO THIS WORLD AND THIS REALM. WHERE TH
SLAYMASTER HAS GONE, CANNOT FOLLOW.
BUT THROUGH YOU, ELIZABETH, I CAN HAVE MY RIGHTFUL VENGEANCE.
THE CHOICE IS YOURS.

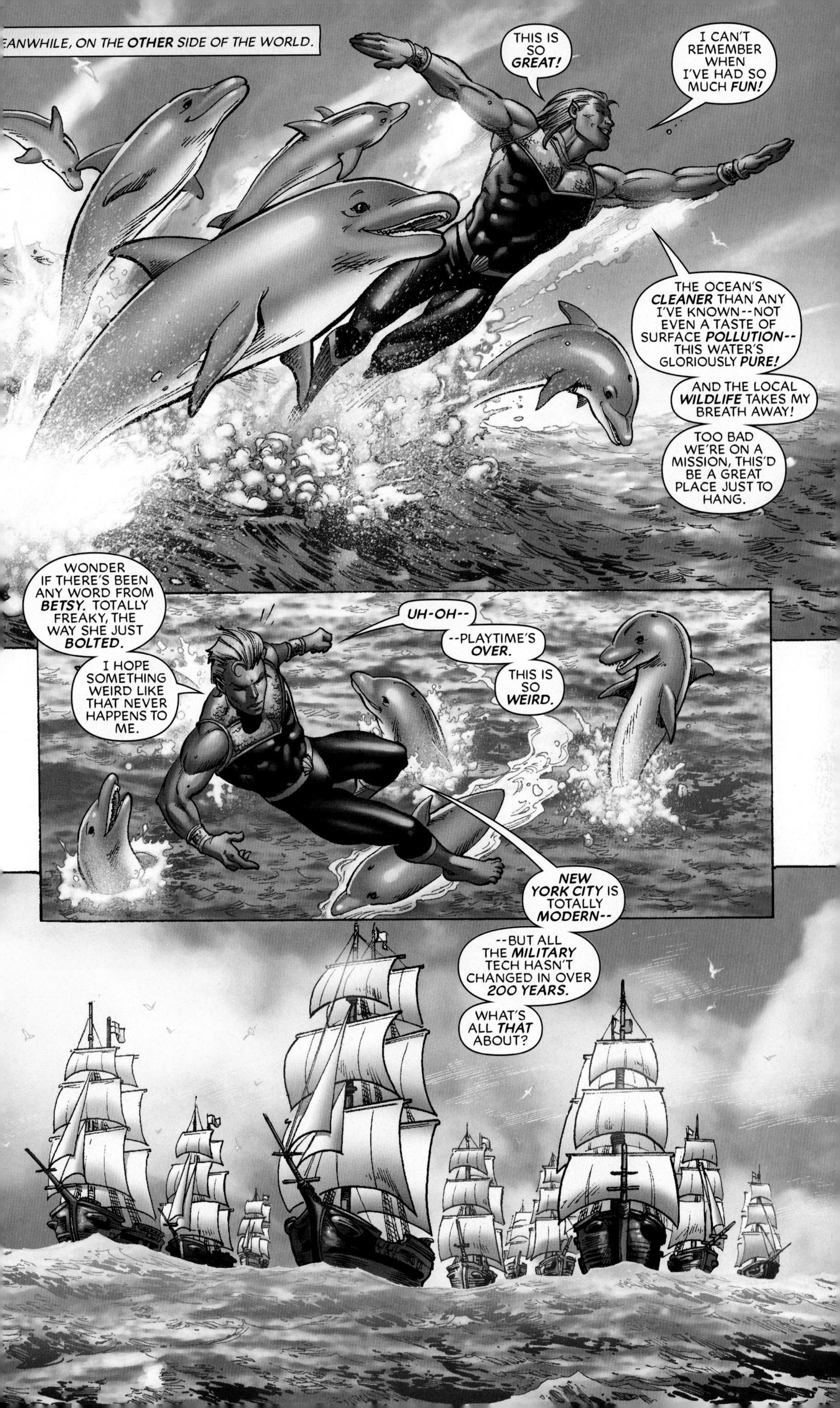

EANWHILE, ON THE OTHER SIDE OF THE WORLD.
THIS IS SO GREAT!
I CAN'T REMEMBER WHEN I'VE HAD SO MUCH FUN!
THE OCEAN'S CLEANER THAN ANY I'VE KNOWN--NOT EVEN A TASTE OF SURFACE POLLUTION-- THIS WATER'S GLORIOUSLY PURE!
AND THE LOCAL WILDLIFE TAKES MY BREATH AWAY!
TOO BAD WE'RE ON A MISSION, THIS'D BE A GREAT PLACE JUST TO HANG.
WONDER IF THERE'S BEEN ANY WORD FROM BETSY. TOTALLY FREAKY, THE WAY SHE JUST BOLTED.
I HOPE SOMETHING WEIRD LIKE THAT NEVER HAPPENS TO ME.
UH-OH--
--PLAYTIME'S OVER.
THIS IS SO WEIRD.
NEW YORK CITY IS TOTALLY MODERN--
--BUT ALL THE MILITARY TECH HASN'T CHANGED IN OVER 200 YEARS.
WHAT'S ALL THAT ABOUT?

HEY-- WHAT'S WITH THE *SHOOTING?*

*TRANSLATED FROM THE *ATLANTEAN*-- MP.

THESE DESIGNS ARE *ANCIENT.*

THEY HAVEN'T EVEN COATED THE HULLS WITH *COPPER* TO LIMIT WATER EROSION.

SIMPLEST THING TO DO IS PUNCH SOME *HOLES* DOWN ALONG THE *KEEL.*

THAT SHOULD PERSUADE THESE *FRENCHMEN* TO TURN BACK FOR *HOME.*

SOME KIND OF *FORCE BLAST.* GOOD THING MY BODY'S BUILT TO WITHSTAND THE PRESSURE DOWN *DEEP*--

--OR THAT SHOT WOULD'VE PUNCHED RIGHT *THROUGH* ME!

THERE'S *ANOTHER* ONE!

SORRY, GUYS, YOU *DON'T* GET TO TAG ME *TWICE.*

SCUBA GEAR--

--AND DEEP-OCEAN *BODY* ARMOR.

SAILING SHIPS AND *HIGH-TECH*--

--WHAT GIVES HERE?

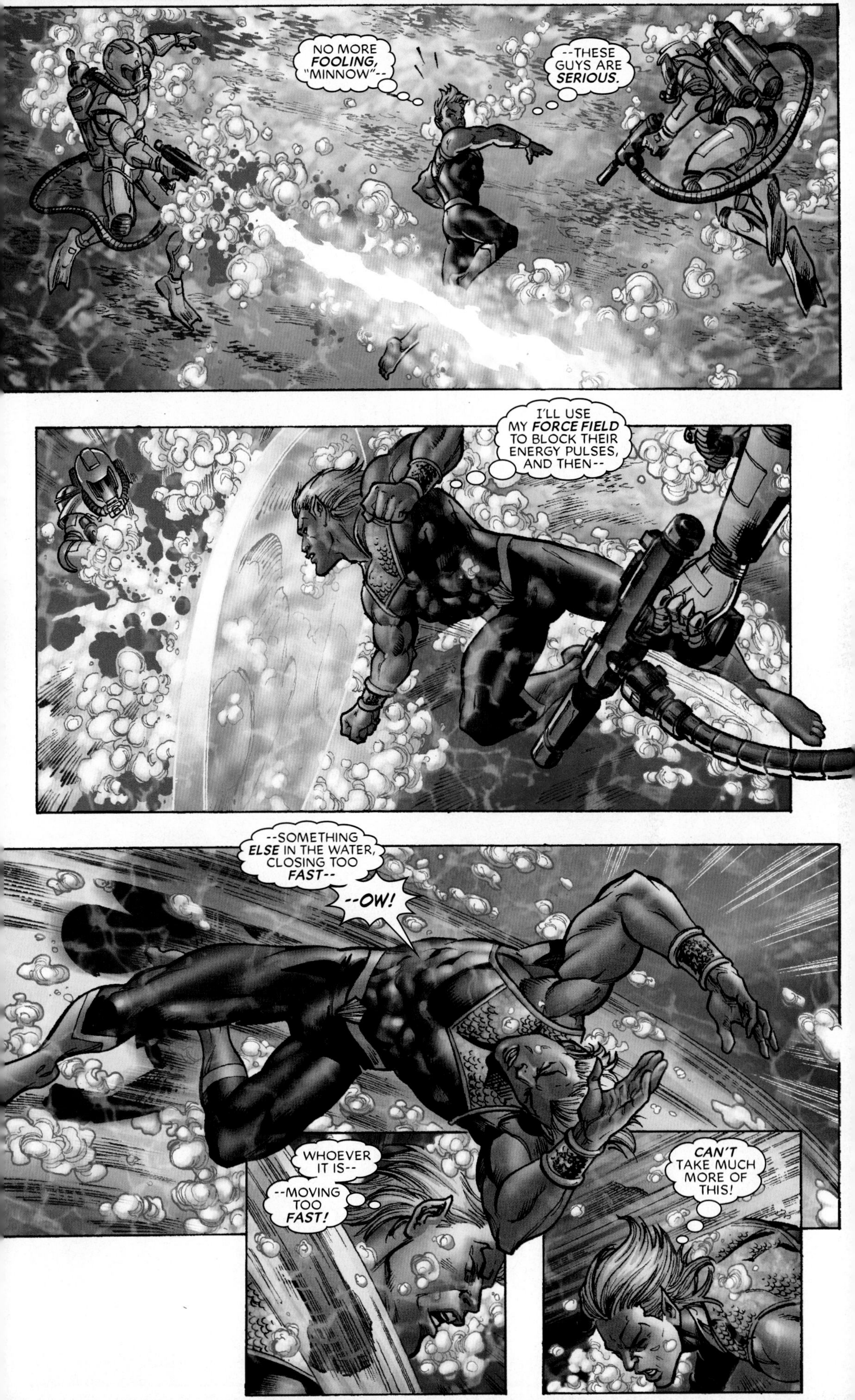
NO MORE FOLING, "MINNOW"--
--THESE GUYS ARE SERIOUS.
I'LL USE MY FORCE FIELD TO BLOCK THEIR ENERGY PULSES, AND THEN--
--SOMETHING ELSE IN THE WATER, CLOSING TOO FAST--
--OW!
WHOEVER IT IS--
--MOVING TOO FAST!
CAN'T TAKE MUCH MORE OF THIS!

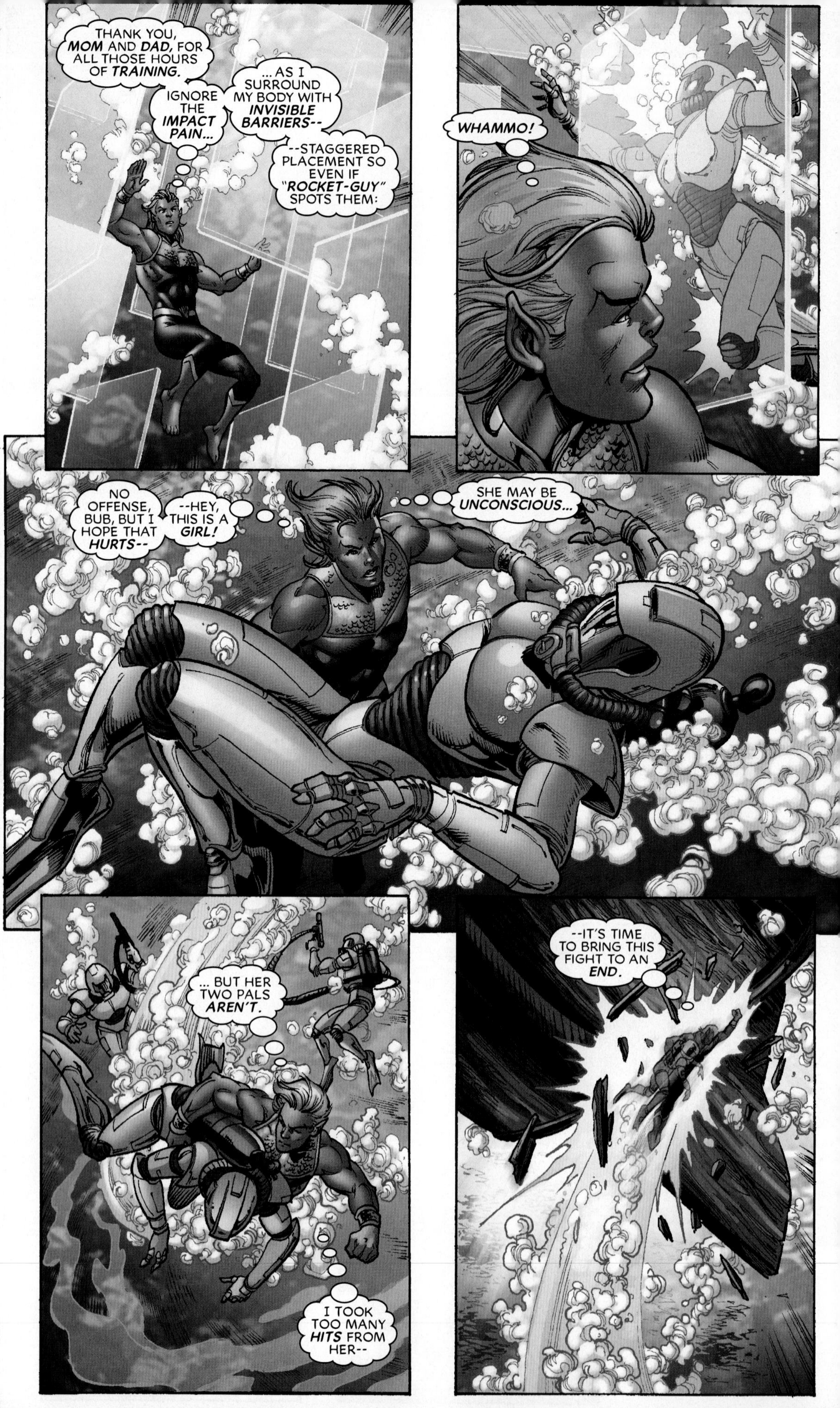
THANK YOU, MOM AND DAD, FOR ALL THOSE HOURS OF TRAINING.
IGNORE THE IMPACT PAIN...
...AS I SURROUND MY BODY WITH INVISIBLE BARRIERS--
--STAGGERED PLACEMENT SO EVEN IF "ROCKET-GUY" SPOTS THEM:
WHAMMO!
NO OFFENSE, BUB, BUT I HOPE THAT HURTS--
--HEY, THIS IS A GIRL!
SHE MAY BE UNCONSCIOUS...
... BUT HER TWO PALS AREN'T.
I TOOK TOO MANY HITS FROM HER--
--IT'S TIME TO BRING THIS FIGHT TO AN END.

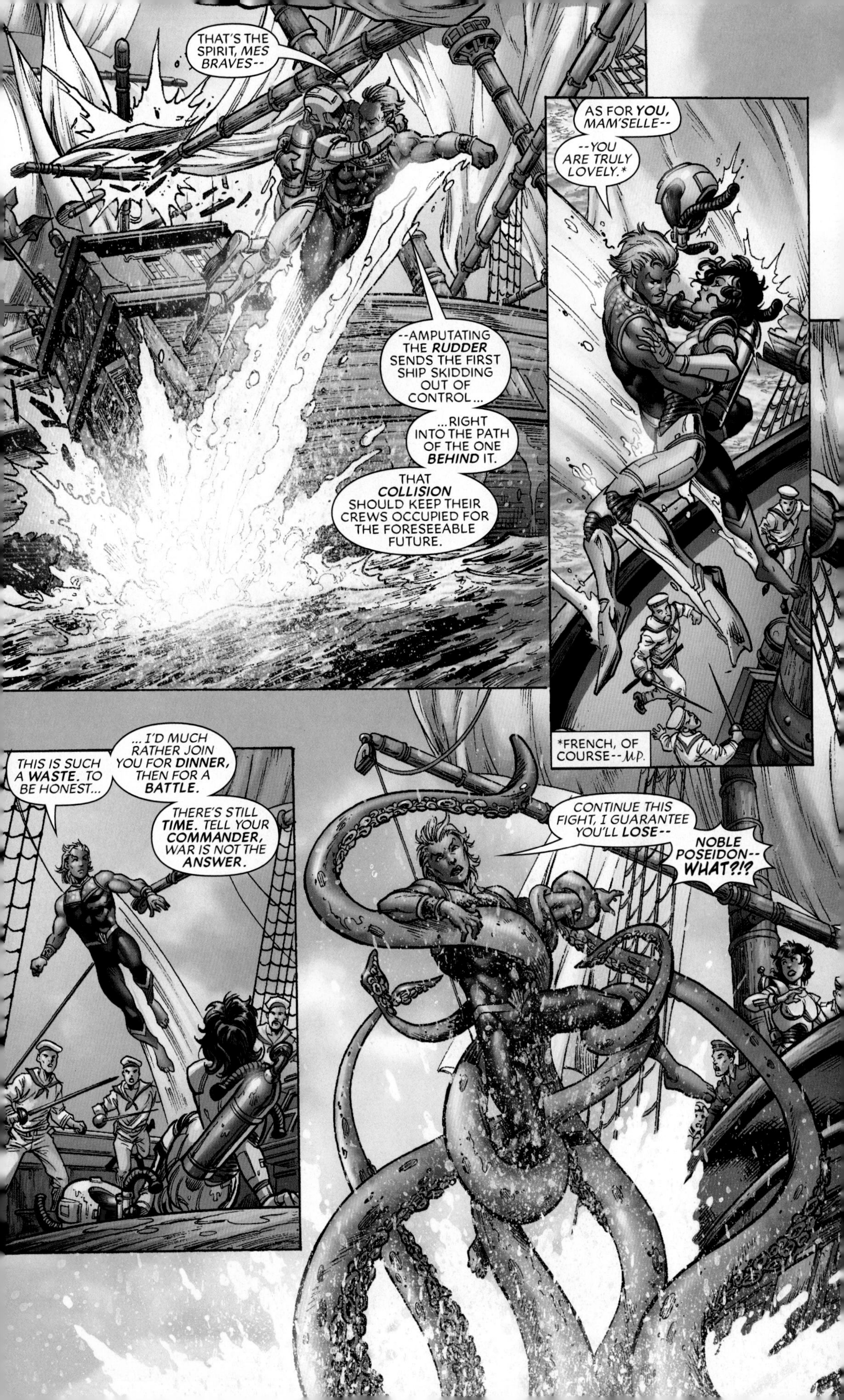
THAT'S THE SPIRIT, MES BRAVES--
--AMPUTATING THE RUDDER SENDS THE FIRST SHIP SKIDDING OUT OF CONTROL...
...RIGHT INTO THE PATH OF THE ONE BEHIND IT.
THAT COLLISION SHOULD KEEP THEIR CREWS OCCUPIED FOR THE FORESEEABLE FUTURE.
AS FOR YOU, MAM'SELLE--
--YOU ARE TRULY LOVELY.*
*FRENCH, OF COURSE--MP.
THIS IS SUCH A WASTE. TO BE HONEST...
...I'D MUCH RATHER JOIN YOU FOR DINNER, THEN FOR A BATTLE.
THERE'S STILL TIME. TELL YOUR COMMANDER, WAR IS NOT THE ANSWER.
CONTINUE THIS FIGHT, I GUARANTEE YOU'LL LOSE--
NOBLE POSEIDON--WHAT?!?

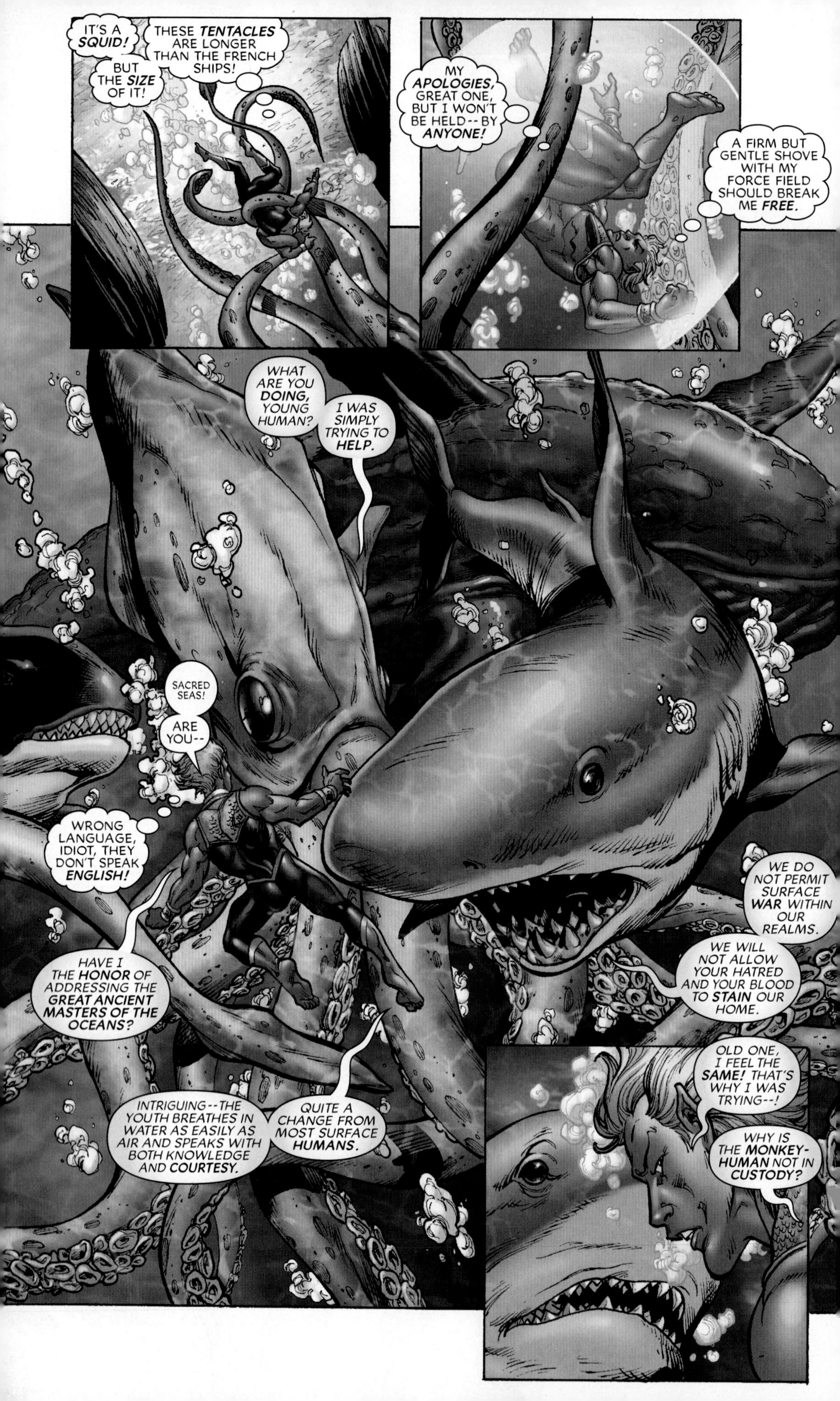
IT'S A SQUID!
BUT THE SIZE OF IT!
THESE TENTACLES ARE LONGER THAN THE FRENCH SHIPS!
MY APOLOGIES, GREAT ONE, BUT I WON'T BE HELD-- BY ANYONE!
A FIRM BUT GENTLE SHOVE WITH MY FORCE FIELD SHOULD BREAK ME FREE.
WHAT ARE YOU DOING, YOUNG HUMAN?
I WAS SIMPLY TRYING TO HELP.
SACRED SEAS!
ARE YOU--
WRONG LANGUAGE, IDIOT, THEY DON'T SPEAK ENGLISH!
HAVE I THE HONOR OF ADDRESSING THE GREAT ANCIENT MASTERS OF THE OCEANS?
INTRIGUING--THE YOUTH BREATHES IN WATER AS EASILY AS AIR AND SPEAKS WITH BOTH KNOWLEDGE AND COURTESY.
QUITE A CHANGE FROM MOST SURFACE HUMANS.
WE DO NOT PERMIT SURFACE WAR WITHIN OUR REALMS.
WE WILL NOT ALLOW YOUR HATRED AND YOUR BLOOD TO STAIN OUR HOME.
OLD ONE, I FEEL THE SAME! THAT'S WHY I WAS TRYING--!
WHY IS THE MONKEY-HUMAN NOT IN CUSTODY?

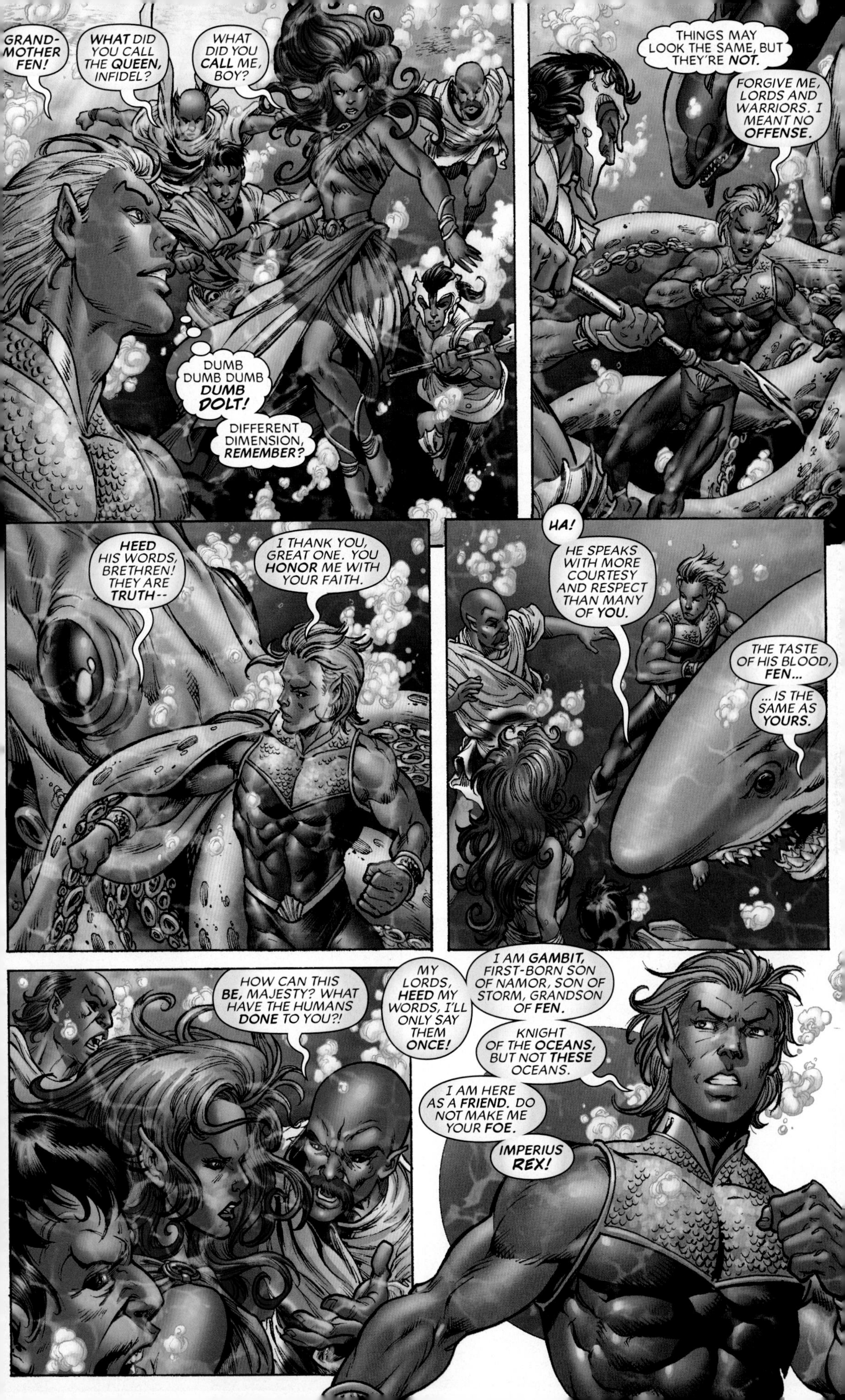
GRAND-MOTHER FEN!
WHAT DID YOU CALL THE QUEEN, INFIDEL?
WHAT DID YOU CALL ME, BOY?
DUMB DUMB DUMB DUMB DOLT!
DIFFERENT DIMENSION, REMEMBER?
THINGS MAY LOOK THE SAME, BUT THEY'RE NOT.
FORGIVE ME, LORDS AND WARRIORS. I MEANT NO OFFENSE.
HEED HIS WORDS, BRETHREN! THEY ARE TRUTH--
I THANK YOU, GREAT ONE. YOU HONOR ME WITH YOUR FAITH.
HA!
HE SPEAKS WITH MORE COURTESY AND RESPECT THAN MANY OF YOU.
THE TASTE OF HIS BLOOD, FEN...
...IS THE SAME AS YOURS.
HOW CAN THIS BE, MAJESTY? WHAT HAVE THE HUMANS DONE TO YOU?!
MY LORDS, HEED MY WORDS, I'LL ONLY SAY THEM ONCE!
I AM GAMBIT, FIRST-BORN SON OF NAMOR, SON OF STORM, GRANDSON OF FEN.
KNIGHT OF THE OCEANS, BUT NOT THESE OCEANS.
I AM HERE AS A FRIEND. DO NOT MAKE ME YOUR FOE.
IMPERIUS REX!

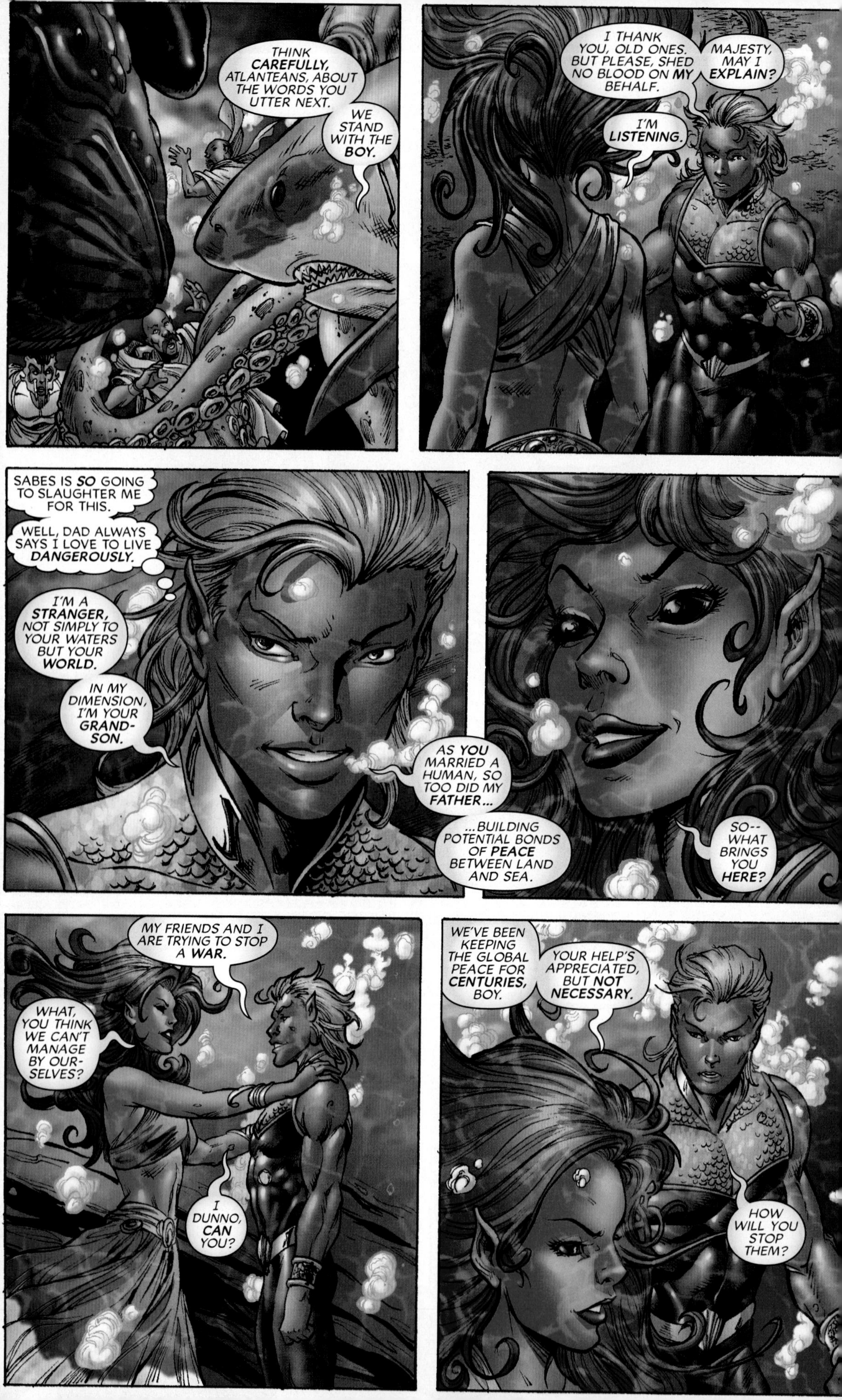
THINK CAREFULLY, ATLANTEANS, ABOUT THE WORDS YOU UTTER NEXT.
WE STAND WITH THE BOY.
I THANK YOU, OLD ONES. BUT PLEASE, SHED NO BLOOD ON MY BEHALF.
MAJESTY, MAY I EXPLAIN?
I'M LISTENING.
SABES IS SO GOING TO SLAUGHTER ME FOR THIS.
WELL, DAD ALWAYS SAYS I LOVE TO LIVE DANGEROUSLY.
I'M A STRANGER, NOT SIMPLY TO YOUR WATERS BUT YOUR WORLD.
IN MY DIMENSION, I'M YOUR GRAND-SON.
AS YOU MARRIED A HUMAN, SO TOO DID MY FATHER...
...BUILDING POTENTIAL BONDS OF PEACE BETWEEN LAND AND SEA.
SO-- WHAT BRINGS YOU HERE?
MY FRIENDS AND I ARE TRYING TO STOP A WAR.
WHAT, YOU THINK WE CAN'T MANAGE BY OUR-SELVES?
I DUNNO, CAN YOU?
WE'VE BEEN KEEPING THE GLOBAL PEACE FOR CENTURIES, BOY.
YOUR HELP'S APPRECIATED, BUT NOT NECESSARY.
HOW WILL YOU STOP THEM?

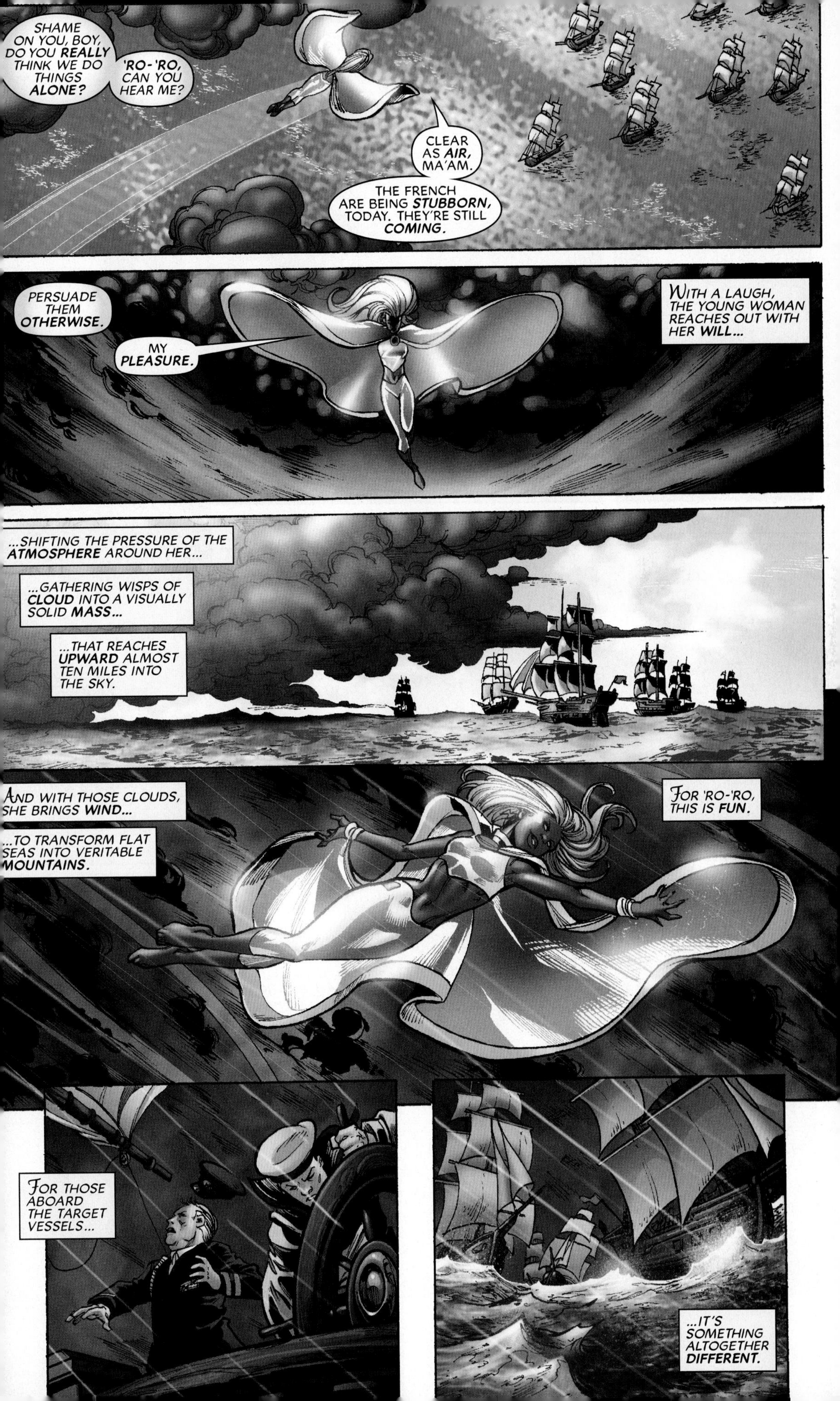

SHAME ON YOU, BOY, DO YOU REALLY THINK WE DO THINGS ALONE?
'RO-'RO, CAN YOU HEAR ME?
CLEAR AS AIR, MA'AM.
THE FRENCH ARE BEING STUBBORN, TODAY. THEY'RE STILL COMING.
PERSUADE THEM OTHERWISE.
MY PLEASURE.
WITH A LAUGH, THE YOUNG WOMAN REACHES OUT WITH HER WILL...
...SHIFTING THE PRESSURE OF THE ATMOSPHERE AROUND HER...
...GATHERING WISPS OF CLOUD INTO A VISUALLY SOLID MASS...
...THAT REACHES UPWARD ALMOST TEN MILES INTO THE SKY.
AND WITH THOSE CLOUDS, SHE BRINGS WIND...
...TO TRANSFORM FLAT SEAS INTO VERITABLE MOUNTAINS.
FOR 'RO-'RO, THIS IS FUN.
FOR THOSE ABOARD THE TARGET VESSELS...
...IT'S SOMETHING ALTOGETHER DIFFERENT.

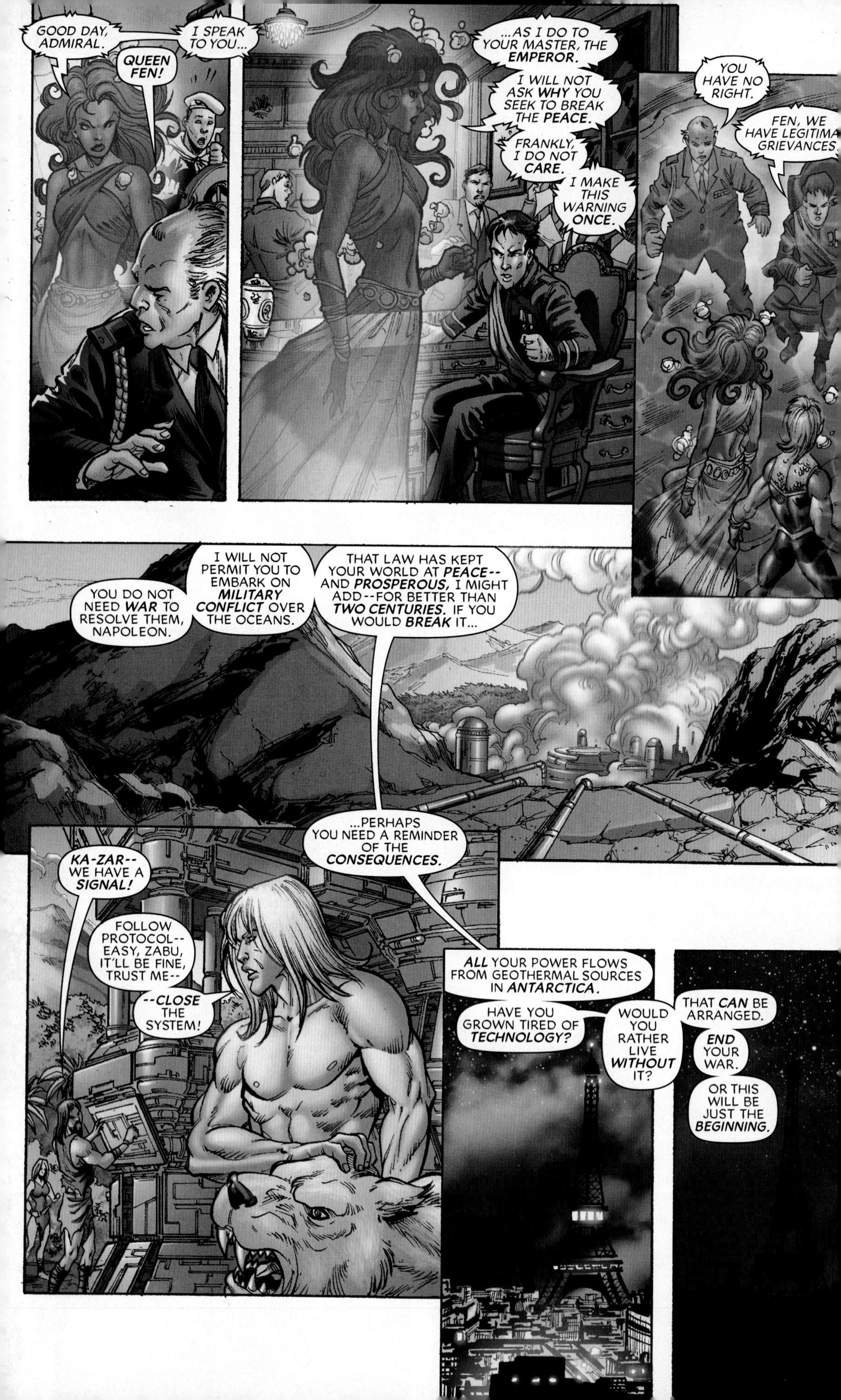
GOOD DAY, ADMIRAL.
I SPEAK TO YOU...
QUEEN FEN!
...AS I DO TO YOUR MASTER, THE EMPEROR.
I WILL NOT ASK WHY YOU SEEK TO BREAK THE PEACE.
FRANKLY, I DO NOT CARE.
I MAKE THIS WARNING ONCE.
YOU HAVE NO RIGHT.
FEN, WE HAVE LEGITIMA GRIEVANCES.
YOU DO NOT NEED WAR TO RESOLVE THEM, NAPOLEON.
I WILL NOT PERMIT YOU TO EMBARK ON MILITARY CONFLICT OVER THE OCEANS.
THAT LAW HAS KEPT YOUR WORLD AT PEACE-- AND PROSPEROUS, I MIGHT ADD--FOR BETTER THAN TWO CENTURIES. IF YOU WOULD BREAK IT...
...PERHAPS YOU NEED A REMINDER OF THE CONSEQUENCES.
KA-ZAR-- WE HAVE A SIGNAL!
FOLLOW PROTOCOL-- EASY, ZABU, IT'LL BE FINE, TRUST ME--
--CLOSE THE SYSTEM!
ALL YOUR POWER FLOWS FROM GEOTHERMAL SOURCES IN ANTARCTICA.
HAVE YOU GROWN TIRED OF TECHNOLOGY?
WOULD YOU RATHER LIVE WITHOUT IT?
THAT CAN BE ARRANGED.
END YOUR WAR.
OR THIS WILL BE JUST THE BEGINNING.

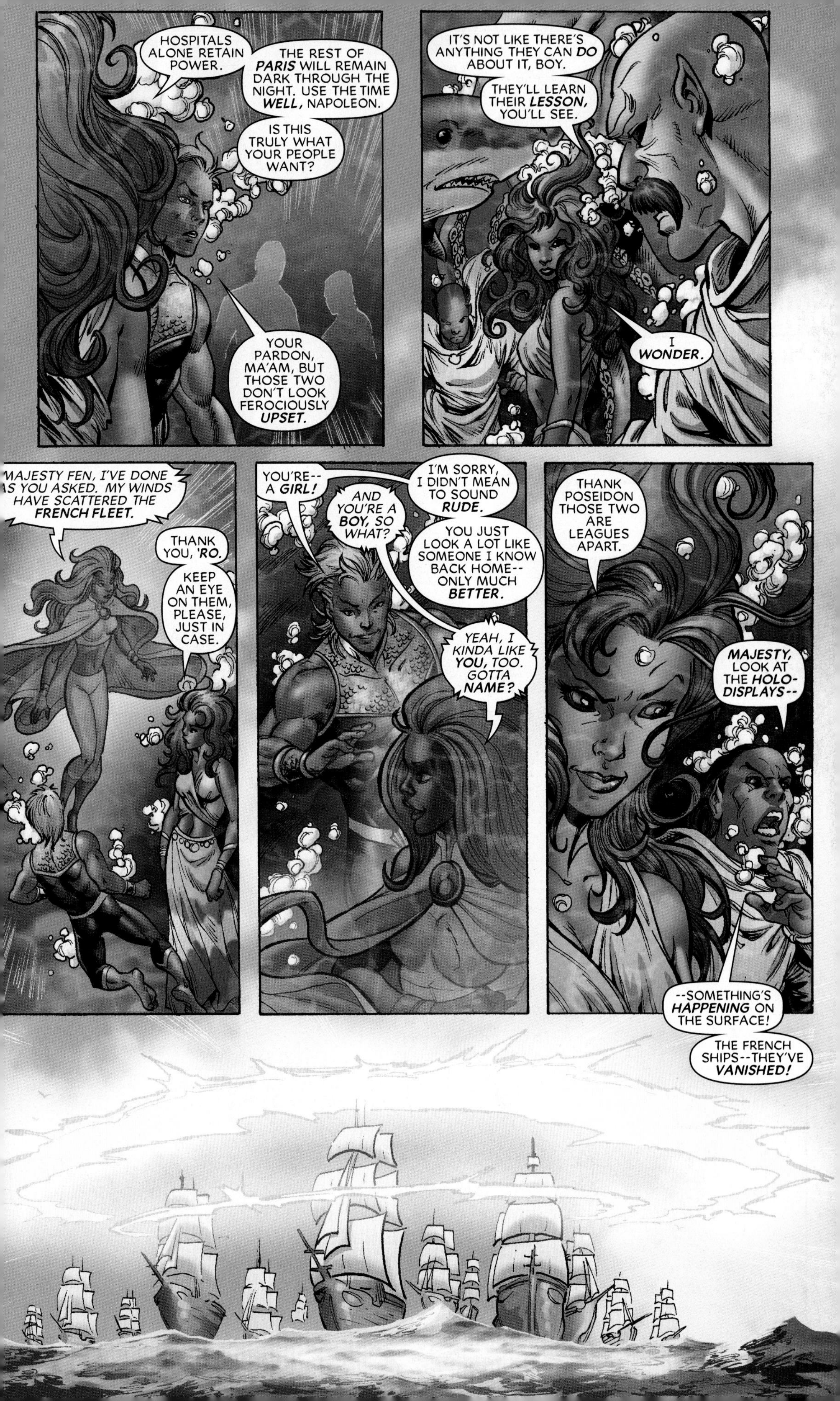
HOSPITALS ALONE RETAIN POWER.
THE REST OF PARIS WILL REMAIN DARK THROUGH THE NIGHT. USE THE TIME WELL, NAPOLEON.
IS THIS TRULY WHAT YOUR PEOPLE WANT?
YOUR PARDON, MA'AM, BUT THOSE TWO DON'T LOOK FEROCIOUSLY UPSET.
IT'S NOT LIKE THERE'S ANYTHING THEY CAN DO ABOUT IT, BOY.
THEY'LL LEARN THEIR LESSON, YOU'LL SEE.
I WONDER.
MAJESTY FEN, I'VE DONE AS YOU ASKED. MY WINDS HAVE SCATTERED THE FRENCH FLEET.
THANK YOU, 'RO.
KEEP AN EYE ON THEM, PLEASE, JUST IN CASE.
YOU'RE-- A GIRL!
I'M SORRY, I DIDN'T MEAN TO SOUND RUDE.
AND YOU'RE A BOY, SO WHAT?
YOU JUST LOOK A LOT LIKE SOMEONE I KNOW BACK HOME-- ONLY MUCH BETTER.
YEAH, I KINDA LIKE YOU, TOO. GOTTA NAME?
THANK POSEIDON THOSE TWO ARE LEAGUES APART.
MAJESTY, LOOK AT THE HOLO-DISPLAYS--
--SOMETHING'S HAPPENING ON THE SURFACE!
THE FRENCH SHIPS--THEY'VE VANISHED!

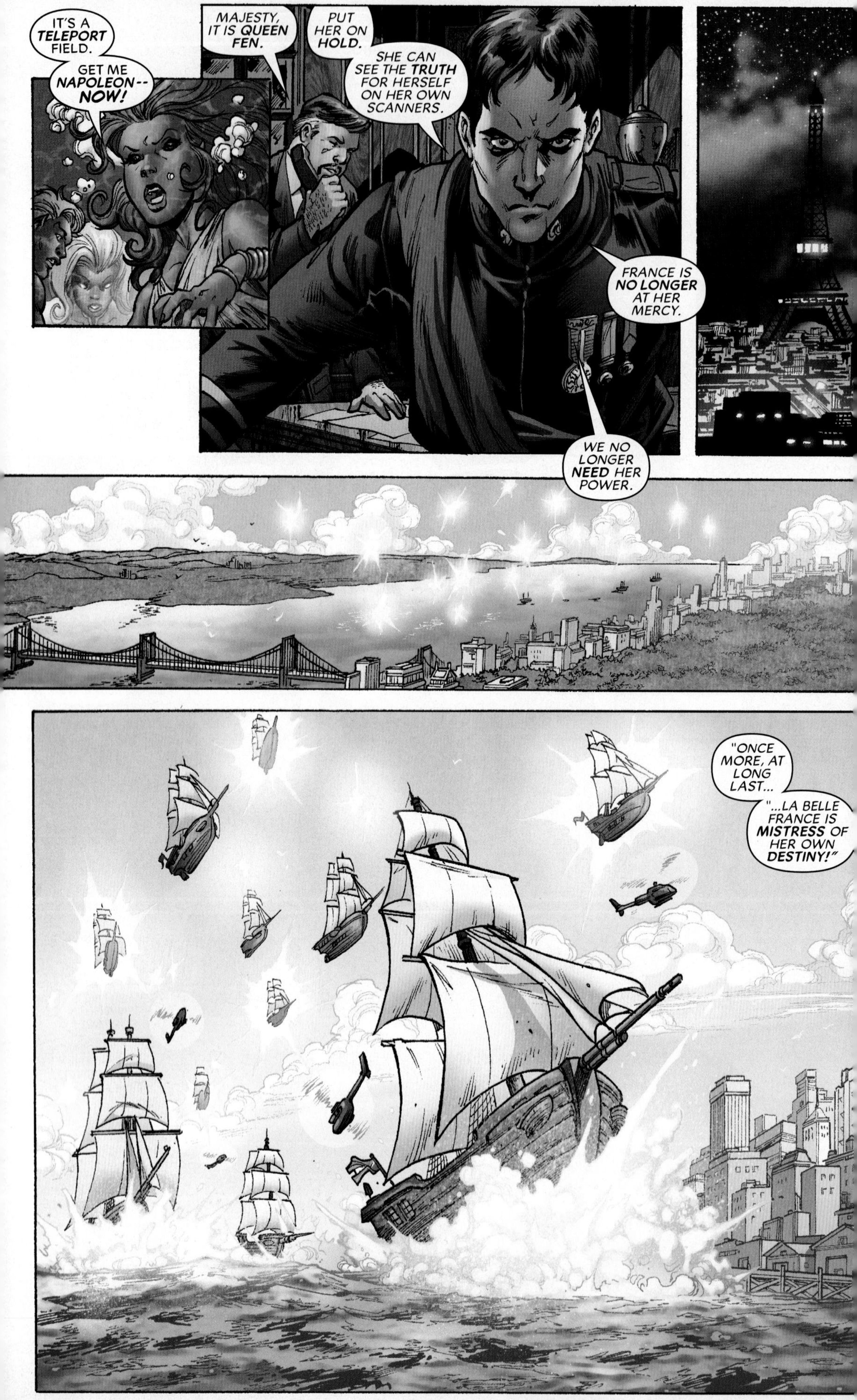
IT'S A TELEPORT FIELD.
GET ME NAPOLEON-- NOW!
MAJESTY, IT IS QUEEN FEN.
PUT HER ON HOLD.
SHE CAN SEE THE TRUTH FOR HERSELF ON HER OWN SCANNERS.
FRANCE IS NO LONGER AT HER MERCY.
WE NO LONGER NEED HER POWER.
"ONCE MORE, AT LONG LAST...
"...LA BELLE FRANCE IS MISTRESS OF HER OWN DESTINY!"

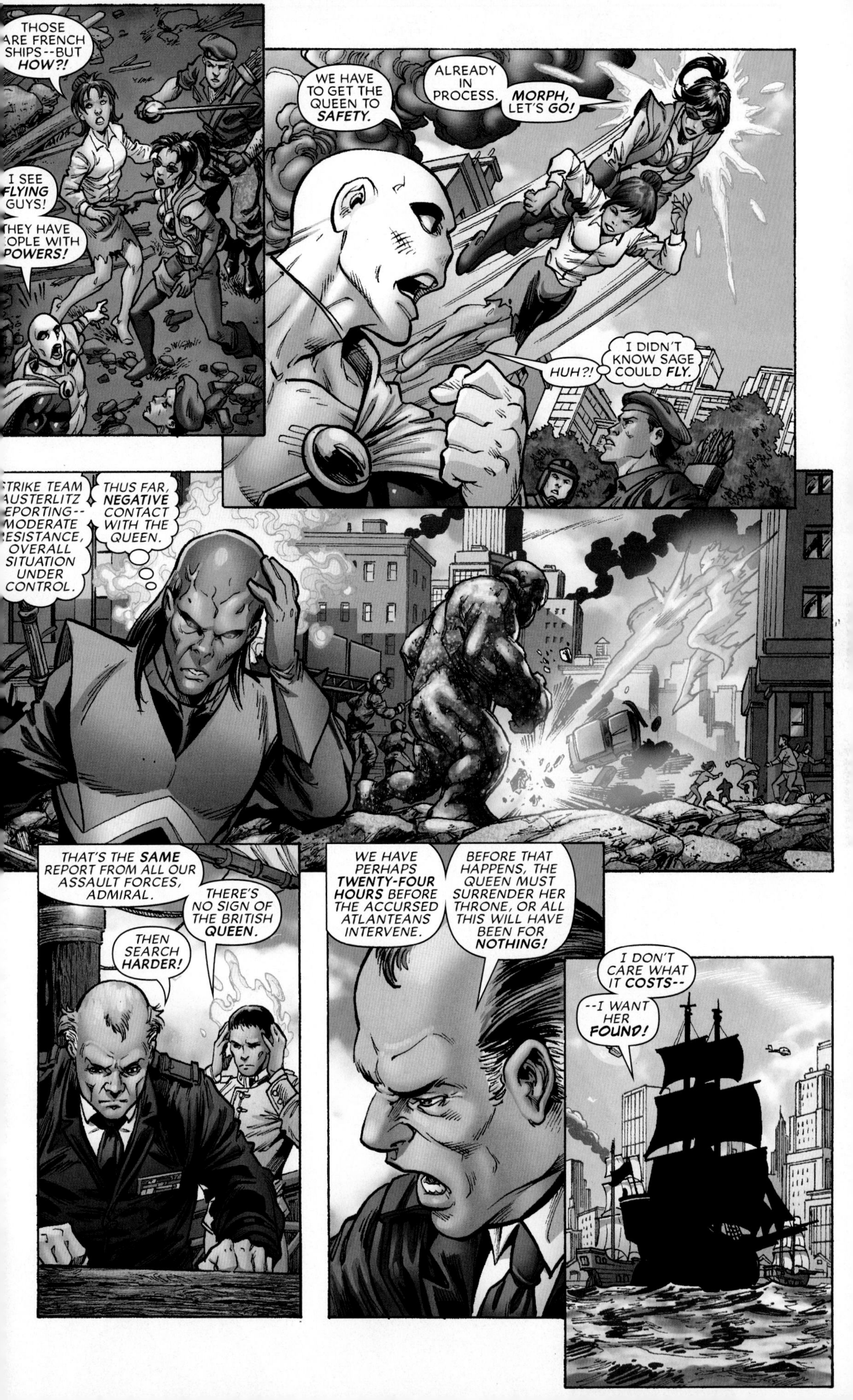
THOSE ARE FRENCH SHIPS--BUT HOW?!
I SEE FLYING GUYS!
THEY HAVE OPLE WITH POWERS!
WE HAVE TO GET THE QUEEN TO SAFETY.
ALREADY IN PROCESS.
MORPH, LET'S GO!
HUH?!
I DIDN'T KNOW SAGE COULD FLY.
TRIKE TEAM AUSTERLITZ EPORTING--MODERATE ESISTANCE, OVERALL SITUATION UNDER CONTROL.
THUS FAR, NEGATIVE CONTACT WITH THE QUEEN.
THAT'S THE SAME REPORT FROM ALL OUR ASSAULT FORCES, ADMIRAL.
THERE'S NO SIGN OF THE BRITISH QUEEN.
THEN SEARCH HARDER!
WE HAVE PERHAPS TWENTY-FOUR HOURS BEFORE THE ACCURSED ATLANTEANS INTERVENE.
BEFORE THAT HAPPENS, THE QUEEN MUST SURRENDER HER THRONE, OR ALL THIS WILL HAVE BEEN FOR NOTHING!
I DON'T CARE WHAT IT COSTS--
--I WANT HER FOUND!

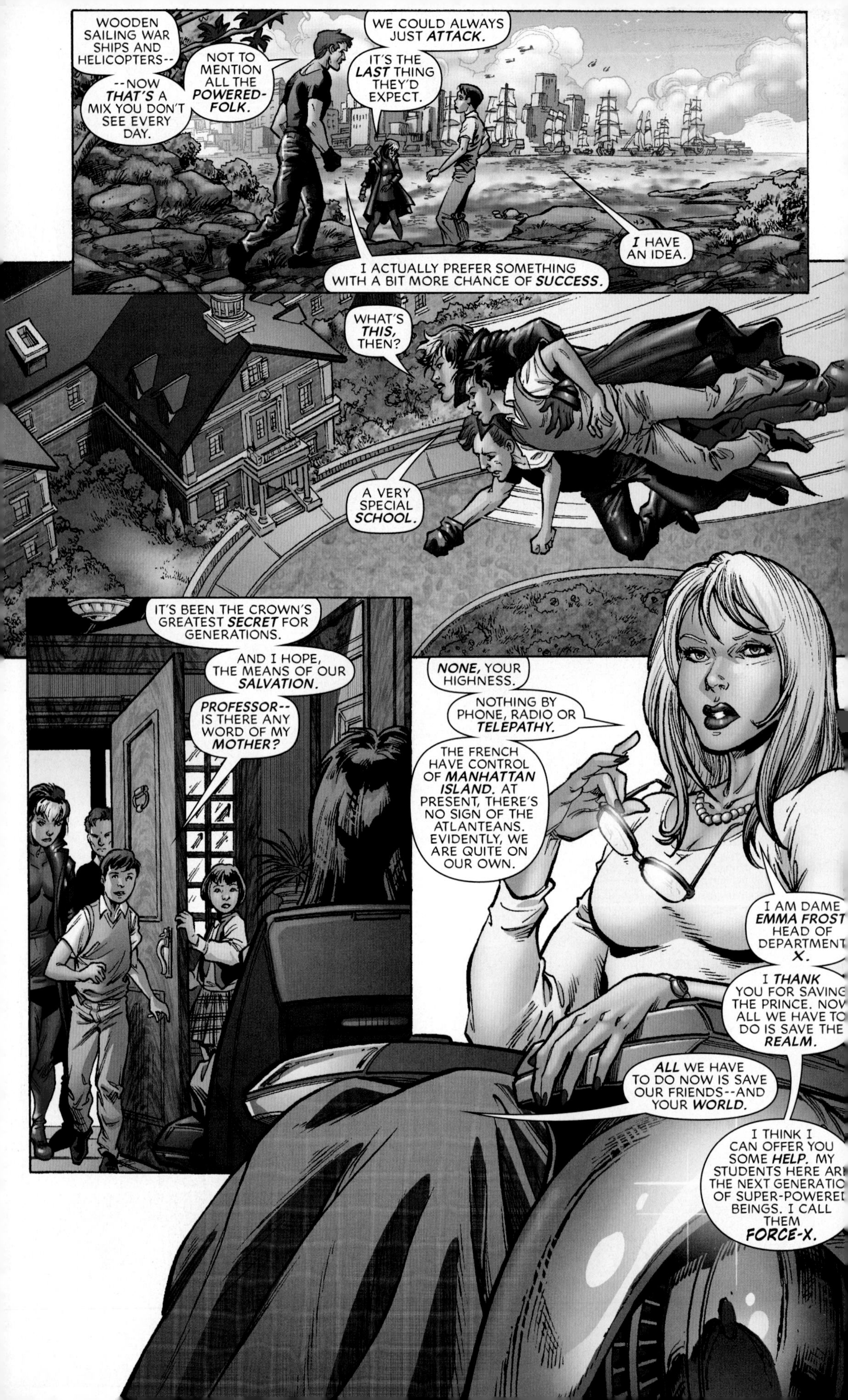
WOODEN SAILING WAR SHIPS AND HELICOPTERS--
--NOW THAT'S A MIX YOU DON'T SEE EVERY DAY.
NOT TO MENTION ALL THE POWERED-FOLK.
WE COULD ALWAYS JUST ATTACK.
IT'S THE LAST THING THEY'D EXPECT.
I ACTUALLY PREFER SOMETHING WITH A BIT MORE CHANCE OF SUCCESS.
I HAVE AN IDEA.
WHAT'S THIS, THEN?
A VERY SPECIAL SCHOOL.
IT'S BEEN THE CROWN'S GREATEST SECRET FOR GENERATIONS.
AND I HOPE, THE MEANS OF OUR SALVATION.
PROFESSOR-- IS THERE ANY WORD OF MY MOTHER?
NONE, YOUR HIGHNESS.
NOTHING BY PHONE, RADIO OR TELEPATHY.
THE FRENCH HAVE CONTROL OF MANHATTAN ISLAND. AT PRESENT, THERE'S NO SIGN OF THE ATLANTEANS. EVIDENTLY, WE ARE QUITE ON OUR OWN.
I AM DAME EMMA FROST HEAD OF DEPARTMENT X.
I THANK YOU FOR SAVING THE PRINCE. NOW ALL WE HAVE TO DO IS SAVE THE REALM.
ALL WE HAVE TO DO NOW IS SAVE OUR FRIENDS--AND YOUR WORLD.
I THINK I CAN OFFER YOU SOME HELP. MY STUDENTS HERE ARE THE NEXT GENERATION OF SUPER-POWERED BEINGS. I CALL THEM FORCE-X.

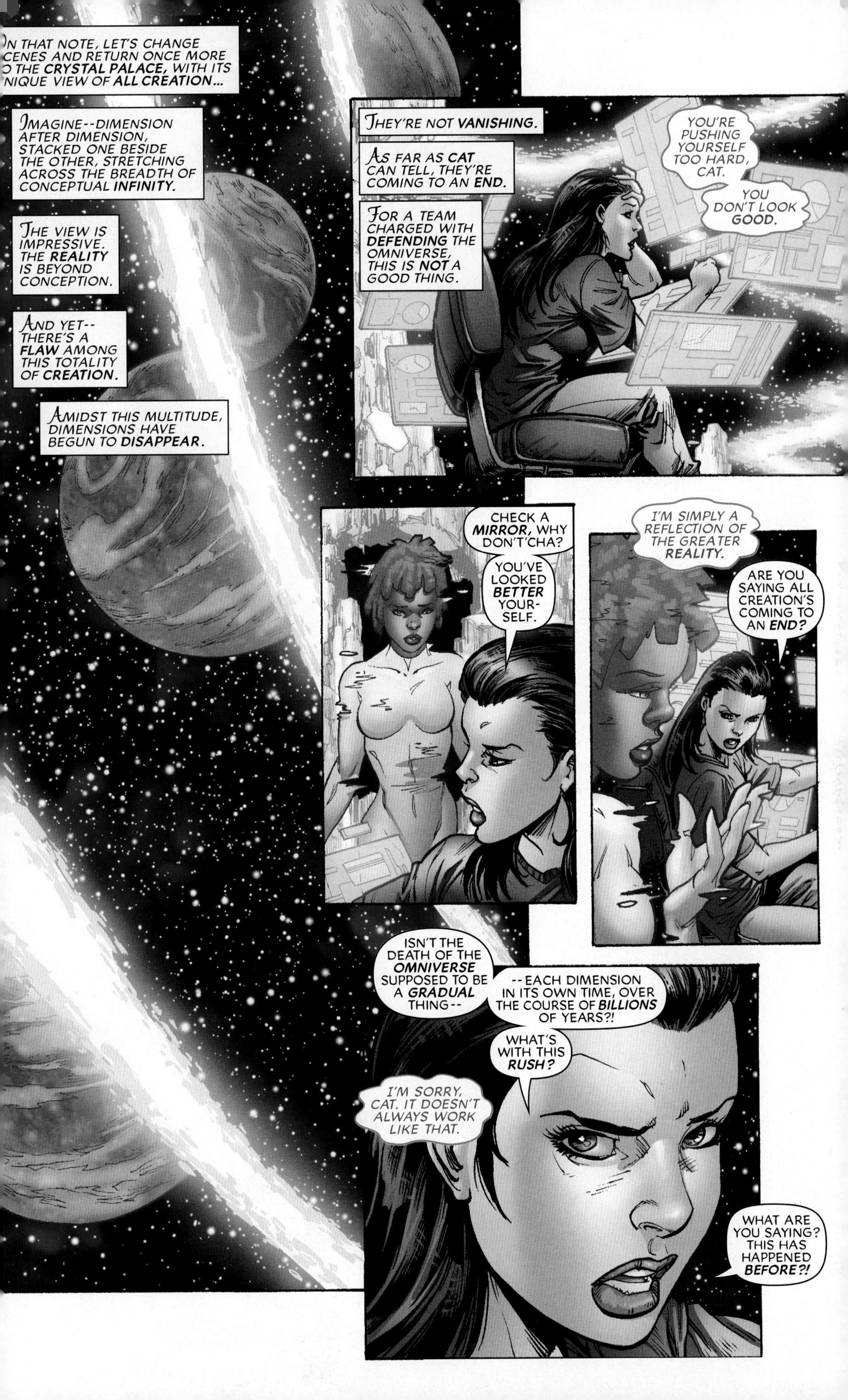
ON THAT NOTE, LET'S CHANGE SCENES AND RETURN ONCE MORE TO THE CRYSTAL PALACE, WITH ITS UNIQUE VIEW OF ALL CREATION...
IMAGINE--DIMENSION AFTER DIMENSION, STACKED ONE BESIDE THE OTHER, STRETCHING ACROSS THE BREADTH OF CONCEPTUAL INFINITY.
THE VIEW IS IMPRESSIVE. THE REALITY IS BEYOND CONCEPTION.
AND YET-- THERE'S A FLAW AMONG THIS TOTALITY OF CREATION.
AMIDST THIS MULTITUDE, DIMENSIONS HAVE BEGUN TO DISAPPEAR.
THEY'RE NOT VANISHING.
AS FAR AS CAT CAN TELL, THEY'RE COMING TO AN END.
FOR A TEAM CHARGED WITH DEFENDING THE OMNIVERSE, THIS IS NOT A GOOD THING.
YOU'RE PUSHING YOURSELF TOO HARD, CAT.
YOU DON'T LOOK GOOD.
CHECK A MIRROR, WHY DON'T'CHA?
YOU'VE LOOKED BETTER YOURSELF.
I'M SIMPLY A REFLECTION OF THE GREATER REALITY.
ARE YOU SAYING ALL CREATION'S COMING TO AN END?
ISN'T THE DEATH OF THE OMNIVERSE SUPPOSED TO BE A GRADUAL THING--
--EACH DIMENSION IN ITS OWN TIME, OVER THE COURSE OF BILLIONS OF YEARS?!
WHAT'S WITH THIS RUSH?
I'M SORRY, CAT. IT DOESN'T ALWAYS WORK LIKE THAT.
WHAT ARE YOU SAYING? THIS HAS HAPPENED BEFORE?!

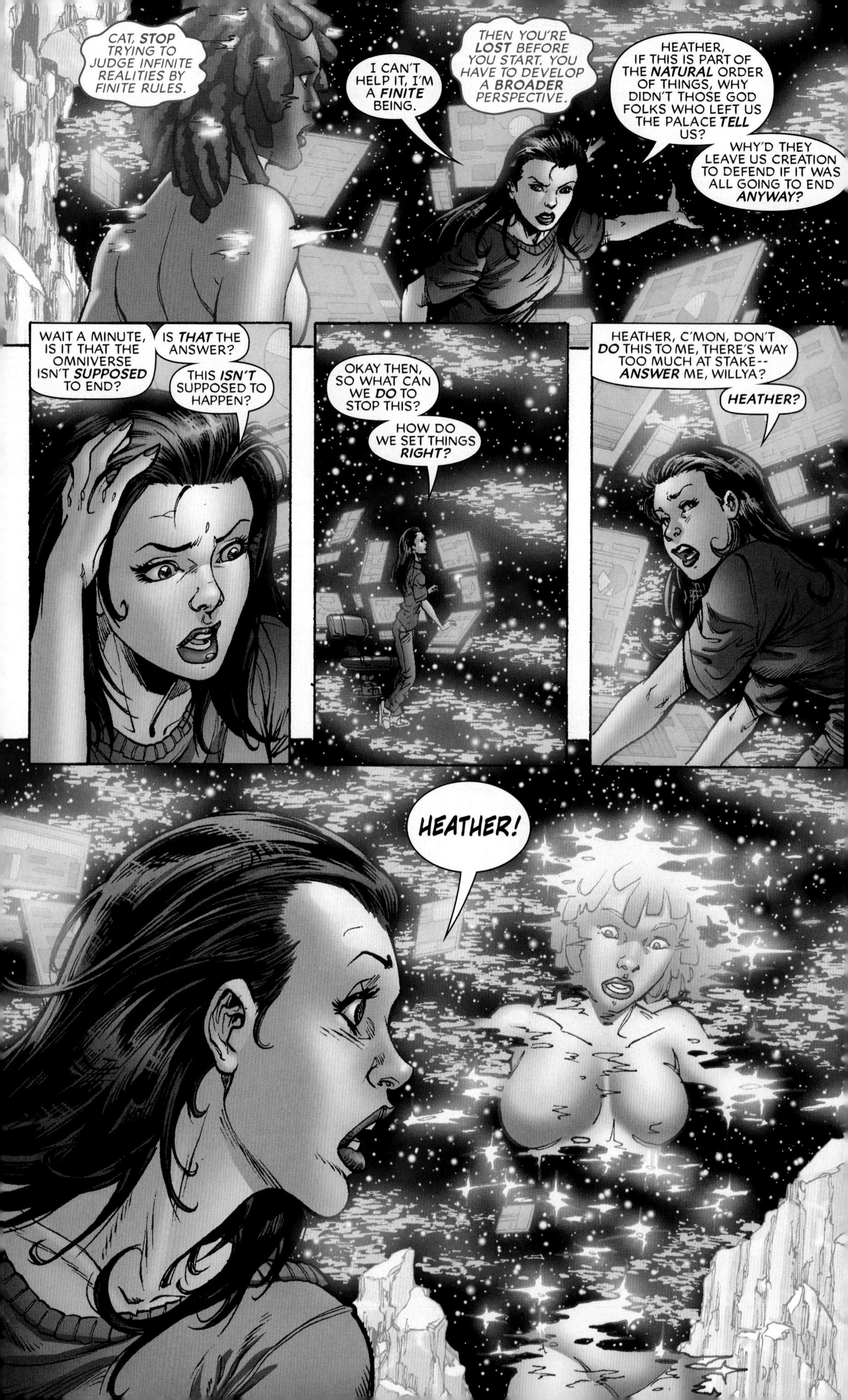
CAT, STOP TRYING TO JUDGE INFINITE REALITIES BY FINITE RULES.
I CAN'T HELP IT, I'M A FINITE BEING.
THEN YOU'RE LOST BEFORE YOU START. YOU HAVE TO DEVELOP A BROADER PERSPECTIVE.
HEATHER, IF THIS IS PART OF THE NATURAL ORDER OF THINGS, WHY DIDN'T THOSE GOD FOLKS WHO LEFT US THE PALACE TELL US?
WHY'D THEY LEAVE US CREATION TO DEFEND IF IT WAS ALL GOING TO END ANYWAY?
WAIT A MINUTE, IS IT THAT THE OMNIVERSE ISN'T SUPPOSED TO END?
IS THAT THE ANSWER?
THIS ISN'T SUPPOSED TO HAPPEN?
OKAY THEN, SO WHAT CAN WE DO TO STOP THIS?
HOW DO WE SET THINGS RIGHT?
HEATHER, C'MON, DON'T DO THIS TO ME, THERE'S WAY TOO MUCH AT STAKE-- ANSWER ME, WILLYA?
HEATHER?
HEATHER!

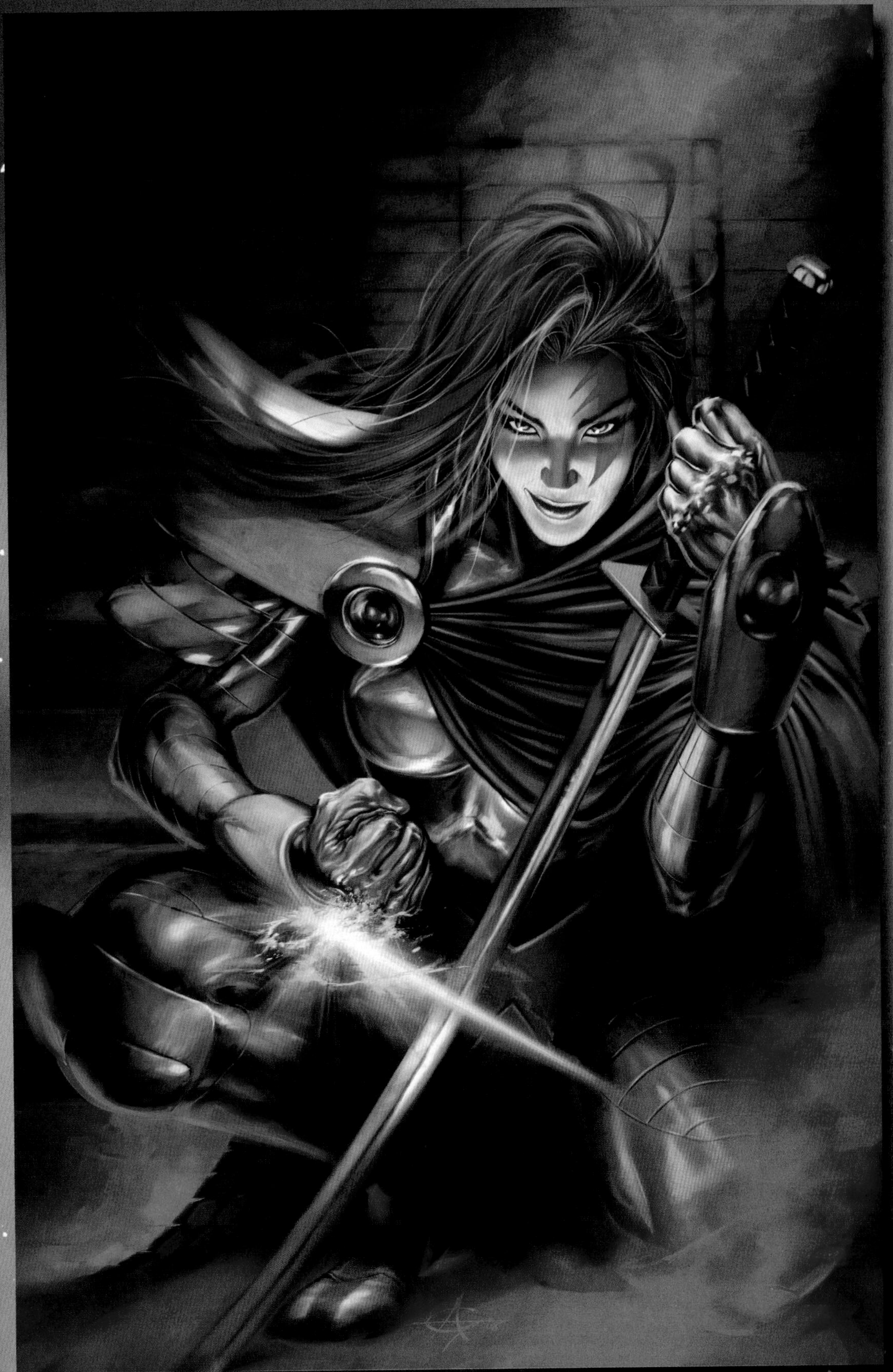

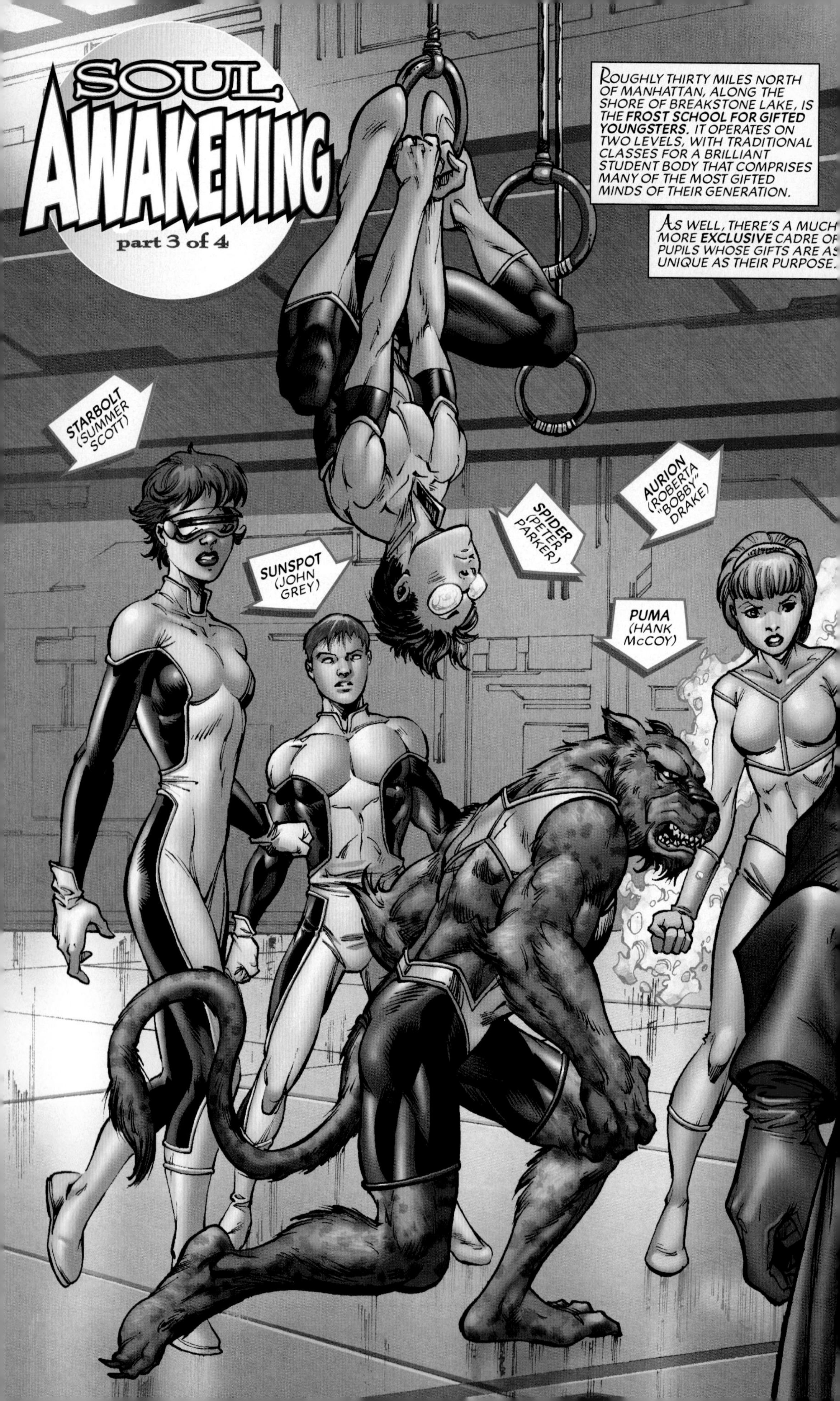
SOUL AWAKENING
part 3 of 4
ROUGHLY THIRTY MILES NORTH OF MANHATTAN, ALONG THE SHORE OF BREAKSTONE LAKE, IS THE FROST SCHOOL FOR GIFTED YOUNGSTERS. IT OPERATES ON TWO LEVELS, WITH TRADITIONAL CLASSES FOR A BRILLIANT STUDENT BODY THAT COMPRISES MANY OF THE MOST GIFTED MINDS OF THEIR GENERATION.
AS WELL, THERE'S A MUCH MORE EXCLUSIVE CADRE OF PUPILS WHOSE GIFTS ARE AS UNIQUE AS THEIR PURPOSE.
STARBOLT (SUMMER SCOTT)
SUNSPOT (JOHN GREY)
SPIDER (PETER PARKER)
AURION (ROBERTA "BOBBY" DRAKE)
PUMA (HANK McCOY)

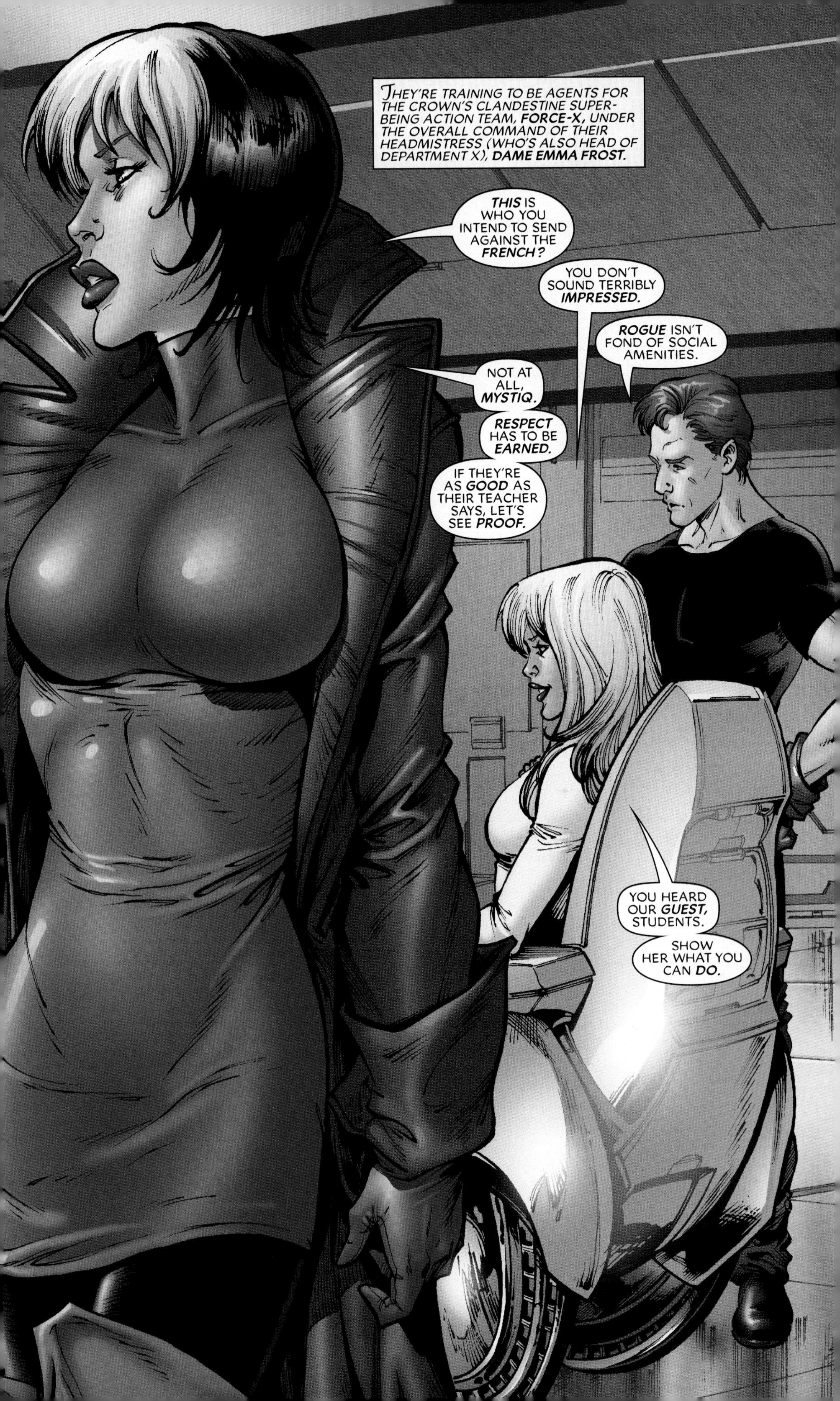
THEY'RE TRAINING TO BE AGENTS FOR THE CROWN'S CLANDESTINE SUPER-BEING ACTION TEAM, FORCE-X, UNDER THE OVERALL COMMAND OF THEIR HEADMISTRESS (WHO'S ALSO HEAD OF DEPARTMENT X), DAME EMMA FROST.
THIS IS WHO YOU INTEND TO SEND AGAINST THE FRENCH?
YOU DON'T SOUND TERRIBLY IMPRESSED.
ROGUE ISN'T FOND OF SOCIAL AMENITIES.
NOT AT ALL, MYSTIQ.
RESPECT HAS TO BE EARNED.
IF THEY'RE AS GOOD AS THEIR TEACHER SAYS, LET'S SEE PROOF.
YOU HEARD OUR GUEST, STUDENTS.
SHOW HER WHAT YOU CAN DO.

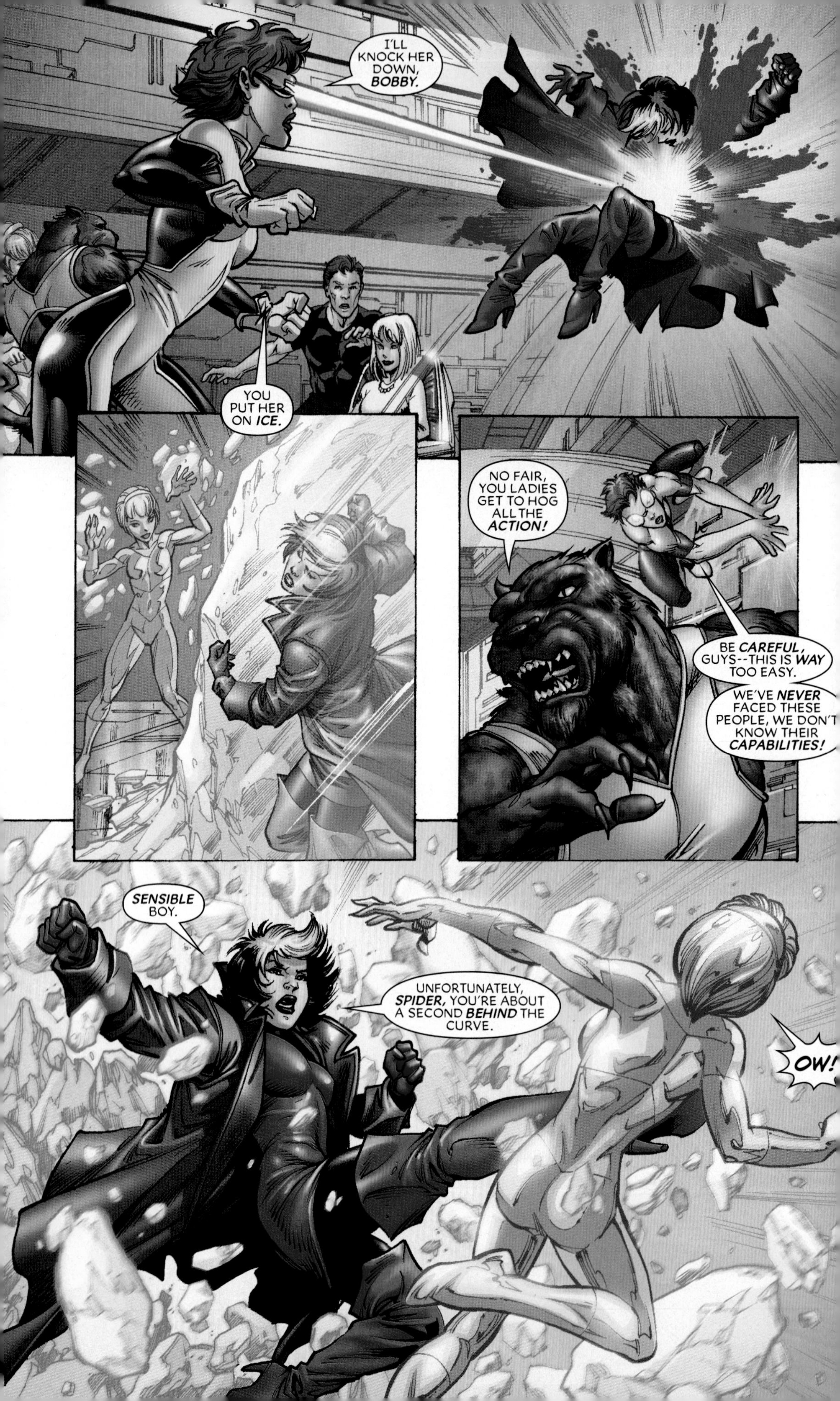
I'LL KNOCK HER DOWN, *BOBBY.*
YOU PUT HER ON *ICE.*
NO FAIR, YOU LADIES GET TO HOG ALL THE *ACTION!*
BE *CAREFUL*, GUYS--THIS IS *WAY* TOO EASY.
WE'VE *NEVER* FACED THESE PEOPLE, WE DON'T KNOW THEIR *CAPABILITIES!*
SENSIBLE BOY.
UNFORTUNATELY, *SPIDER,* YOU'RE ABOUT A SECOND *BEHIND* THE CURVE.
OW!

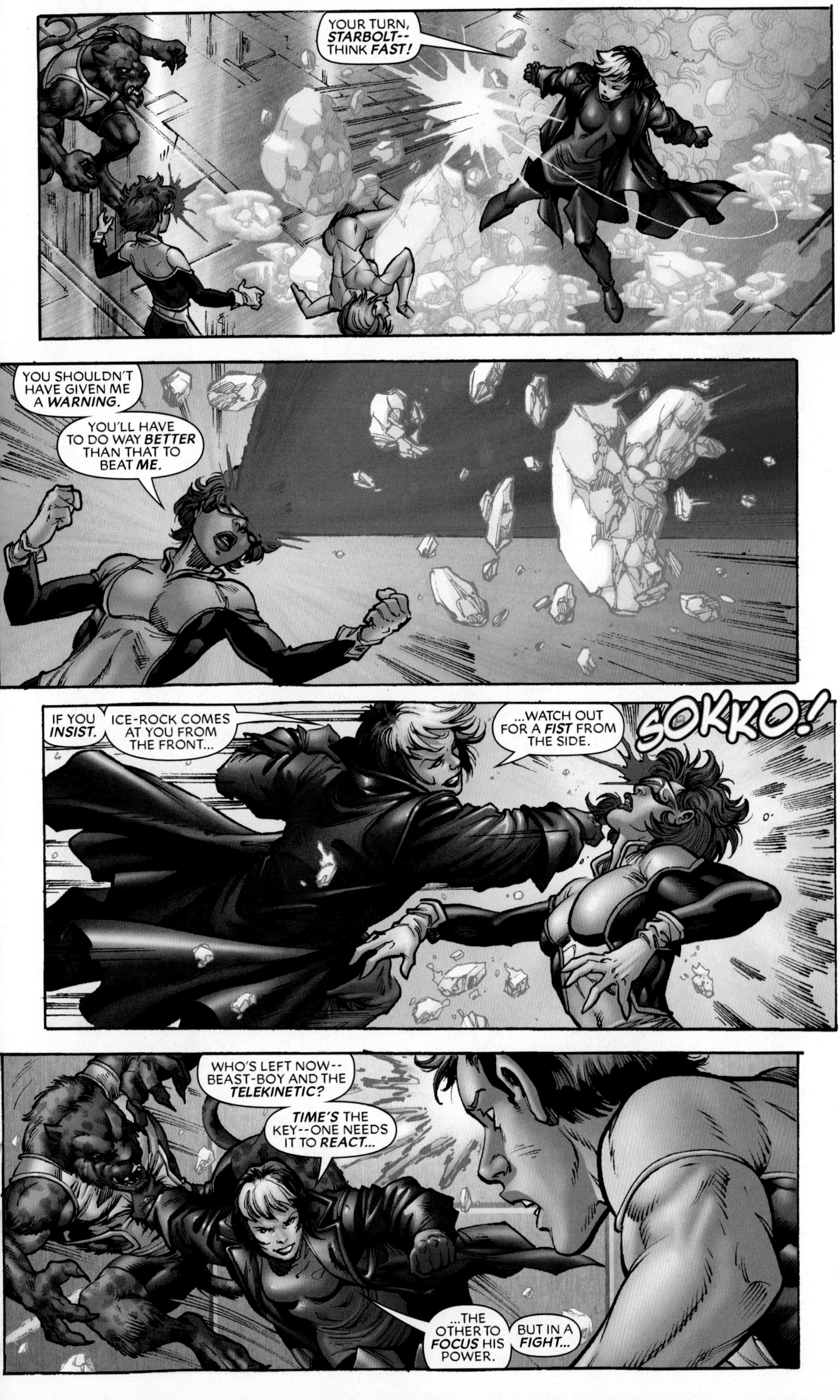
YOUR TURN, STARBOLT-- THINK FAST!
YOU SHOULDN'T HAVE GIVEN ME A WARNING.
YOU'LL HAVE TO DO WAY BETTER THAN THAT TO BEAT ME.
IF YOU INSIST.
ICE-ROCK COMES AT YOU FROM THE FRONT...
...WATCH OUT FOR A FIST FROM THE SIDE.
SOKKO!
WHO'S LEFT NOW-- BEAST-BOY AND THE TELEKINETIC?
TIME'S THE KEY--ONE NEEDS IT TO REACT...
...THE OTHER TO FOCUS HIS POWER.
BUT IN A FIGHT...

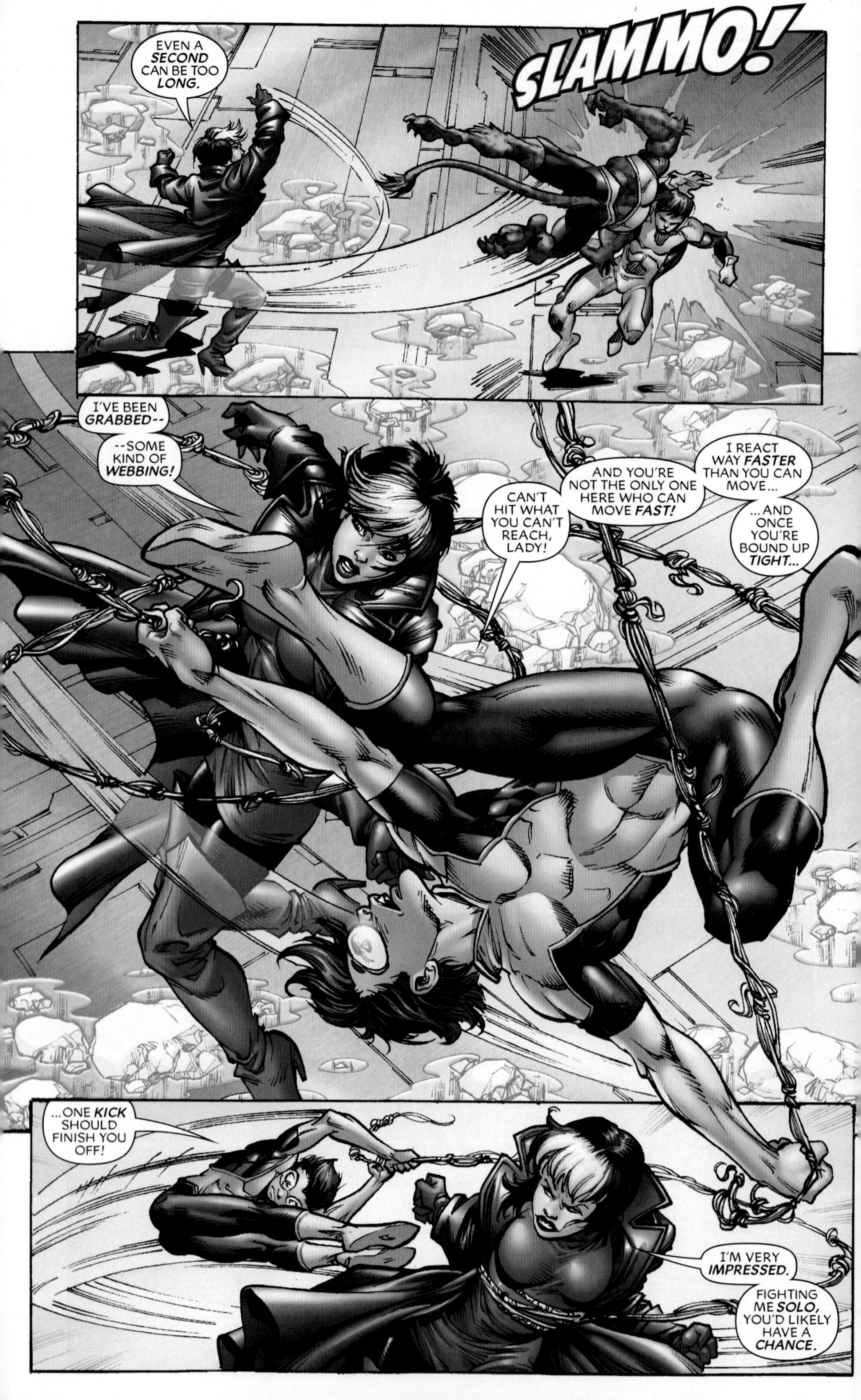

EVEN A SECOND CAN BE TOO LONG.
SLAMMO!
I'VE BEEN GRABBED--
--SOME KIND OF WEBBING!
CAN'T HIT WHAT YOU CAN'T REACH, LADY!
AND YOU'RE NOT THE ONLY ONE HERE WHO CAN MOVE FAST!
I REACT WAY FASTER THAN YOU CAN MOVE...
...AND ONCE YOU'RE BOUND UP TIGHT...
...ONE KICK SHOULD FINISH YOU OFF!
I'M VERY IMPRESSED.
FIGHTING ME SOLO, YOU'D LIKELY HAVE A CHANCE.

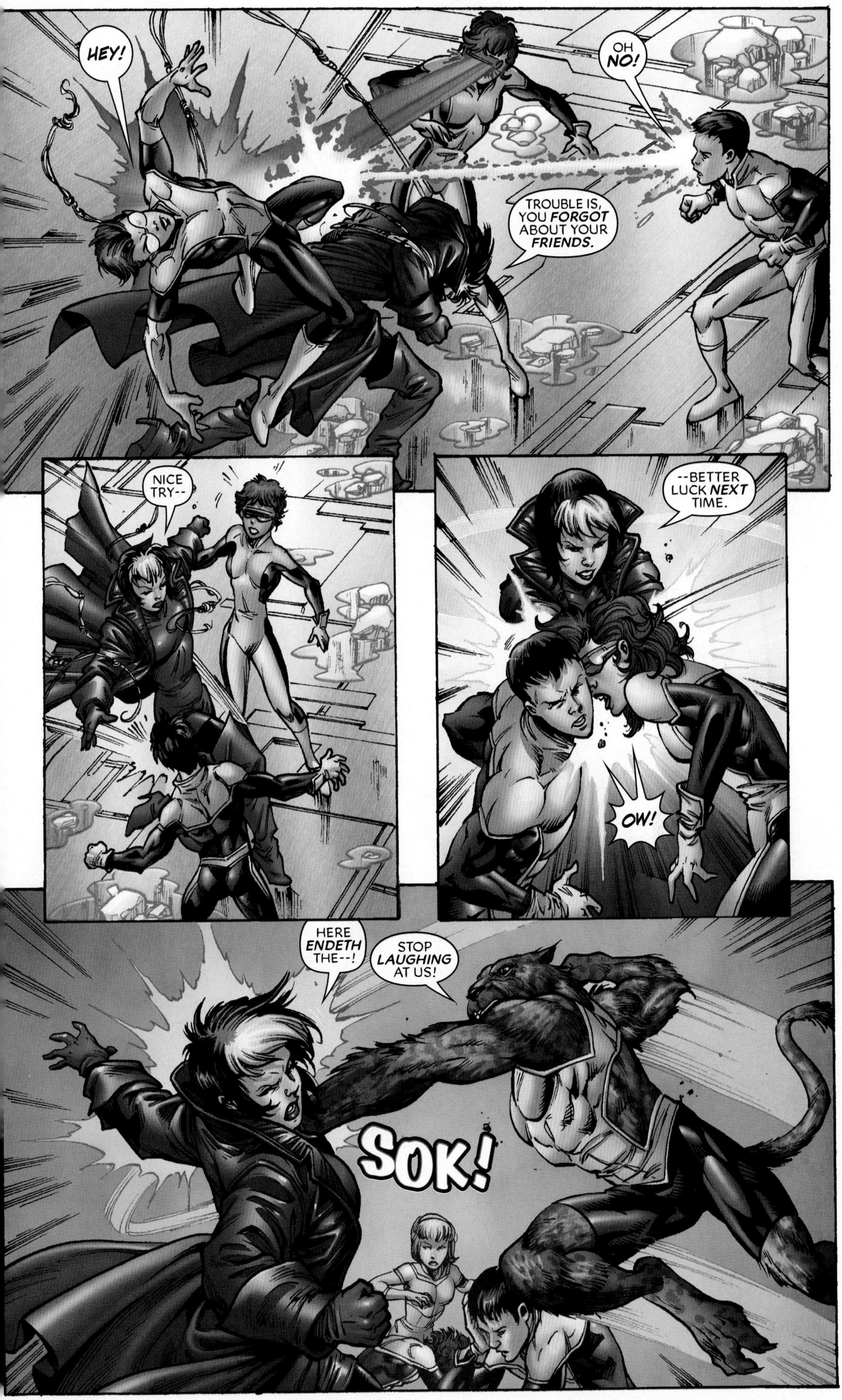
HEY!
OH NO!
TROUBLE IS, YOU FORGOT ABOUT YOUR FRIENDS.
NICE TRY--
--BETTER LUCK NEXT TIME.
OW!
HERE ENDETH THE--!
STOP LAUGHING AT US!
SOK!

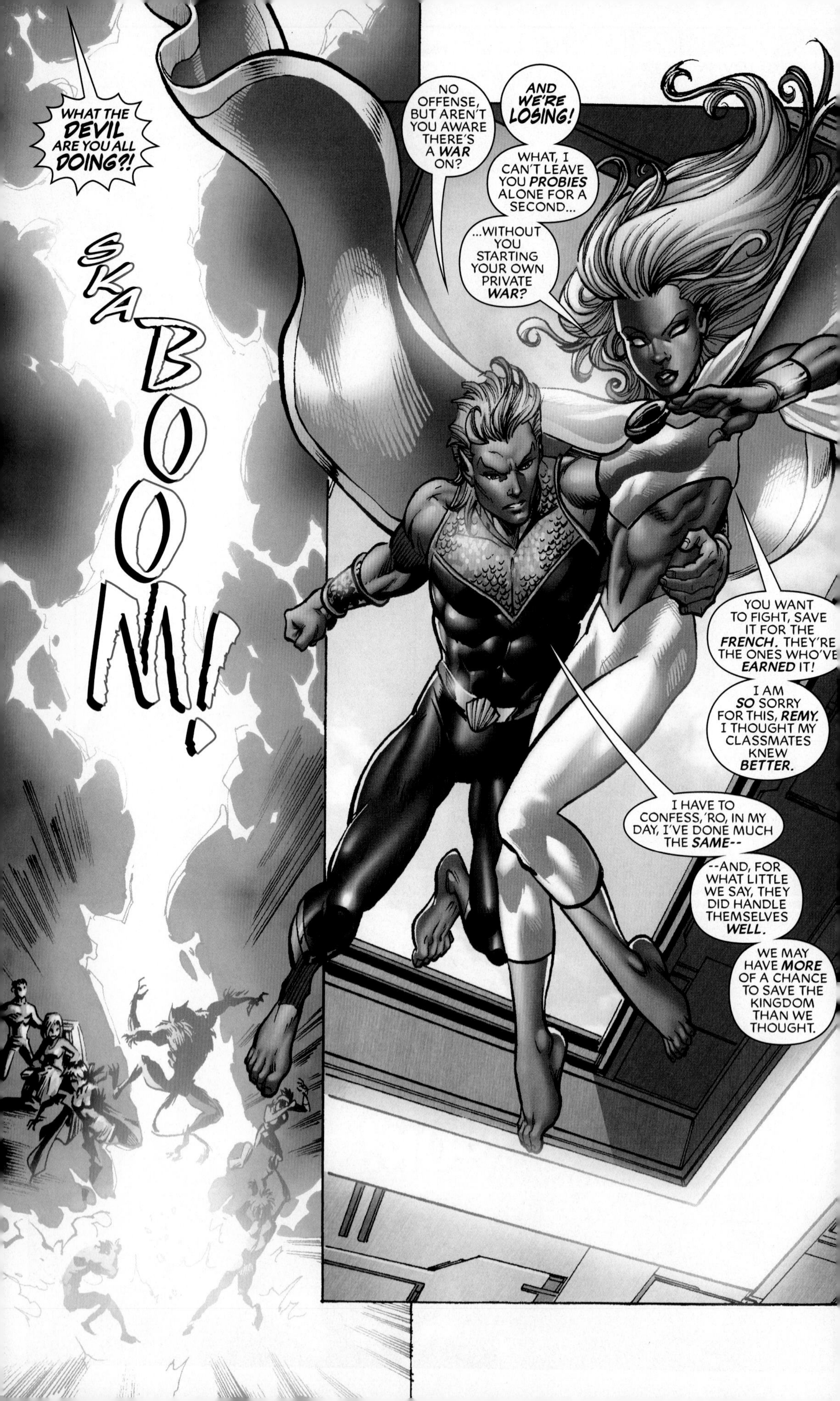
WHAT THE DEVIL ARE YOU ALL DOING?!
SKABOOM!
NO OFFENSE, BUT AREN'T YOU AWARE THERE'S A WAR ON?
AND WE'RE LOSING!
WHAT, I CAN'T LEAVE YOU PROBIES ALONE FOR A SECOND...
...WITHOUT YOU STARTING YOUR OWN PRIVATE WAR?
YOU WANT TO FIGHT, SAVE IT FOR THE FRENCH. THEY'RE THE ONES WHO'VE EARNED IT!
I AM SO SORRY FOR THIS, REMY. I THOUGHT MY CLASSMATES KNEW BETTER.
I HAVE TO CONFESS, 'RO, IN MY DAY, I'VE DONE MUCH THE SAME--
--AND, FOR WHAT LITTLE WE SAY, THEY DID HANDLE THEMSELVES WELL.
WE MAY HAVE MORE OF A CHANCE TO SAVE THE KINGDOM THAN WE THOUGHT.

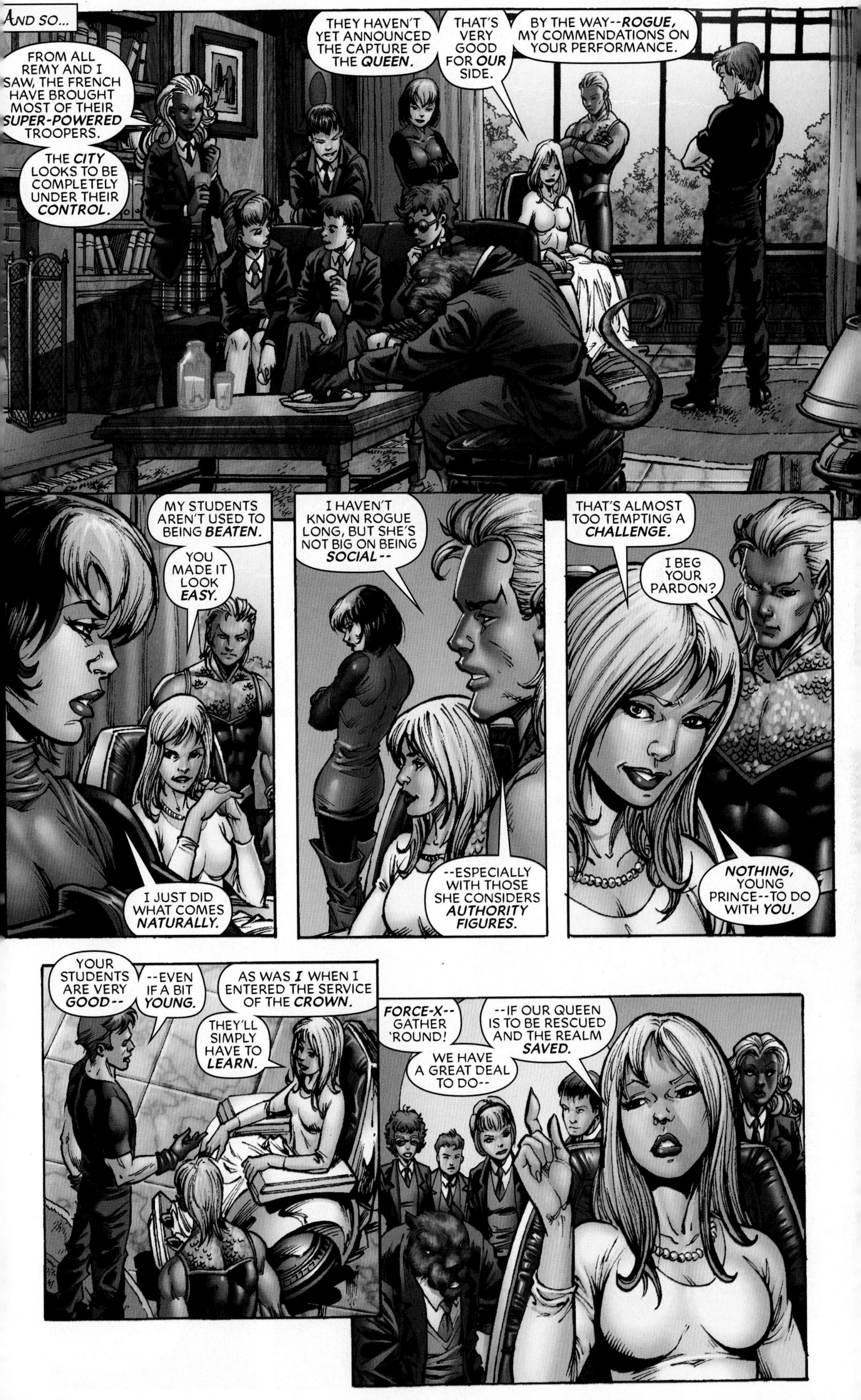

AND SO...
FROM ALL REMY AND I SAW, THE FRENCH HAVE BROUGHT MOST OF THEIR SUPER-POWERED TROOPERS.
THE CITY LOOKS TO BE COMPLETELY UNDER THEIR CONTROL.
THEY HAVEN'T YET ANNOUNCED THE CAPTURE OF THE QUEEN.
THAT'S VERY GOOD FOR OUR SIDE.
BY THE WAY--ROGUE, MY COMMENDATIONS ON YOUR PERFORMANCE.
MY STUDENTS AREN'T USED TO BEING BEATEN.
YOU MADE IT LOOK EASY.
I JUST DID WHAT COMES NATURALLY.
I HAVEN'T KNOWN ROGUE LONG, BUT SHE'S NOT BIG ON BEING SOCIAL--
--ESPECIALLY WITH THOSE SHE CONSIDERS AUTHORITY FIGURES.
THAT'S ALMOST TOO TEMPTING A CHALLENGE.
I BEG YOUR PARDON?
NOTHING, YOUNG PRINCE--TO DO WITH YOU.
YOUR STUDENTS ARE VERY GOOD--
--EVEN IF A BIT YOUNG.
AS WAS I WHEN I ENTERED THE SERVICE OF THE CROWN.
THEY'LL SIMPLY HAVE TO LEARN.
FORCE-X--GATHER 'ROUND!
WE HAVE A GREAT DEAL TO DO--
--IF OUR QUEEN IS TO BE RESCUED AND THE REALM SAVED.

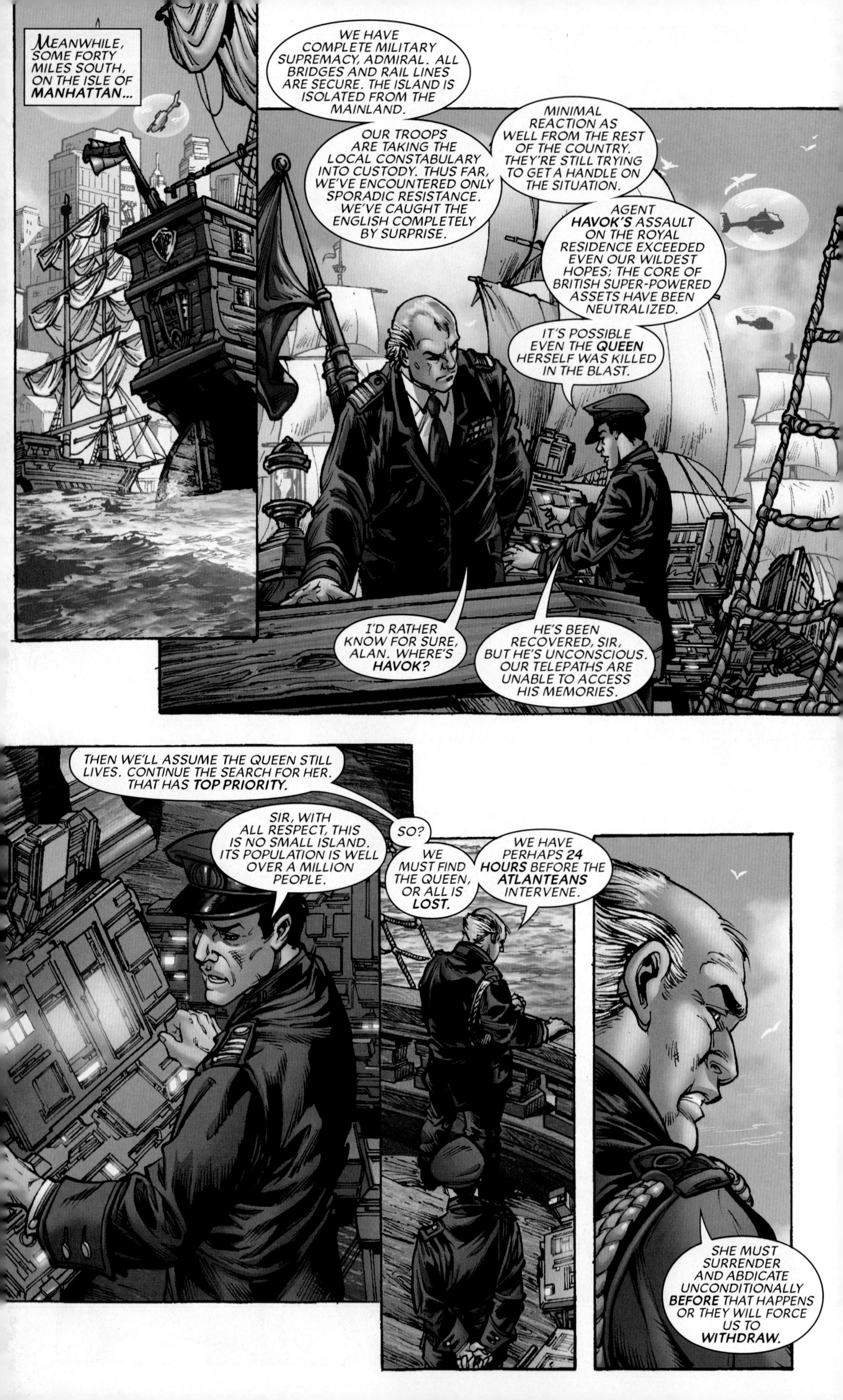
MEANWHILE, SOME FORTY MILES SOUTH, ON THE ISLE OF MANHATTAN...
WE HAVE COMPLETE MILITARY SUPREMACY, ADMIRAL. ALL BRIDGES AND RAIL LINES ARE SECURE. THE ISLAND IS ISOLATED FROM THE MAINLAND.
OUR TROOPS ARE TAKING THE LOCAL CONSTABULARY INTO CUSTODY. THUS FAR, WE'VE ENCOUNTERED ONLY SPORADIC RESISTANCE. WE'VE CAUGHT THE ENGLISH COMPLETELY BY SURPRISE.
MINIMAL REACTION AS WELL FROM THE REST OF THE COUNTRY. THEY'RE STILL TRYING TO GET A HANDLE ON THE SITUATION.
AGENT HAVOK'S ASSAULT ON THE ROYAL RESIDENCE EXCEEDED EVEN OUR WILDEST HOPES; THE CORE OF BRITISH SUPER-POWERED ASSETS HAVE BEEN NEUTRALIZED.
IT'S POSSIBLE EVEN THE QUEEN HERSELF WAS KILLED IN THE BLAST.
I'D RATHER KNOW FOR SURE, ALAN. WHERE'S HAVOK?
HE'S BEEN RECOVERED, SIR, BUT HE'S UNCONSCIOUS. OUR TELEPATHS ARE UNABLE TO ACCESS HIS MEMORIES.
THEN WE'LL ASSUME THE QUEEN STILL LIVES. CONTINUE THE SEARCH FOR HER. THAT HAS TOP PRIORITY.
SIR, WITH ALL RESPECT, THIS IS NO SMALL ISLAND. ITS POPULATION IS WELL OVER A MILLION PEOPLE.
SO?
WE MUST FIND THE QUEEN, OR ALL IS LOST.
WE HAVE PERHAPS 24 HOURS BEFORE THE ATLANTEANS INTERVENE.
SHE MUST SURRENDER AND ABDICATE UNCONDITIONALLY BEFORE THAT HAPPENS OR THEY WILL FORCE US TO WITHDRAW.

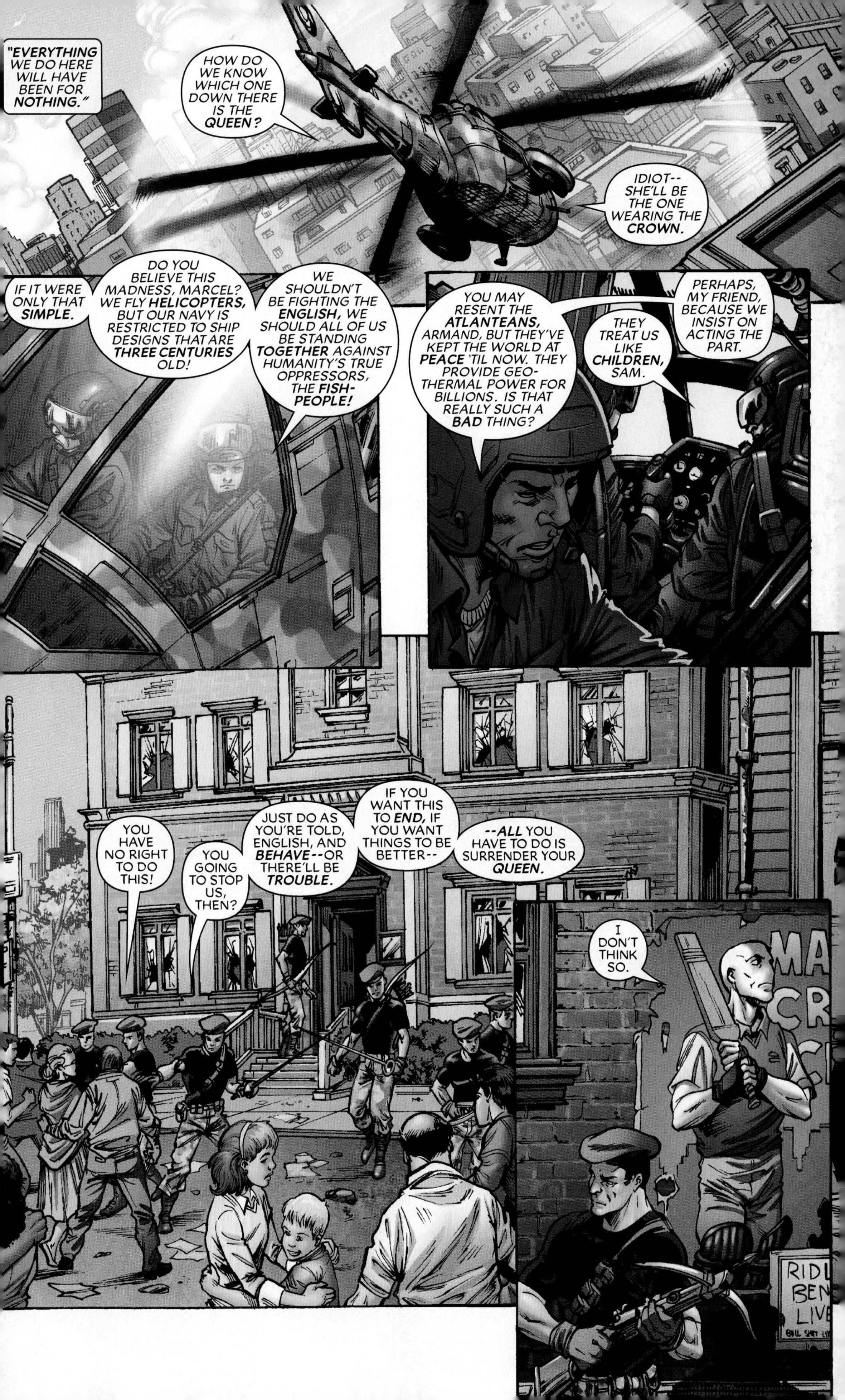
"EVERYTHING WE DO HERE WILL HAVE BEEN FOR NOTHING."
HOW DO WE KNOW WHICH ONE DOWN THERE IS THE QUEEN?
IDIOT--SHE'LL BE THE ONE WEARING THE CROWN.
IF IT WERE ONLY THAT SIMPLE.
DO YOU BELIEVE THIS MADNESS, MARCEL? WE FLY HELICOPTERS, BUT OUR NAVY IS RESTRICTED TO SHIP DESIGNS THAT ARE THREE CENTURIES OLD!
WE SHOULDN'T BE FIGHTING THE ENGLISH, WE SHOULD ALL OF US BE STANDING TOGETHER AGAINST HUMANITY'S TRUE OPPRESSORS, THE FISH-PEOPLE!
YOU MAY RESENT THE ATLANTEANS, ARMAND, BUT THEY'VE KEPT THE WORLD AT PEACE 'TIL NOW. THEY PROVIDE GEO-THERMAL POWER FOR BILLIONS. IS THAT REALLY SUCH A BAD THING?
THEY TREAT US LIKE CHILDREN, SAM.
PERHAPS, MY FRIEND, BECAUSE WE INSIST ON ACTING THE PART.
YOU HAVE NO RIGHT TO DO THIS!
YOU GOING TO STOP US, THEN?
JUST DO AS YOU'RE TOLD, ENGLISH, AND BEHAVE--OR THERE'LL BE TROUBLE.
IF YOU WANT THIS TO END, IF YOU WANT THINGS TO BE BETTER--
--ALL YOU HAVE TO DO IS SURRENDER YOUR QUEEN.
I DON'T THINK SO.

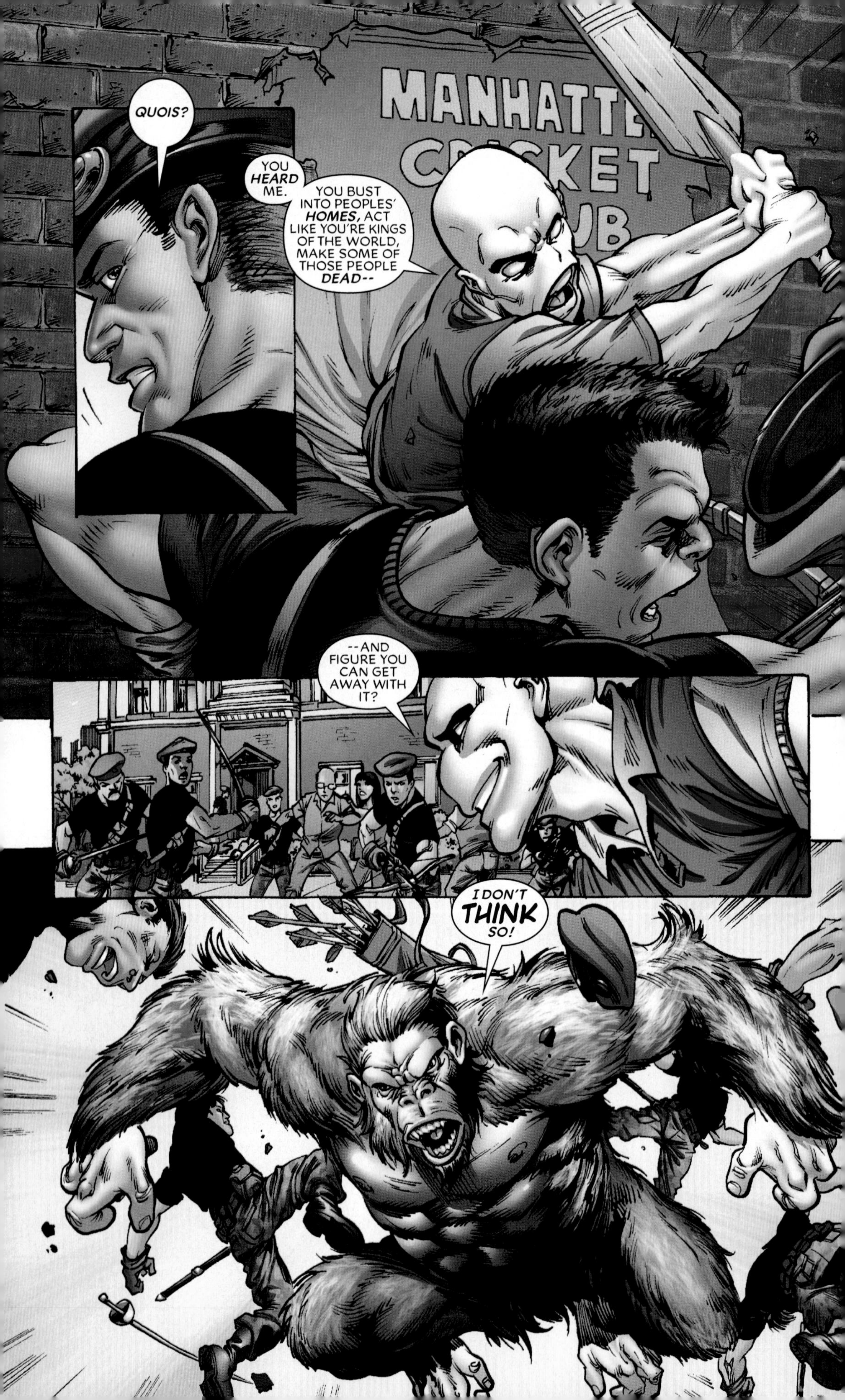
MANHATTEN CRICKET CLUB
QUOIS?
YOU HEARD ME.
YOU BUST INTO PEOPLES' HOMES, ACT LIKE YOU'RE KINGS OF THE WORLD, MAKE SOME OF THOSE PEOPLE DEAD--
--AND FIGURE YOU CAN GET AWAY WITH IT?
I DON'T THINK SO!

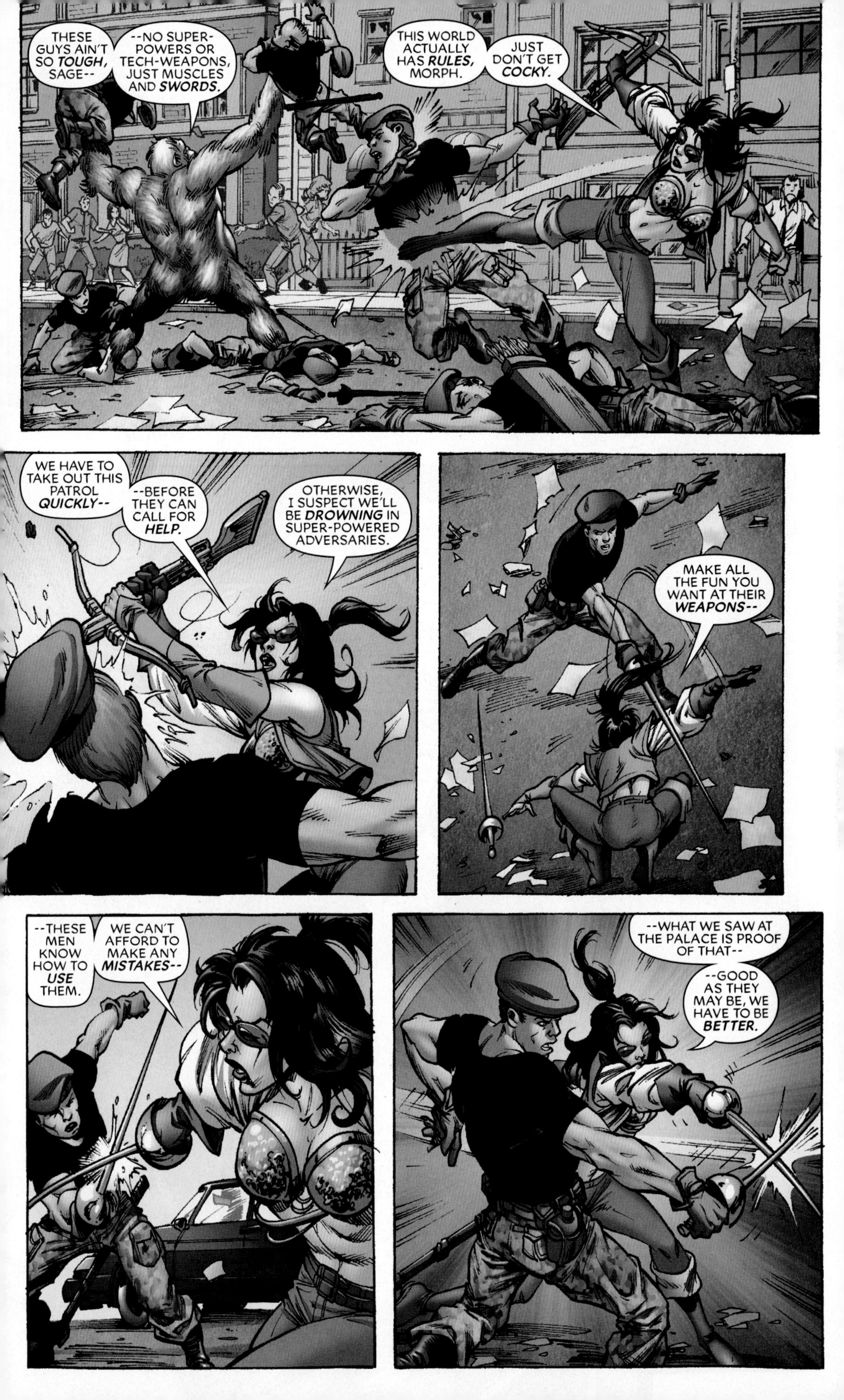

THESE GUYS AIN'T SO TOUGH, SAGE--
--NO SUPER-POWERS OR TECH-WEAPONS, JUST MUSCLES AND SWORDS.
THIS WORLD ACTUALLY HAS RULES, MORPH.
JUST DON'T GET COCKY.
WE HAVE TO TAKE OUT THIS PATROL QUICKLY--
--BEFORE THEY CAN CALL FOR HELP.
OTHERWISE, I SUSPECT WE'LL BE DROWNING IN SUPER-POWERED ADVERSARIES.
MAKE ALL THE FUN YOU WANT AT THEIR WEAPONS--
--THESE MEN KNOW HOW TO USE THEM.
WE CAN'T AFFORD TO MAKE ANY MISTAKES--
--WHAT WE SAW AT THE PALACE IS PROOF OF THAT--
--GOOD AS THEY MAY BE, WE HAVE TO BE BETTER.

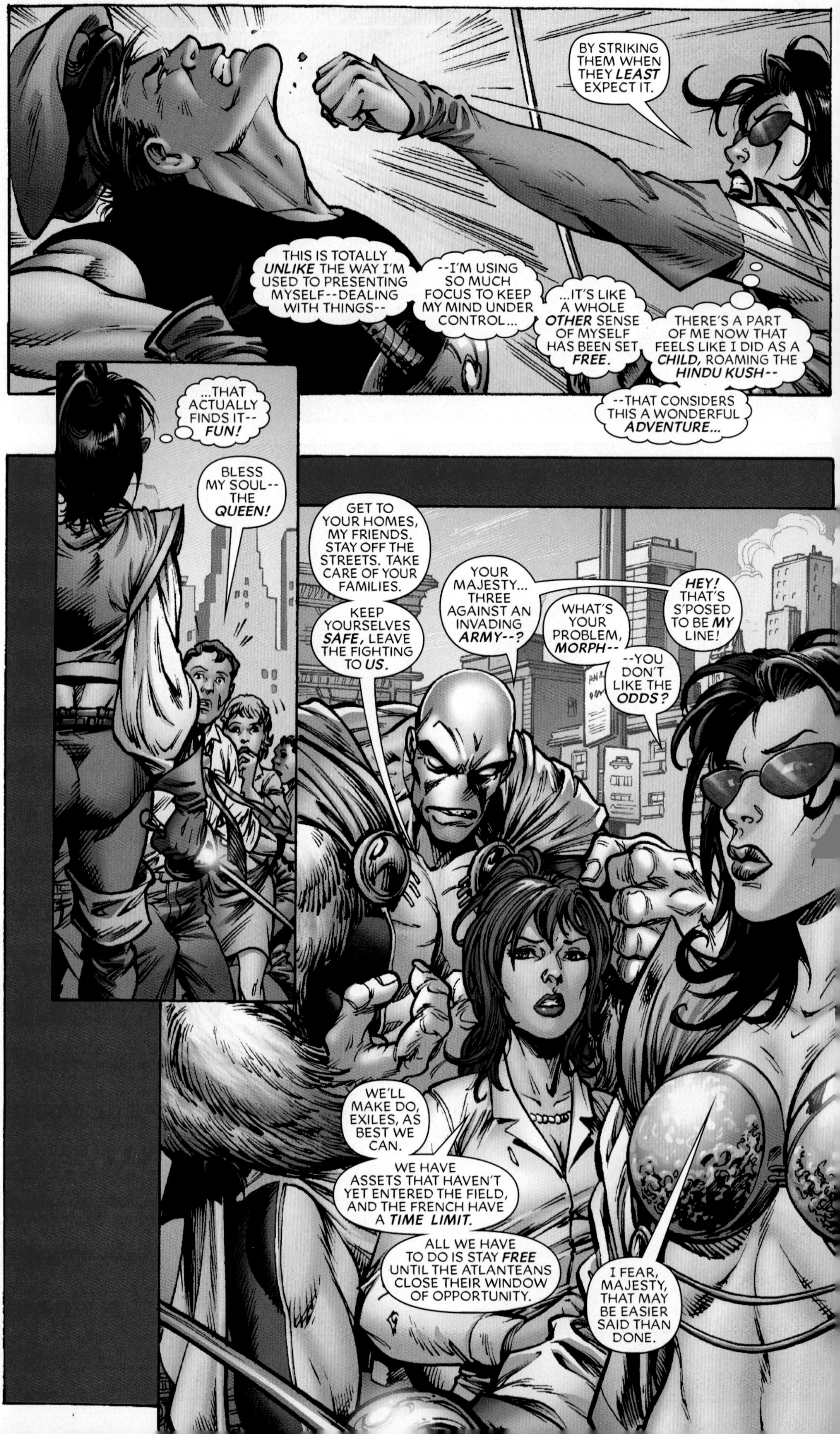
BY STRIKING THEM WHEN THEY LEAST EXPECT IT.
THIS IS TOTALLY UNLIKE THE WAY I'M USED TO PRESENTING MYSELF--DEALING WITH THINGS--
--I'M USING SO MUCH FOCUS TO KEEP MY MIND UNDER CONTROL...
...IT'S LIKE A WHOLE OTHER SENSE OF MYSELF HAS BEEN SET FREE.
THERE'S A PART OF ME NOW THAT FEELS LIKE I DID AS A CHILD, ROAMING THE HINDU KUSH--
--THAT CONSIDERS THIS A WONDERFUL ADVENTURE...
...THAT ACTUALLY FINDS IT--FUN!
BLESS MY SOUL--THE QUEEN!
GET TO YOUR HOMES, MY FRIENDS. STAY OFF THE STREETS. TAKE CARE OF YOUR FAMILIES.
KEEP YOURSELVES SAFE, LEAVE THE FIGHTING TO US.
YOUR MAJESTY... THREE AGAINST AN INVADING ARMY--?
HEY! THAT'S S'POSED TO BE MY LINE!
WHAT'S YOUR PROBLEM, MORPH--
--YOU DON'T LIKE THE ODDS?
WE'LL MAKE DO, EXILES, AS BEST WE CAN.
WE HAVE ASSETS THAT HAVEN'T YET ENTERED THE FIELD, AND THE FRENCH HAVE A TIME LIMIT.
ALL WE HAVE TO DO IS STAY FREE UNTIL THE ATLANTEANS CLOSE THEIR WINDOW OF OPPORTUNITY.
I FEAR, MAJESTY, THAT MAY BE EASIER SAID THAN DONE.

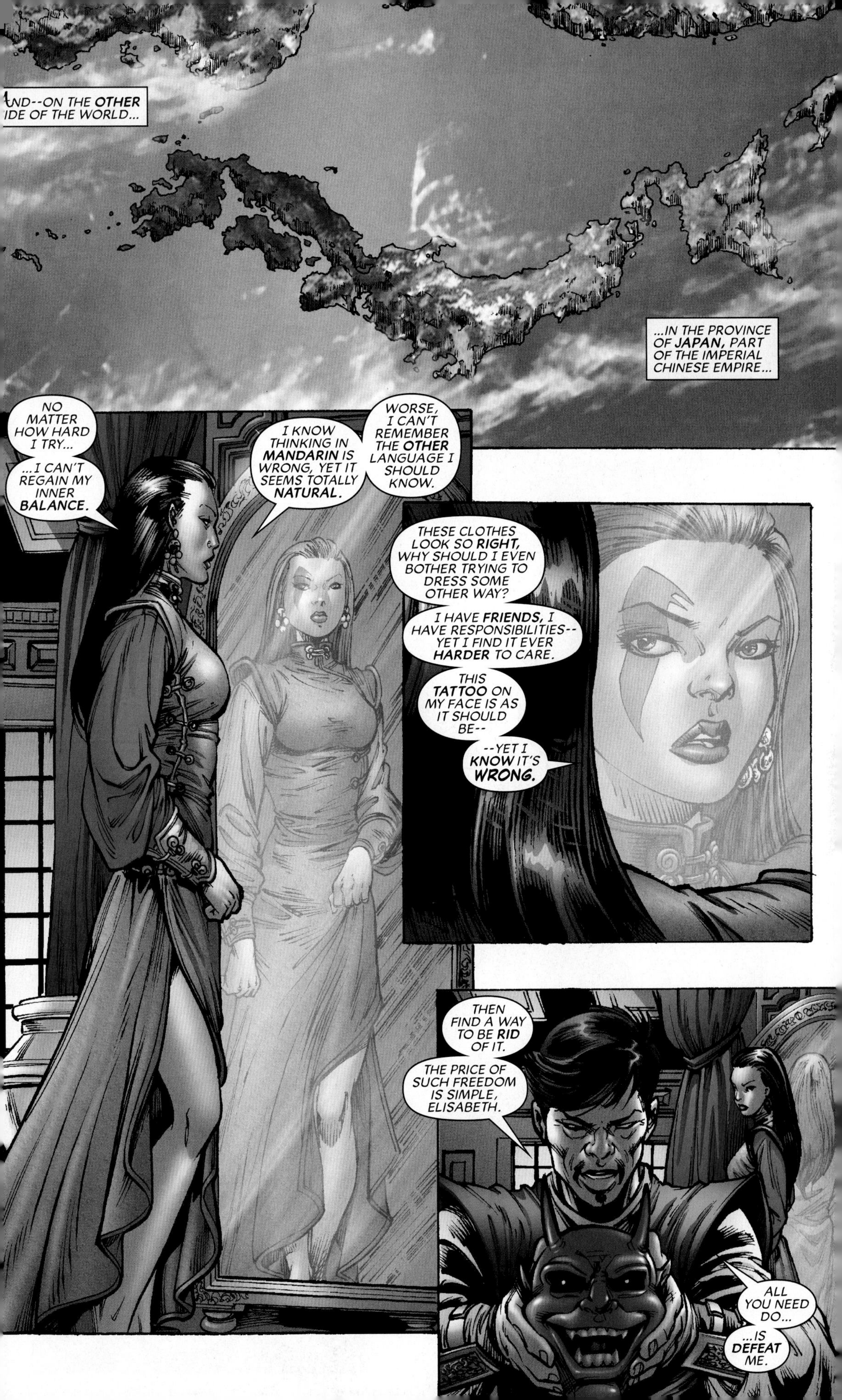
AND--ON THE OTHER SIDE OF THE WORLD...
...IN THE PROVINCE OF JAPAN, PART OF THE IMPERIAL CHINESE EMPIRE...
NO MATTER HOW HARD I TRY...
...I CAN'T REGAIN MY INNER BALANCE.
I KNOW THINKING IN MANDARIN IS WRONG, YET IT SEEMS TOTALLY NATURAL.
WORSE, I CAN'T REMEMBER THE OTHER LANGUAGE I SHOULD KNOW.
THESE CLOTHES LOOK SO RIGHT, WHY SHOULD I EVEN BOTHER TRYING TO DRESS SOME OTHER WAY?
I HAVE FRIENDS, I HAVE RESPONSIBILITIES--YET I FIND IT EVER HARDER TO CARE.
THIS TATTOO ON MY FACE IS AS IT SHOULD BE--
--YET I KNOW IT'S WRONG.
THEN FIND A WAY TO BE RID OF IT.
THE PRICE OF SUCH FREEDOM IS SIMPLE, ELISABETH.
ALL YOU NEED DO...
...IS DEFEAT ME.

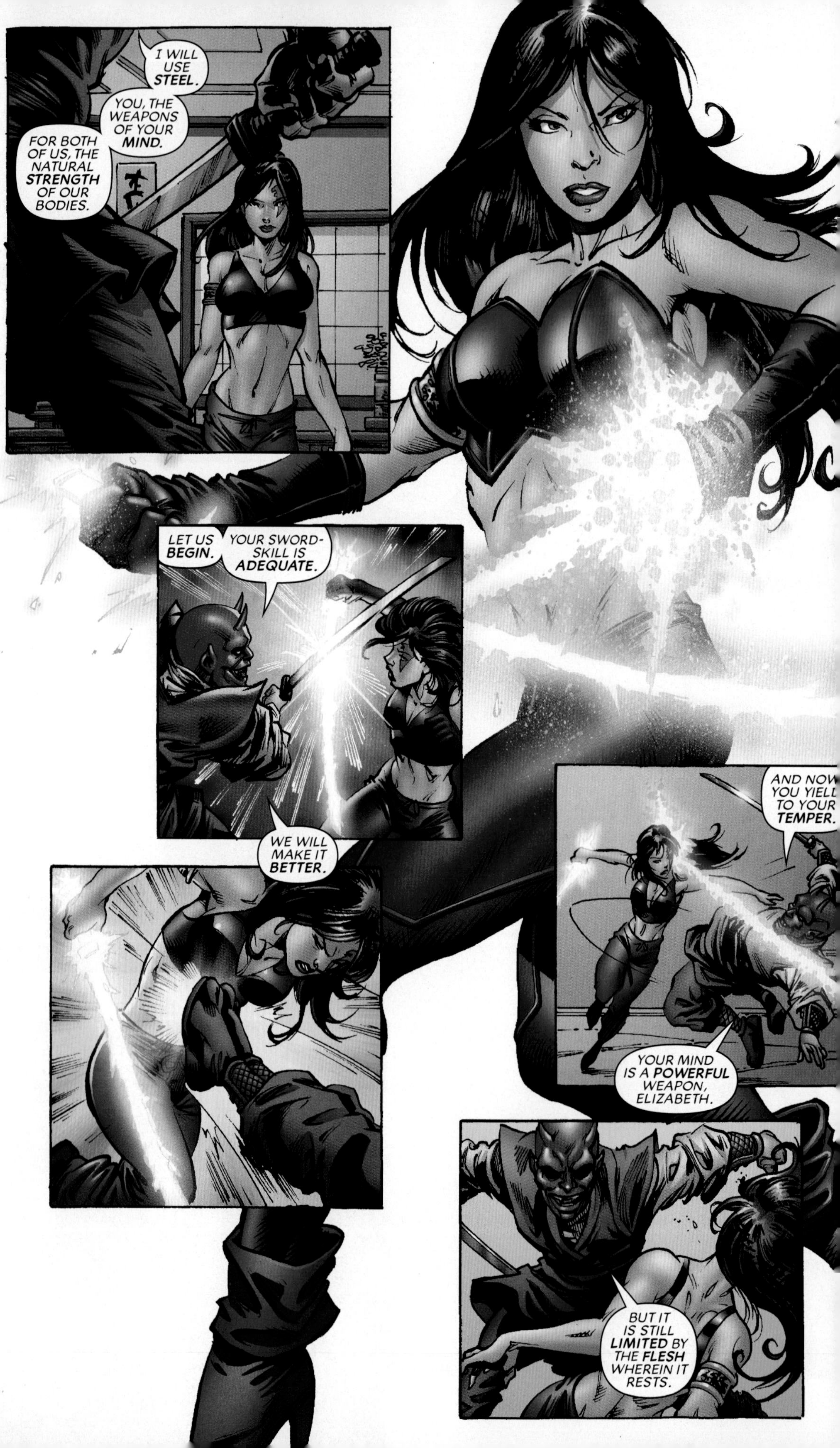
I WILL USE STEEL.
YOU, THE WEAPONS OF YOUR MIND.
FOR BOTH OF US, THE NATURAL STRENGTH OF OUR BODIES.
LET US BEGIN.
YOUR SWORD-SKILL IS ADEQUATE.
WE WILL MAKE IT BETTER.
AND NOW YOU YIELD TO YOUR TEMPER.
YOUR MIND IS A POWERFUL WEAPON, ELIZABETH.
BUT IT IS STILL LIMITED BY THE FLESH WHEREIN IT RESTS.

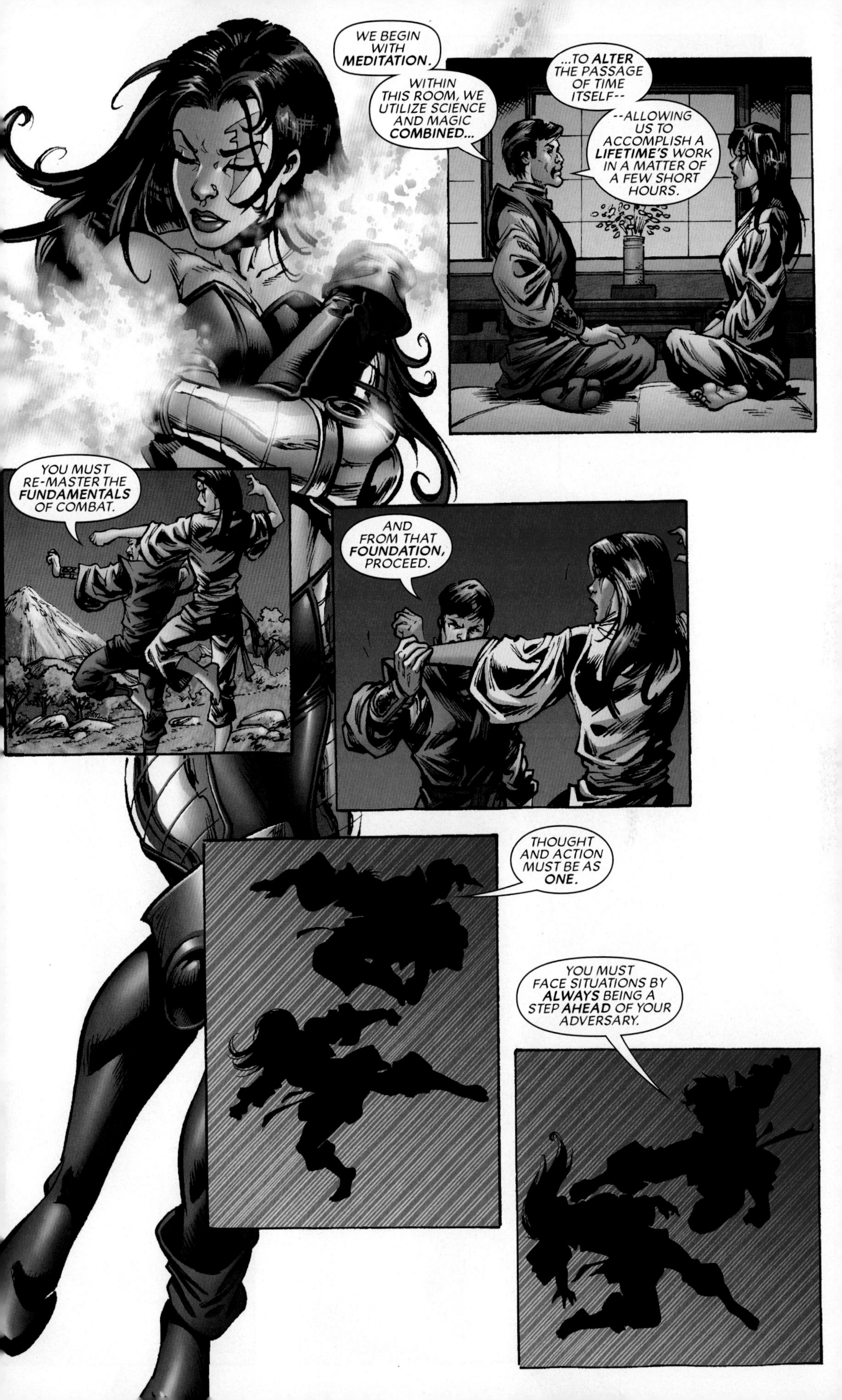
WE BEGIN WITH MEDITATION.
WITHIN THIS ROOM, WE UTILIZE SCIENCE AND MAGIC COMBINED...
...TO ALTER THE PASSAGE OF TIME ITSELF--
--ALLOWING US TO ACCOMPLISH A LIFETIME'S WORK IN A MATTER OF A FEW SHORT HOURS.
YOU MUST RE-MASTER THE FUNDAMENTALS OF COMBAT.
AND FROM THAT FOUNDATION, PROCEED.
THOUGHT AND ACTION MUST BE AS ONE.
YOU MUST FACE SITUATIONS BY ALWAYS BEING A STEP AHEAD OF YOUR ADVERSARY.

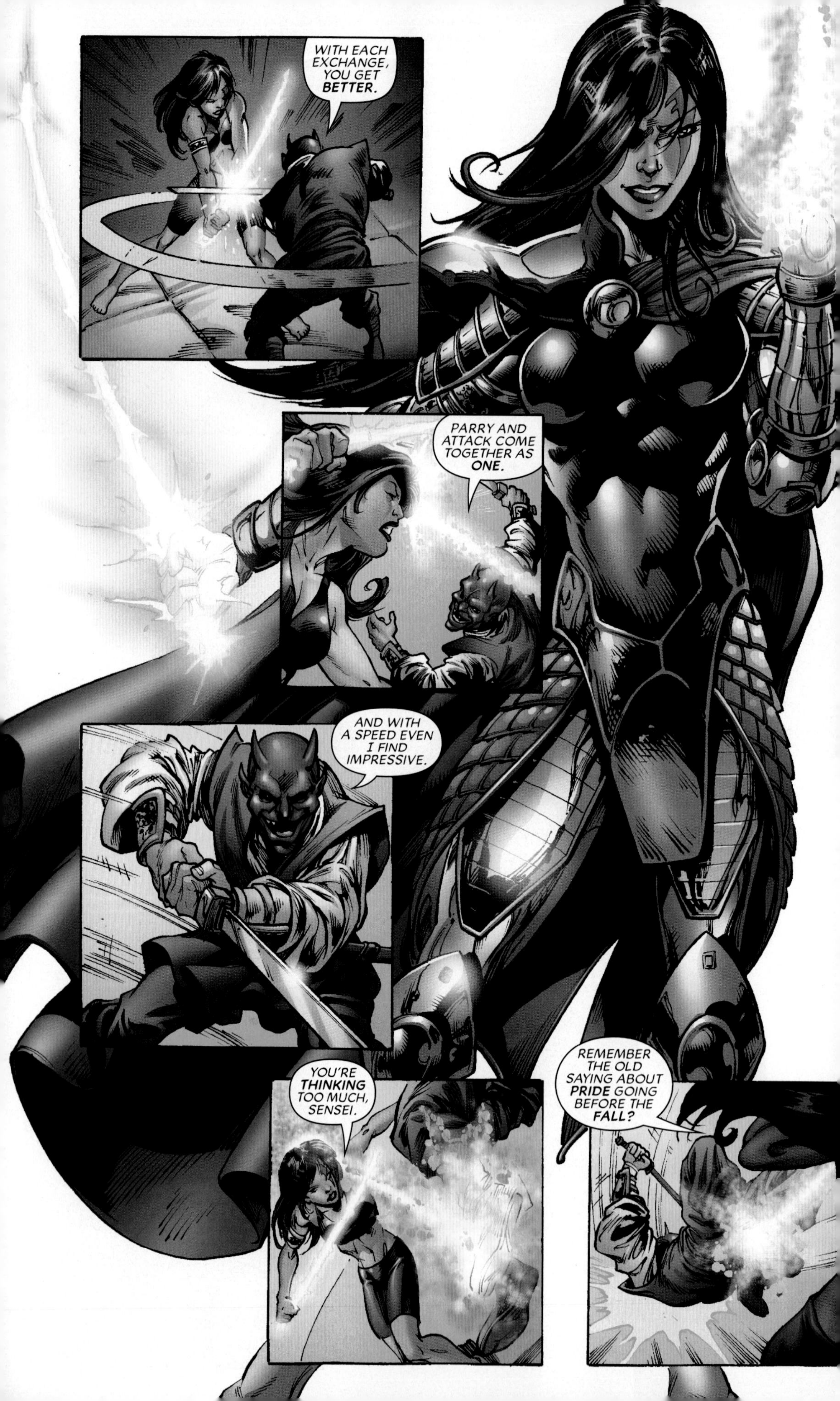
WITH EACH EXCHANGE, YOU GET BETTER.
PARRY AND ATTACK COME TOGETHER AS ONE.
AND WITH A SPEED EVEN I FIND IMPRESSIVE.
YOU'RE THINKING TOO MUCH, SENSEI.
REMEMBER THE OLD SAYING ABOUT PRIDE GOING BEFORE THE FALL?

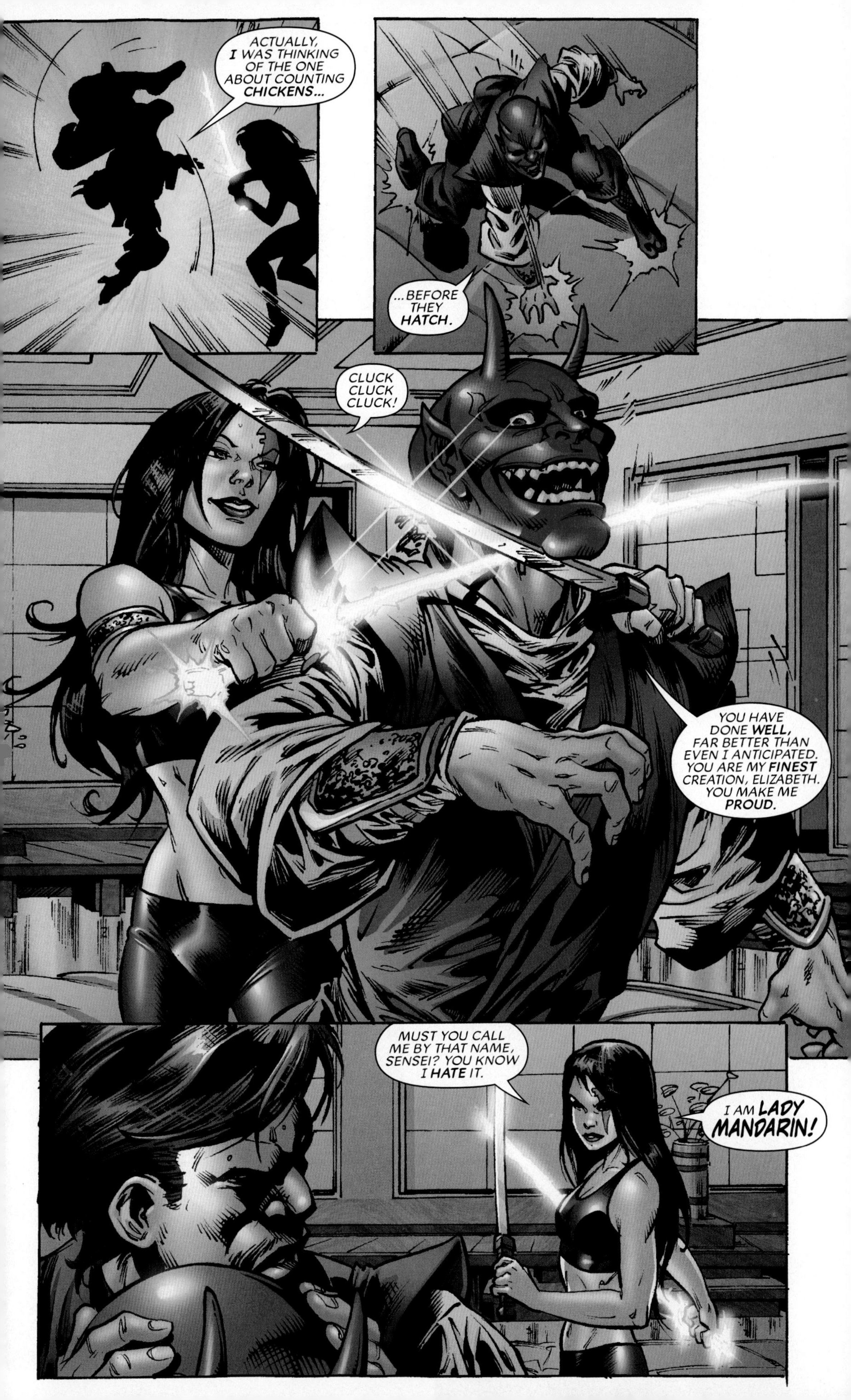
ACTUALLY, I WAS THINKING OF THE ONE ABOUT COUNTING CHICKENS...
...BEFORE THEY HATCH.
CLUCK CLUCK CLUCK!
YOU HAVE DONE WELL, FAR BETTER THAN EVEN I ANTICIPATED. YOU ARE MY FINEST CREATION, ELIZABETH. YOU MAKE ME PROUD.
MUST YOU CALL ME BY THAT NAME, SENSEI? YOU KNOW I HATE IT.
I AM LADY MANDARIN!

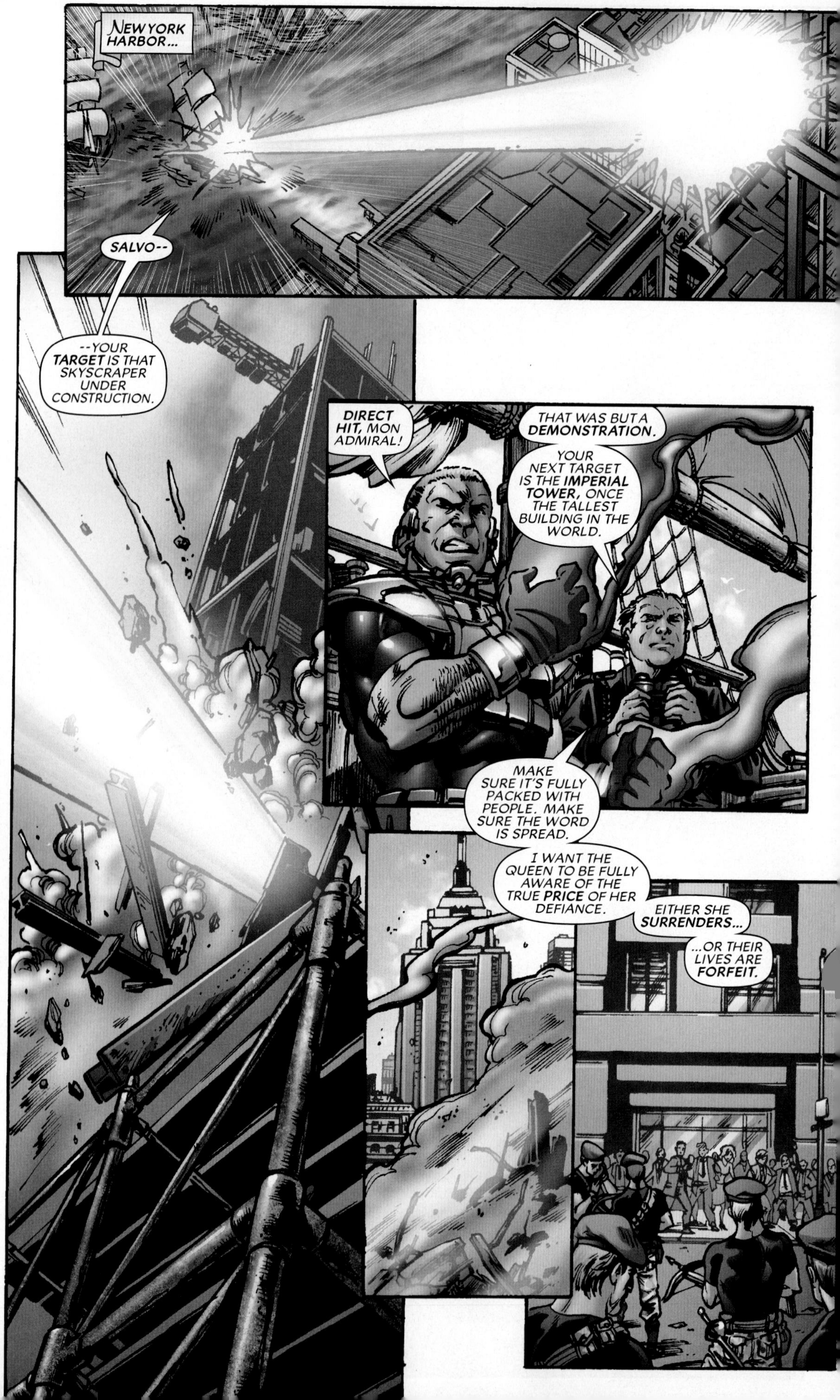
NEW YORK HARBOR...
SALVO--
--YOUR TARGET IS THAT SKYSCRAPER UNDER CONSTRUCTION.
DIRECT HIT, MON ADMIRAL!
THAT WAS BUT A DEMONSTRATION.
YOUR NEXT TARGET IS THE IMPERIAL TOWER, ONCE THE TALLEST BUILDING IN THE WORLD.
MAKE SURE IT'S FULLY PACKED WITH PEOPLE. MAKE SURE THE WORD IS SPREAD.
I WANT THE QUEEN TO BE FULLY AWARE OF THE TRUE PRICE OF HER DEFIANCE.
EITHER SHE SURRENDERS...
...OR THEIR LIVES ARE FORFEIT.

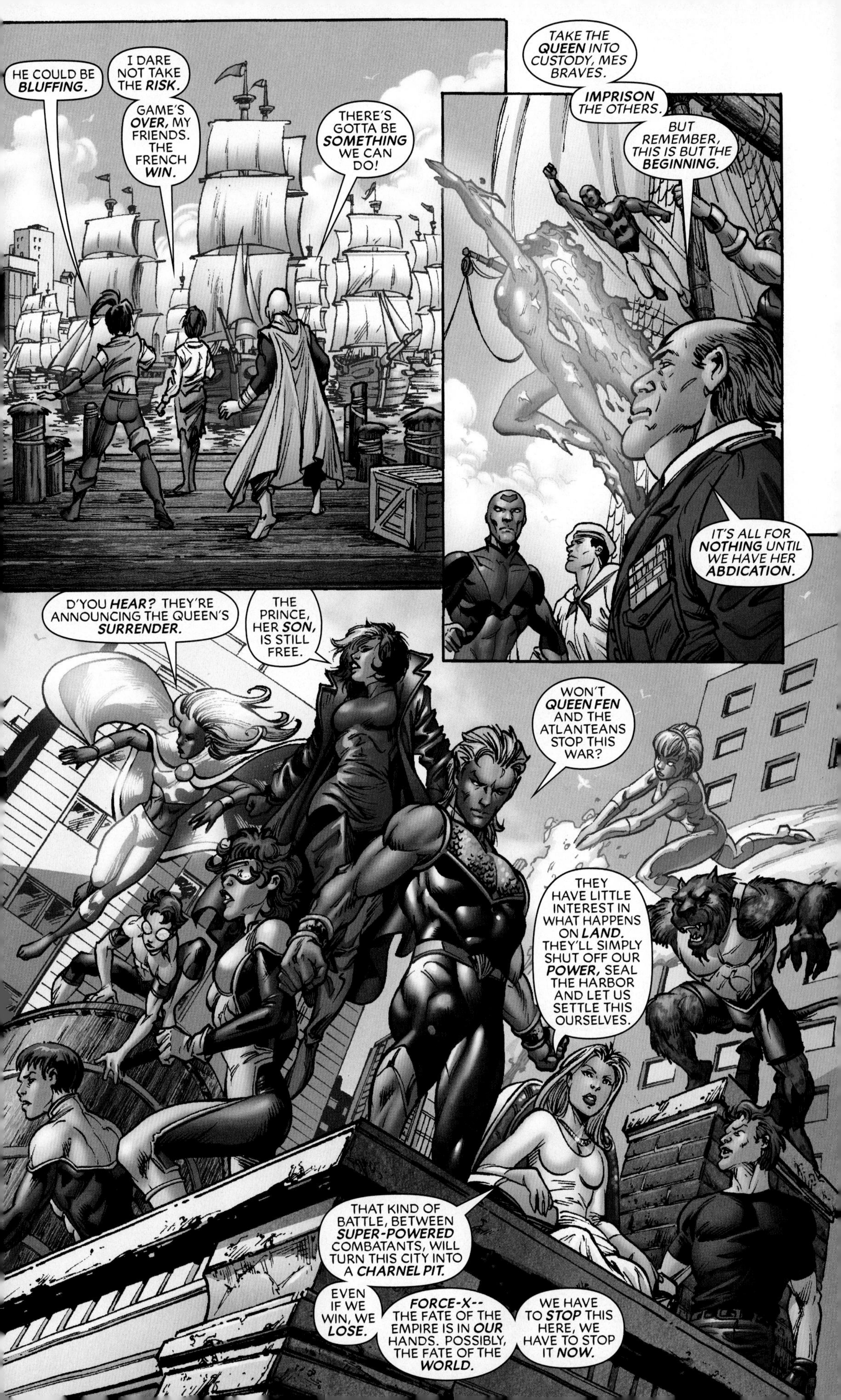
HE COULD BE BLUFFING.
I DARE NOT TAKE THE RISK.
GAME'S OVER, MY FRIENDS. THE FRENCH WIN.
THERE'S GOTTA BE SOMETHING WE CAN DO!
TAKE THE QUEEN INTO CUSTODY, MES BRAVES.
IMPRISON THE OTHERS.
BUT REMEMBER, THIS IS BUT THE BEGINNING.
IT'S ALL FOR NOTHING UNTIL WE HAVE HER ABDICATION.
D'YOU HEAR? THEY'RE ANNOUNCING THE QUEEN'S SURRENDER.
THE PRINCE, HER SON, IS STILL FREE.
WON'T QUEEN FEN AND THE ATLANTEANS STOP THIS WAR?
THEY HAVE LITTLE INTEREST IN WHAT HAPPENS ON LAND. THEY'LL SIMPLY SHUT OFF OUR POWER, SEAL THE HARBOR AND LET US SETTLE THIS OURSELVES.
THAT KIND OF BATTLE, BETWEEN SUPER-POWERED COMBATANTS, WILL TURN THIS CITY INTO A CHARNEL PIT.
EVEN IF WE WIN, WE LOSE.
FORCE-X-- THE FATE OF THE EMPIRE IS IN OUR HANDS. POSSIBLY, THE FATE OF THE WORLD.
WE HAVE TO STOP THIS HERE, WE HAVE TO STOP IT NOW.

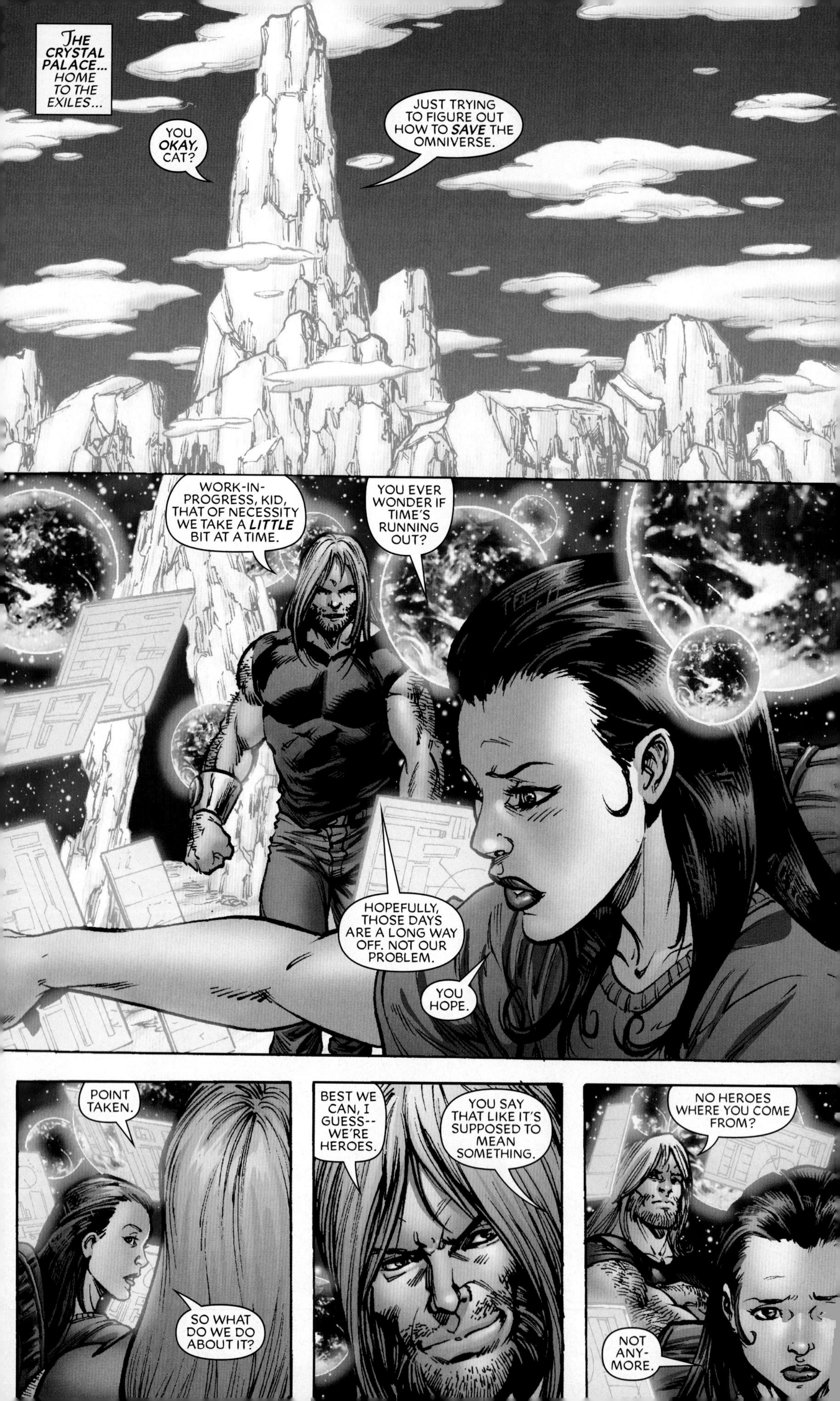
THE CRYSTAL PALACE... HOME TO THE EXILES...
YOU OKAY, CAT?
JUST TRYING TO FIGURE OUT HOW TO SAVE THE OMNIVERSE.
WORK-IN-PROGRESS, KID, THAT OF NECESSITY WE TAKE A LITTLE BIT AT A TIME.
YOU EVER WONDER IF TIME'S RUNNING OUT?
HOPEFULLY, THOSE DAYS ARE A LONG WAY OFF. NOT OUR PROBLEM.
YOU HOPE.
POINT TAKEN.
SO WHAT DO WE DO ABOUT IT?
BEST WE CAN, I GUESS-- WE'RE HEROES.
YOU SAY THAT LIKE IT'S SUPPOSED TO MEAN SOMETHING.
NO HEROES WHERE YOU COME FROM?
NOT ANY-MORE.

TOO BAD. FACT IS, CAT, YOU TAKE A *STAND.*

YOU FIGURE WHAT'S *RIGHT*--

--WHAT BRINGS THE MOST BENEFIT TO THE MOST PEOPLE, WHAT DOES THE LEAST HARM--

--WHAT ULTIMATELY LEADS TO THE *BEST FUTURE.*

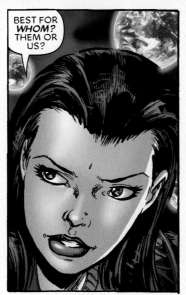

BEST FOR *WHOM?* THEM OR *US?*

NO STOCK ANSWER FOR THAT ONE. YOU MAKE A CHOICE, YOU LIVE WITH THE CONSEQUENCES.

IT'S THAT SIMPLE.

AND THAT *HARD.*

THAT'S A LOT OF THINKING.

ME, I FOLLOW MY *INSTINCTS.* RATIONAL THOUGHT USUALLY GETS IN THE *WAY.*

YOU EVER GET IT *WRONG?*

NOPE.

NO SECOND THOUGHTS? NO *REGRETS?*

NOPE.

THANKS, BOSS. I'LL KEEP THAT IN MIND.

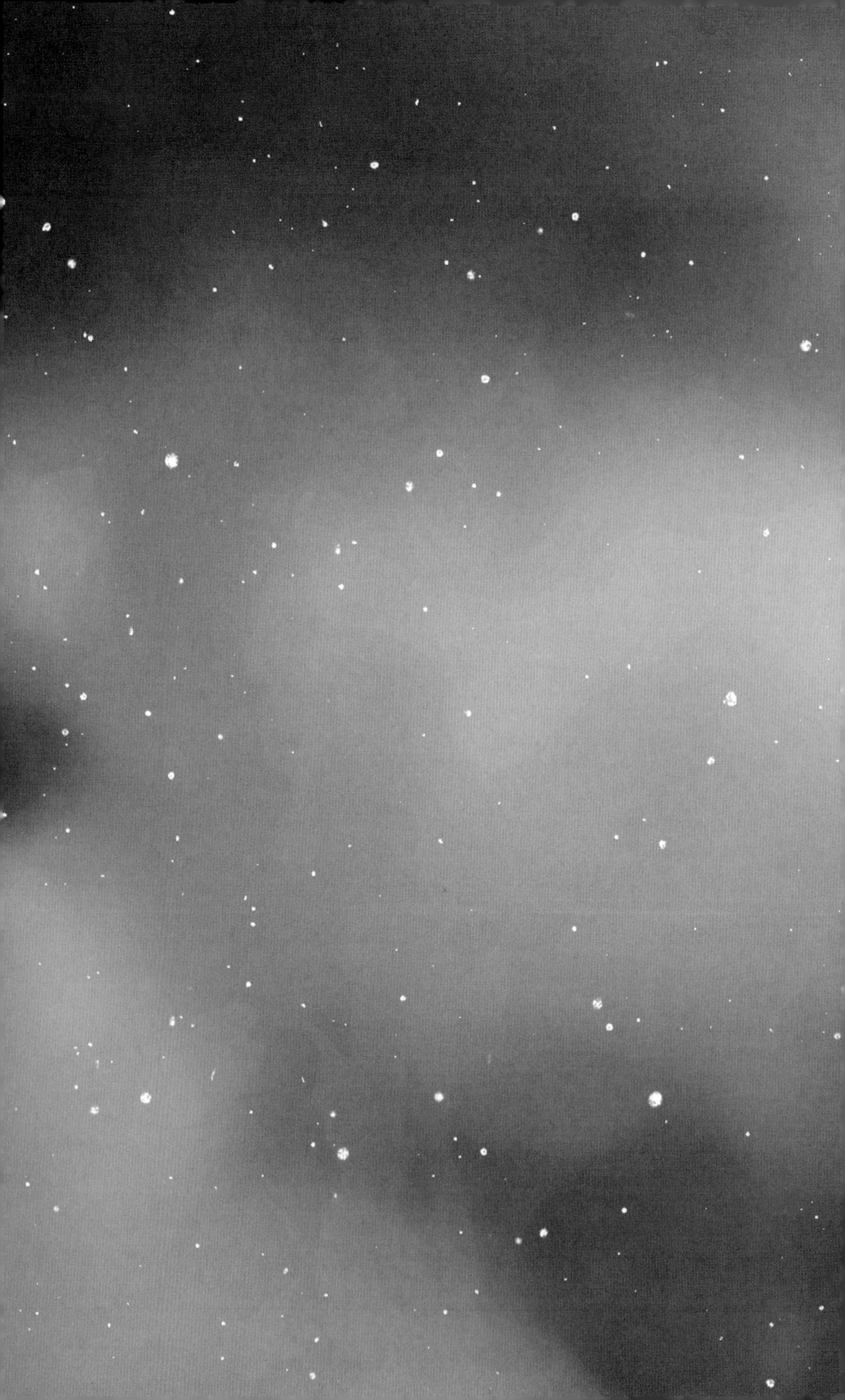

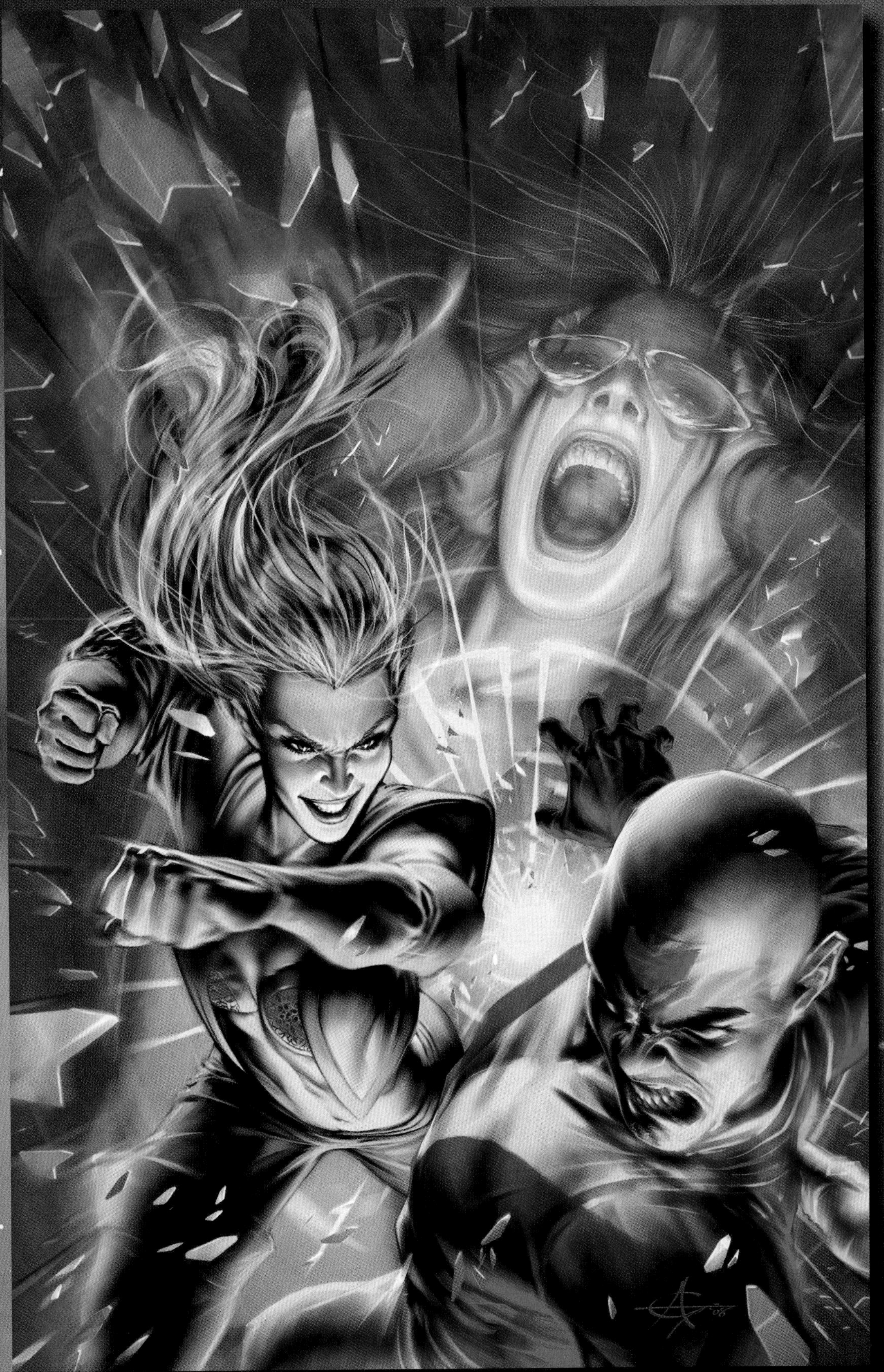

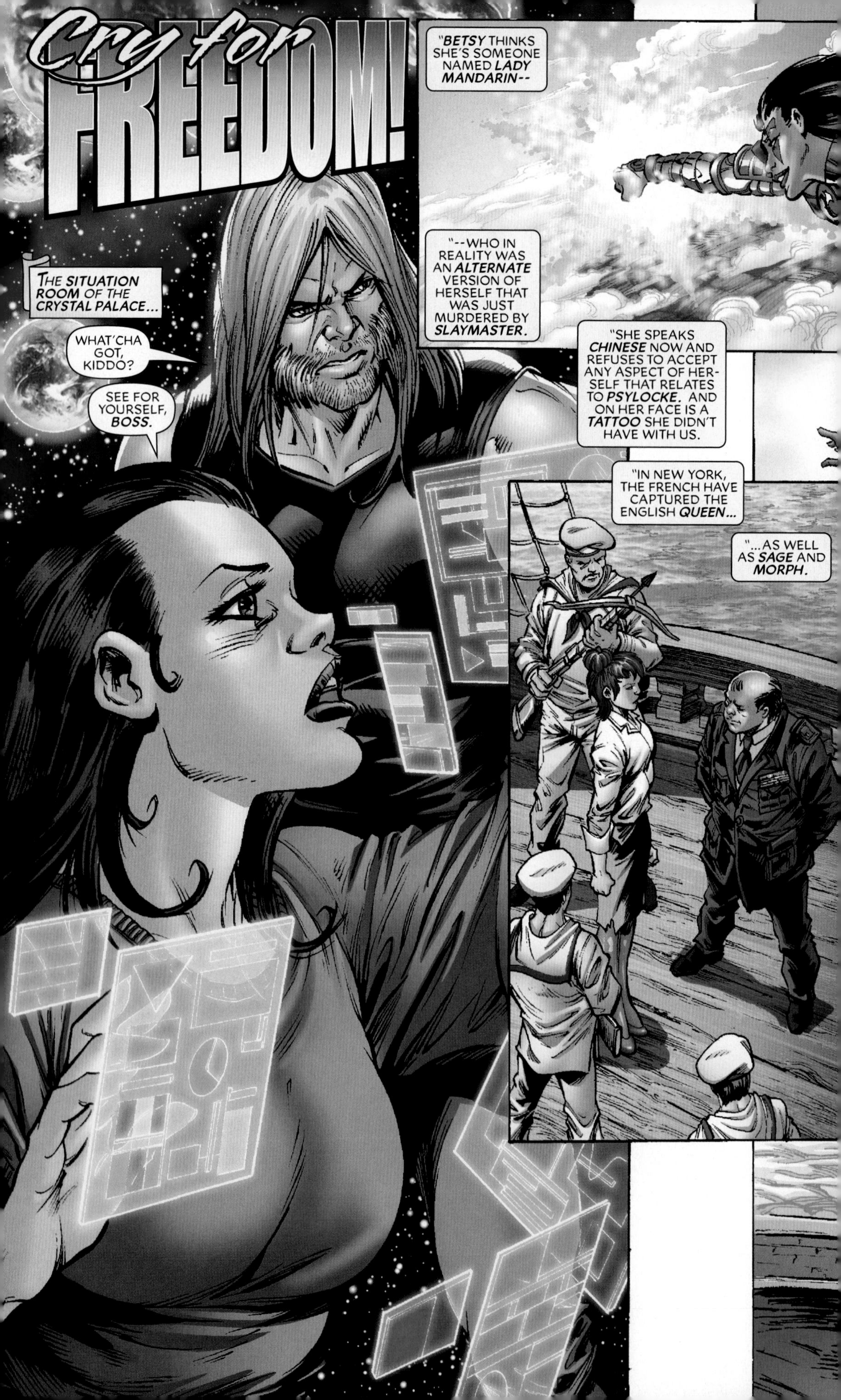

Cry for FREEDOM!
THE SITUATION ROOM OF THE CRYSTAL PALACE...
WHAT'CHA GOT, KIDDO?
SEE FOR YOURSELF, BOSS.
"BETSY THINKS SHE'S SOMEONE NAMED LADY MANDARIN--
"--WHO IN REALITY WAS AN ALTERNATE VERSION OF HERSELF THAT WAS JUST MURDERED BY SLAYMASTER.
"SHE SPEAKS CHINESE NOW AND REFUSES TO ACCEPT ANY ASPECT OF HER-SELF THAT RELATES TO PSYLOCKE. AND ON HER FACE IS A TATTOO SHE DIDN'T HAVE WITH US.
"IN NEW YORK, THE FRENCH HAVE CAPTURED THE ENGLISH QUEEN...
"...AS WELL AS SAGE AND MORPH.

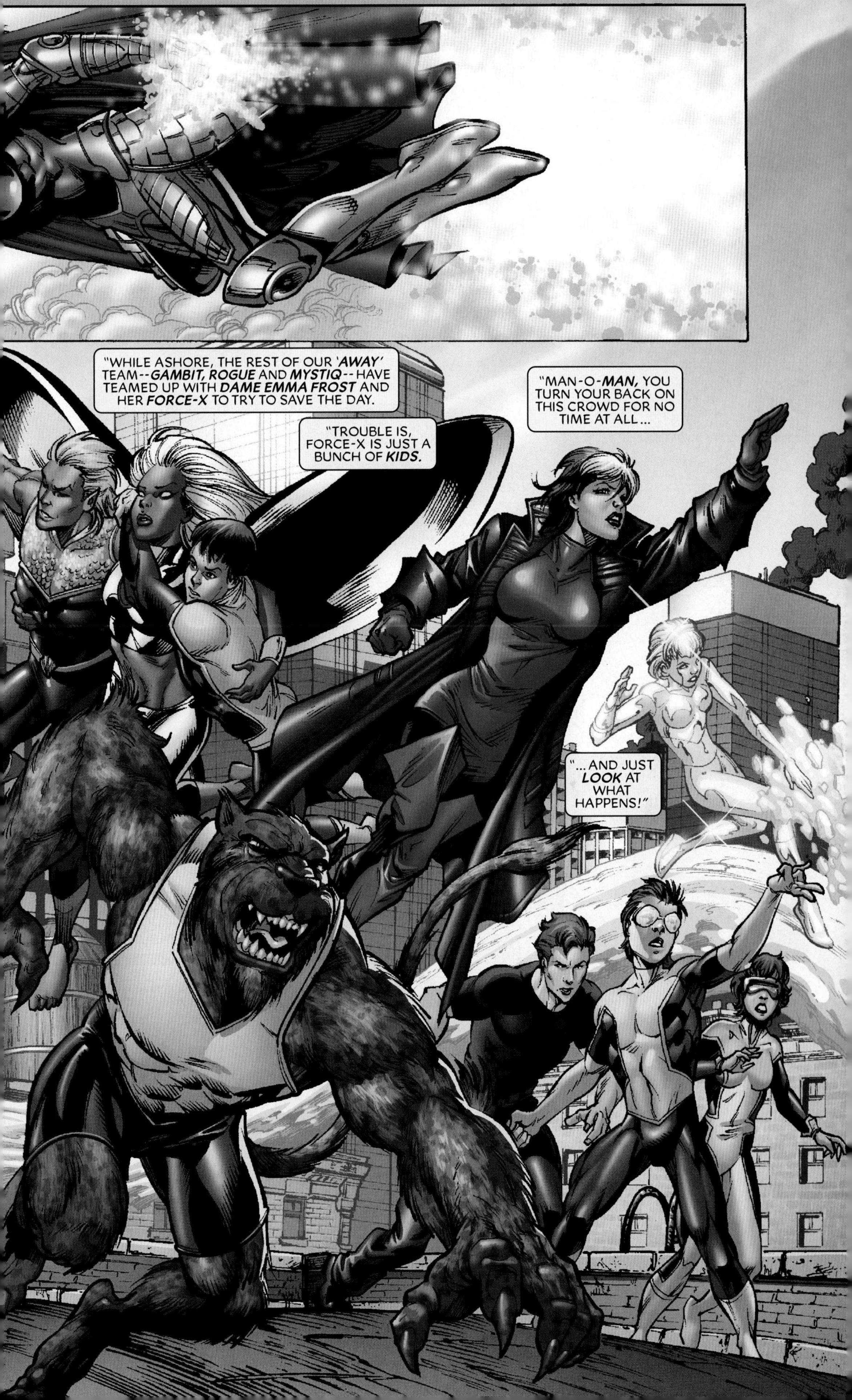
"WHILE ASHORE, THE REST OF OUR 'AWAY' TEAM--GAMBIT, ROGUE AND MYSTIQ--HAVE TEAMED UP WITH DAME EMMA FROST AND HER FORCE-X TO TRY TO SAVE THE DAY.
"TROUBLE IS, FORCE-X IS JUST A BUNCH OF KIDS.
"MAN-O-MAN, YOU TURN YOUR BACK ON THIS CROWD FOR NO TIME AT ALL...
"...AND JUST LOOK AT WHAT HAPPENS!"

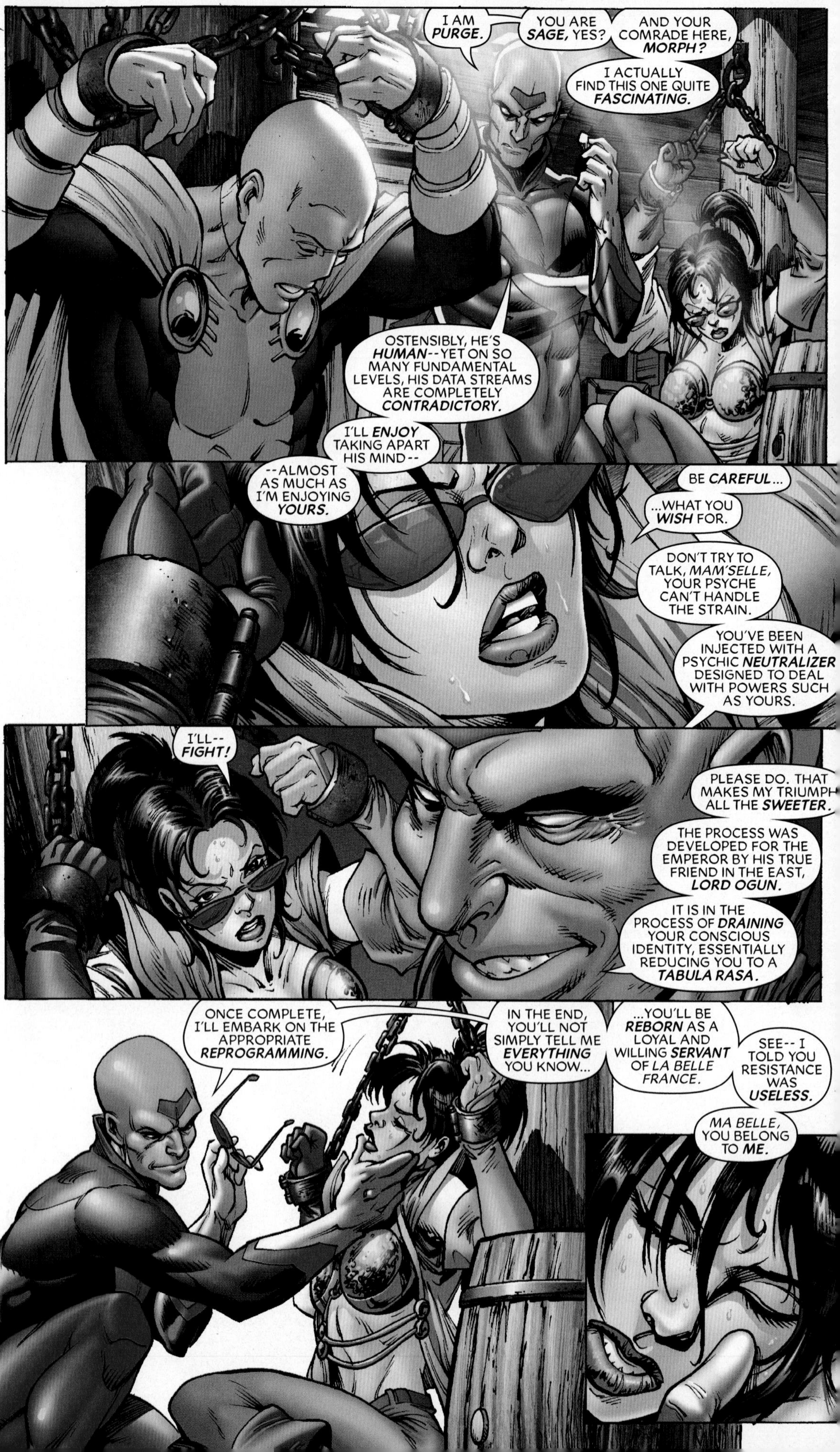

I AM PURGE.
YOU ARE SAGE, YES?
AND YOUR COMRADE HERE, MORPH?
I ACTUALLY FIND THIS ONE QUITE FASCINATING.
OSTENSIBLY, HE'S HUMAN--YET ON SO MANY FUNDAMENTAL LEVELS, HIS DATA STREAMS ARE COMPLETELY CONTRADICTORY.
I'LL ENJOY TAKING APART HIS MIND--
--ALMOST AS MUCH AS I'M ENJOYING YOURS.
BE CAREFUL...
...WHAT YOU WISH FOR.
DON'T TRY TO TALK, MAM'SELLE, YOUR PSYCHE CAN'T HANDLE THE STRAIN.
YOU'VE BEEN INJECTED WITH A PSYCHIC NEUTRALIZER DESIGNED TO DEAL WITH POWERS SUCH AS YOURS.
I'LL-- FIGHT!
PLEASE DO. THAT MAKES MY TRIUMPH ALL THE SWEETER.
THE PROCESS WAS DEVELOPED FOR THE EMPEROR BY HIS TRUE FRIEND IN THE EAST, LORD OGUN.
IT IS IN THE PROCESS OF DRAINING YOUR CONSCIOUS IDENTITY, ESSENTIALLY REDUCING YOU TO A TABULA RASA.
ONCE COMPLETE, I'LL EMBARK ON THE APPROPRIATE REPROGRAMMING.
IN THE END, YOU'LL NOT SIMPLY TELL ME EVERYTHING YOU KNOW...
...YOU'LL BE REBORN AS A LOYAL AND WILLING SERVANT OF LA BELLE FRANCE.
SEE-- I TOLD YOU RESISTANCE WAS USELESS.
MA BELLE, YOU BELONG TO ME.

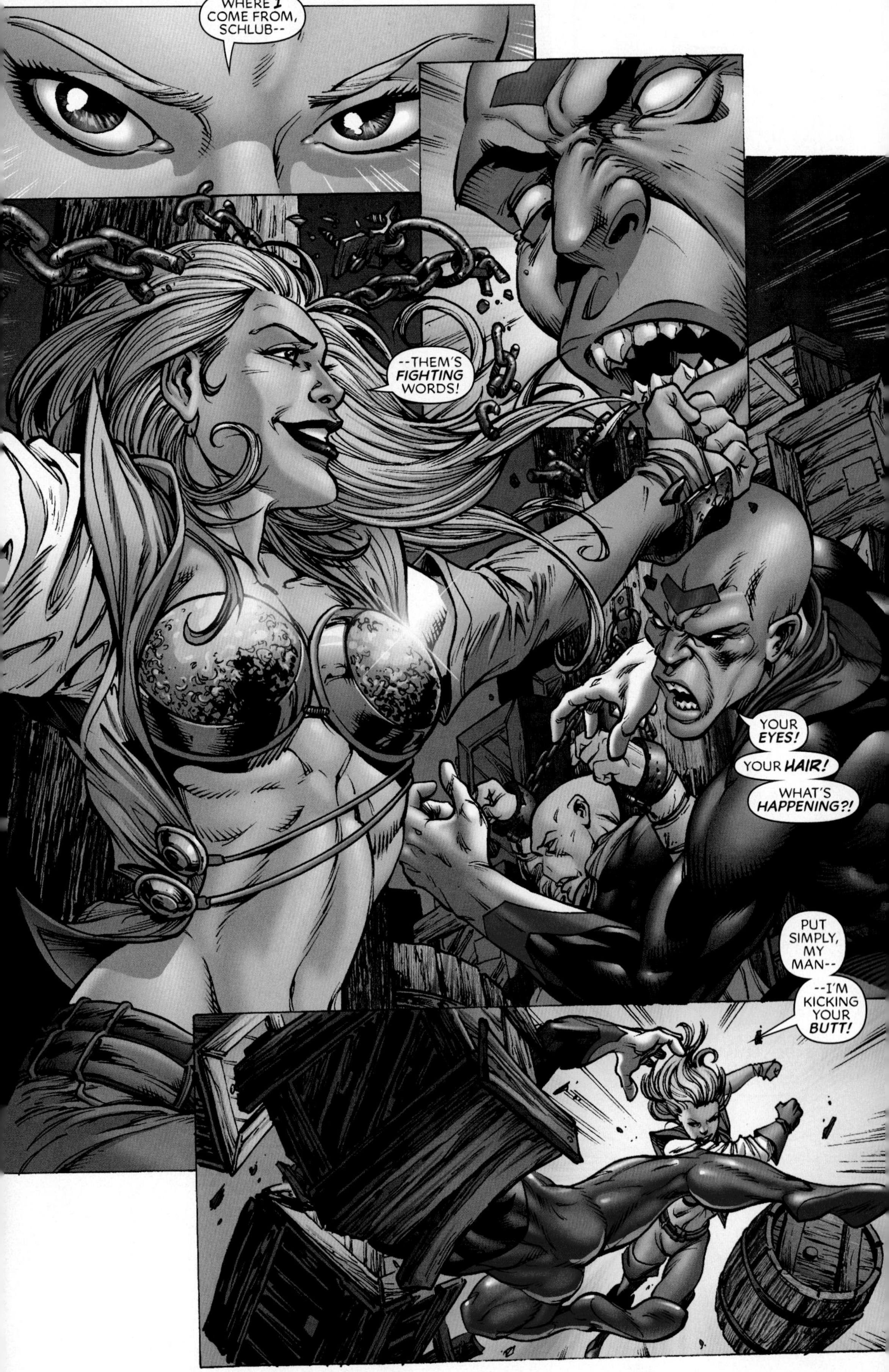
WHERE I COME FROM, SCHLUB--
--THEM'S FIGHTING WORDS!
YOUR EYES!
YOUR HAIR!
WHAT'S HAPPENING?!
PUT SIMPLY, MY MAN--
--I'M KICKING YOUR BUTT!

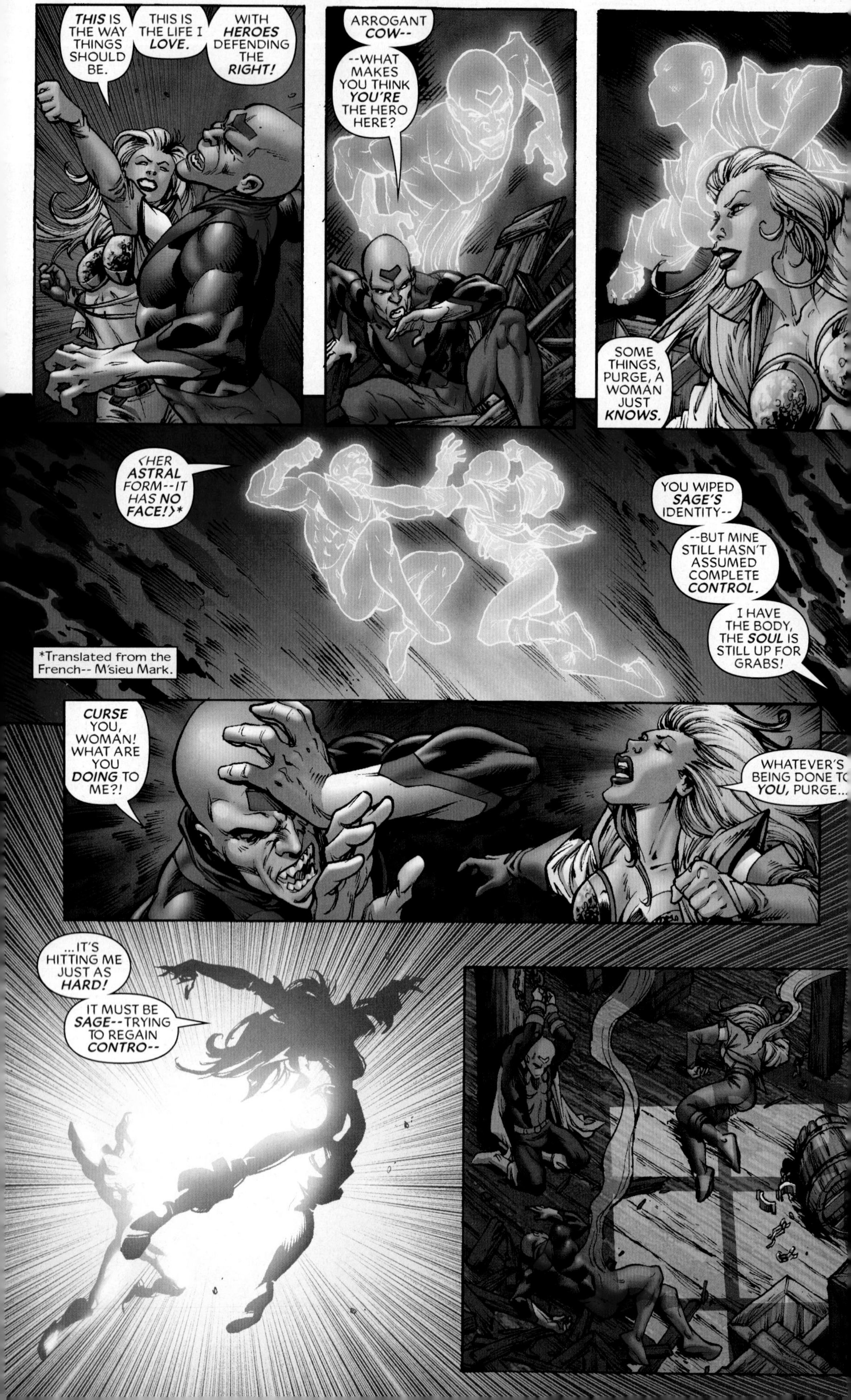
THIS IS THE WAY THINGS SHOULD BE.
THIS IS THE LIFE I LOVE.
WITH HEROES DEFENDING THE RIGHT!
ARROGANT COW--
--WHAT MAKES YOU THINK YOU'RE THE HERO HERE?
SOME THINGS, PURGE, A WOMAN JUST KNOWS.
<HER ASTRAL FORM--IT HAS NO FACE!>*
YOU WIPED SAGE'S IDENTITY--
--BUT MINE STILL HASN'T ASSUMED COMPLETE CONTROL.
I HAVE THE BODY, THE SOUL IS STILL UP FOR GRABS!
*Translated from the French-- M'sieu Mark.
CURSE YOU, WOMAN! WHAT ARE YOU DOING TO ME?!
WHATEVER'S BEING DONE TO YOU, PURGE...
...IT'S HITTING ME JUST AS HARD!
IT MUST BE SAGE--TRYING TO REGAIN CONTRO--

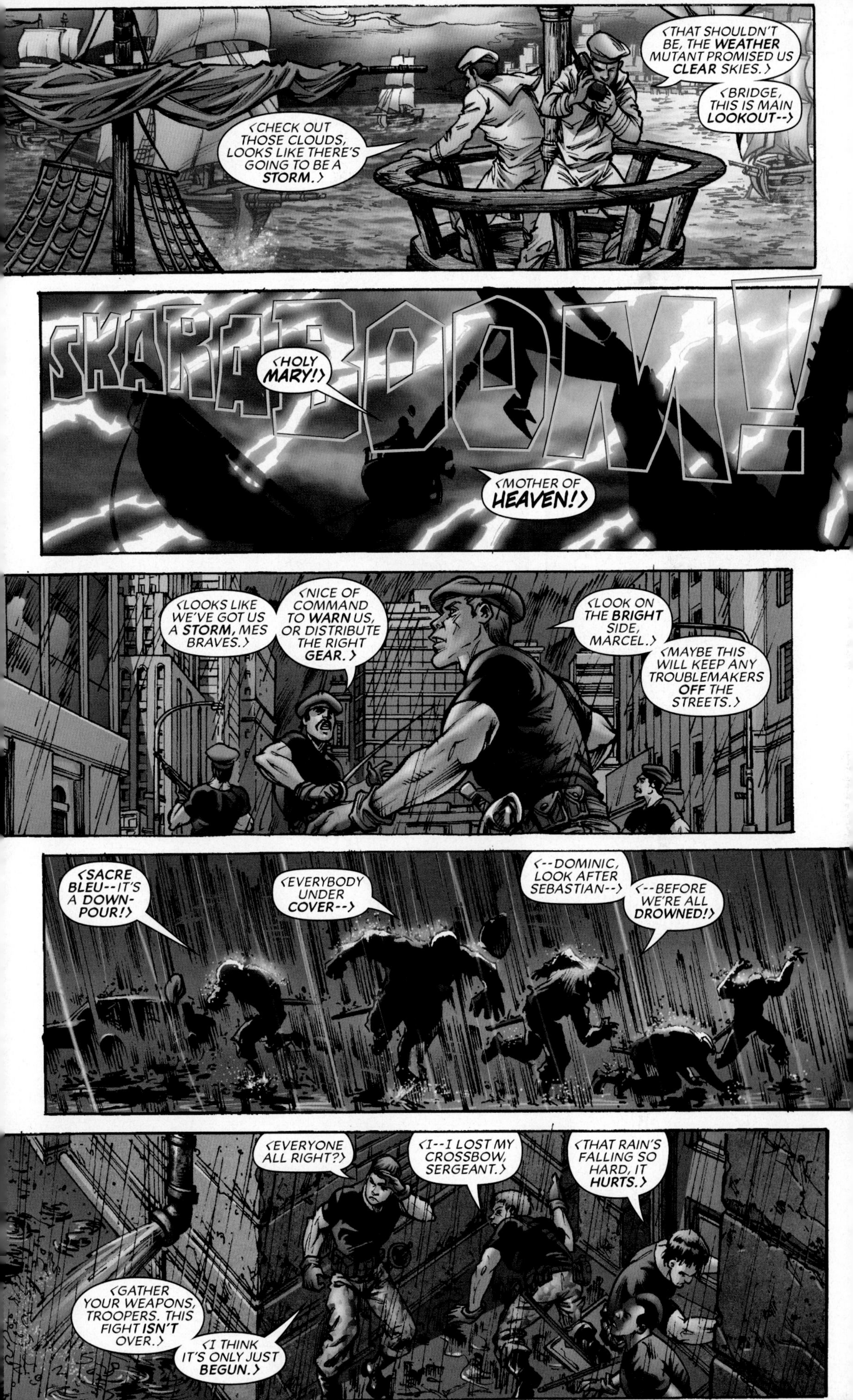

<CHECK OUT THOSE CLOUDS, LOOKS LIKE THERE'S GOING TO BE A STORM.>
<THAT SHOULDN'T BE, THE WEATHER MUTANT PROMISED US CLEAR SKIES.>
<BRIDGE, THIS IS MAIN LOOKOUT-->
SKARABOOM!
<HOLY MARY!>
<MOTHER OF HEAVEN!>
<LOOKS LIKE WE'VE GOT US A STORM, MES BRAVES.>
<NICE OF COMMAND TO WARN US, OR DISTRIBUTE THE RIGHT GEAR.>
<LOOK ON THE BRIGHT SIDE, MARCEL.>
<MAYBE THIS WILL KEEP ANY TROUBLEMAKERS OFF THE STREETS.>
<SACRE BLEU--IT'S A DOWN-POUR!>
<EVERYBODY UNDER COVER-->
<--DOMINIC, LOOK AFTER SEBASTIAN-->
<--BEFORE WE'RE ALL DROWNED!>
<EVERYONE ALL RIGHT?>
<I--I LOST MY CROSSBOW, SERGEANT.>
<THAT RAIN'S FALLING SO HARD, IT HURTS.>
<GATHER YOUR WEAPONS, TROOPERS. THIS FIGHT ISN'T OVER.>
<I THINK IT'S ONLY JUST BEGUN.>

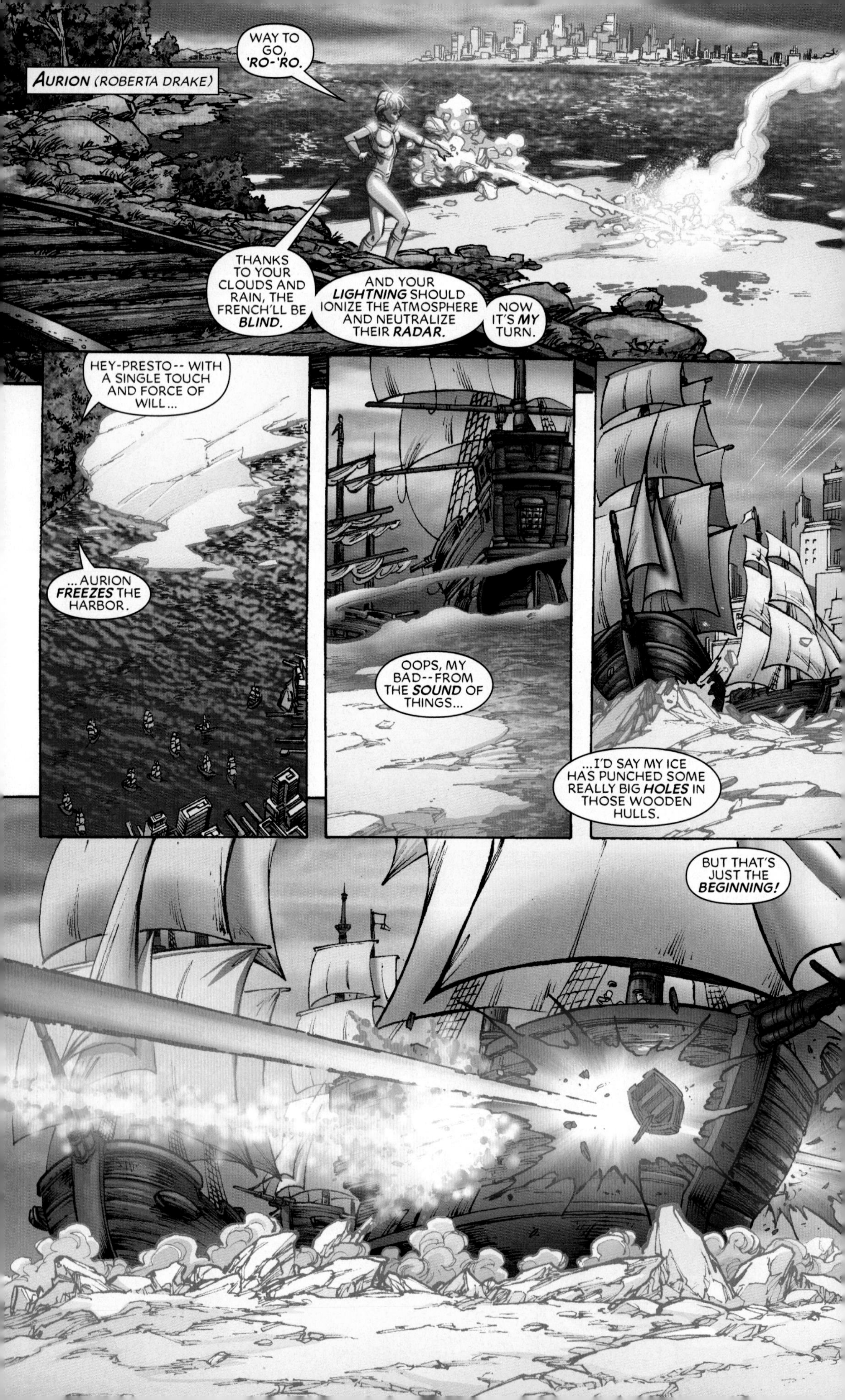
AURION (ROBERTA DRAKE)
WAY TO GO, 'RO-'RO.
THANKS TO YOUR CLOUDS AND RAIN, THE FRENCH'LL BE BLIND.
AND YOUR LIGHTNING SHOULD IONIZE THE ATMOSPHERE AND NEUTRALIZE THEIR RADAR.
NOW IT'S MY TURN.
HEY-PRESTO-- WITH A SINGLE TOUCH AND FORCE OF WILL...
...AURION FREEZES THE HARBOR.
OOPS, MY BAD--FROM THE SOUND OF THINGS...
...I'D SAY MY ICE HAS PUNCHED SOME REALLY BIG HOLES IN THOSE WOODEN HULLS.
BUT THAT'S JUST THE BEGINNING!

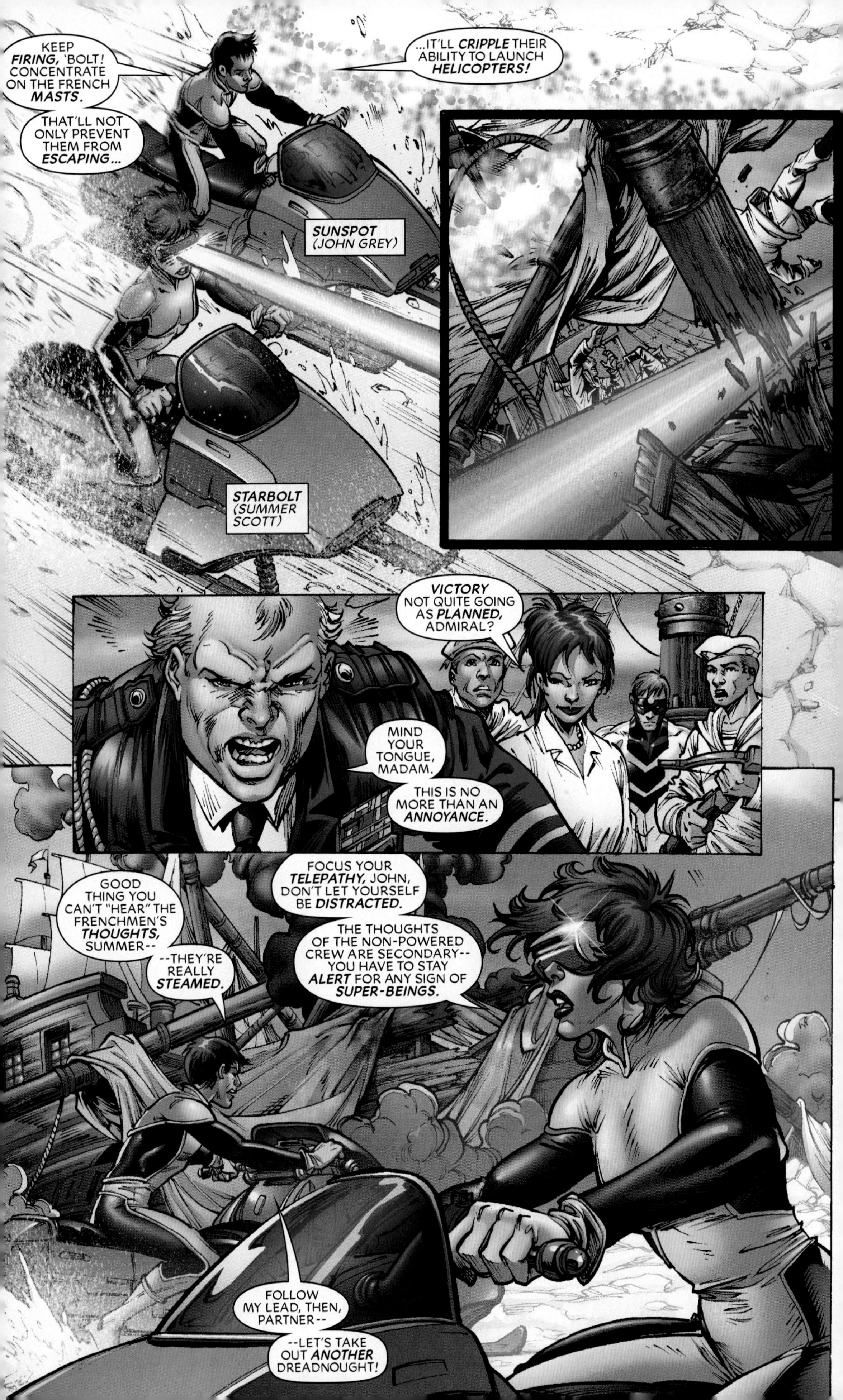
KEEP FIRING, 'BOLT! CONCENTRATE ON THE FRENCH MASTS.
THAT'LL NOT ONLY PREVENT THEM FROM ESCAPING...
...IT'LL CRIPPLE THEIR ABILITY TO LAUNCH HELICOPTERS!
SUNSPOT (JOHN GREY)
STARBOLT (SUMMER SCOTT)
VICTORY NOT QUITE GOING AS PLANNED, ADMIRAL?
MIND YOUR TONGUE, MADAM.
THIS IS NO MORE THAN AN ANNOYANCE.
GOOD THING YOU CAN'T "HEAR" THE FRENCHMEN'S THOUGHTS, SUMMER--
--THEY'RE REALLY STEAMED.
FOCUS YOUR TELEPATHY, JOHN, DON'T LET YOURSELF BE DISTRACTED.
THE THOUGHTS OF THE NON-POWERED CREW ARE SECONDARY--YOU HAVE TO STAY ALERT FOR ANY SIGN OF SUPER-BEINGS.
FOLLOW MY LEAD, THEN, PARTNER--
--LET'S TAKE OUT ANOTHER DREADNOUGHT!

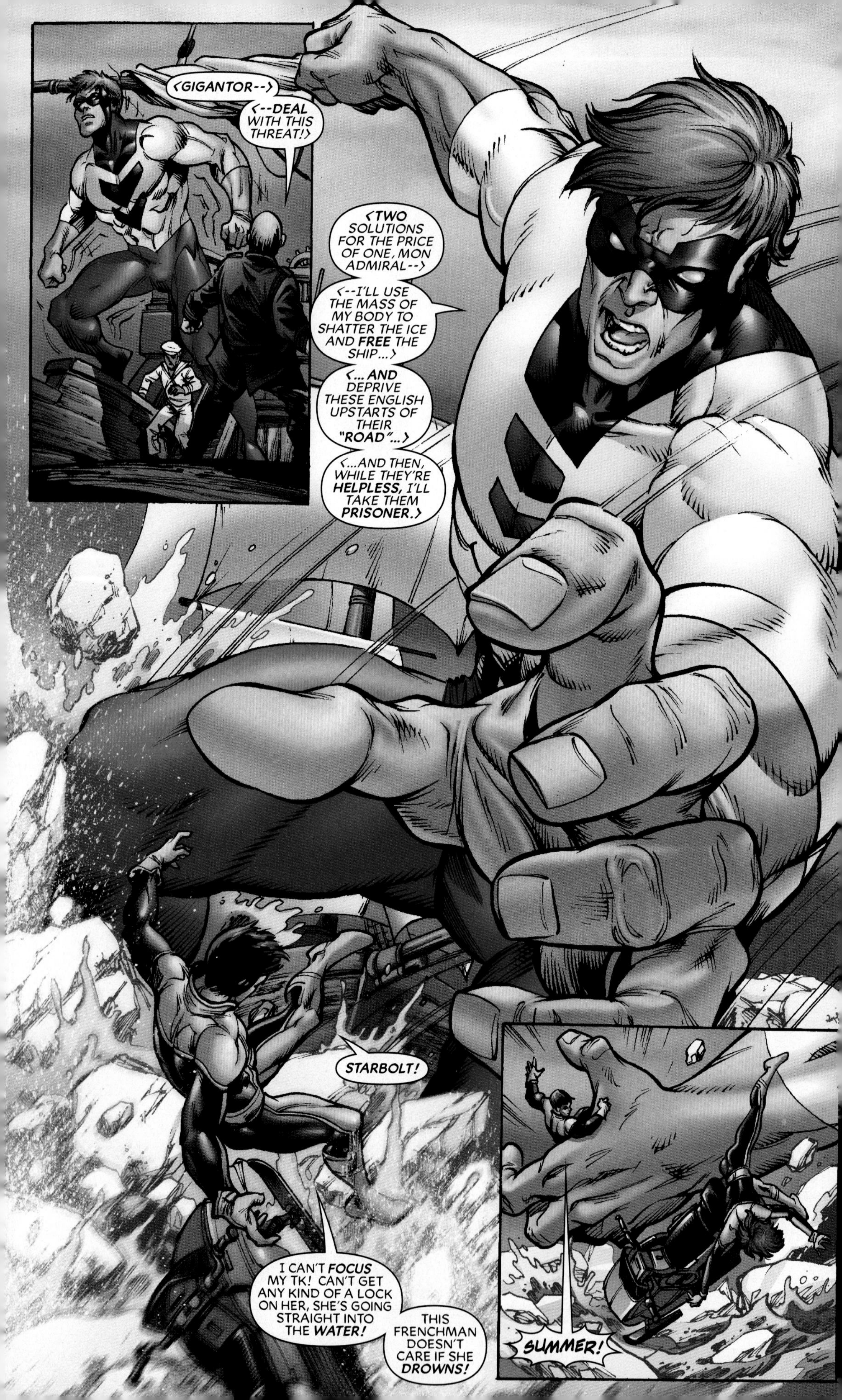

<GIGANTOR-->
<--DEAL WITH THIS THREAT!>
<TWO SOLUTIONS FOR THE PRICE OF ONE, MON ADMIRAL-->
<--I'LL USE THE MASS OF MY BODY TO SHATTER THE ICE AND FREE THE SHIP...>
<... AND DEPRIVE THESE ENGLISH UPSTARTS OF THEIR "ROAD"...>
<...AND THEN, WHILE THEY'RE HELPLESS, I'LL TAKE THEM PRISONER.>
STARBOLT!
I CAN'T FOCUS MY TK! CAN'T GET ANY KIND OF A LOCK ON HER, SHE'S GOING STRAIGHT INTO THE WATER!
THIS FRENCHMAN DOESN'T CARE IF SHE DROWNS!
SUMMER!

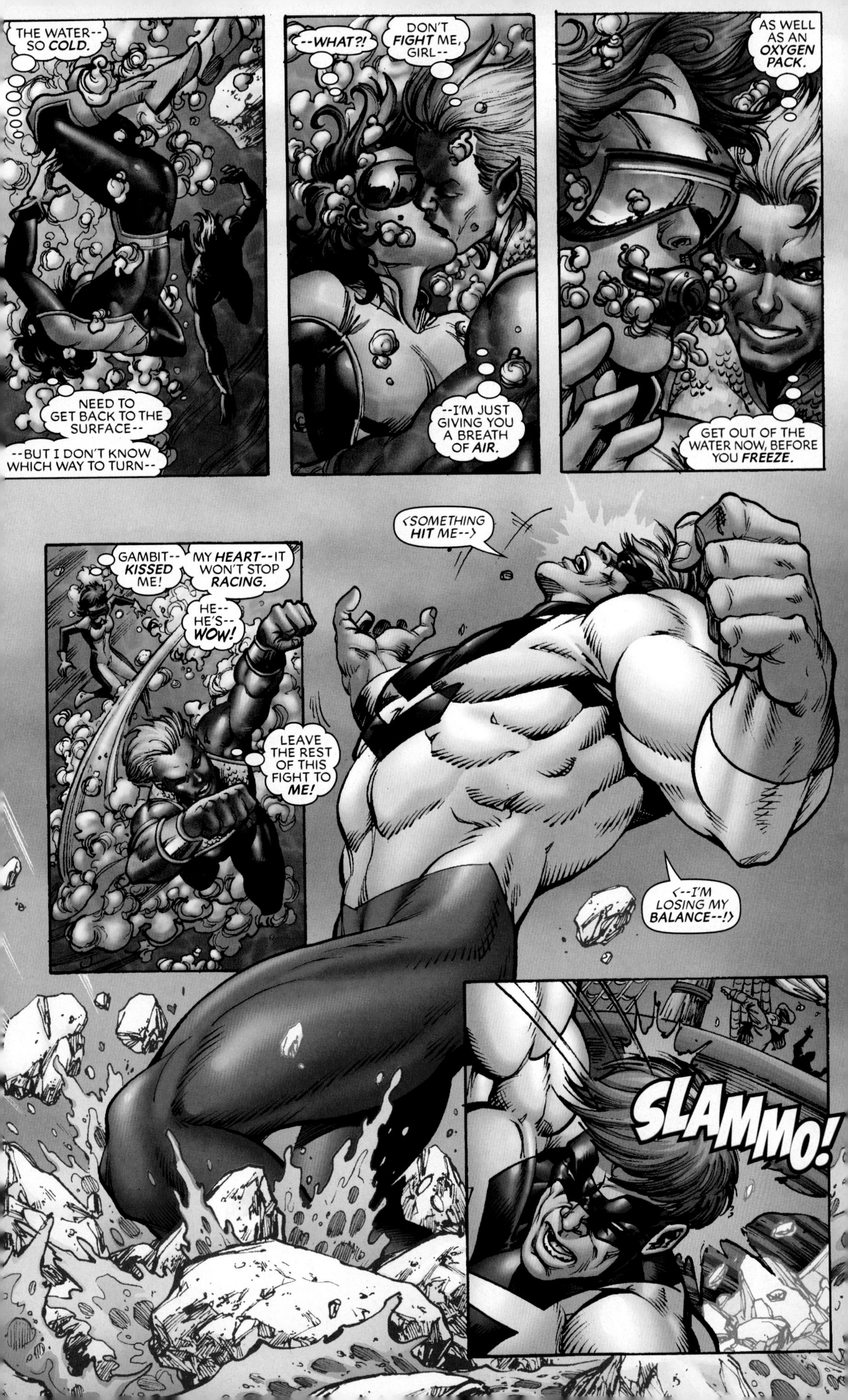
THE WATER-- SO COLD.
NEED TO GET BACK TO THE SURFACE--
--BUT I DON'T KNOW WHICH WAY TO TURN--
--WHAT?!
DON'T FIGHT ME, GIRL--
--I'M JUST GIVING YOU A BREATH OF AIR.
AS WELL AS AN OXYGEN PACK.
GET OUT OF THE WATER NOW, BEFORE YOU FREEZE.
GAMBIT--KISSED ME!
MY HEART--IT WON'T STOP RACING.
HE-- HE'S-- WOW!
LEAVE THE REST OF THIS FIGHT TO ME!
<SOMETHING HIT ME-->
<--I'M LOSING MY BALANCE--!>
SLAMMO!

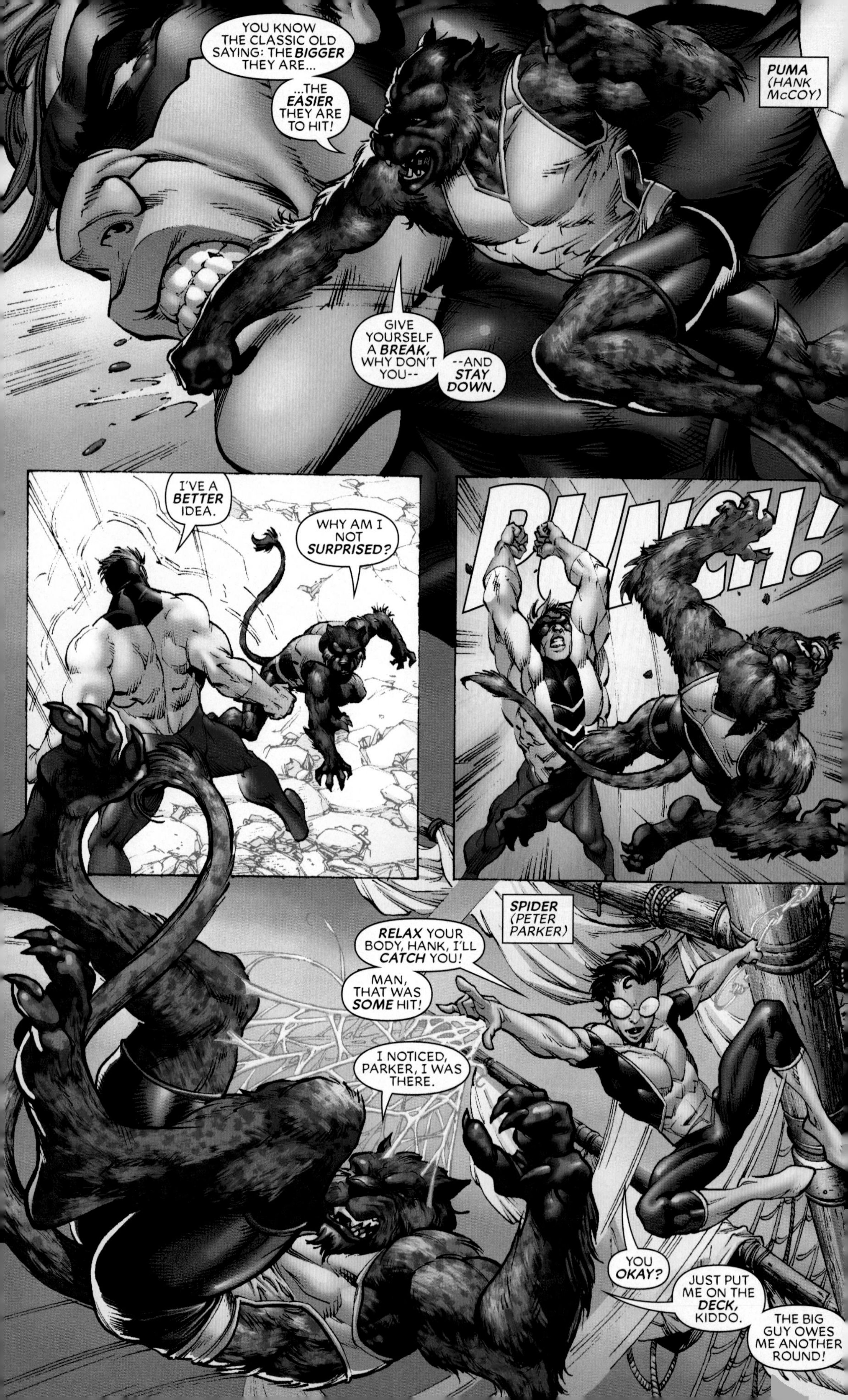
YOU KNOW THE CLASSIC OLD SAYING: THE BIGGER THEY ARE...
...THE EASIER THEY ARE TO HIT!
PUMA (HANK McCOY)
GIVE YOURSELF A BREAK, WHY DON'T YOU--
--AND STAY DOWN.
I'VE A BETTER IDEA.
WHY AM I NOT SURPRISED?
BUNCH!
SPIDER (PETER PARKER)
RELAX YOUR BODY, HANK, I'LL CATCH YOU!
MAN, THAT WAS SOME HIT!
I NOTICED, PARKER, I WAS THERE.
YOU OKAY?
JUST PUT ME ON THE DECK, KIDDO.
THE BIG GUY OWES ME ANOTHER ROUND!

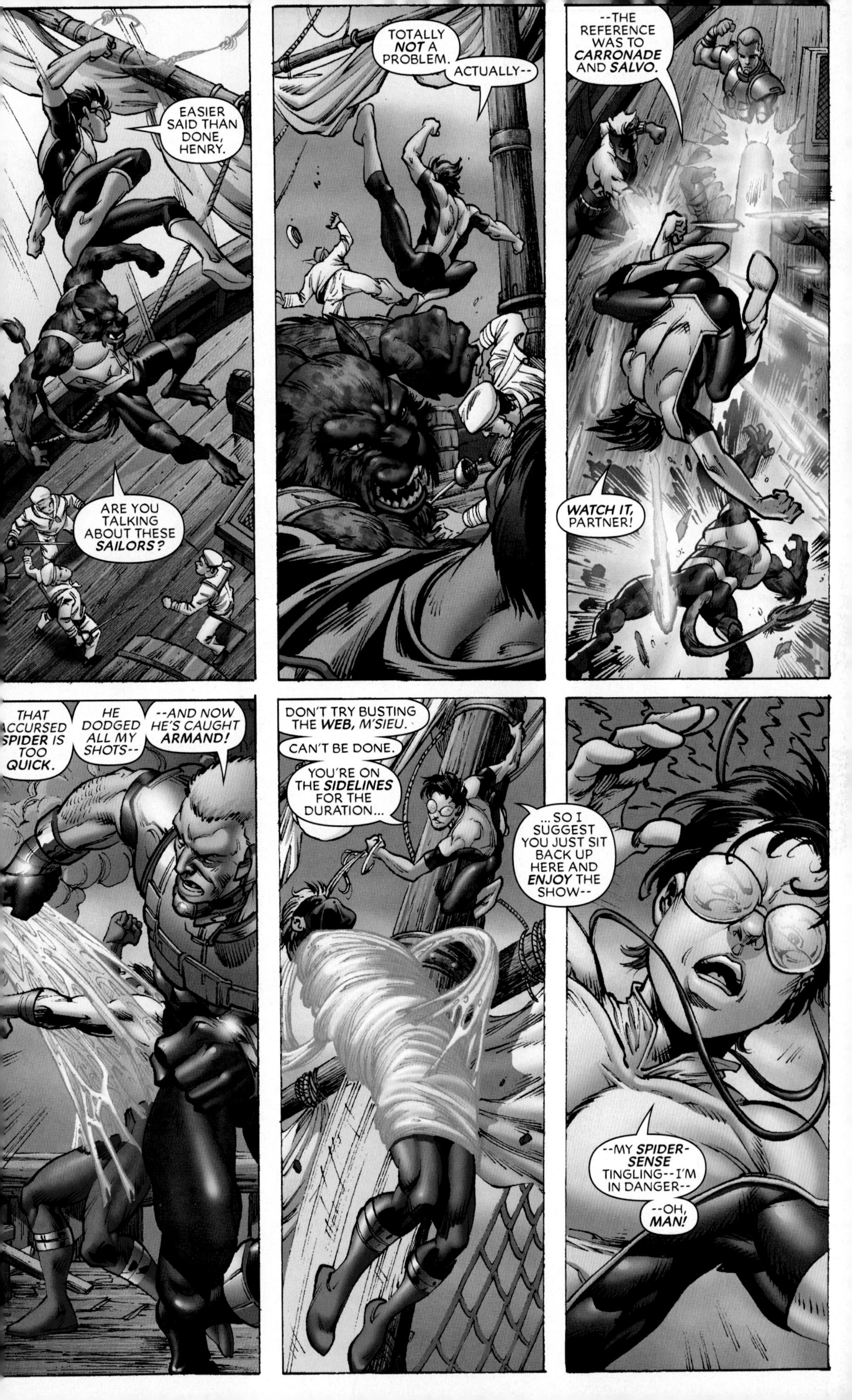
EASIER SAID THAN DONE, HENRY.
ARE YOU TALKING ABOUT THESE SAILORS?
TOTALLY NOT A PROBLEM.
ACTUALLY--
--THE REFERENCE WAS TO CARRONADE AND SALVO.
WATCH IT, PARTNER!
THAT ACCURSED SPIDER IS TOO QUICK.
HE DODGED ALL MY SHOTS--
--AND NOW HE'S CAUGHT ARMAND!
DON'T TRY BUSTING THE WEB, M'SIEU.
CAN'T BE DONE.
YOU'RE ON THE SIDELINES FOR THE DURATION...
...SO I SUGGEST YOU JUST SIT BACK UP HERE AND ENJOY THE SHOW--
--MY SPIDER-SENSE TINGLING--I'M IN DANGER--
--OH, MAN!

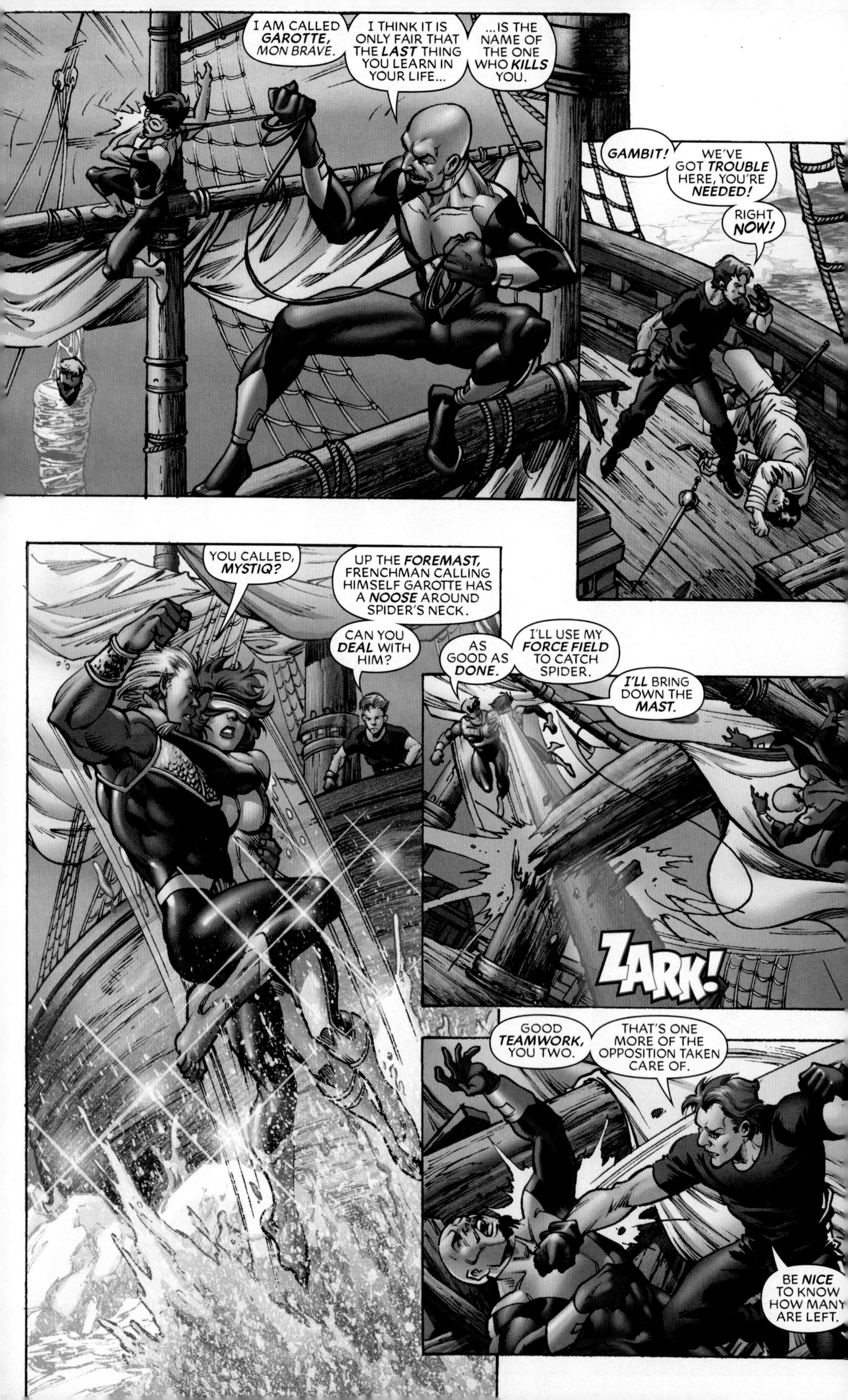
I AM CALLED GAROTTE, MON BRAVE.
I THINK IT IS ONLY FAIR THAT THE LAST THING YOU LEARN IN YOUR LIFE...
...IS THE NAME OF THE ONE WHO KILLS YOU.
GAMBIT!
WE'VE GOT TROUBLE HERE, YOU'RE NEEDED!
RIGHT NOW!
YOU CALLED, MYSTIQ?
UP THE FOREMAST, FRENCHMAN CALLING HIMSELF GAROTTE HAS A NOOSE AROUND SPIDER'S NECK.
CAN YOU DEAL WITH HIM?
AS GOOD AS DONE.
I'LL USE MY FORCE FIELD TO CATCH SPIDER.
I'LL BRING DOWN THE MAST.
ZARK!
GOOD TEAMWORK, YOU TWO.
THAT'S ONE MORE OF THE OPPOSITION TAKEN CARE OF.
BE NICE TO KNOW HOW MANY ARE LEFT.

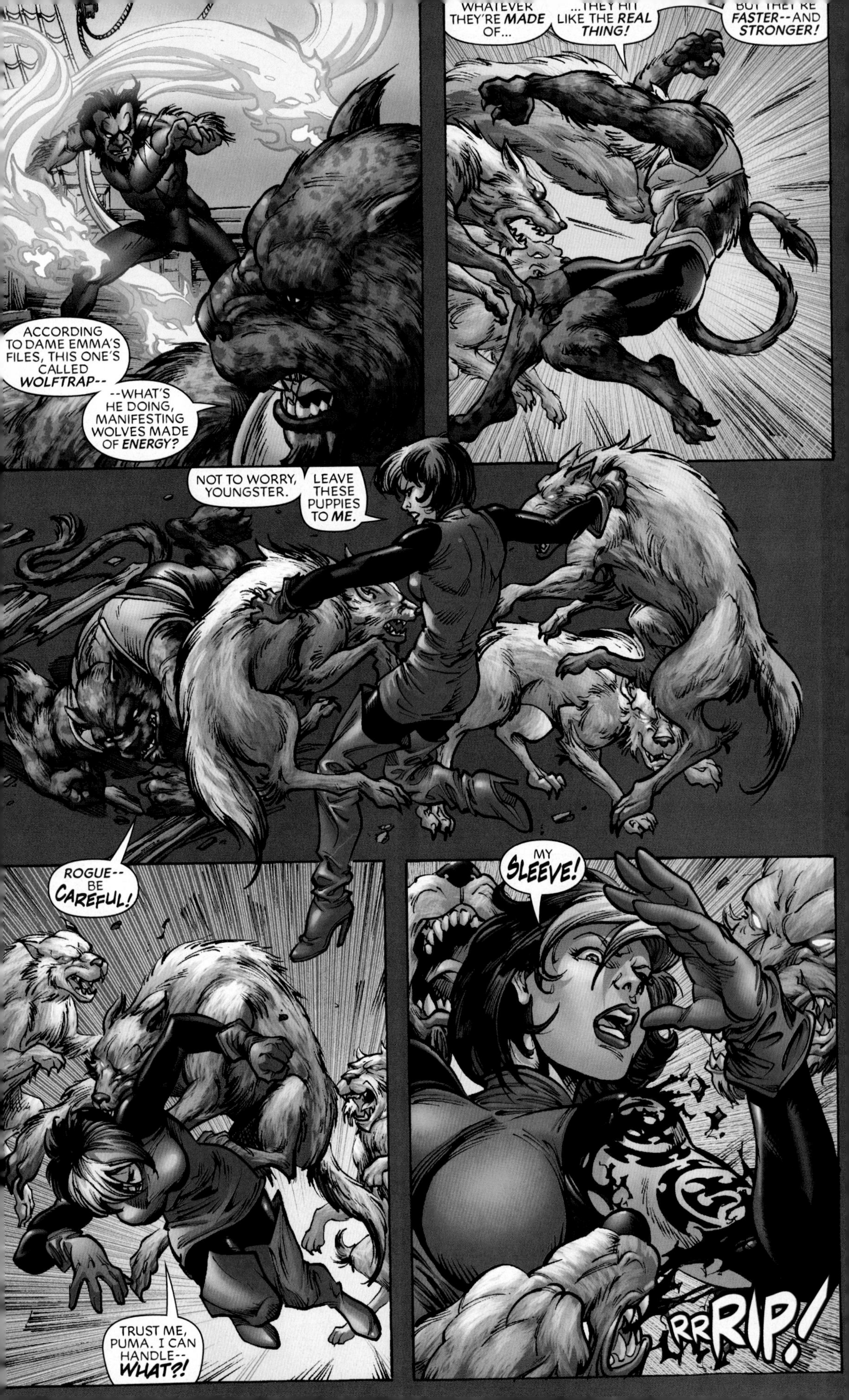
ACCORDING TO DAME EMMA'S FILES, THIS ONE'S CALLED WOLFTRAP--
--WHAT'S HE DOING, MANIFESTING WOLVES MADE OF ENERGY?
WHATEVER THEY'RE MADE OF...
...THEY HIT LIKE THE REAL THING!
BUT THEY'RE FASTER--AND STRONGER!
NOT TO WORRY, YOUNGSTER.
LEAVE THESE PUPPIES TO ME.
ROGUE--BE CAREFUL!
TRUST ME, PUMA. I CAN HANDLE-- WHAT?!
MY SLEEVE!
RRRIP!

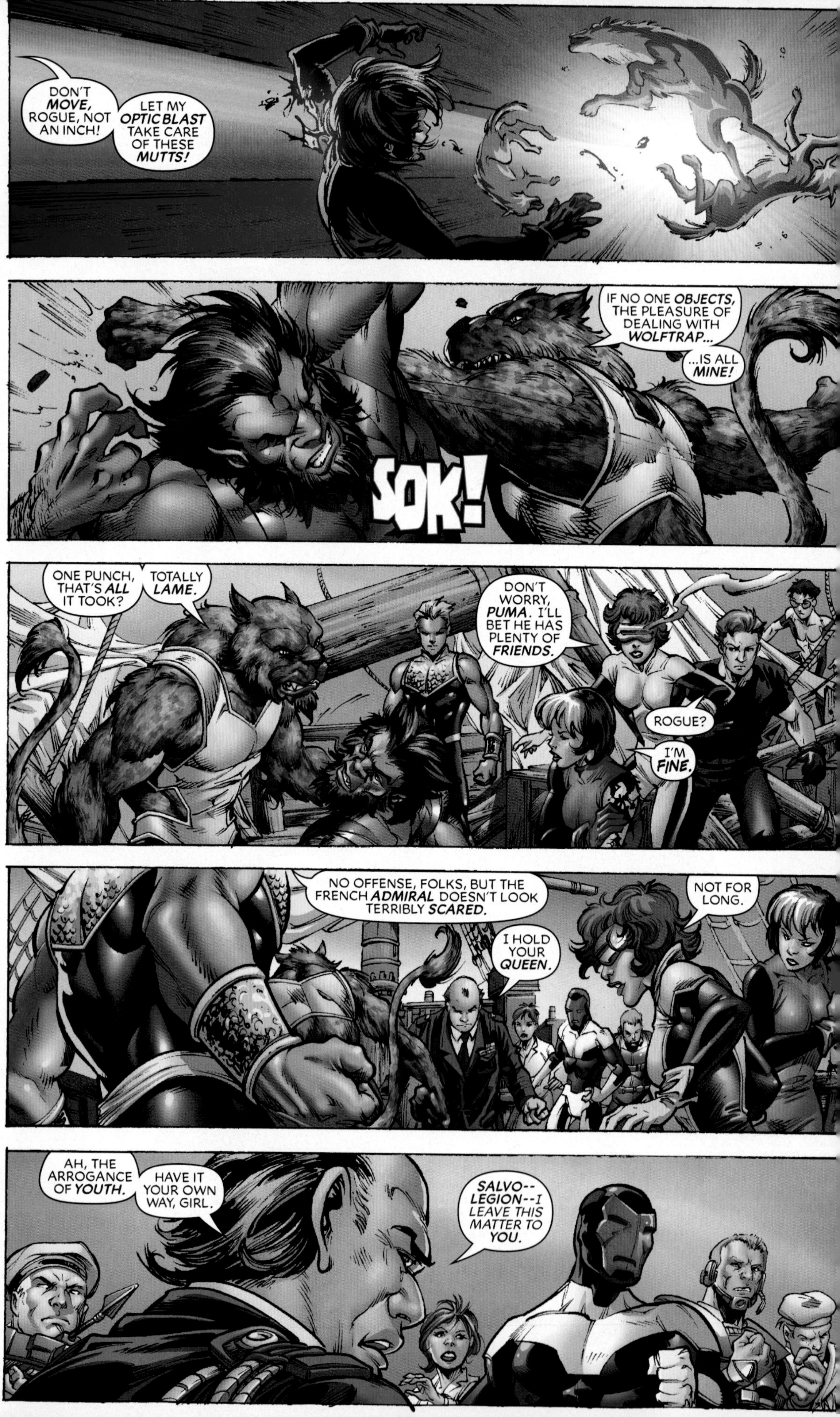
DON'T MOVE, ROGUE, NOT AN INCH!
LET MY OPTIC BLAST TAKE CARE OF THESE MUTTS!
IF NO ONE OBJECTS, THE PLEASURE OF DEALING WITH WOLFTRAP...
...IS ALL MINE!
SOK!
ONE PUNCH, THAT'S ALL IT TOOK?
TOTALLY LAME.
DON'T WORRY, PUMA. I'LL BET HE HAS PLENTY OF FRIENDS.
ROGUE?
I'M FINE.
NO OFFENSE, FOLKS, BUT THE FRENCH ADMIRAL DOESN'T LOOK TERRIBLY SCARED.
I HOLD YOUR QUEEN.
NOT FOR LONG.
AH, THE ARROGANCE OF YOUTH.
HAVE IT YOUR OWN WAY, GIRL.
SALVO--LEGION--I LEAVE THIS MATTER TO YOU.

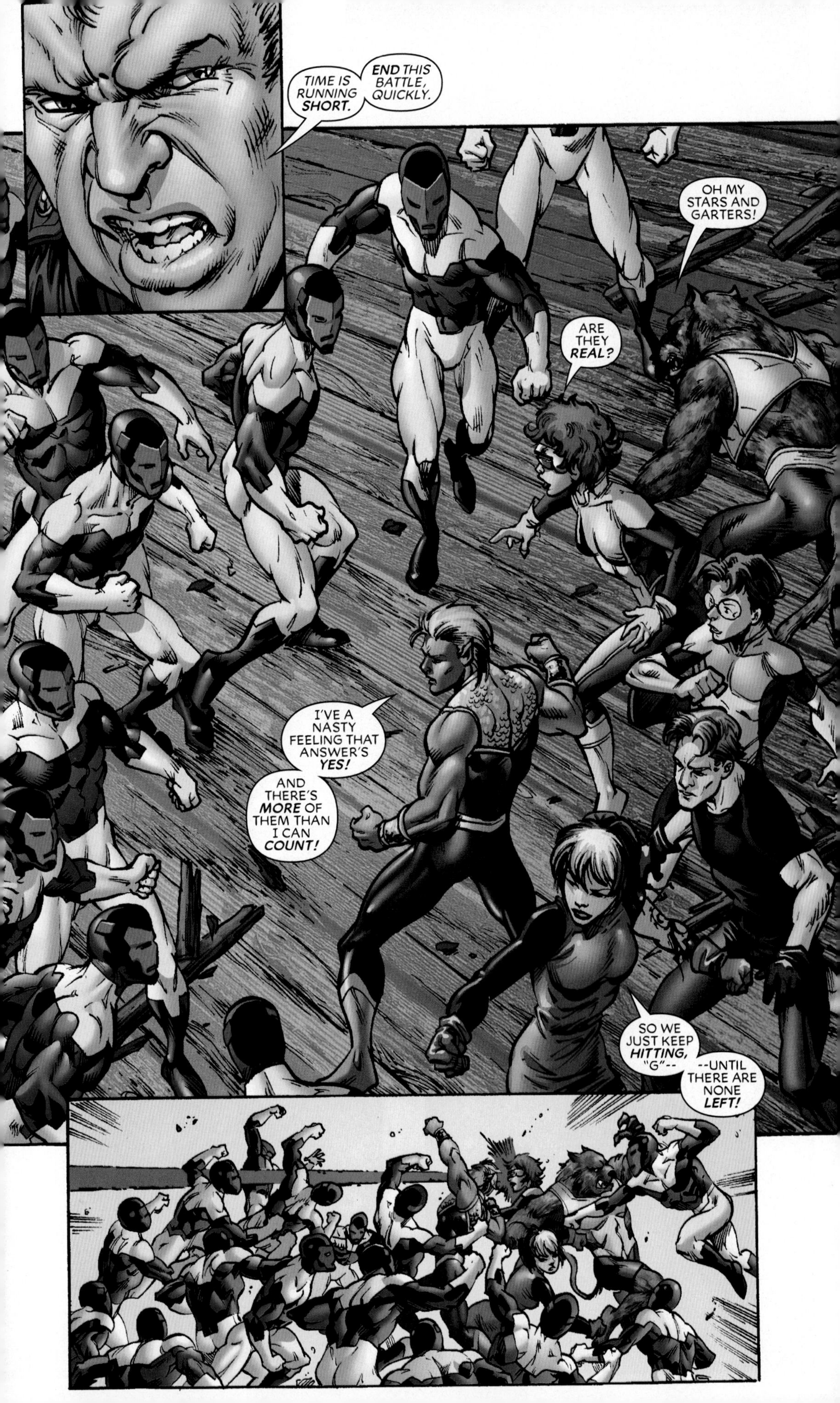
TIME IS RUNNING SHORT.
END THIS BATTLE, QUICKLY.
OH MY STARS AND GARTERS!
ARE THEY REAL?
I'VE A NASTY FEELING THAT ANSWER'S YES!
AND THERE'S MORE OF THEM THAN I CAN COUNT!
SO WE JUST KEEP HITTING, "G"--
--UNTIL THERE ARE NONE LEFT!

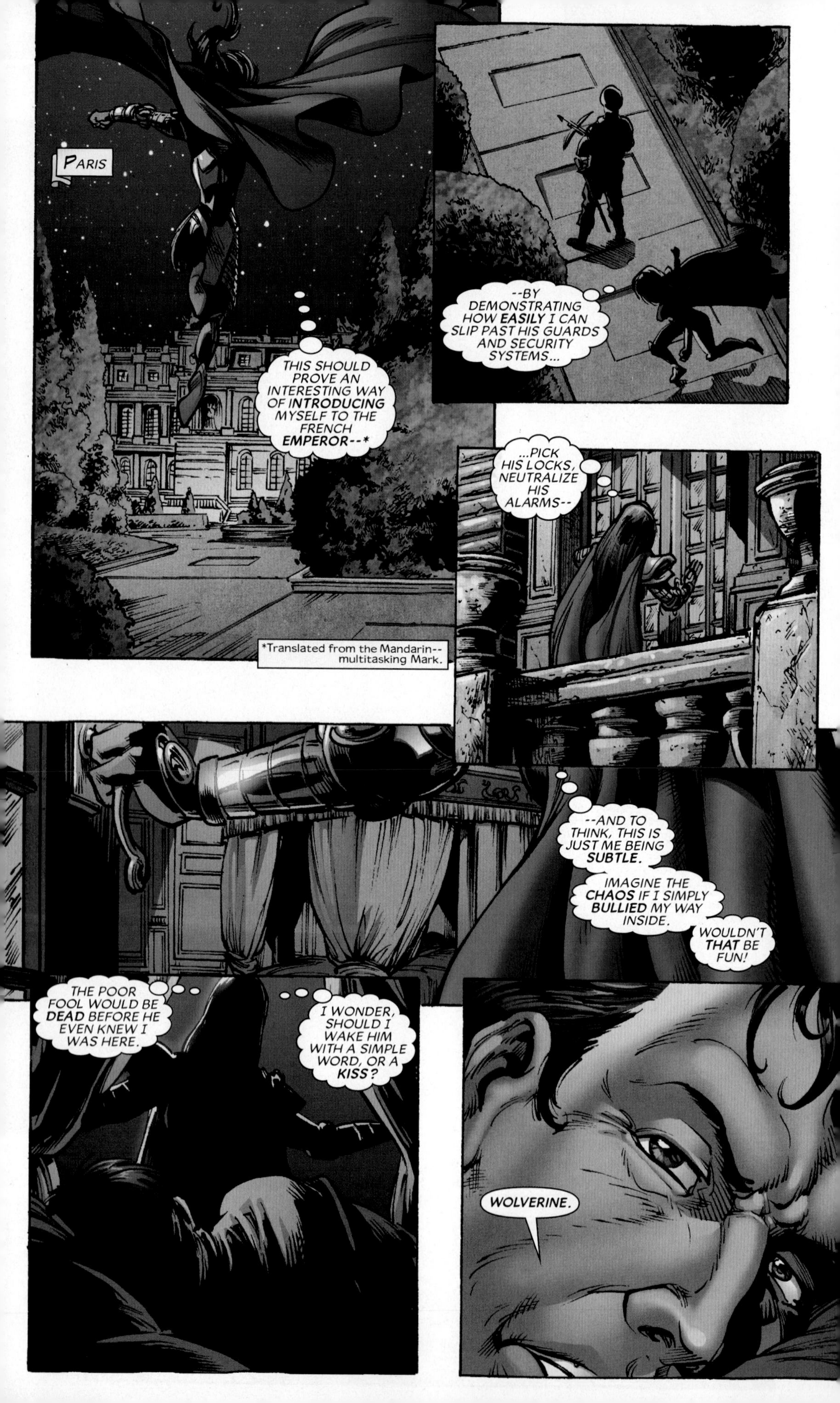
PARIS
THIS SHOULD PROVE AN INTERESTING WAY OF INTRODUCING MYSELF TO THE FRENCH EMPEROR--*
*Translated from the Mandarin-- multitasking Mark.
--BY DEMONSTRATING HOW EASILY I CAN SLIP PAST HIS GUARDS AND SECURITY SYSTEMS...
...PICK HIS LOCKS, NEUTRALIZE HIS ALARMS--
--AND TO THINK, THIS IS JUST ME BEING SUBTLE.
IMAGINE THE CHAOS IF I SIMPLY BULLIED MY WAY INSIDE.
WOULDN'T THAT BE FUN!
THE POOR FOOL WOULD BE DEAD BEFORE HE EVEN KNEW I WAS HERE.
I WONDER, SHOULD I WAKE HIM WITH A SIMPLE WORD, OR A KISS?
WOLVERINE.

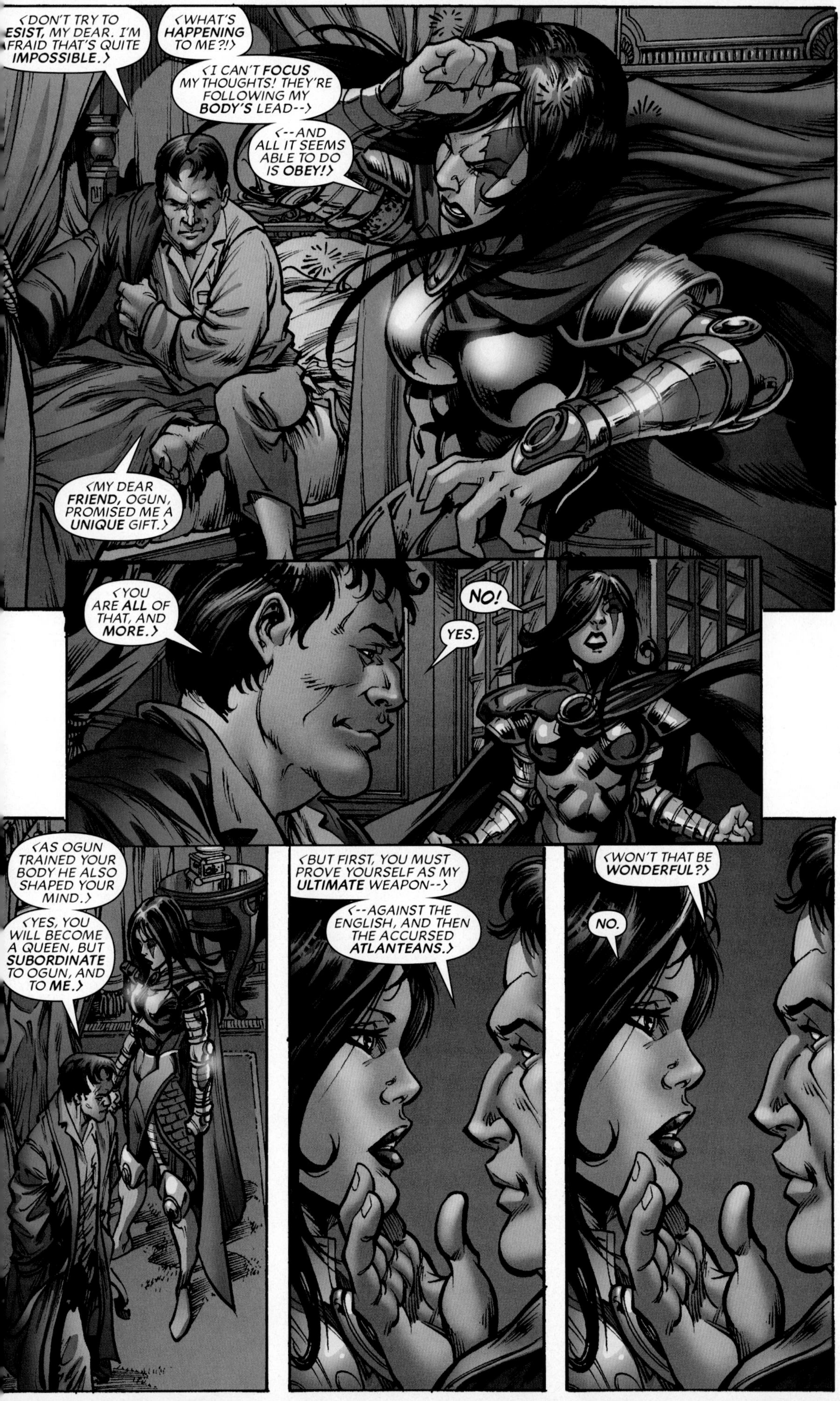

<DON'T TRY TO ESIST, MY DEAR. I'M FRAID THAT'S QUITE IMPOSSIBLE.>
<WHAT'S HAPPENING TO ME?!>
<I CAN'T FOCUS MY THOUGHTS! THEY'RE FOLLOWING MY BODY'S LEAD-->
<--AND ALL IT SEEMS ABLE TO DO IS OBEY!>
<MY DEAR FRIEND, OGUN, PROMISED ME A UNIQUE GIFT.>
<YOU ARE ALL OF THAT, AND MORE.>
NO!
YES.
<AS OGUN TRAINED YOUR BODY HE ALSO SHAPED YOUR MIND.>
<YES, YOU WILL BECOME A QUEEN, BUT SUBORDINATE TO OGUN, AND TO ME.>
<BUT FIRST, YOU MUST PROVE YOURSELF AS MY ULTIMATE WEAPON-->
<--AGAINST THE ENGLISH, AND THEN THE ACCURSED ATLANTEANS.>
<WON'T THAT BE WONDERFUL?>
NO.

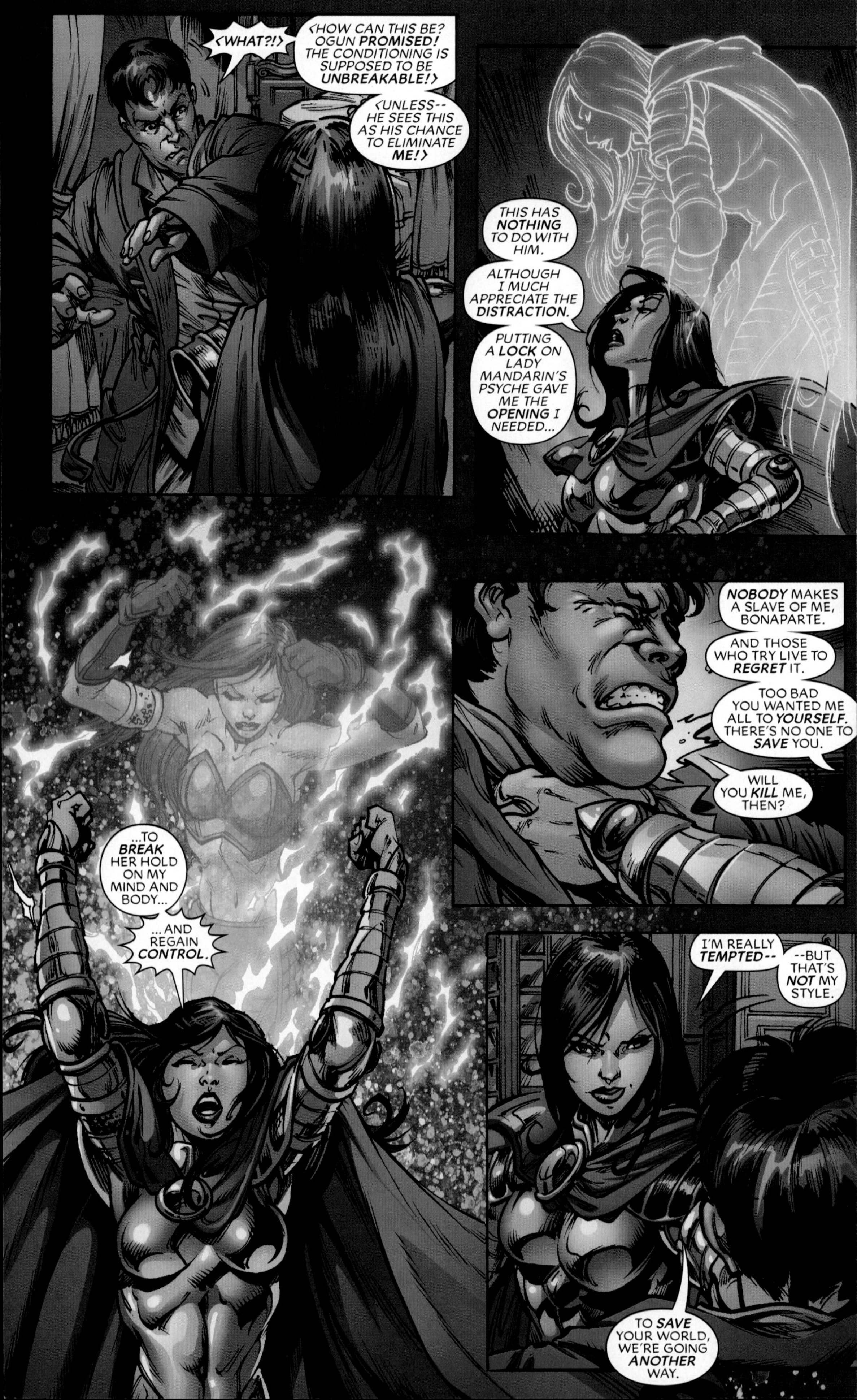

‹WHAT?!›
‹HOW CAN THIS BE? OGUN PROMISED! THE CONDITIONING IS SUPPOSED TO BE UNBREAKABLE!›
‹UNLESS-- HE SEES THIS AS HIS CHANCE TO ELIMINATE ME!›
THIS HAS NOTHING TO DO WITH HIM.
ALTHOUGH I MUCH APPRECIATE THE DISTRACTION.
PUTTING A LOCK ON LADY MANDARIN'S PSYCHE GAVE ME THE OPENING I NEEDED...
...TO BREAK HER HOLD ON MY MIND AND BODY...
...AND REGAIN CONTROL.
NOBODY MAKES A SLAVE OF ME, BONAPARTE.
AND THOSE WHO TRY LIVE TO REGRET IT.
TOO BAD YOU WANTED ME ALL TO YOURSELF. THERE'S NO ONE TO SAVE YOU.
WILL YOU KILL ME, THEN?
I'M REALLY TEMPTED--
--BUT THAT'S NOT MY STYLE.
TO SAVE YOUR WORLD, WE'RE GOING ANOTHER WAY.

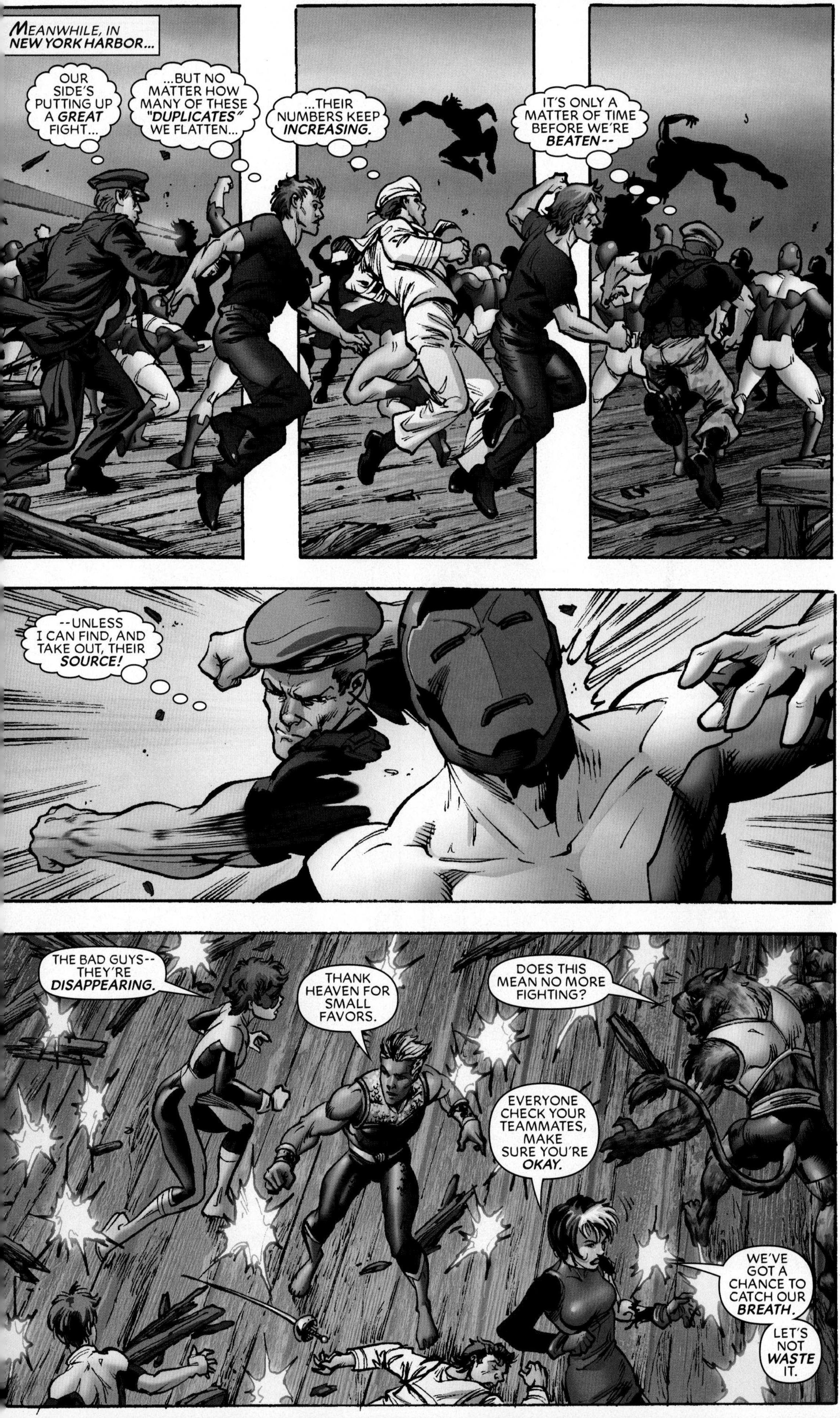
MEANWHILE, IN NEW YORK HARBOR...
OUR SIDE'S PUTTING UP A GREAT FIGHT...
...BUT NO MATTER HOW MANY OF THESE "DUPLICATES" WE FLATTEN...
...THEIR NUMBERS KEEP INCREASING.
IT'S ONLY A MATTER OF TIME BEFORE WE'RE BEATEN--
--UNLESS I CAN FIND, AND TAKE OUT, THEIR SOURCE!
THE BAD GUYS--THEY'RE DISAPPEARING.
THANK HEAVEN FOR SMALL FAVORS.
DOES THIS MEAN NO MORE FIGHTING?
EVERYONE CHECK YOUR TEAMMATES, MAKE SURE YOU'RE OKAY.
WE'VE GOT A CHANCE TO CATCH OUR BREATH.
LET'S NOT WASTE IT.

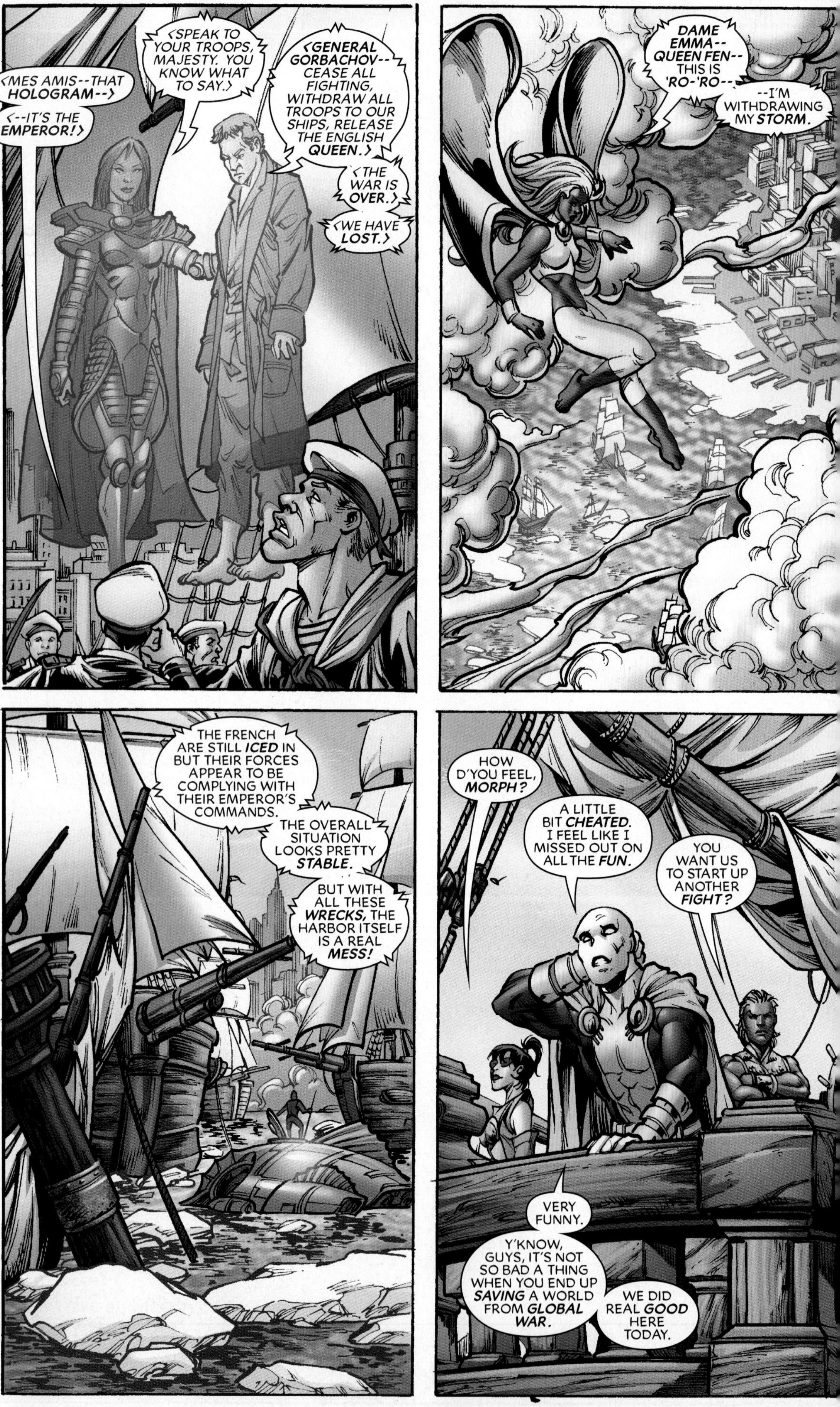
<MES AMIS--THAT HOLOGRAM-->
<--IT'S THE EMPEROR!>
<SPEAK TO YOUR TROOPS, MAJESTY. YOU KNOW WHAT TO SAY.>
<GENERAL GORBACHOV-- CEASE ALL FIGHTING, WITHDRAW ALL TROOPS TO OUR SHIPS, RELEASE THE ENGLISH QUEEN.>
<THE WAR IS OVER.>
<WE HAVE LOST.>
DAME EMMA-- QUEEN FEN-- THIS IS 'RO-'RO--
--I'M WITHDRAWING MY STORM.
THE FRENCH ARE STILL ICED IN BUT THEIR FORCES APPEAR TO BE COMPLYING WITH THEIR EMPEROR'S COMMANDS.
THE OVERALL SITUATION LOOKS PRETTY STABLE.
BUT WITH ALL THESE WRECKS, THE HARBOR ITSELF IS A REAL MESS!
HOW D'YOU FEEL, MORPH?
A LITTLE BIT CHEATED. I FEEL LIKE I MISSED OUT ON ALL THE FUN.
YOU WANT US TO START UP ANOTHER FIGHT?
VERY FUNNY.
Y'KNOW, GUYS, IT'S NOT SO BAD A THING WHEN YOU END UP SAVING A WORLD FROM GLOBAL WAR.
WE DID REAL GOOD HERE TODAY.

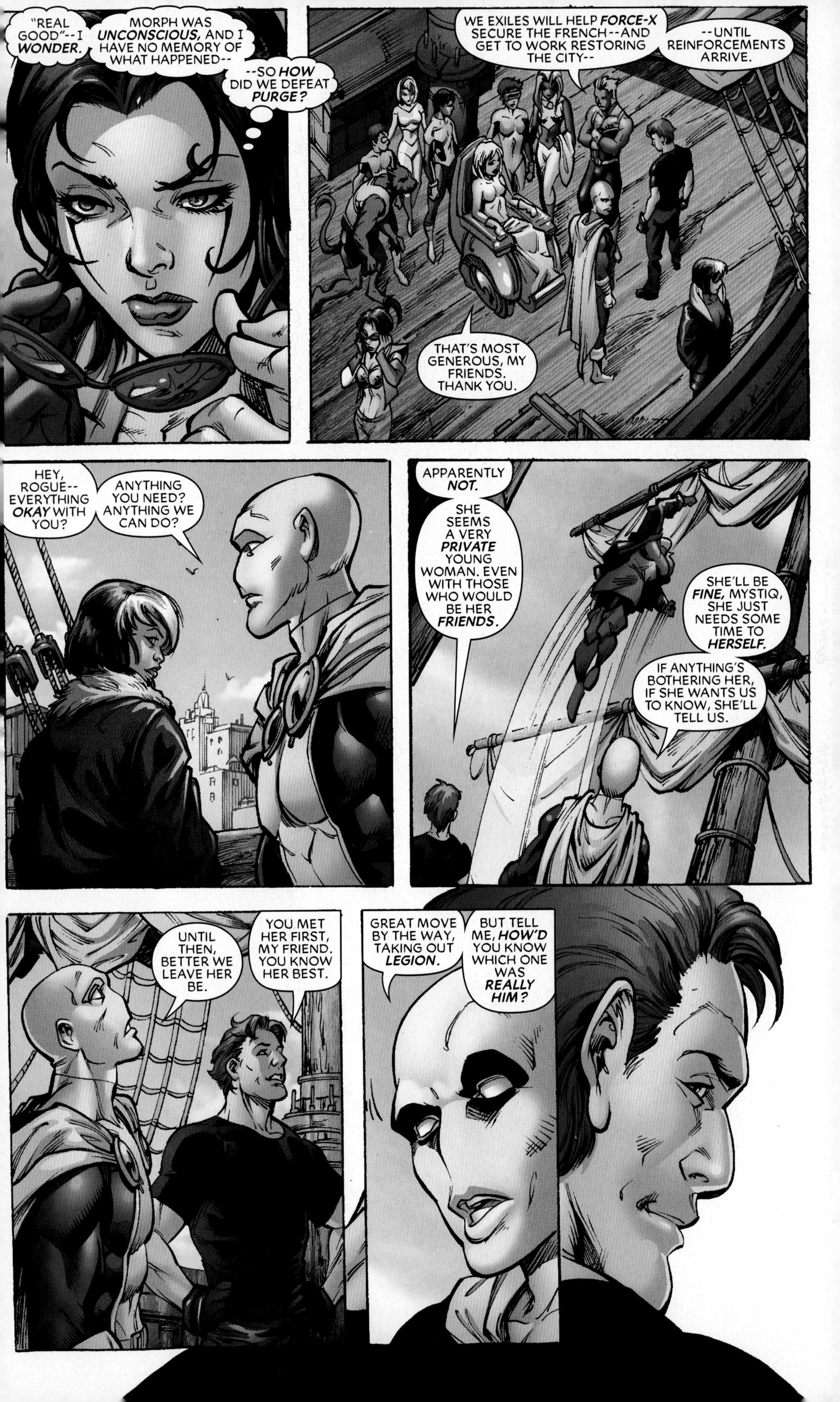

"REAL GOOD"--I WONDER.
MORPH WAS UNCONSCIOUS, AND I HAVE NO MEMORY OF WHAT HAPPENED--
--SO HOW DID WE DEFEAT PURGE?
WE EXILES WILL HELP FORCE-X SECURE THE FRENCH--AND GET TO WORK RESTORING THE CITY--
--UNTIL REINFORCEMENTS ARRIVE.
THAT'S MOST GENEROUS, MY FRIENDS. THANK YOU.
HEY, ROGUE--EVERYTHING OKAY WITH YOU?
ANYTHING YOU NEED? ANYTHING WE CAN DO?
APPARENTLY NOT.
SHE SEEMS A VERY PRIVATE YOUNG WOMAN. EVEN WITH THOSE WHO WOULD BE HER FRIENDS.
SHE'LL BE FINE, MYSTIQ, SHE JUST NEEDS SOME TIME TO HERSELF.
IF ANYTHING'S BOTHERING HER, IF SHE WANTS US TO KNOW, SHE'LL TELL US.
UNTIL THEN, BETTER WE LEAVE HER BE.
YOU MET HER FIRST, MY FRIEND. YOU KNOW HER BEST.
GREAT MOVE BY THE WAY, TAKING OUT LEGION.
BUT TELL ME, HOW'D YOU KNOW WHICH ONE WAS REALLY HIM?

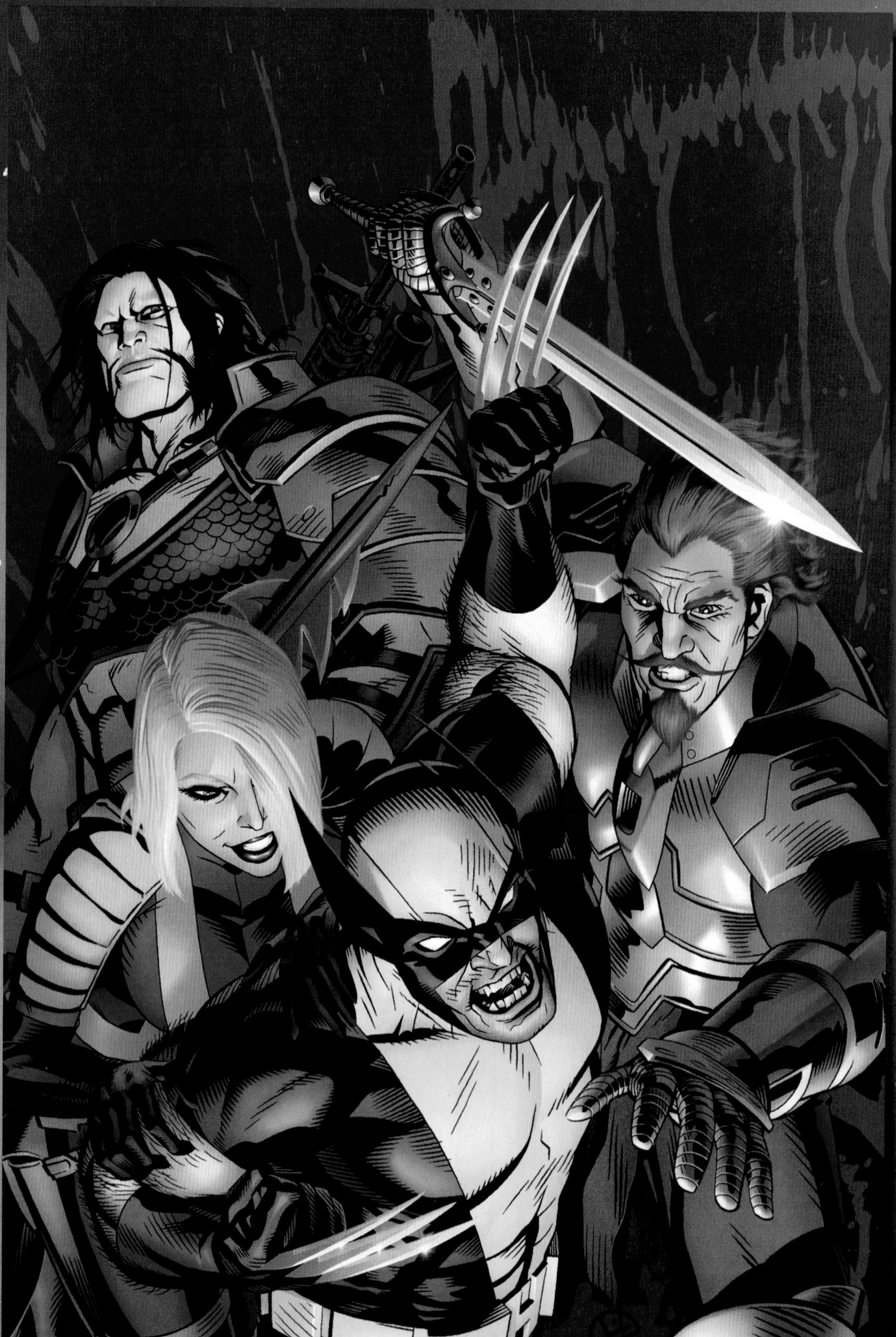

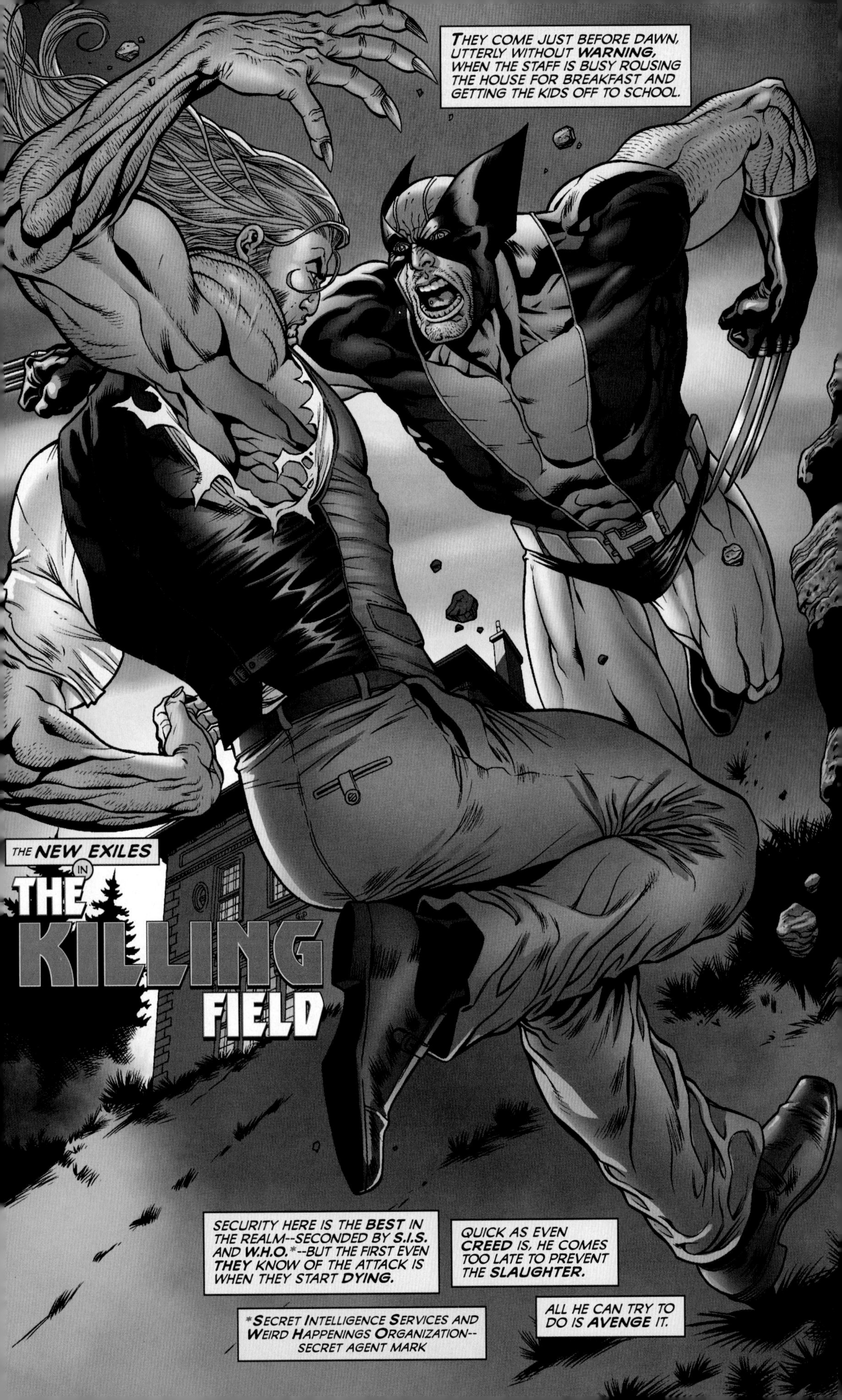

THEY COME JUST BEFORE DAWN, UTTERLY WITHOUT WARNING, WHEN THE STAFF IS BUSY ROUSING THE HOUSE FOR BREAKFAST AND GETTING THE KIDS OFF TO SCHOOL.
THE NEW EXILES IN
THE KILLING FIELD
SECURITY HERE IS THE BEST IN THE REALM--SECONDED BY S.I.S. AND W.H.O.*--BUT THE FIRST EVEN THEY KNOW OF THE ATTACK IS WHEN THEY START DYING.
QUICK AS EVEN CREED IS, HE COMES TOO LATE TO PREVENT THE SLAUGHTER.
*SECRET INTELLIGENCE SERVICES AND WEIRD HAPPENINGS ORGANIZATION-- SECRET AGENT MARK
ALL HE CAN TRY TO DO IS AVENGE IT.

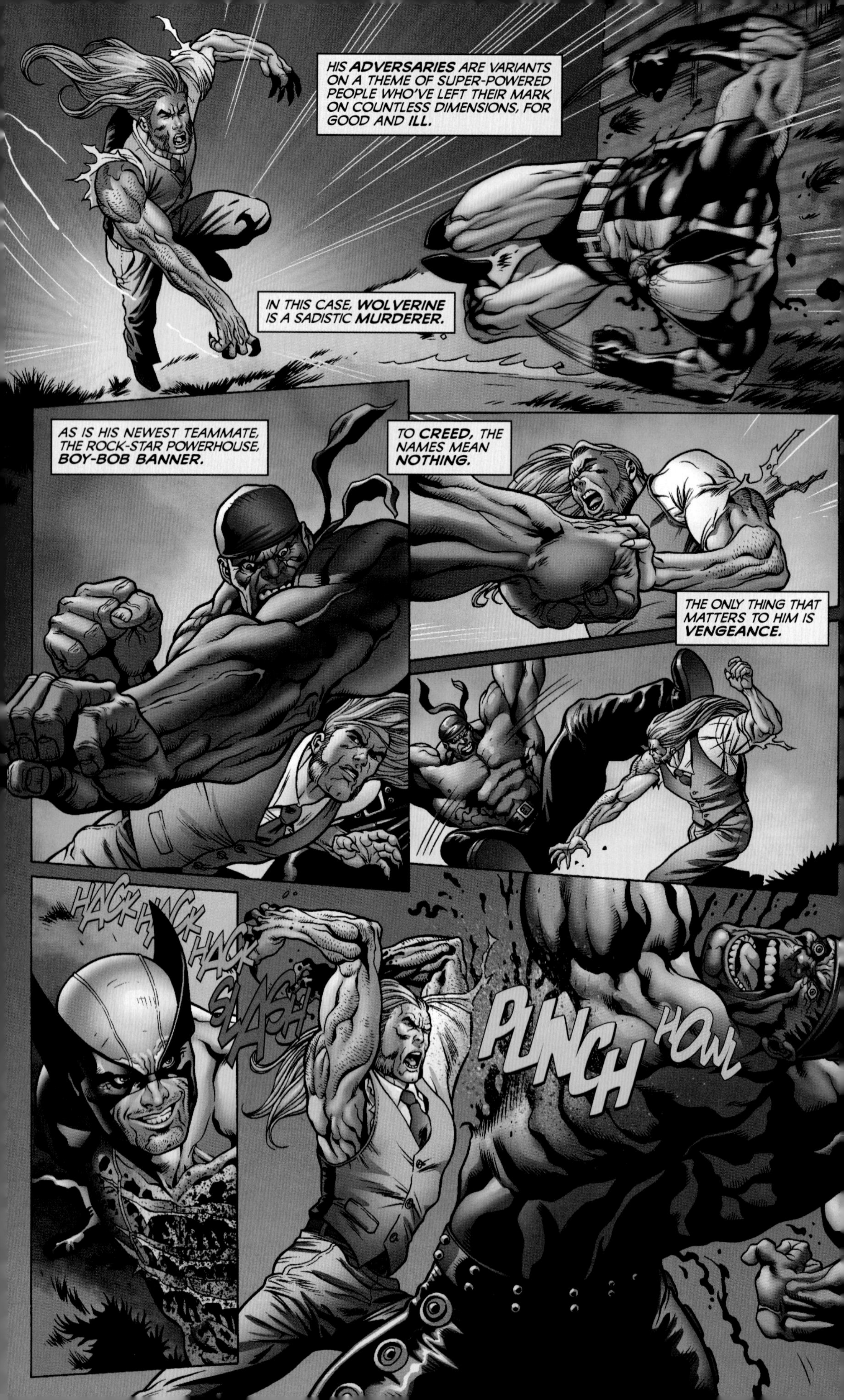

HIS **ADVERSARIES** ARE VARIANTS ON A THEME OF SUPER-POWERED PEOPLE WHO'VE LEFT THEIR MARK ON COUNTLESS DIMENSIONS, FOR GOOD AND **ILL**.
IN THIS CASE, **WOLVERINE** IS A SADISTIC **MURDERER**.
AS IS HIS NEWEST TEAMMATE, THE ROCK-STAR POWERHOUSE, **BOY-BOB BANNER**.
TO **CREED**, THE NAMES MEAN **NOTHING**.
THE ONLY THING THAT MATTERS TO HIM IS **VENGEANCE**.
HACK
HACK
HACK
SLASH
PUNCH
HOWL

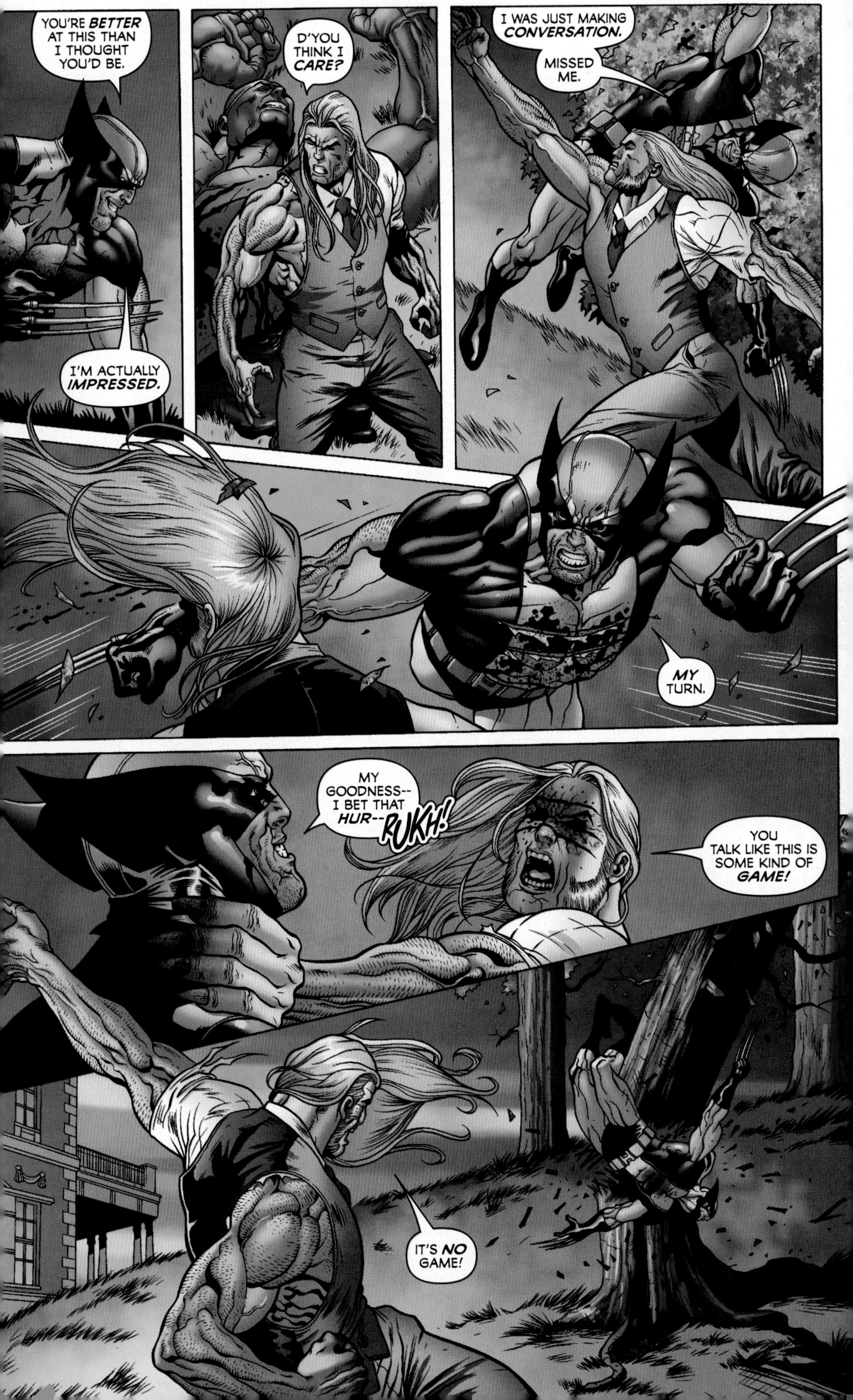
YOU'RE *BETTER* AT THIS THAN I THOUGHT YOU'D BE.
I'M ACTUALLY *IMPRESSED.*
D'YOU THINK I *CARE?*
I WAS JUST MAKING *CONVERSATION.*
MISSED ME.
MY TURN.
MY GOODNESS-- I BET THAT *HUR--*
RUKH!
YOU TALK LIKE THIS IS SOME KIND OF *GAME!*
IT'S *NO* GAME!

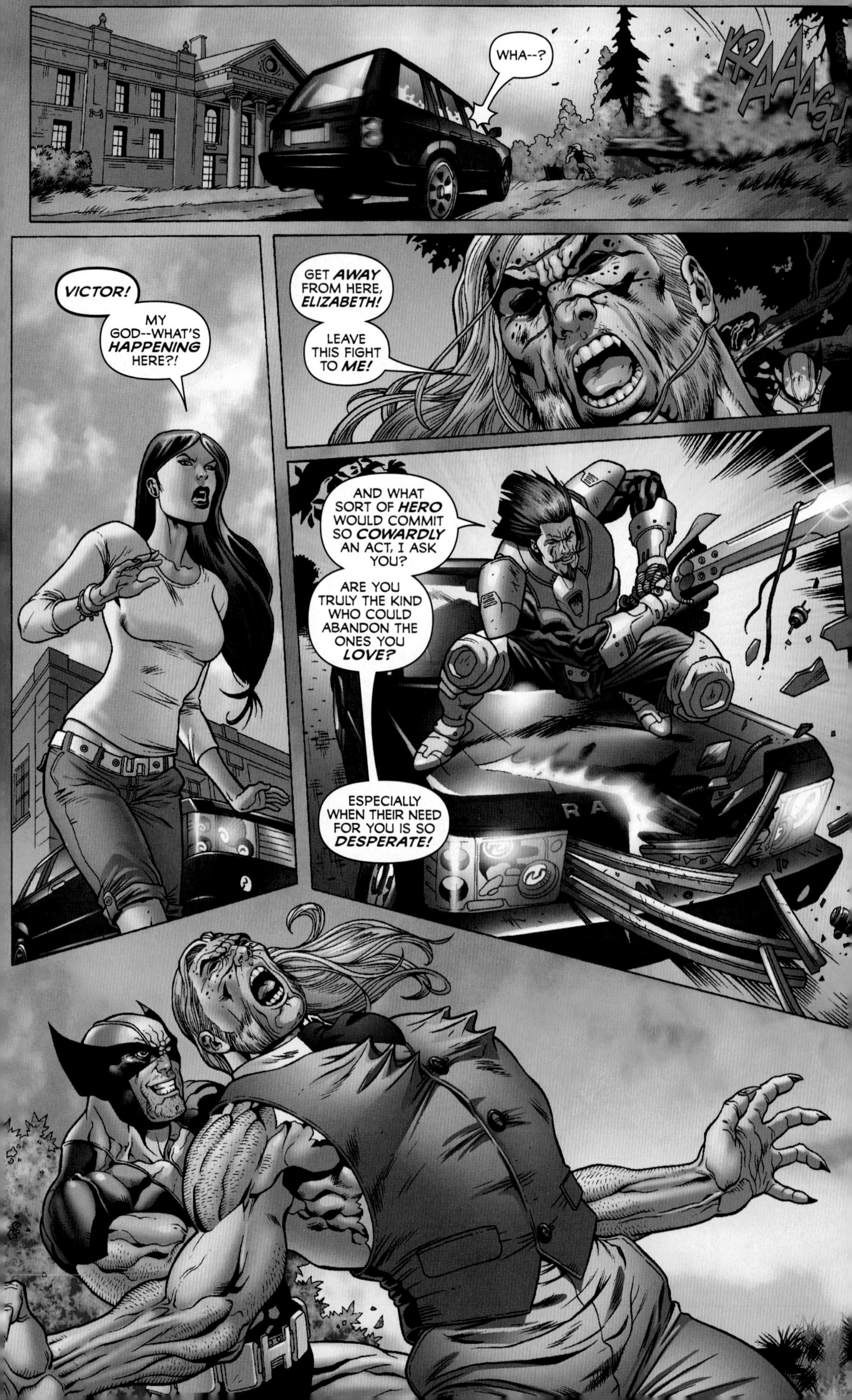

WHA--?
KRAAASH
VICTOR!
MY GOD--WHAT'S HAPPENING HERE?!
GET AWAY FROM HERE, ELIZABETH!
LEAVE THIS FIGHT TO ME!
AND WHAT SORT OF HERO WOULD COMMIT SO COWARDLY AN ACT, I ASK YOU?
ARE YOU TRULY THE KIND WHO COULD ABANDON THE ONES YOU LOVE?
ESPECIALLY WHEN THEIR NEED FOR YOU IS SO DESPERATE!

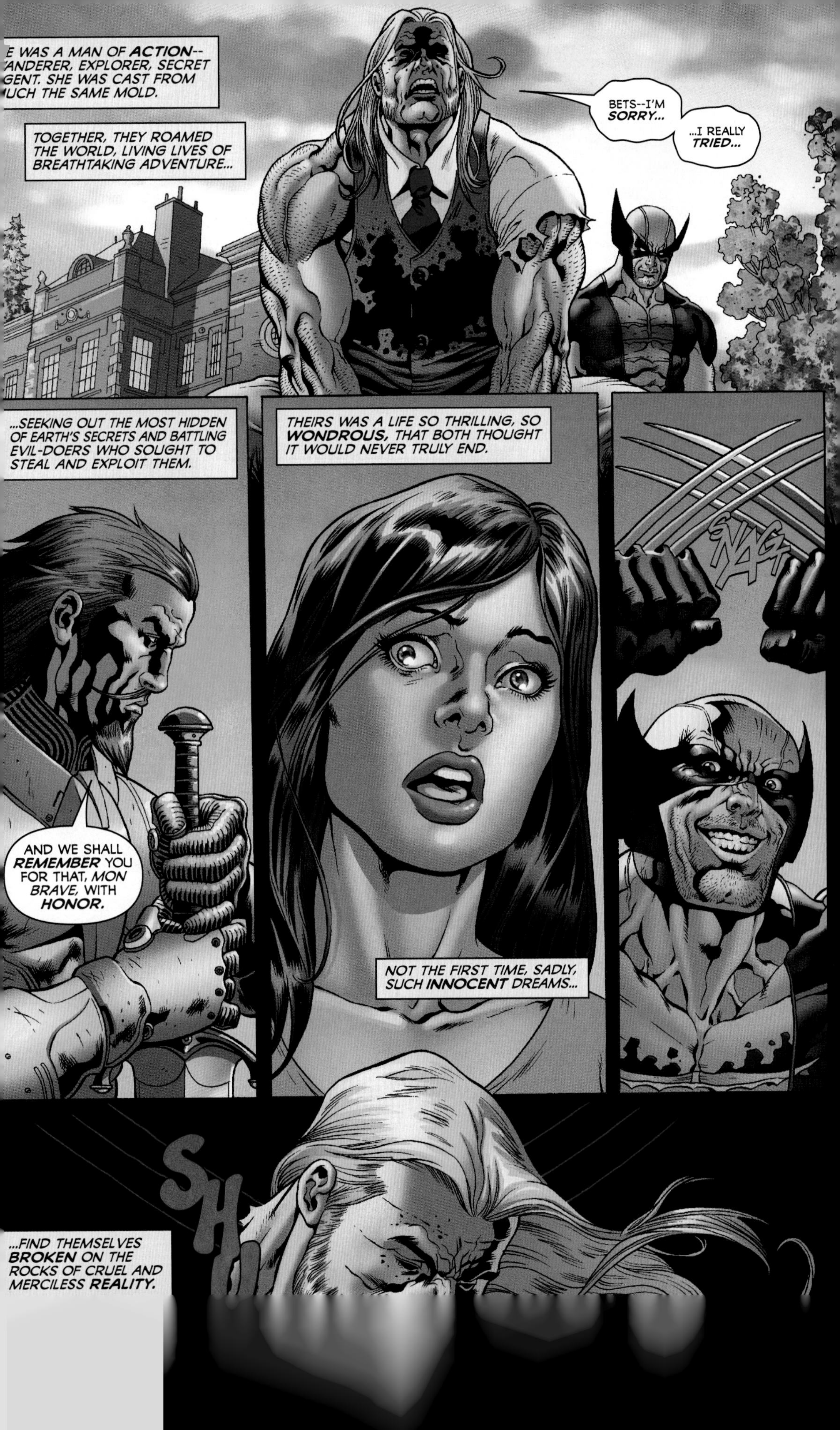
E WAS A MAN OF ACTION-- ANDERER, EXPLORER, SECRET GENT. SHE WAS CAST FROM UCH THE SAME MOLD.
TOGETHER, THEY ROAMED THE WORLD, LIVING LIVES OF BREATHTAKING ADVENTURE...
BETS--I'M SORRY...
...I REALLY TRIED...
...SEEKING OUT THE MOST HIDDEN OF EARTH'S SECRETS AND BATTLING EVIL-DOERS WHO SOUGHT TO STEAL AND EXPLOIT THEM.
AND WE SHALL REMEMBER YOU FOR THAT, MON BRAVE, WITH HONOR.
THEIRS WAS A LIFE SO THRILLING, SO WONDROUS, THAT BOTH THOUGHT IT WOULD NEVER TRULY END.
NOT THE FIRST TIME, SADLY, SUCH INNOCENT DREAMS...
...FIND THEMSELVES BROKEN ON THE ROCKS OF CRUEL AND MERCILESS REALITY.

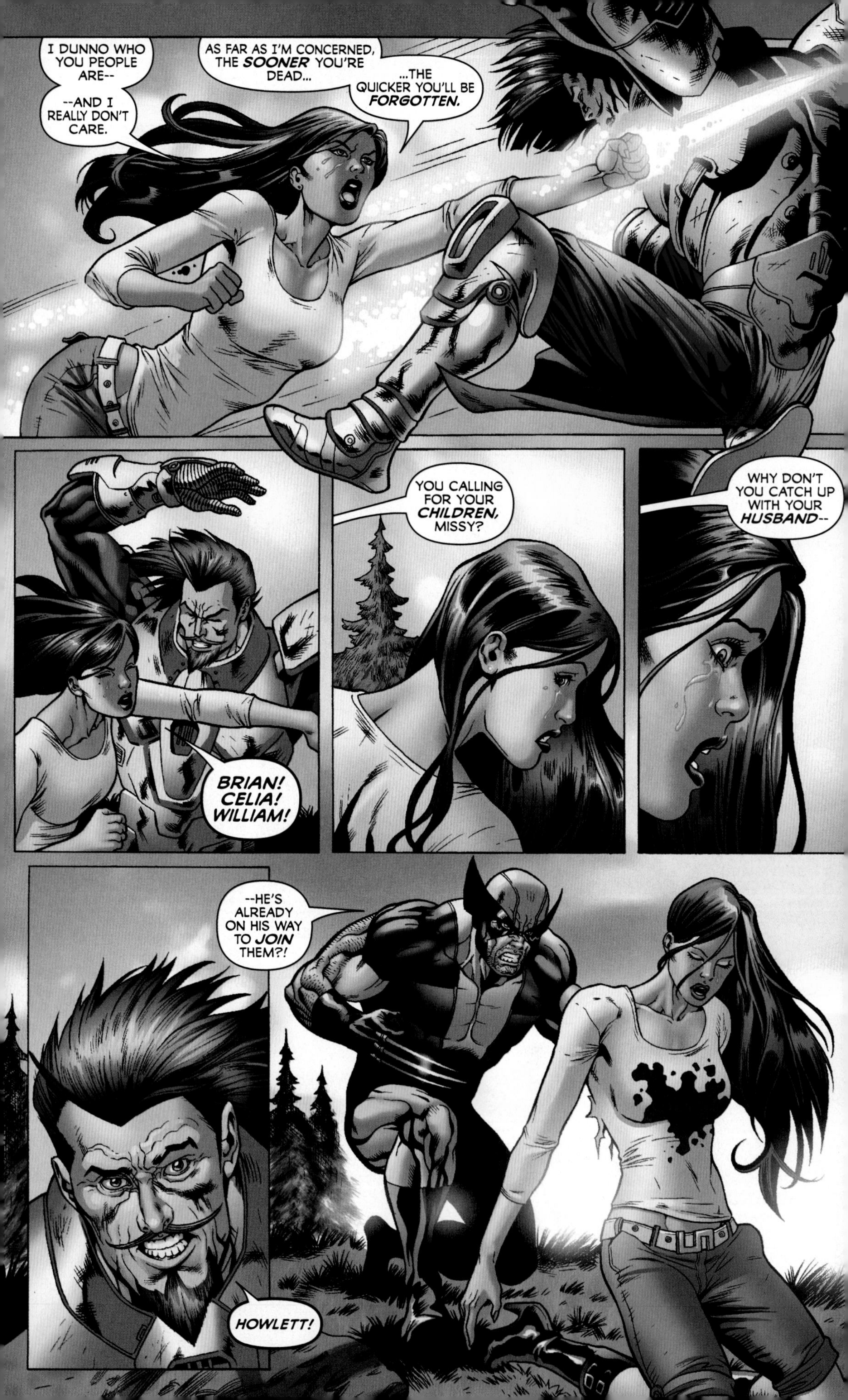
I DUNNO WHO YOU PEOPLE ARE--
--AND I REALLY DON'T CARE.
AS FAR AS I'M CONCERNED, THE SOONER YOU'RE DEAD...
...THE QUICKER YOU'LL BE FORGOTTEN.
BRIAN! CELIA! WILLIAM!
YOU CALLING FOR YOUR CHILDREN, MISSY?
WHY DON'T YOU CATCH UP WITH YOUR HUSBAND--
--HE'S ALREADY ON HIS WAY TO JOIN THEM?!
HOWLETT!

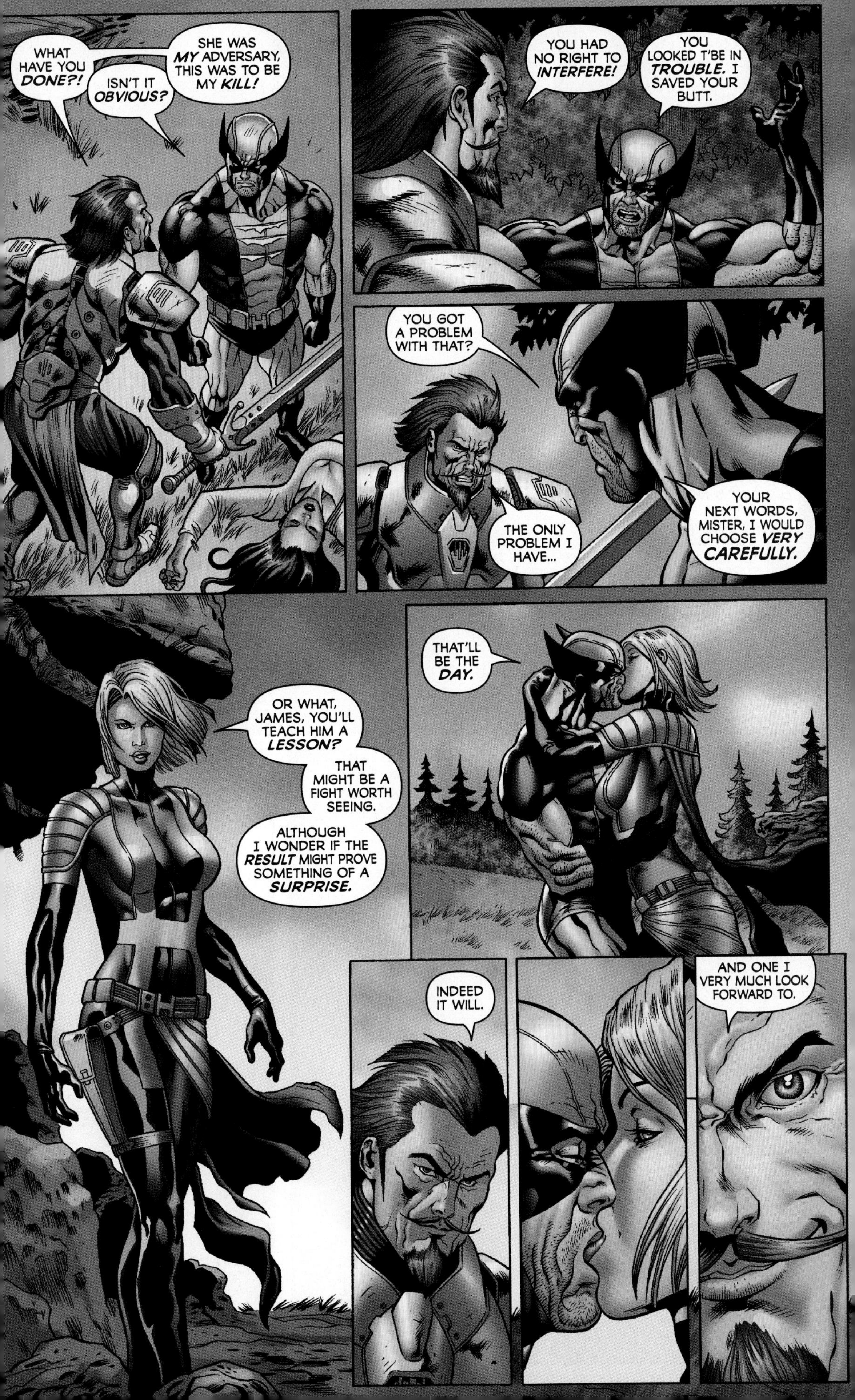

WHAT HAVE YOU DONE?!
ISN'T IT OBVIOUS?
SHE WAS MY ADVERSARY, THIS WAS TO BE MY KILL!
YOU HAD NO RIGHT TO INTERFERE!
YOU LOOKED T'BE IN TROUBLE. I SAVED YOUR BUTT.
YOU GOT A PROBLEM WITH THAT?
THE ONLY PROBLEM I HAVE...
YOUR NEXT WORDS, MISTER, I WOULD CHOOSE VERY CAREFULLY.
OR WHAT, JAMES, YOU'LL TEACH HIM A LESSON?
THAT MIGHT BE A FIGHT WORTH SEEING.
ALTHOUGH I WONDER IF THE RESULT MIGHT PROVE SOMETHING OF A SURPRISE.
THAT'LL BE THE DAY.
INDEED IT WILL.
AND ONE I VERY MUCH LOOK FORWARD TO.

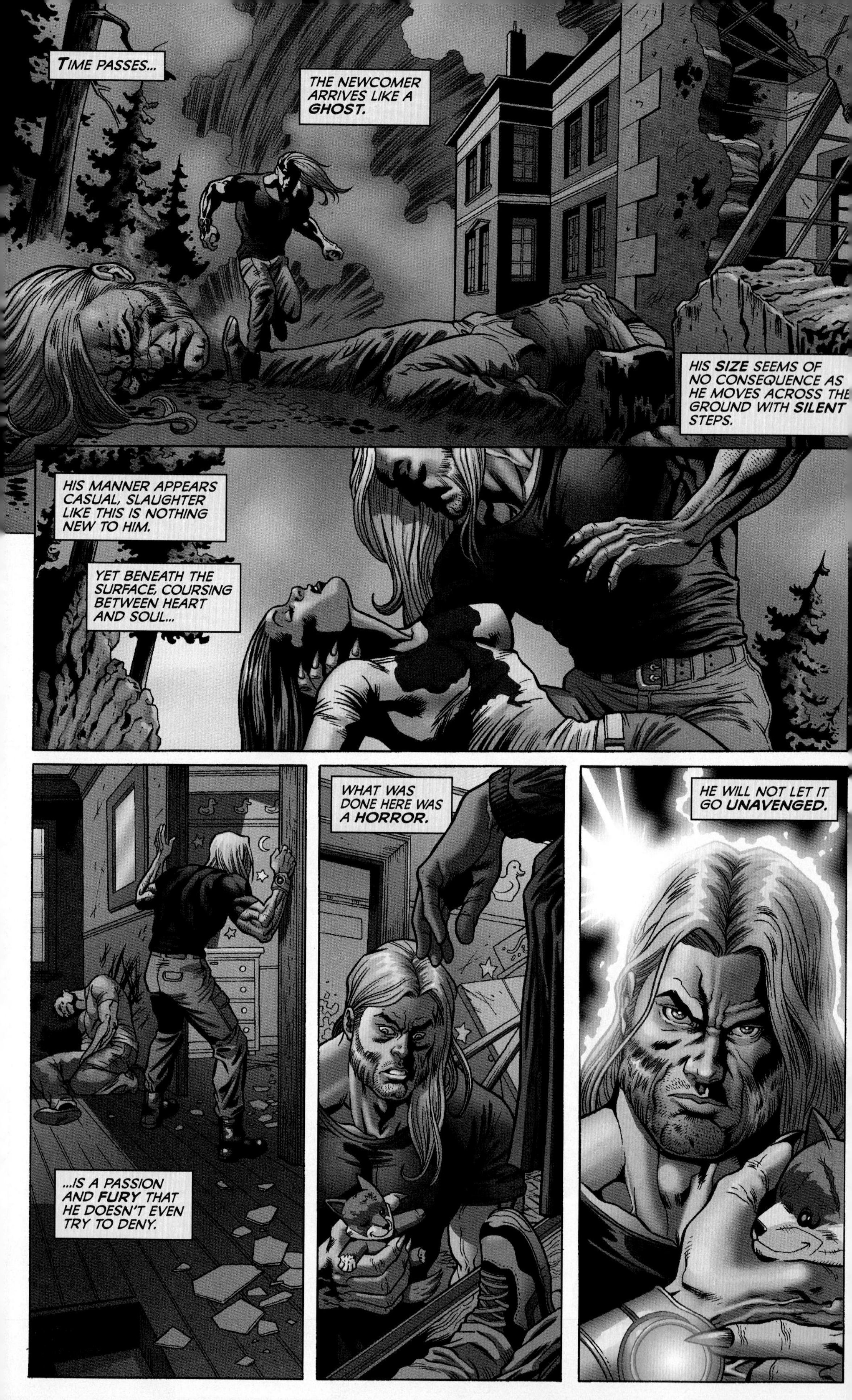

TIME PASSES...
THE NEWCOMER ARRIVES LIKE A **GHOST.**
HIS **SIZE** SEEMS OF NO CONSEQUENCE AS HE MOVES ACROSS THE GROUND WITH **SILENT** STEPS.
HIS MANNER APPEARS CASUAL, SLAUGHTER LIKE THIS IS NOTHING NEW TO HIM.
YET BENEATH THE SURFACE, COURSING BETWEEN HEART AND SOUL...
...IS A PASSION AND **FURY** THAT HE DOESN'T EVEN TRY TO DENY.
WHAT WAS DONE HERE WAS A **HORROR.**
HE WILL NOT LET IT GO **UNAVENGED.**

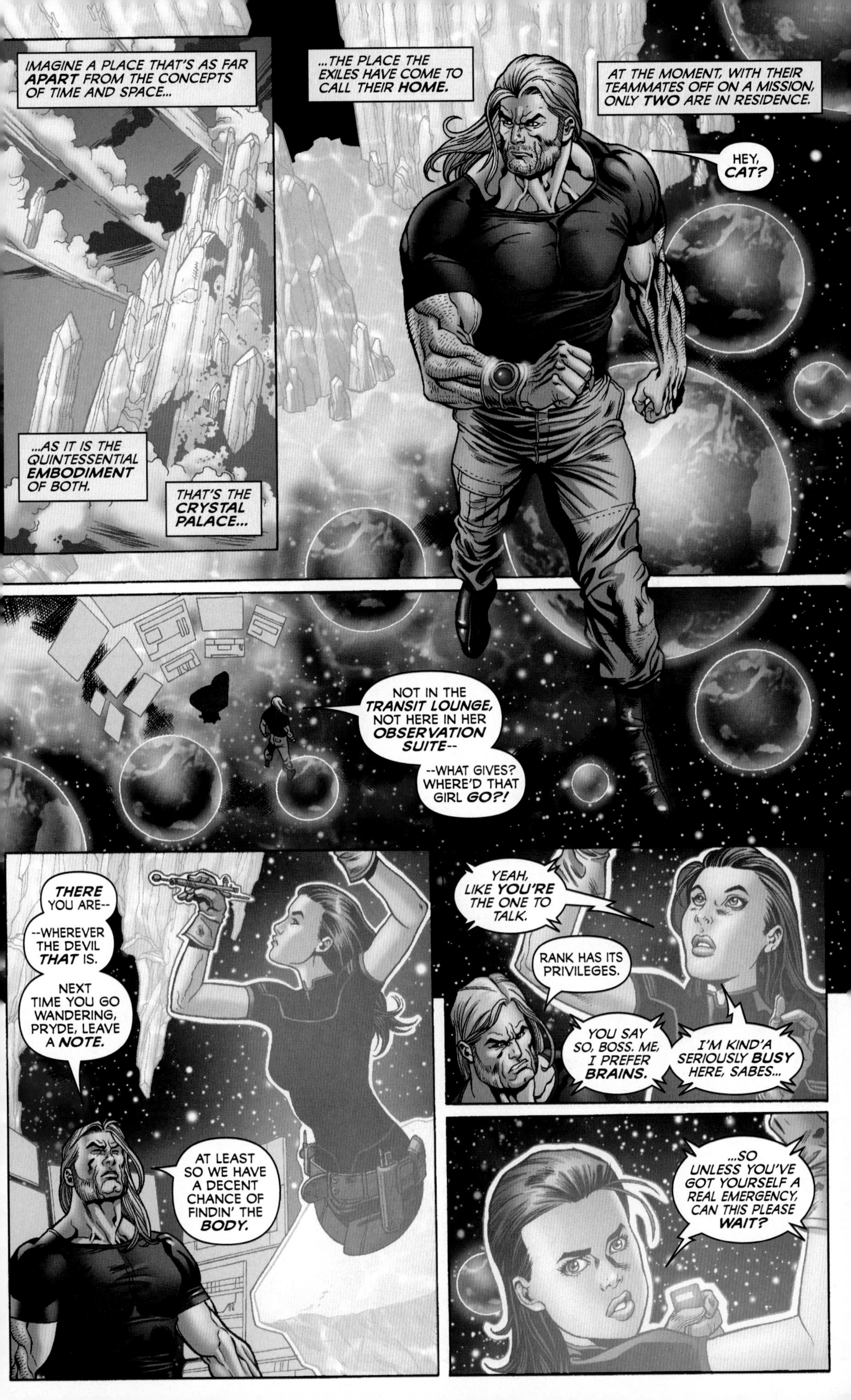
IMAGINE A PLACE THAT'S AS FAR APART FROM THE CONCEPTS OF TIME AND SPACE...
...AS IT IS THE QUINTESSENTIAL EMBODIMENT OF BOTH.
THAT'S THE CRYSTAL PALACE...
...THE PLACE THE EXILES HAVE COME TO CALL THEIR HOME.
AT THE MOMENT, WITH THEIR TEAMMATES OFF ON A MISSION, ONLY TWO ARE IN RESIDENCE.
HEY, CAT?
NOT IN THE TRANSIT LOUNGE, NOT HERE IN HER OBSERVATION SUITE--
--WHAT GIVES? WHERE'D THAT GIRL GO?!
THERE YOU ARE--
--WHEREVER THE DEVIL THAT IS.
NEXT TIME YOU GO WANDERING, PRYDE, LEAVE A NOTE.
AT LEAST SO WE HAVE A DECENT CHANCE OF FINDIN' THE BODY.
YEAH, LIKE YOU'RE THE ONE TO TALK.
RANK HAS ITS PRIVILEGES.
YOU SAY SO, BOSS. ME, I PREFER BRAINS.
I'M KIND'A SERIOUSLY BUSY HERE, SABES...
...SO UNLESS YOU'VE GOT YOURSELF A REAL EMERGENCY, CAN THIS PLEASE WAIT?

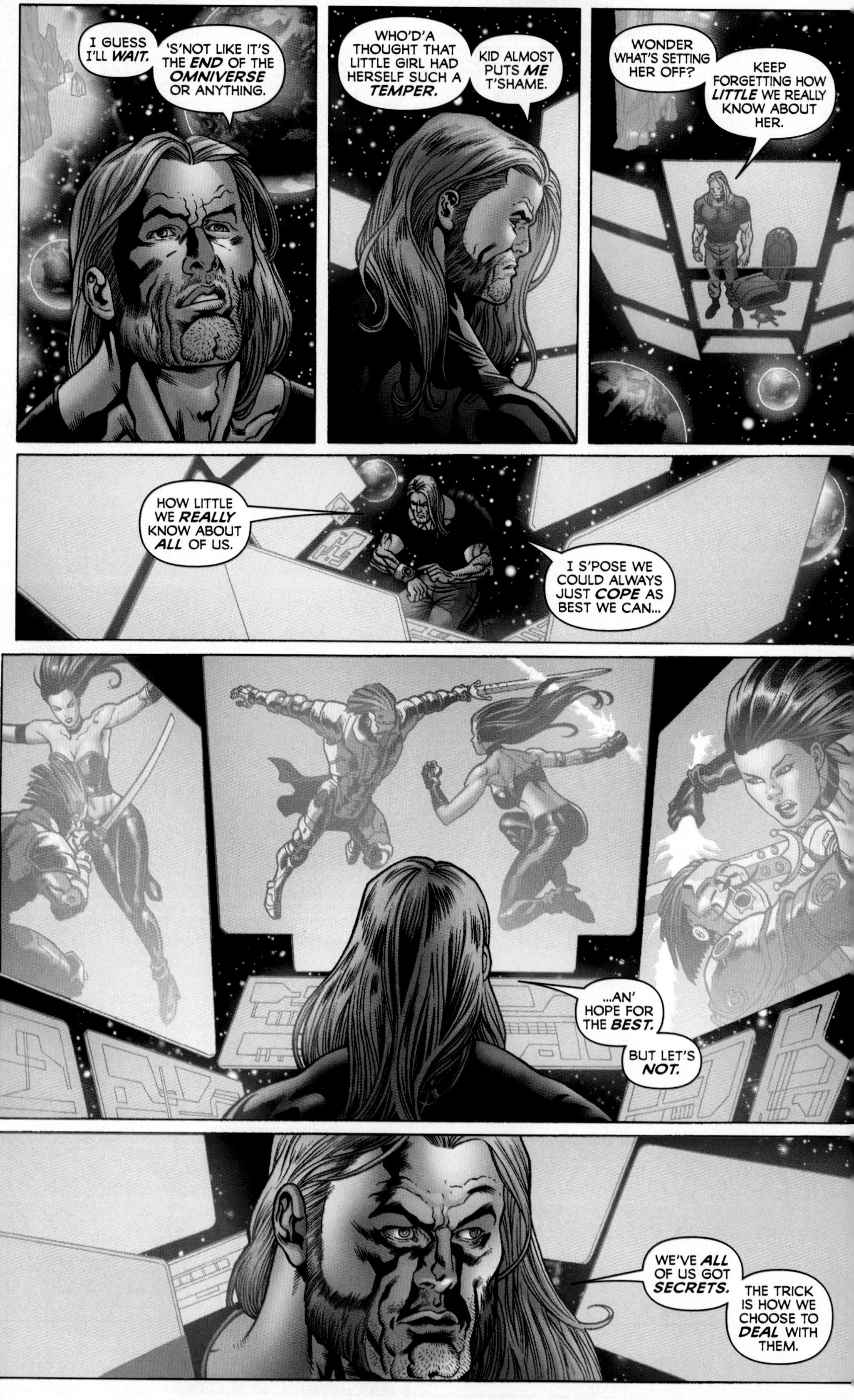
I GUESS I'LL *WAIT.*
'S'NOT LIKE IT'S THE *END* OF THE *OMNIVERSE* OR ANYTHING.
WHO'D'A THOUGHT THAT LITTLE GIRL HAD HERSELF SUCH A *TEMPER.*
KID ALMOST PUTS *ME* T'SHAME.
WONDER WHAT'S SETTING HER OFF?
KEEP FORGETTING HOW *LITTLE* WE REALLY KNOW ABOUT HER.
HOW LITTLE WE *REALLY* KNOW ABOUT *ALL* OF US.
I S'POSE WE COULD ALWAYS JUST *COPE* AS BEST WE CAN...
...AN' HOPE FOR THE *BEST.*
BUT LET'S *NOT.*
WE'VE *ALL* OF US GOT *SECRETS.*
THE TRICK IS HOW WE CHOOSE TO *DEAL* WITH THEM.

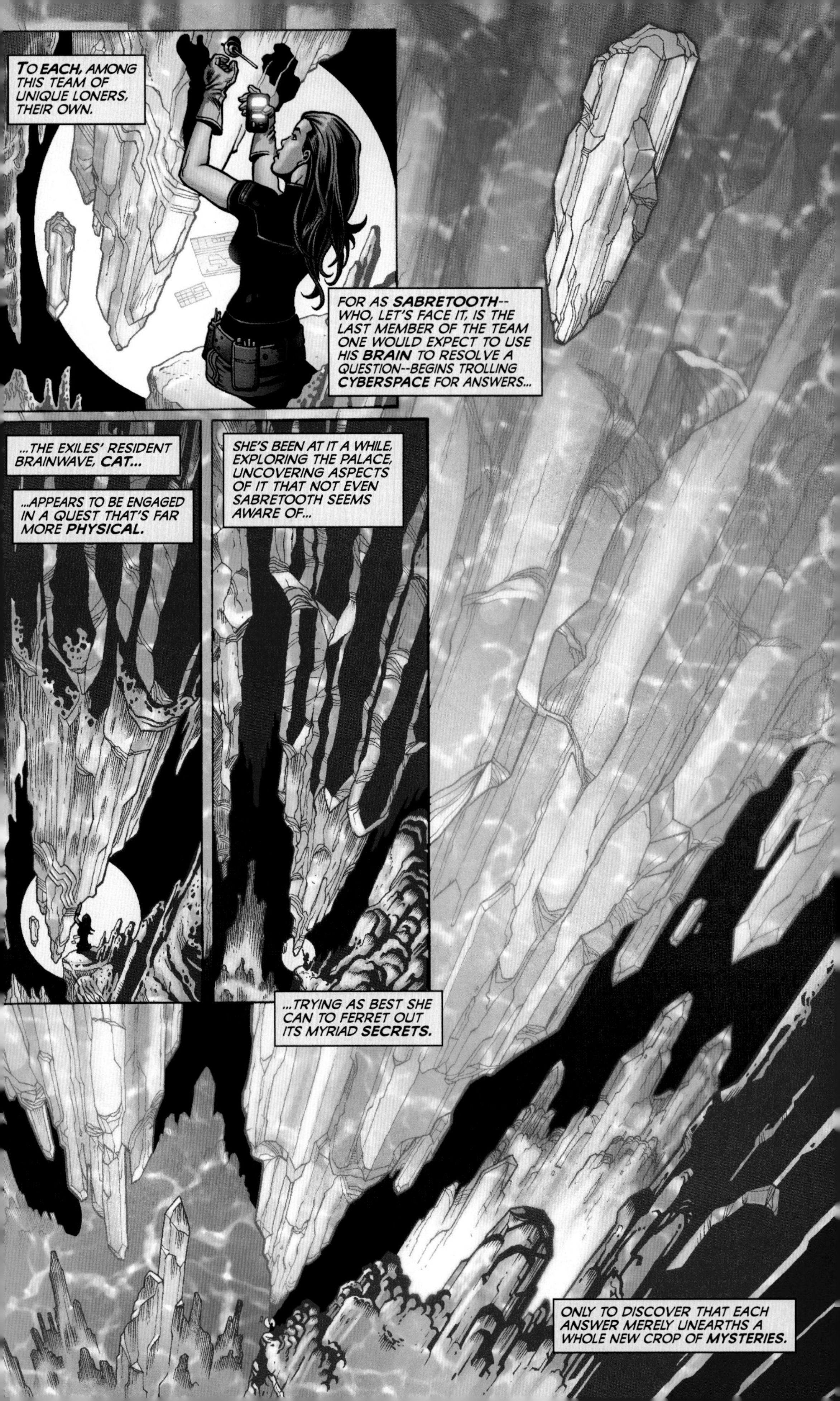

TO EACH, AMONG THIS TEAM OF UNIQUE LONERS, THEIR OWN.
FOR AS SABRETOOTH-- WHO, LET'S FACE IT, IS THE LAST MEMBER OF THE TEAM ONE WOULD EXPECT TO USE HIS BRAIN TO RESOLVE A QUESTION--BEGINS TROLLING CYBERSPACE FOR ANSWERS...
...THE EXILES' RESIDENT BRAINWAVE, CAT...
...APPEARS TO BE ENGAGED IN A QUEST THAT'S FAR MORE PHYSICAL.
SHE'S BEEN AT IT A WHILE, EXPLORING THE PALACE, UNCOVERING ASPECTS OF IT THAT NOT EVEN SABRETOOTH SEEMS AWARE OF...
...TRYING AS BEST SHE CAN TO FERRET OUT ITS MYRIAD SECRETS.
ONLY TO DISCOVER THAT EACH ANSWER MERELY UNEARTHS A WHOLE NEW CROP OF MYSTERIES.

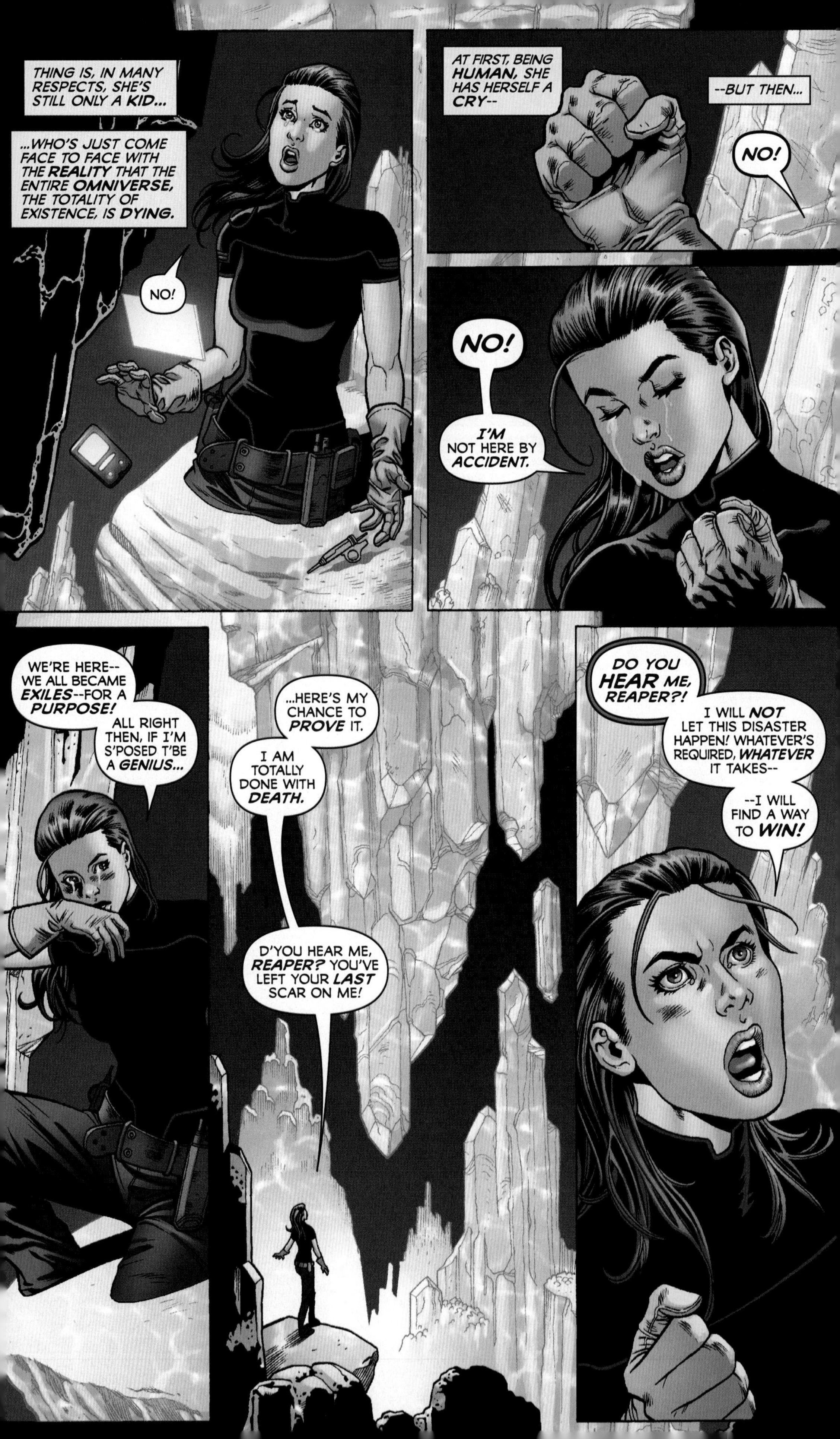
THING IS, IN MANY RESPECTS, SHE'S STILL ONLY A KID...
...WHO'S JUST COME FACE TO FACE WITH THE REALITY THAT THE ENTIRE OMNIVERSE, THE TOTALITY OF EXISTENCE, IS DYING.
NO!
AT FIRST, BEING HUMAN, SHE HAS HERSELF A CRY--
--BUT THEN...
NO!
NO!
I'M NOT HERE BY ACCIDENT.
WE'RE HERE-- WE ALL BECAME EXILES--FOR A PURPOSE!
ALL RIGHT THEN, IF I'M S'POSED T'BE A GENIUS...
...HERE'S MY CHANCE TO PROVE IT.
I AM TOTALLY DONE WITH DEATH.
D'YOU HEAR ME, REAPER? YOU'VE LEFT YOUR LAST SCAR ON ME!
DO YOU HEAR ME, REAPER?!
I WILL NOT LET THIS DISASTER HAPPEN! WHATEVER'S REQUIRED, WHATEVER IT TAKES--
--I WILL FIND A WAY TO WIN!

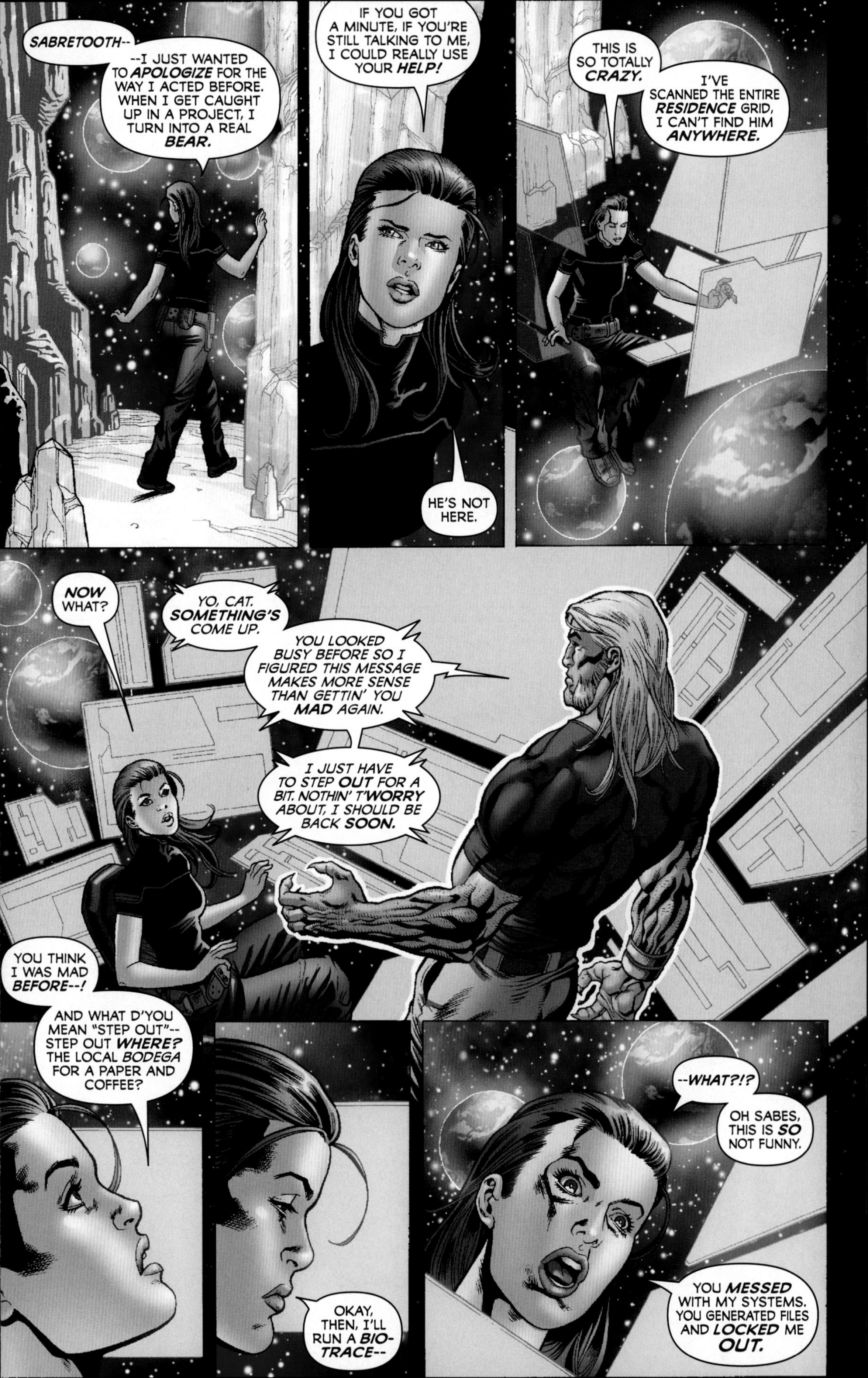
SABRETOOTH--
--I JUST WANTED TO APOLOGIZE FOR THE WAY I ACTED BEFORE. WHEN I GET CAUGHT UP IN A PROJECT, I TURN INTO A REAL BEAR.
IF YOU GOT A MINUTE, IF YOU'RE STILL TALKING TO ME, I COULD REALLY USE YOUR HELP!
HE'S NOT HERE.
THIS IS SO TOTALLY CRAZY.
I'VE SCANNED THE ENTIRE RESIDENCE GRID, I CAN'T FIND HIM ANYWHERE.
NOW WHAT?
YO, CAT. SOMETHING'S COME UP.
YOU LOOKED BUSY BEFORE SO I FIGURED THIS MESSAGE MAKES MORE SENSE THAN GETTIN' YOU MAD AGAIN.
I JUST HAVE TO STEP OUT FOR A BIT. NOTHIN' T'WORRY ABOUT, I SHOULD BE BACK SOON.
YOU THINK I WAS MAD BEFORE--!
AND WHAT D'YOU MEAN "STEP OUT"-- STEP OUT WHERE? THE LOCAL BODEGA FOR A PAPER AND COFFEE?
OKAY, THEN, I'LL RUN A BIO-TRACE--
--WHAT?!?
OH SABES, THIS IS SO NOT FUNNY.
YOU MESSED WITH MY SYSTEMS. YOU GENERATED FILES AND LOCKED ME OUT.

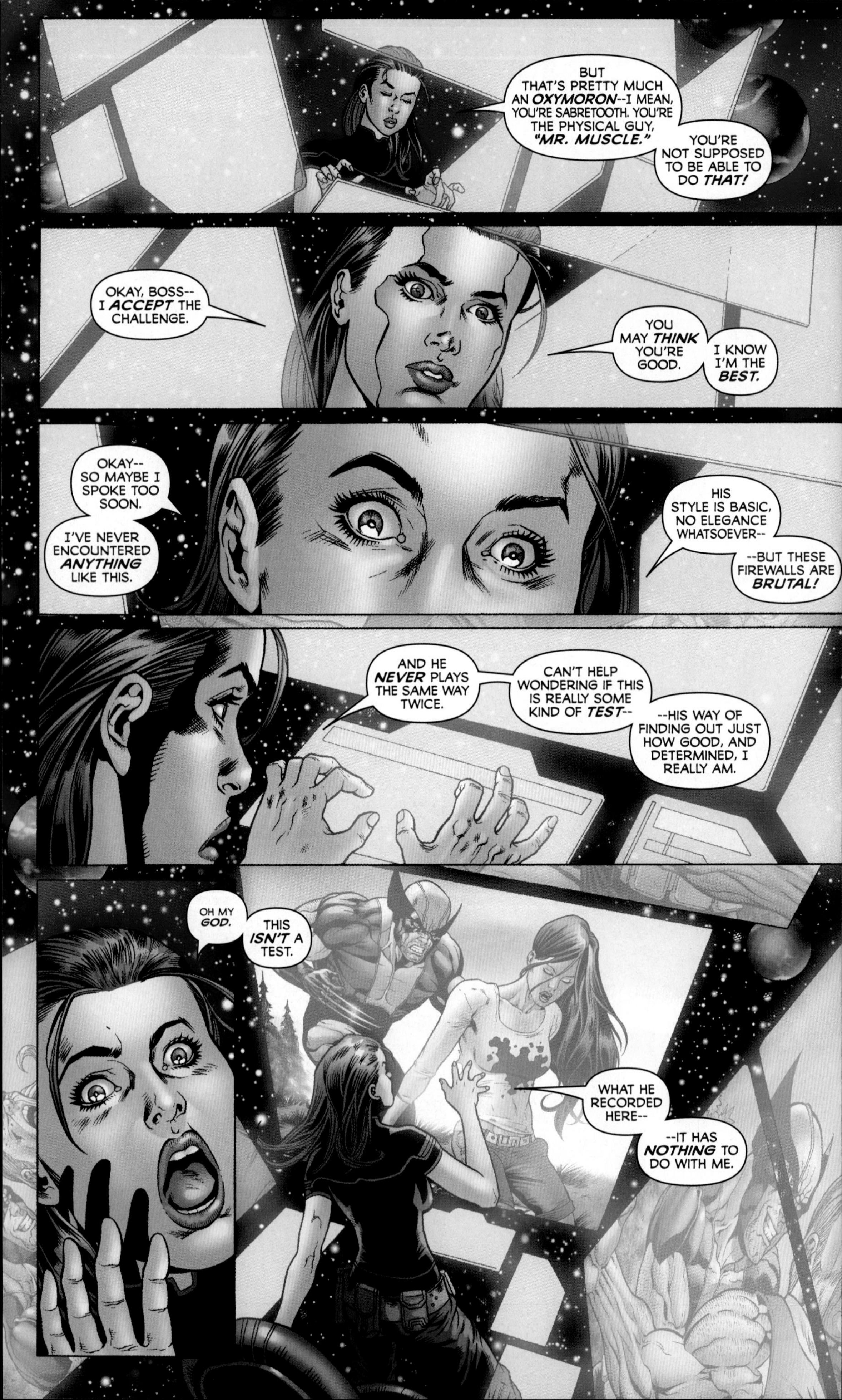
BUT THAT'S PRETTY MUCH AN OXYMORON--I MEAN, YOU'RE SABRETOOTH. YOU'RE THE PHYSICAL GUY, "MR. MUSCLE."
YOU'RE NOT SUPPOSED TO BE ABLE TO DO THAT!
OKAY, BOSS-- I ACCEPT THE CHALLENGE.
YOU MAY THINK YOU'RE GOOD.
I KNOW I'M THE BEST.
OKAY-- SO MAYBE I SPOKE TOO SOON.
I'VE NEVER ENCOUNTERED ANYTHING LIKE THIS.
HIS STYLE IS BASIC, NO ELEGANCE WHATSOEVER--
--BUT THESE FIREWALLS ARE BRUTAL!
AND HE NEVER PLAYS THE SAME WAY TWICE.
CAN'T HELP WONDERING IF THIS IS REALLY SOME KIND OF TEST--
--HIS WAY OF FINDING OUT JUST HOW GOOD, AND DETERMINED, I REALLY AM.
OH MY GOD.
THIS ISN'T A TEST.
WHAT HE RECORDED HERE--
--IT HAS NOTHING TO DO WITH ME.

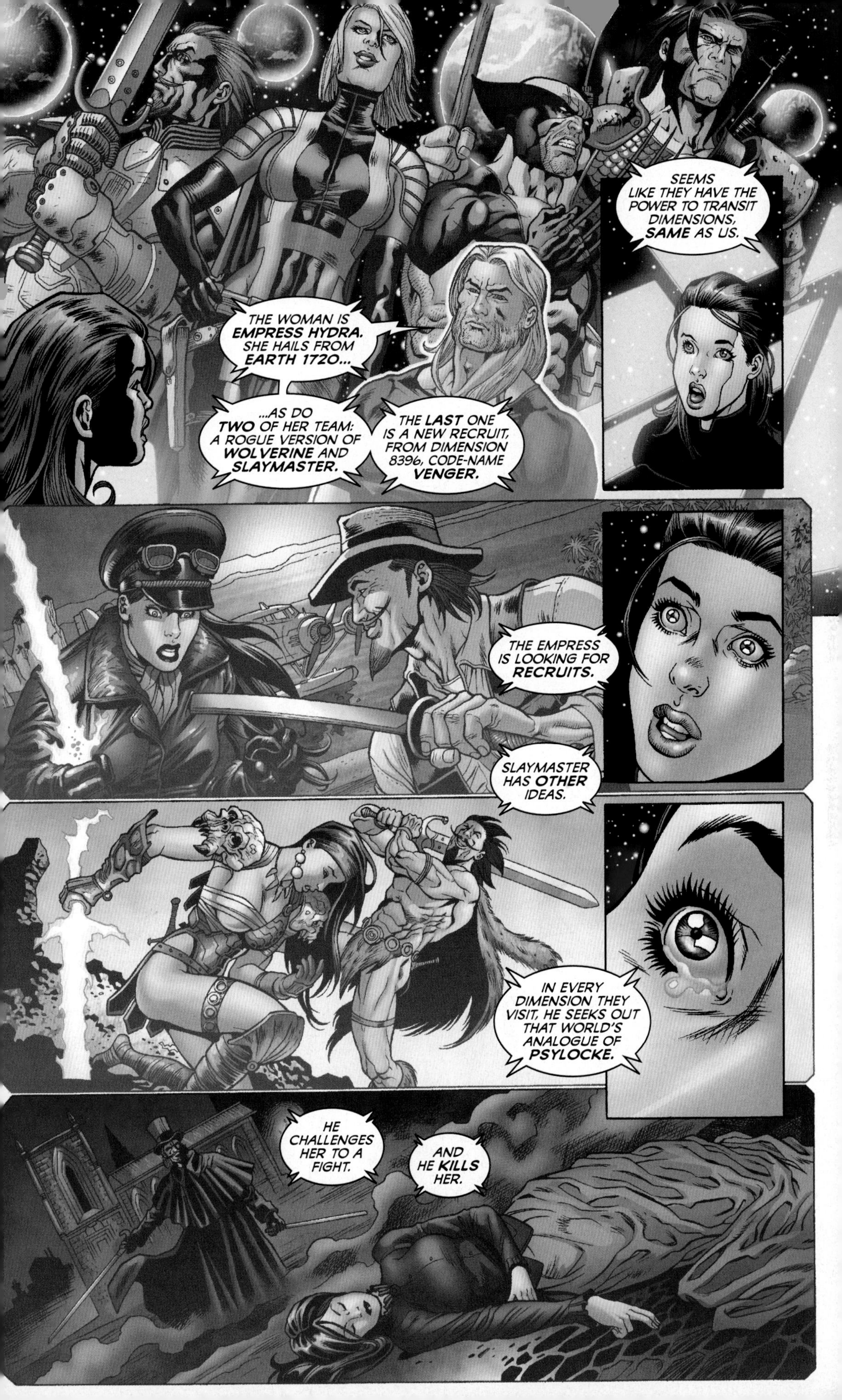
THE WOMAN IS EMPRESS HYDRA. SHE HAILS FROM EARTH 1720...
...AS DO TWO OF HER TEAM: A ROGUE VERSION OF WOLVERINE AND SLAYMASTER.
THE LAST ONE IS A NEW RECRUIT, FROM DIMENSION 8396, CODE-NAME VENGER.
SEEMS LIKE THEY HAVE THE POWER TO TRANSIT DIMENSIONS, SAME AS US.
THE EMPRESS IS LOOKING FOR RECRUITS.
SLAYMASTER HAS OTHER IDEAS.
IN EVERY DIMENSION THEY VISIT, HE SEEKS OUT THAT WORLD'S ANALOGUE OF PSYLOCKE.
HE CHALLENGES HER TO A FIGHT.
AND HE KILLS HER.

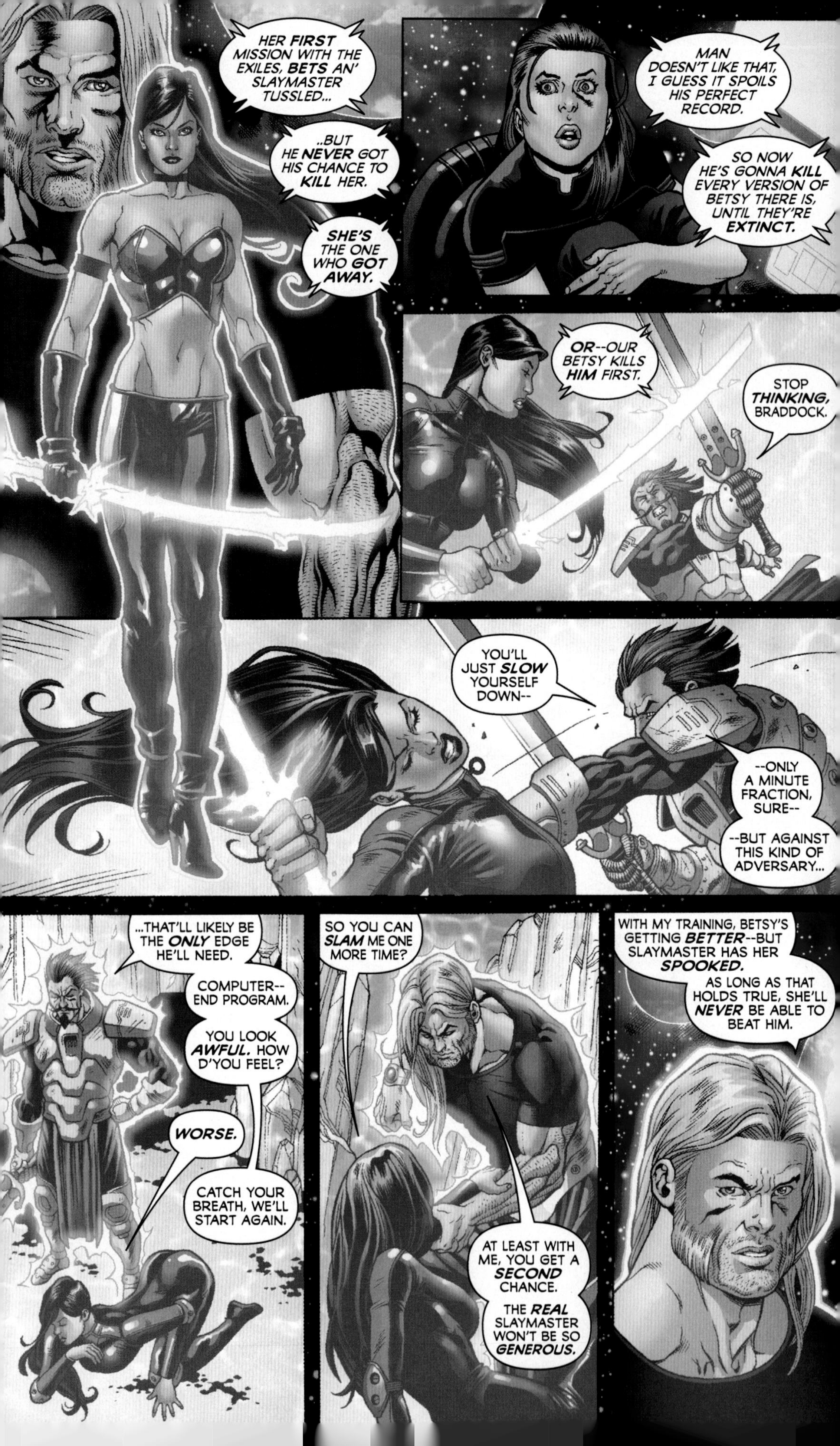
HER FIRST MISSION WITH THE EXILES, BETS AN' SLAYMASTER TUSSLED...
..BUT HE NEVER GOT HIS CHANCE TO KILL HER.
SHE'S THE ONE WHO GOT AWAY.
MAN DOESN'T LIKE THAT, I GUESS IT SPOILS HIS PERFECT RECORD.
SO NOW HE'S GONNA KILL EVERY VERSION OF BETSY THERE IS, UNTIL THEY'RE EXTINCT.
OR--OUR BETSY KILLS HIM FIRST.
STOP THINKING, BRADDOCK.
YOU'LL JUST SLOW YOURSELF DOWN--
--ONLY A MINUTE FRACTION, SURE--
--BUT AGAINST THIS KIND OF ADVERSARY...
...THAT'LL LIKELY BE THE ONLY EDGE HE'LL NEED.
COMPUTER-- END PROGRAM.
YOU LOOK AWFUL. HOW D'YOU FEEL?
WORSE.
CATCH YOUR BREATH, WE'LL START AGAIN.
SO YOU CAN SLAM ME ONE MORE TIME?
AT LEAST WITH ME, YOU GET A SECOND CHANCE.
THE REAL SLAYMASTER WON'T BE SO GENEROUS.
WITH MY TRAINING, BETSY'S GETTING BETTER--BUT SLAYMASTER HAS HER SPOOKED.
AS LONG AS THAT HOLDS TRUE, SHE'LL NEVER BE ABLE TO BEAT HIM.

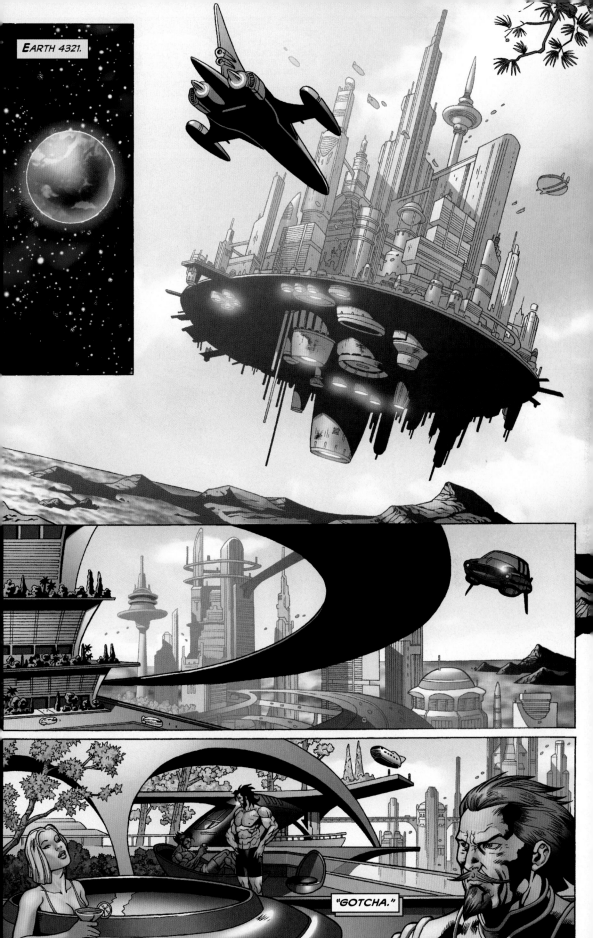

EARTH 4321.

"GOTCHA."

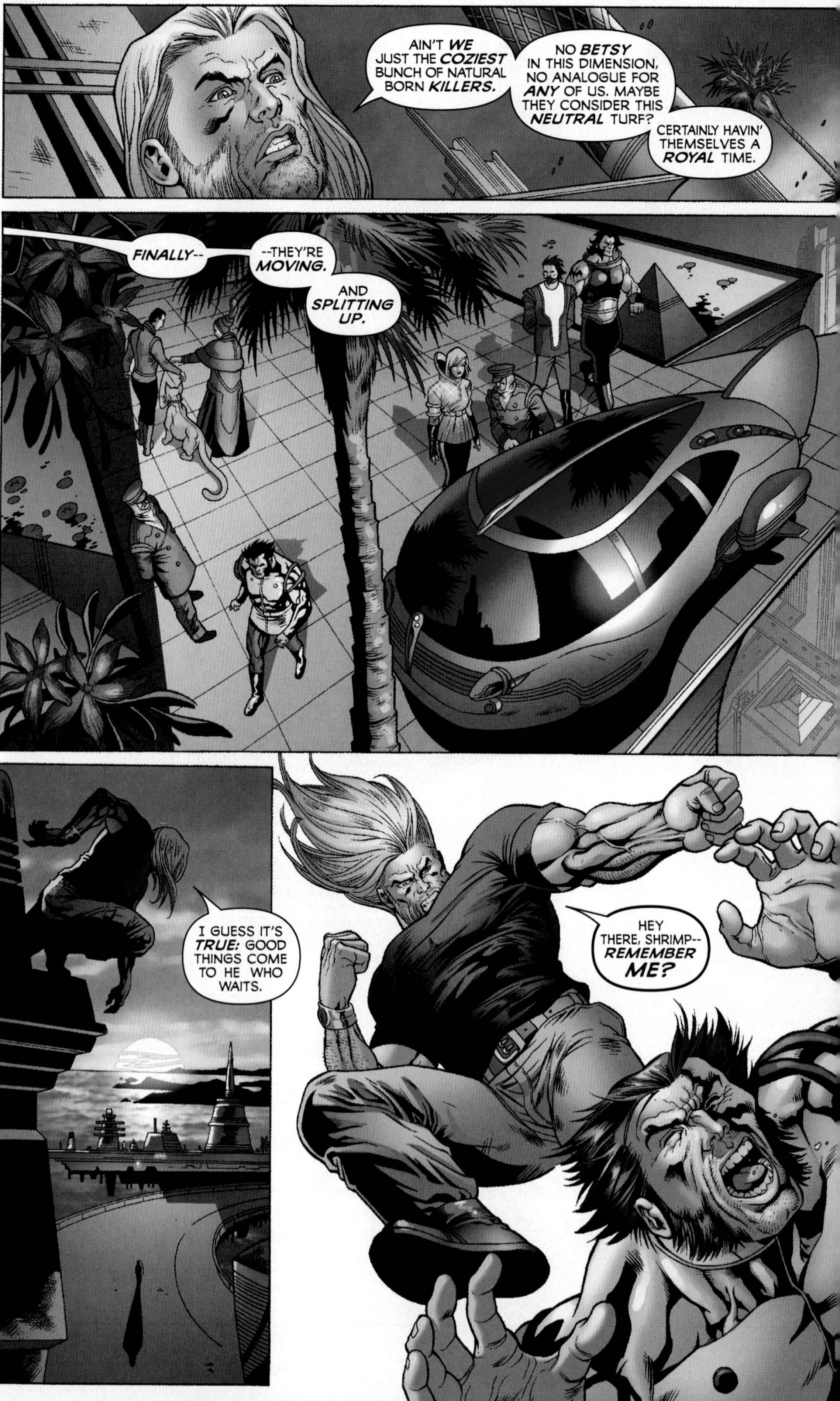
AIN'T WE JUST THE COZIEST BUNCH OF NATURAL BORN KILLERS.
NO BETSY IN THIS DIMENSION, NO ANALOGUE FOR ANY OF US. MAYBE THEY CONSIDER THIS NEUTRAL TURF?
CERTAINLY HAVIN' THEMSELVES A ROYAL TIME.
FINALLY--
--THEY'RE MOVING.
AND SPLITTING UP.
I GUESS IT'S TRUE: GOOD THINGS COME TO HE WHO WAITS.
HEY THERE, SHRIMP-- REMEMBER ME?

GOTTA SAY, I'VE BEEN LOOKING FORWARD TO THIS MOMENT.

IN CASE YOU'RE WONDERING, I'M BALANCING THE SCALES FOR THAT VERSION OF *ME* YOU KILLED A WHILE BACK.

AND FOR THE WOMAN HE *LOVED.*

AN' THEIR *KIDS.*

I *REGRET* THAT CIRCUMSTANCES REQUIRE ME TO *INTERVENE...*

...BUT I'M AFRAID I *CANNOT* ALLOW YOU TO TAKE MY COMRADE'S *LIFE.*

SHOK

OR EVEN TO DO HIM *HARM.*

EVEN *WE* HAVE OUR CODE OF *HONOR.*

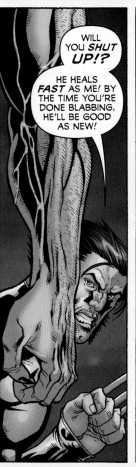

WILL YOU *SHUT UP!?*

HE HEALS *FAST* AS ME! BY THE TIME YOU'RE DONE BLABBING, HE'LL BE GOOD AS NEW!

I DON'T NEED T'BE *HEALED,* RUNT--

--T'SIGN OFF ON THE LIKES OF *YOU!*

WE'RE A *LONG* WAY UP, WOLVERINE.

HOW D'YOU FEEL ABOUT FLYING--

--OR BETTER YET, A REALLY *HARD* LANDING?

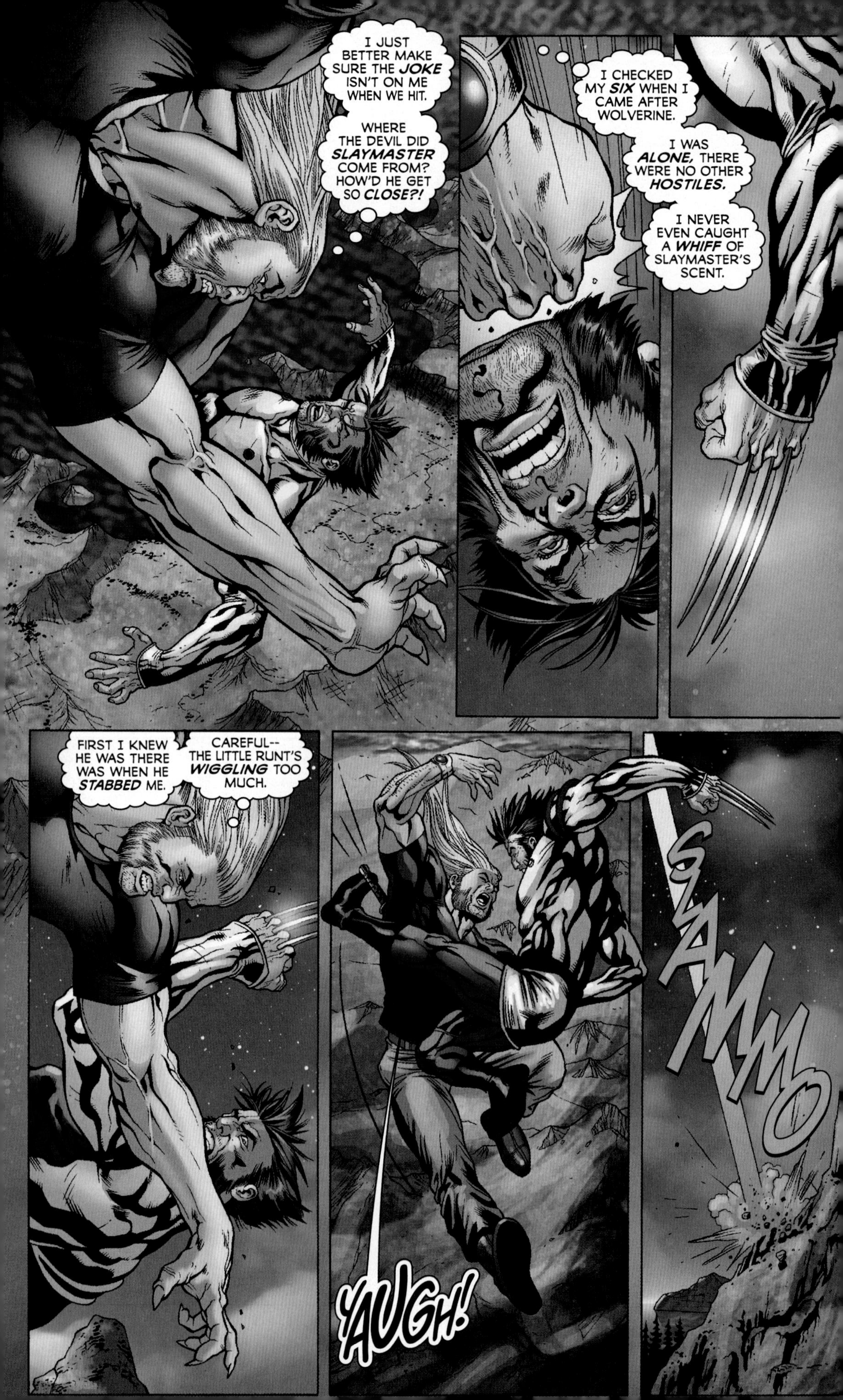

I JUST BETTER MAKE SURE THE JOKE ISN'T ON ME WHEN WE HIT.
WHERE THE DEVIL DID SLAYMASTER COME FROM? HOW'D HE GET SO CLOSE?!
I CHECKED MY SIX WHEN I CAME AFTER WOLVERINE.
I WAS ALONE, THERE WERE NO OTHER HOSTILES.
I NEVER EVEN CAUGHT A WHIFF OF SLAYMASTER'S SCENT.
FIRST I KNEW HE WAS THERE WAS WHEN HE STABBED ME.
CAREFUL-- THE LITTLE RUNT'S WIGGLING TOO MUCH.
'AUGH!
SWAMMO

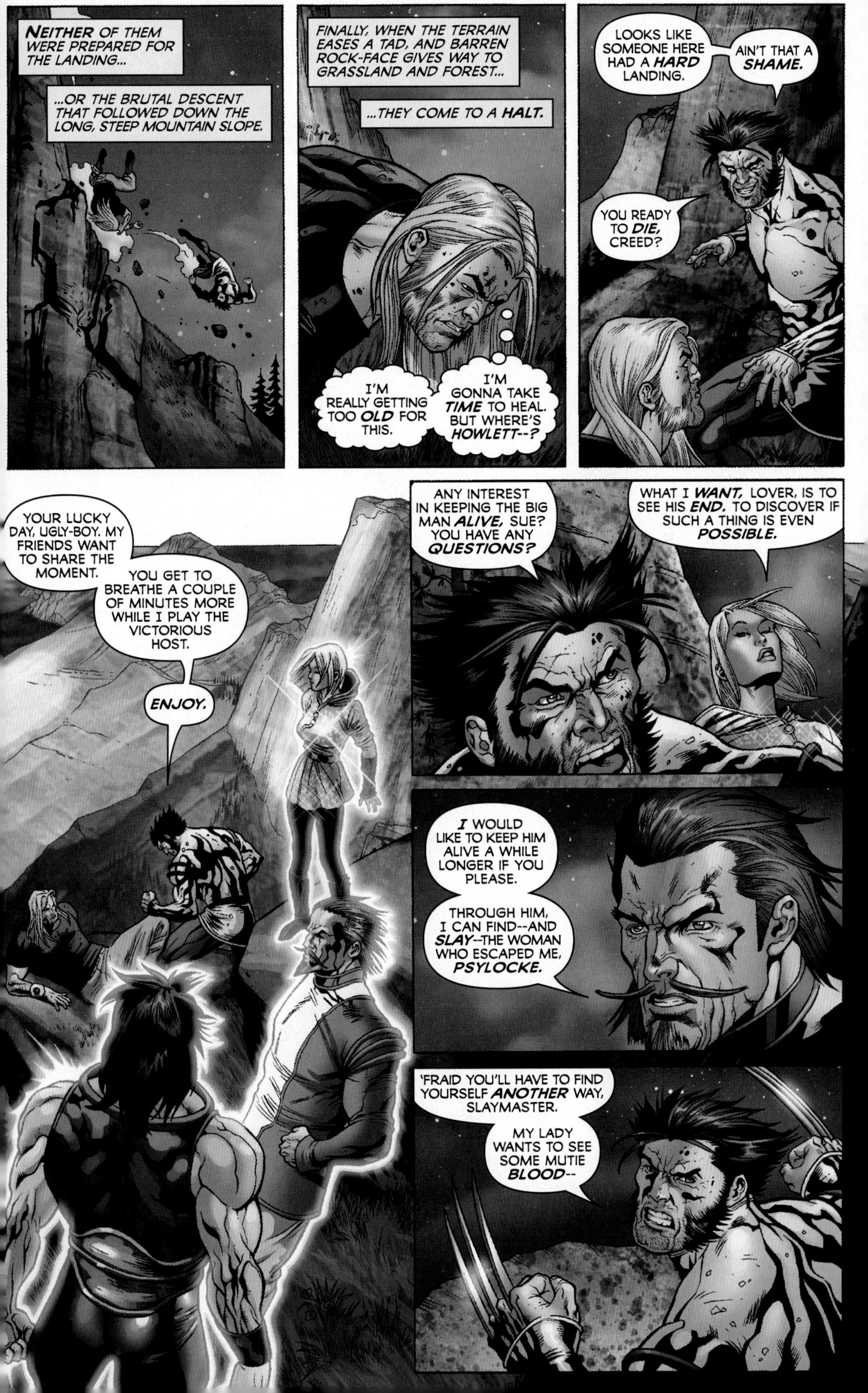
NEITHER OF THEM WERE PREPARED FOR THE LANDING...
...OR THE BRUTAL DESCENT THAT FOLLOWED DOWN THE LONG, STEEP MOUNTAIN SLOPE.
FINALLY, WHEN THE TERRAIN EASES A TAD, AND BARREN ROCK-FACE GIVES WAY TO GRASSLAND AND FOREST...
...THEY COME TO A HALT.
I'M REALLY GETTING TOO OLD FOR THIS.
I'M GONNA TAKE TIME TO HEAL. BUT WHERE'S HOWLETT--?
LOOKS LIKE SOMEONE HERE HAD A HARD LANDING.
AIN'T THAT A SHAME.
YOU READY TO DIE, CREED?
YOUR LUCKY DAY, UGLY-BOY. MY FRIENDS WANT TO SHARE THE MOMENT.
YOU GET TO BREATHE A COUPLE OF MINUTES MORE WHILE I PLAY THE VICTORIOUS HOST.
ENJOY.
ANY INTEREST IN KEEPING THE BIG MAN ALIVE, SUE? YOU HAVE ANY QUESTIONS?
WHAT I WANT, LOVER, IS TO SEE HIS END. TO DISCOVER IF SUCH A THING IS EVEN POSSIBLE.
I WOULD LIKE TO KEEP HIM ALIVE A WHILE LONGER IF YOU PLEASE.
THROUGH HIM, I CAN FIND--AND SLAY--THE WOMAN WHO ESCAPED ME, PSYLOCKE.
'FRAID YOU'LL HAVE TO FIND YOURSELF ANOTHER WAY, SLAYMASTER.
MY LADY WANTS TO SEE SOME MUTIE BLOOD--

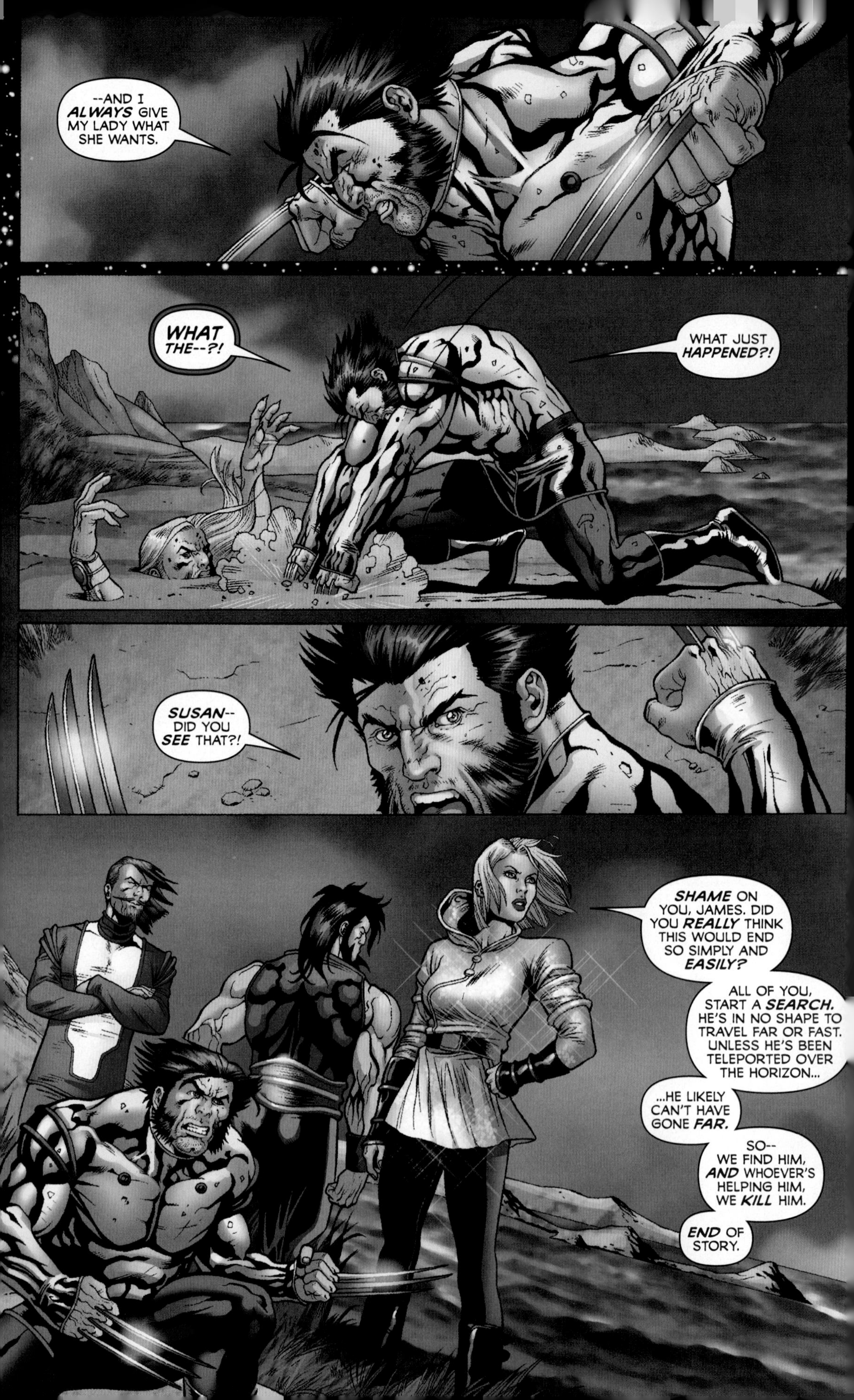
--AND I ALWAYS GIVE MY LADY WHAT SHE WANTS.
WHAT THE--?!
WHAT JUST HAPPENED?!
SUSAN-- DID YOU SEE THAT?!
SHAME ON YOU, JAMES. DID YOU REALLY THINK THIS WOULD END SO SIMPLY AND EASILY?
ALL OF YOU, START A SEARCH. HE'S IN NO SHAPE TO TRAVEL FAR OR FAST. UNLESS HE'S BEEN TELEPORTED OVER THE HORIZON...
...HE LIKELY CAN'T HAVE GONE FAR.
SO-- WE FIND HIM, AND WHOEVER'S HELPING HIM, WE KILL HIM.
END OF STORY.

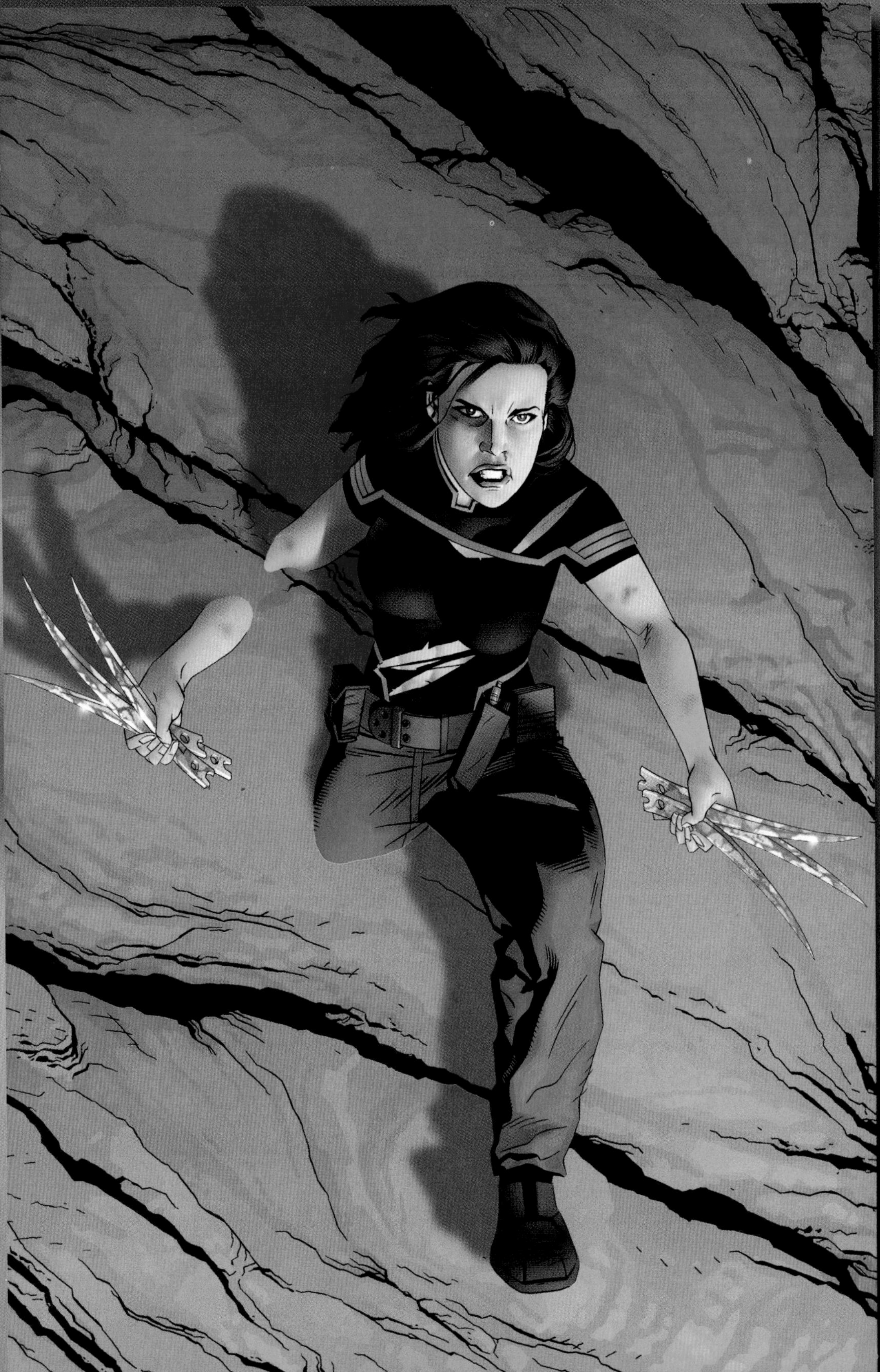

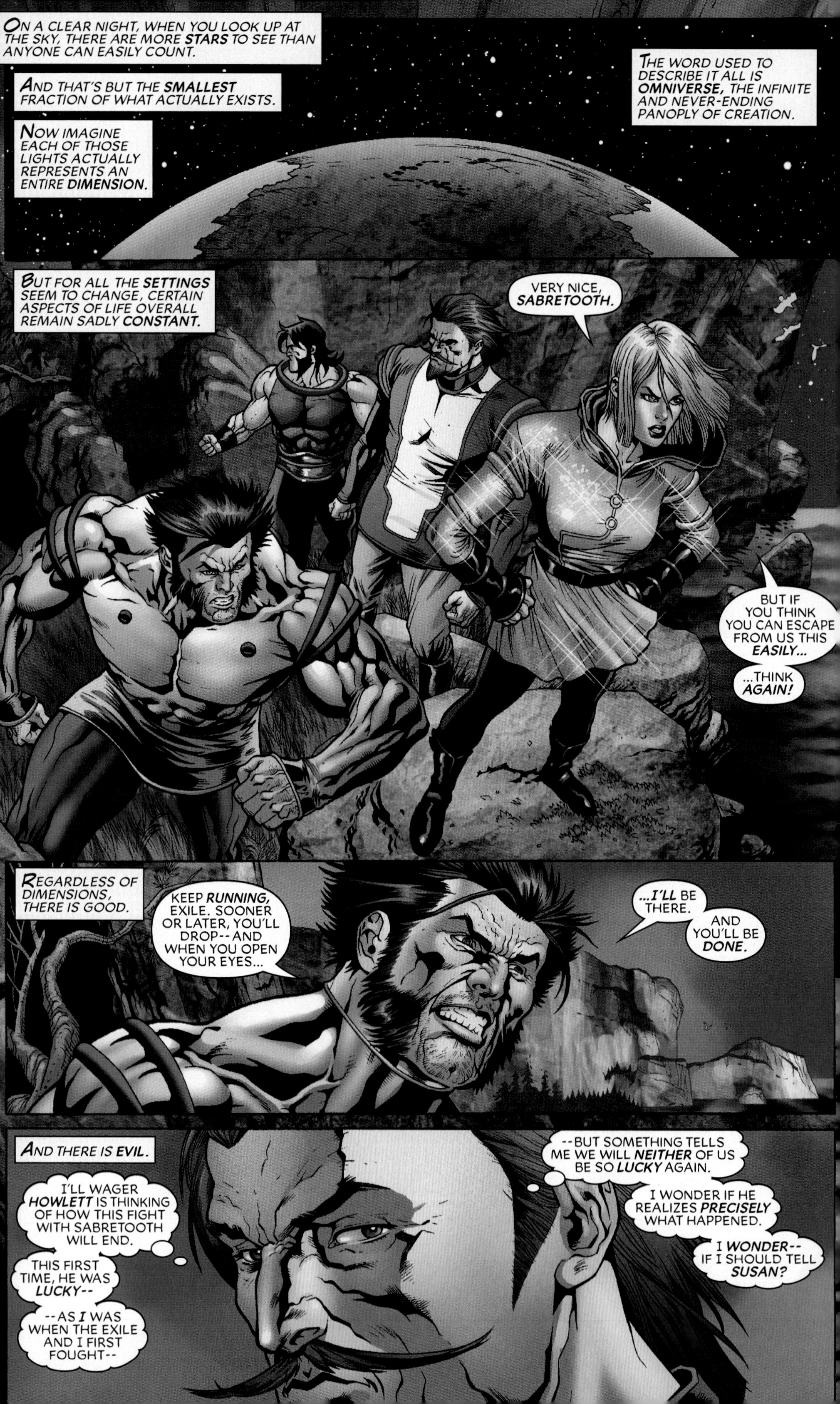

ON A CLEAR NIGHT, WHEN YOU LOOK UP AT THE SKY, THERE ARE MORE STARS TO SEE THAN ANYONE CAN EASILY COUNT.
AND THAT'S BUT THE SMALLEST FRACTION OF WHAT ACTUALLY EXISTS.
NOW IMAGINE EACH OF THOSE LIGHTS ACTUALLY REPRESENTS AN ENTIRE DIMENSION.
THE WORD USED TO DESCRIBE IT ALL IS OMNIVERSE, THE INFINITE AND NEVER-ENDING PANOPLY OF CREATION.
BUT FOR ALL THE SETTINGS SEEM TO CHANGE, CERTAIN ASPECTS OF LIFE OVERALL REMAIN SADLY CONSTANT.
VERY NICE, SABRETOOTH.
BUT IF YOU THINK YOU CAN ESCAPE FROM US THIS EASILY...
...THINK AGAIN!
REGARDLESS OF DIMENSIONS, THERE IS GOOD.
KEEP RUNNING, EXILE. SOONER OR LATER, YOU'LL DROP-- AND WHEN YOU OPEN YOUR EYES...
...I'LL BE THERE.
AND YOU'LL BE DONE.
AND THERE IS EVIL.
I'LL WAGER HOWLETT IS THINKING OF HOW THIS FIGHT WITH SABRETOOTH WILL END.
THIS FIRST TIME, HE WAS LUCKY--
--AS I WAS WHEN THE EXILE AND I FIRST FOUGHT--
--BUT SOMETHING TELLS ME WE WILL NEITHER OF US BE SO LUCKY AGAIN.
I WONDER IF HE REALIZES PRECISELY WHAT HAPPENED.
I WONDER-- IF I SHOULD TELL SUSAN?

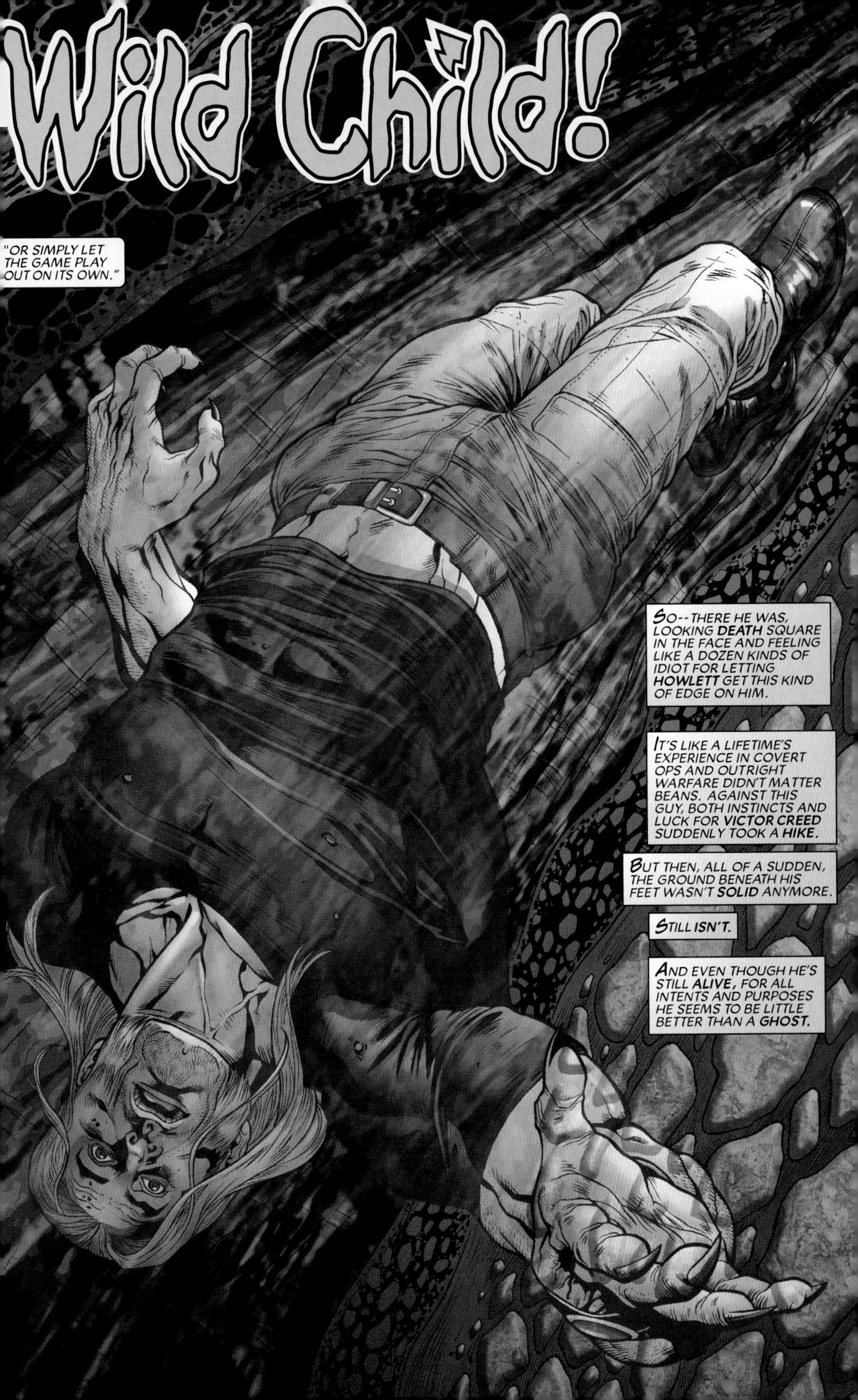
Wild Child!
"OR SIMPLY LET THE GAME PLAY OUT ON ITS OWN."
SO--THERE HE WAS, LOOKING DEATH SQUARE IN THE FACE AND FEELING LIKE A DOZEN KINDS OF IDIOT FOR LETTING HOWLETT GET THIS KIND OF EDGE ON HIM.
IT'S LIKE A LIFETIME'S EXPERIENCE IN COVERT OPS AND OUTRIGHT WARFARE DIDN'T MATTER BEANS. AGAINST THIS GUY, BOTH INSTINCTS AND LUCK FOR VICTOR CREED SUDDENLY TOOK A HIKE.
BUT THEN, ALL OF A SUDDEN, THE GROUND BENEATH HIS FEET WASN'T SOLID ANYMORE.
STILL ISN'T.
AND EVEN THOUGH HE'S STILL ALIVE, FOR ALL INTENTS AND PURPOSES HE SEEMS TO BE LITTLE BETTER THAN A GHOST.

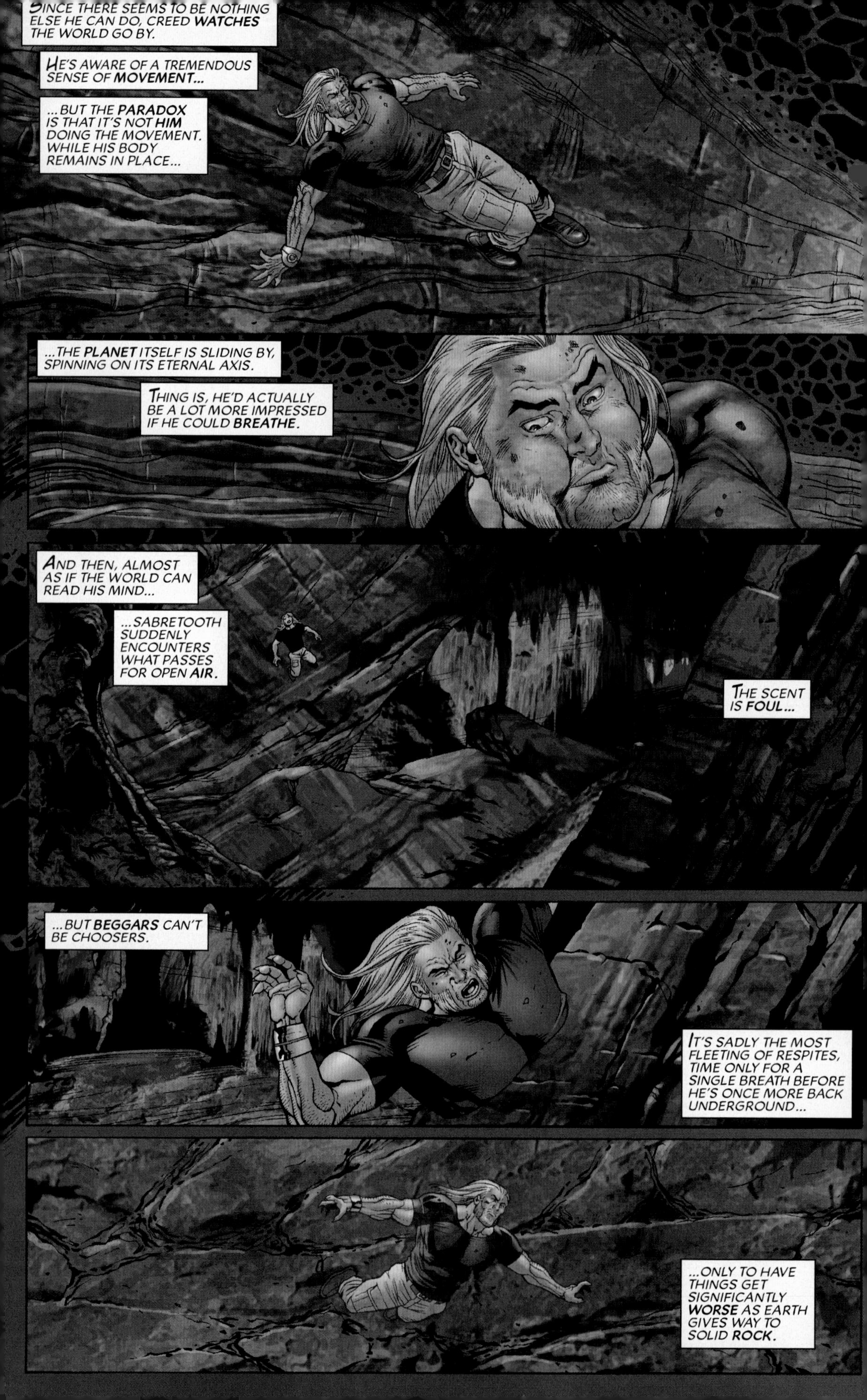
SINCE THERE SEEMS TO BE NOTHING ELSE HE CAN DO, CREED WATCHES THE WORLD GO BY.
HE'S AWARE OF A TREMENDOUS SENSE OF MOVEMENT...
...BUT THE PARADOX IS THAT IT'S NOT HIM DOING THE MOVEMENT. WHILE HIS BODY REMAINS IN PLACE...
...THE PLANET ITSELF IS SLIDING BY, SPINNING ON ITS ETERNAL AXIS.
THING IS, HE'D ACTUALLY BE A LOT MORE IMPRESSED IF HE COULD BREATHE.
AND THEN, ALMOST AS IF THE WORLD CAN READ HIS MIND...
...SABRETOOTH SUDDENLY ENCOUNTERS WHAT PASSES FOR OPEN AIR.
THE SCENT IS FOUL...
...BUT BEGGARS CAN'T BE CHOOSERS.
IT'S SADLY THE MOST FLEETING OF RESPITES, TIME ONLY FOR A SINGLE BREATH BEFORE HE'S ONCE MORE BACK UNDERGROUND...
...ONLY TO HAVE THINGS GET SIGNIFICANTLY WORSE AS EARTH GIVES WAY TO SOLID ROCK.

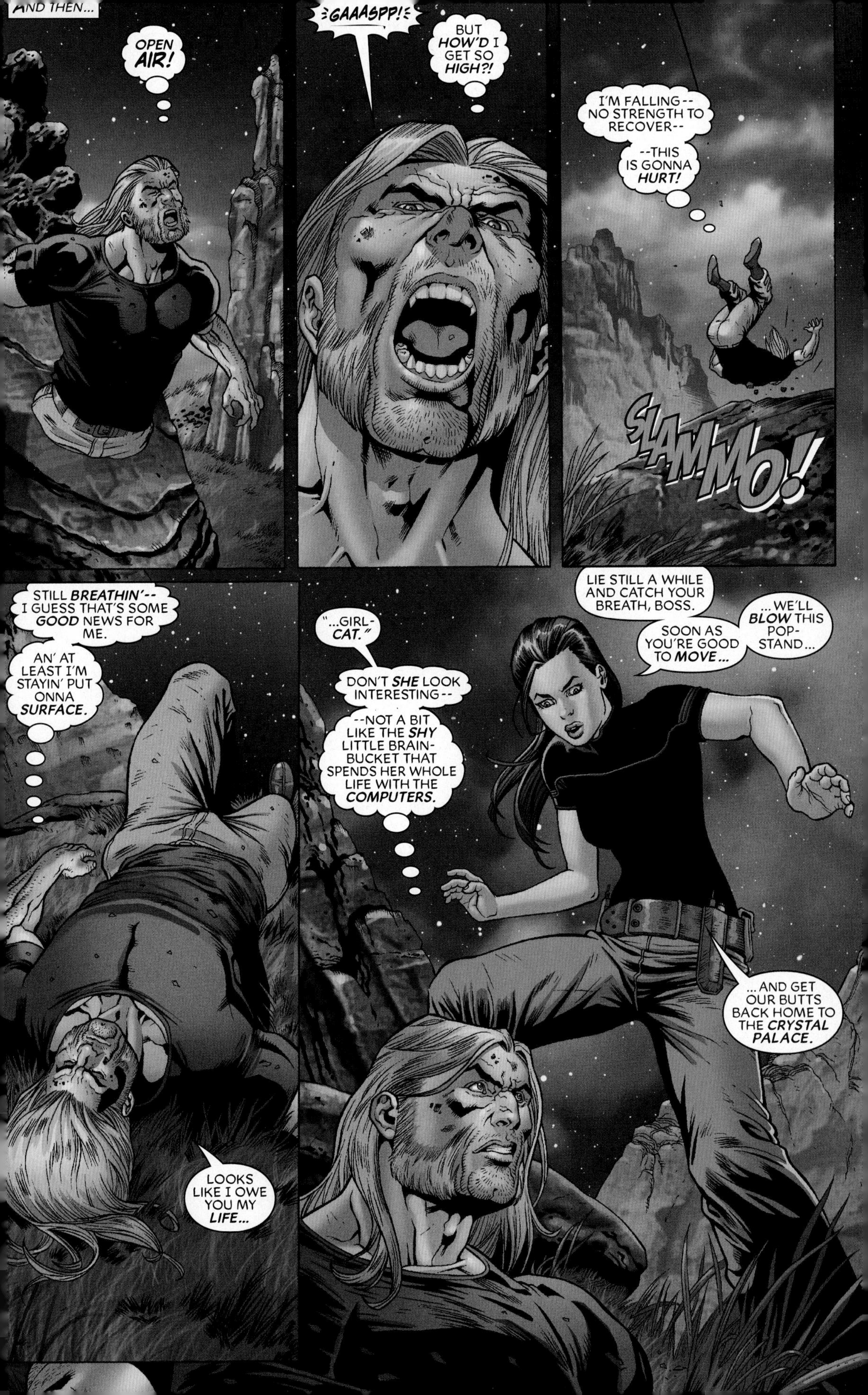
AND THEN...
OPEN AIR!
GAAASPP!
BUT HOW'D I GET SO HIGH?!
I'M FALLING-- NO STRENGTH TO RECOVER--
--THIS IS GONNA HURT!
SLAMMO!
STILL BREATHIN'-- I GUESS THAT'S SOME GOOD NEWS FOR ME.
AN' AT LEAST I'M STAYIN' PUT ONNA SURFACE.
LOOKS LIKE I OWE YOU MY LIFE...
"...GIRL-CAT."
DON'T SHE LOOK INTERESTING--
--NOT A BIT LIKE THE SHY LITTLE BRAIN-BUCKET THAT SPENDS HER WHOLE LIFE WITH THE COMPUTERS.
LIE STILL A WHILE AND CATCH YOUR BREATH, BOSS.
SOON AS YOU'RE GOOD TO MOVE...
...WE'LL BLOW THIS POP-STAND...
...AND GET OUR BUTTS BACK HOME TO THE CRYSTAL PALACE.

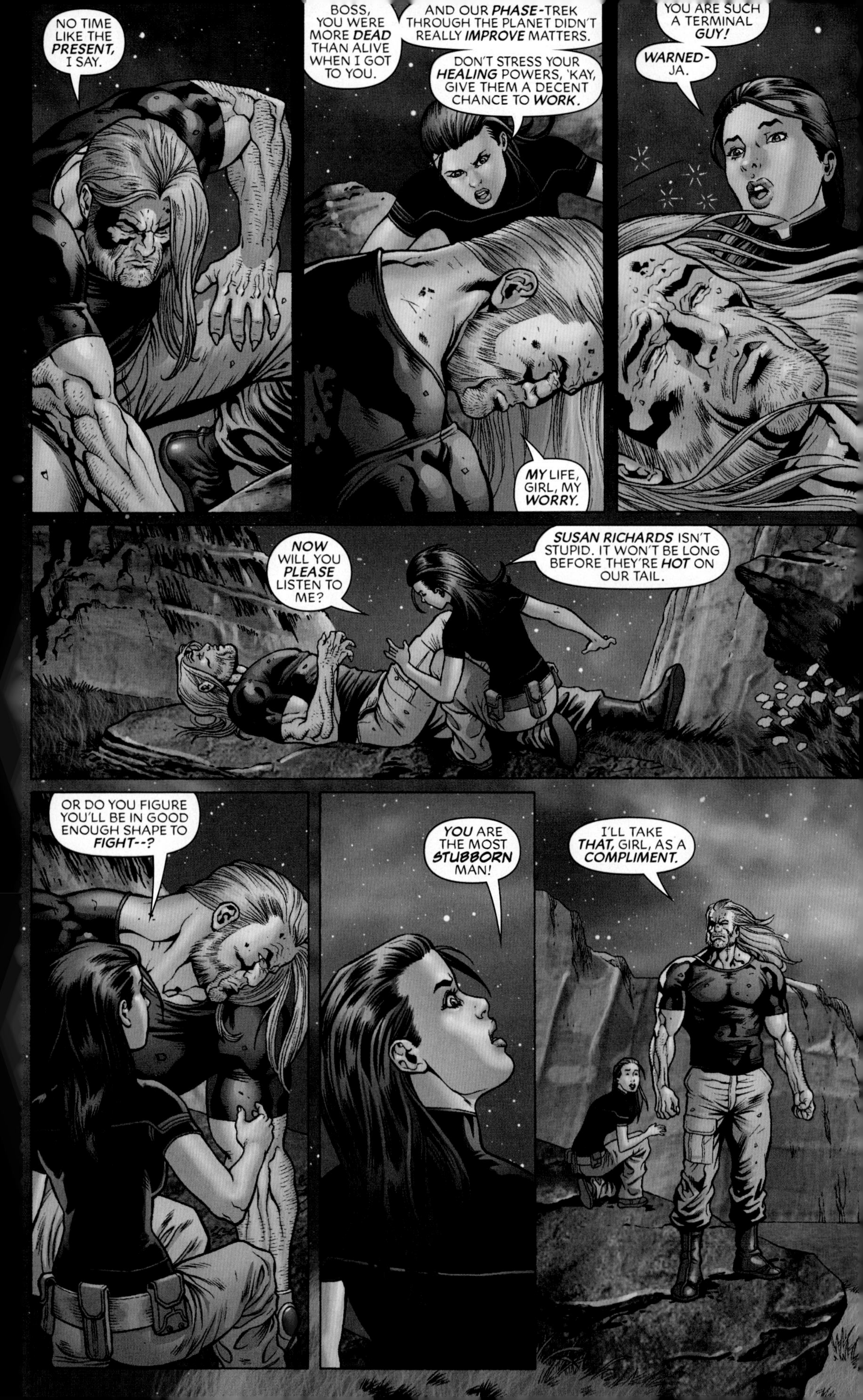
NO TIME LIKE THE PRESENT, I SAY.
BOSS, YOU WERE MORE DEAD THAN ALIVE WHEN I GOT TO YOU.
AND OUR PHASE-TREK THROUGH THE PLANET DIDN'T REALLY IMPROVE MATTERS.
DON'T STRESS YOUR HEALING POWERS, 'KAY, GIVE THEM A DECENT CHANCE TO WORK.
MY LIFE, GIRL, MY WORRY.
YOU ARE SUCH A TERMINAL GUY!
WARNED-JA.
NOW WILL YOU PLEASE LISTEN TO ME?
SUSAN RICHARDS ISN'T STUPID. IT WON'T BE LONG BEFORE THEY'RE HOT ON OUR TAIL.
OR DO YOU FIGURE YOU'LL BE IN GOOD ENOUGH SHAPE TO FIGHT--?
YOU ARE THE MOST STUBBORN MAN!
I'LL TAKE THAT, GIRL, AS A COMPLIMENT.

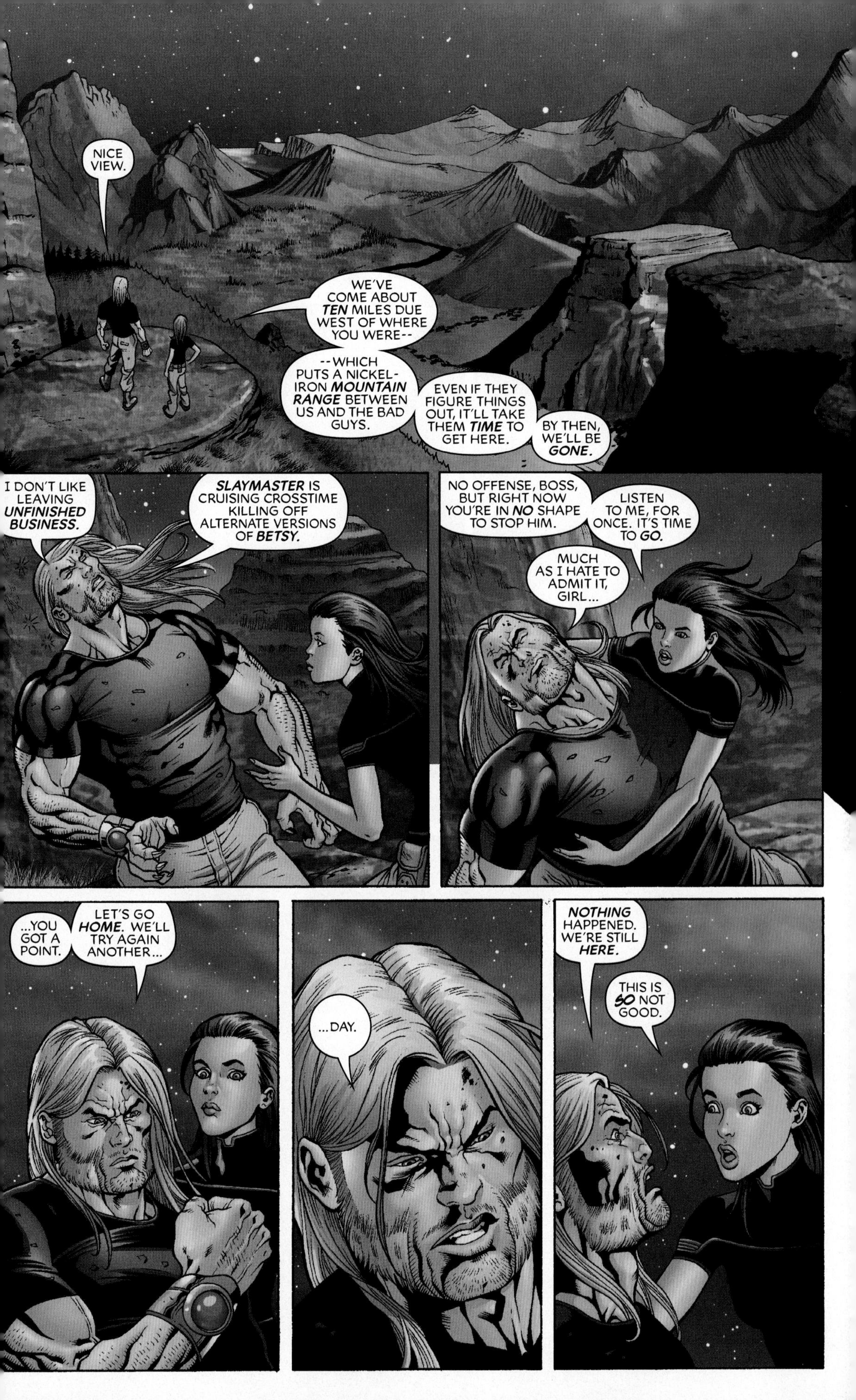
NICE VIEW.
WE'VE COME ABOUT TEN MILES DUE WEST OF WHERE YOU WERE--
--WHICH PUTS A NICKEL-IRON MOUNTAIN RANGE BETWEEN US AND THE BAD GUYS.
EVEN IF THEY FIGURE THINGS OUT, IT'LL TAKE THEM TIME TO GET HERE.
BY THEN, WE'LL BE GONE.
I DON'T LIKE LEAVING UNFINISHED BUSINESS.
SLAYMASTER IS CRUISING CROSSTIME KILLING OFF ALTERNATE VERSIONS OF BETSY.
NO OFFENSE, BOSS, BUT RIGHT NOW YOU'RE IN NO SHAPE TO STOP HIM.
LISTEN TO ME, FOR ONCE. IT'S TIME TO GO.
MUCH AS I HATE TO ADMIT IT, GIRL...
...YOU GOT A POINT.
LET'S GO HOME. WE'LL TRY AGAIN ANOTHER...
...DAY.
NOTHING HAPPENED. WE'RE STILL HERE.
THIS IS SO NOT GOOD.

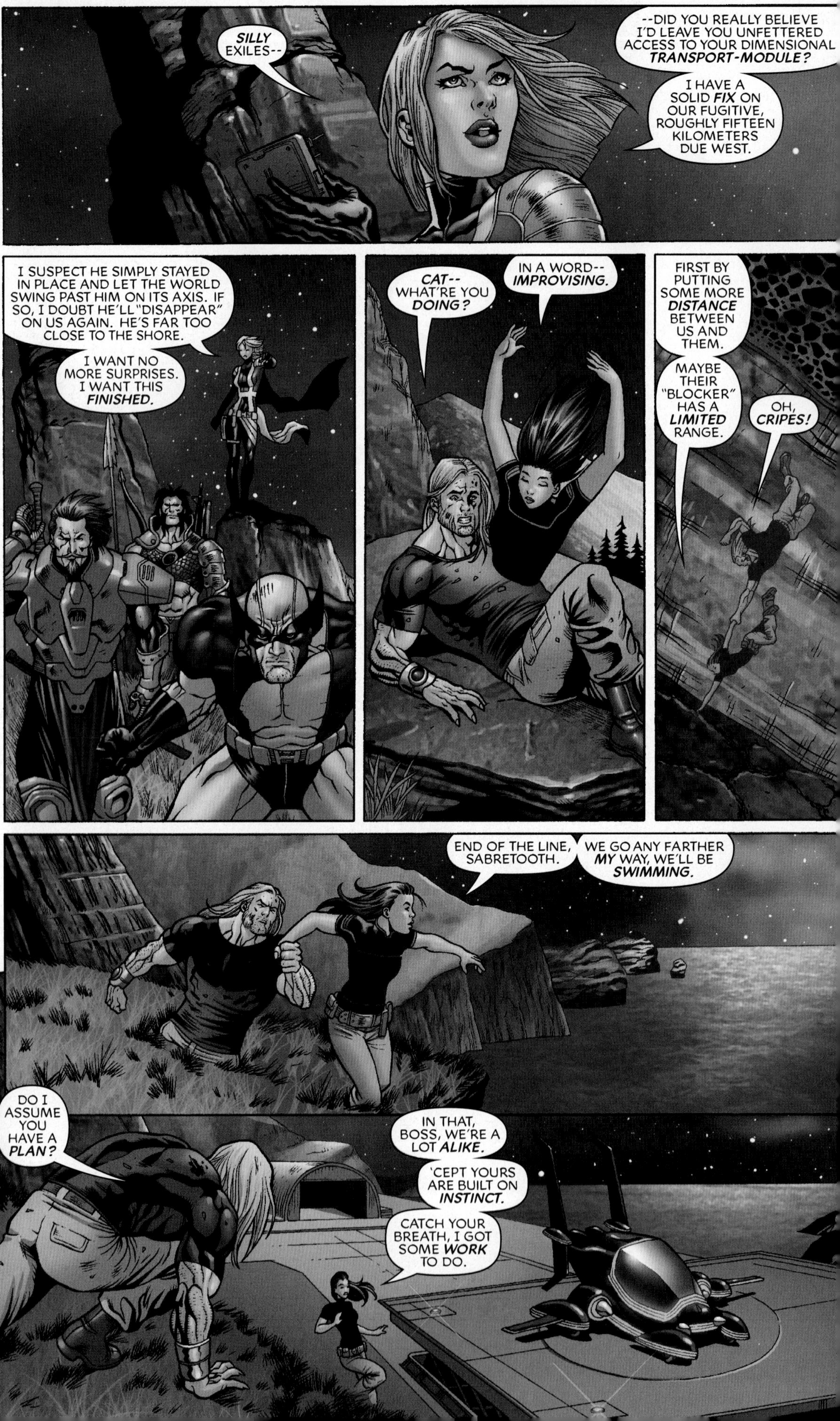
SILLY EXILES--
--DID YOU REALLY BELIEVE I'D LEAVE YOU UNFETTERED ACCESS TO YOUR DIMENSIONAL TRANSPORT-MODULE?
I HAVE A SOLID FIX ON OUR FUGITIVE, ROUGHLY FIFTEEN KILOMETERS DUE WEST.
I SUSPECT HE SIMPLY STAYED IN PLACE AND LET THE WORLD SWING PAST HIM ON ITS AXIS. IF SO, I DOUBT HE'LL "DISAPPEAR" ON US AGAIN. HE'S FAR TOO CLOSE TO THE SHORE.
I WANT NO MORE SURPRISES. I WANT THIS FINISHED.
CAT-- WHAT'RE YOU DOING?
IN A WORD-- IMPROVISING.
FIRST BY PUTTING SOME MORE DISTANCE BETWEEN US AND THEM.
MAYBE THEIR "BLOCKER" HAS A LIMITED RANGE.
OH, CRIPES!
END OF THE LINE, SABRETOOTH.
WE GO ANY FARTHER MY WAY, WE'LL BE SWIMMING.
DO I ASSUME YOU HAVE A PLAN?
IN THAT, BOSS, WE'RE A LOT ALIKE.
'CEPT YOURS ARE BUILT ON INSTINCT.
CATCH YOUR BREATH, I GOT SOME WORK TO DO.

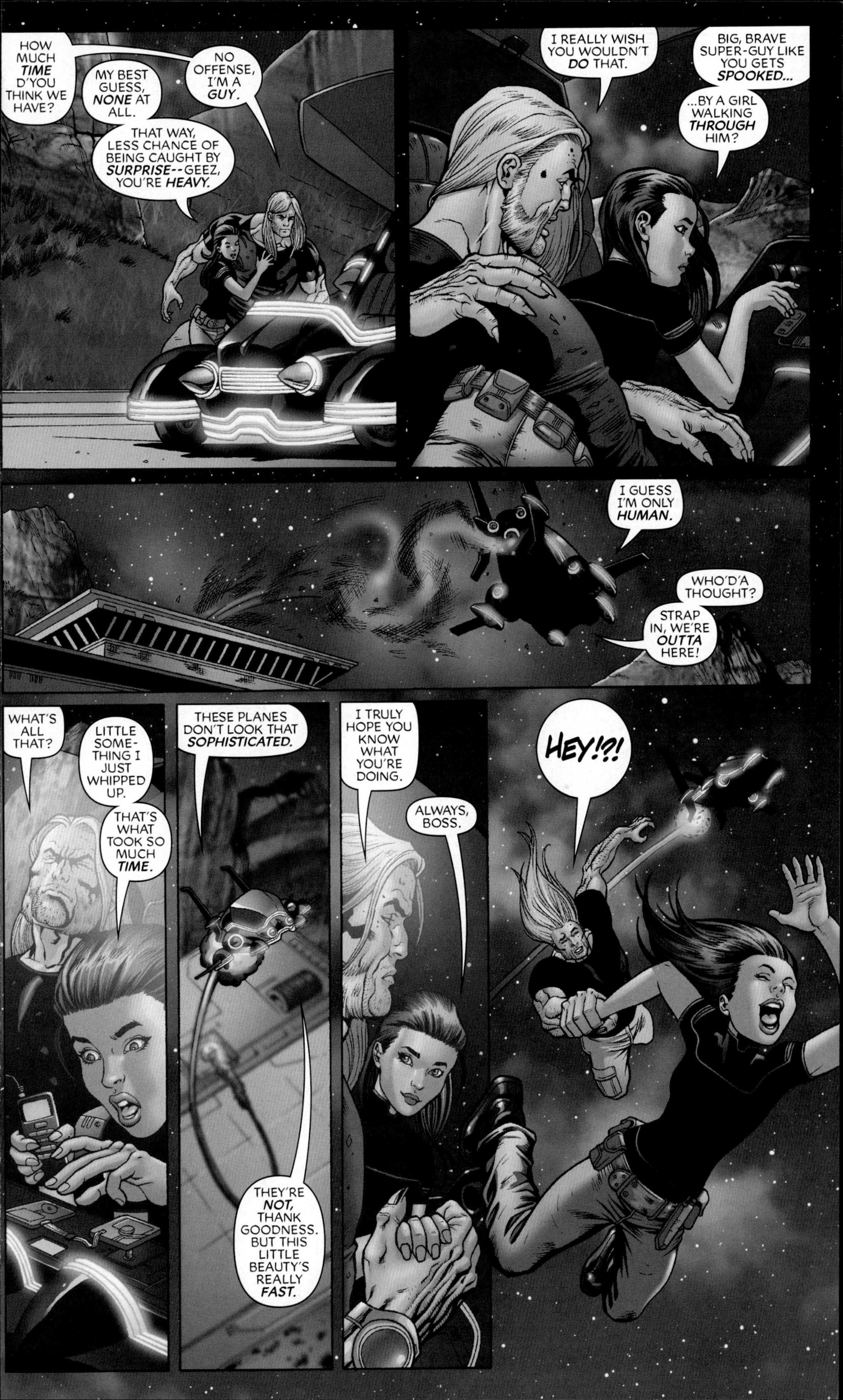
HOW MUCH TIME D'YOU THINK WE HAVE?
MY BEST GUESS, NONE AT ALL.
THAT WAY, LESS CHANCE OF BEING CAUGHT BY SURPRISE--GEEZ, YOU'RE HEAVY.
NO OFFENSE, I'M A GUY.
I REALLY WISH YOU WOULDN'T DO THAT.
BIG, BRAVE SUPER-GUY LIKE YOU GETS SPOOKED...
...BY A GIRL WALKING THROUGH HIM?
I GUESS I'M ONLY HUMAN.
WHO'D'A THOUGHT?
STRAP IN, WE'RE OUTTA HERE!
WHAT'S ALL THAT?
LITTLE SOME-THING I JUST WHIPPED UP.
THAT'S WHAT TOOK SO MUCH TIME.
THESE PLANES DON'T LOOK THAT SOPHISTICATED.
THEY'RE NOT, THANK GOODNESS. BUT THIS LITTLE BEAUTY'S REALLY FAST.
I TRULY HOPE YOU KNOW WHAT YOU'RE DOING.
ALWAYS, BOSS.
HEY!?!

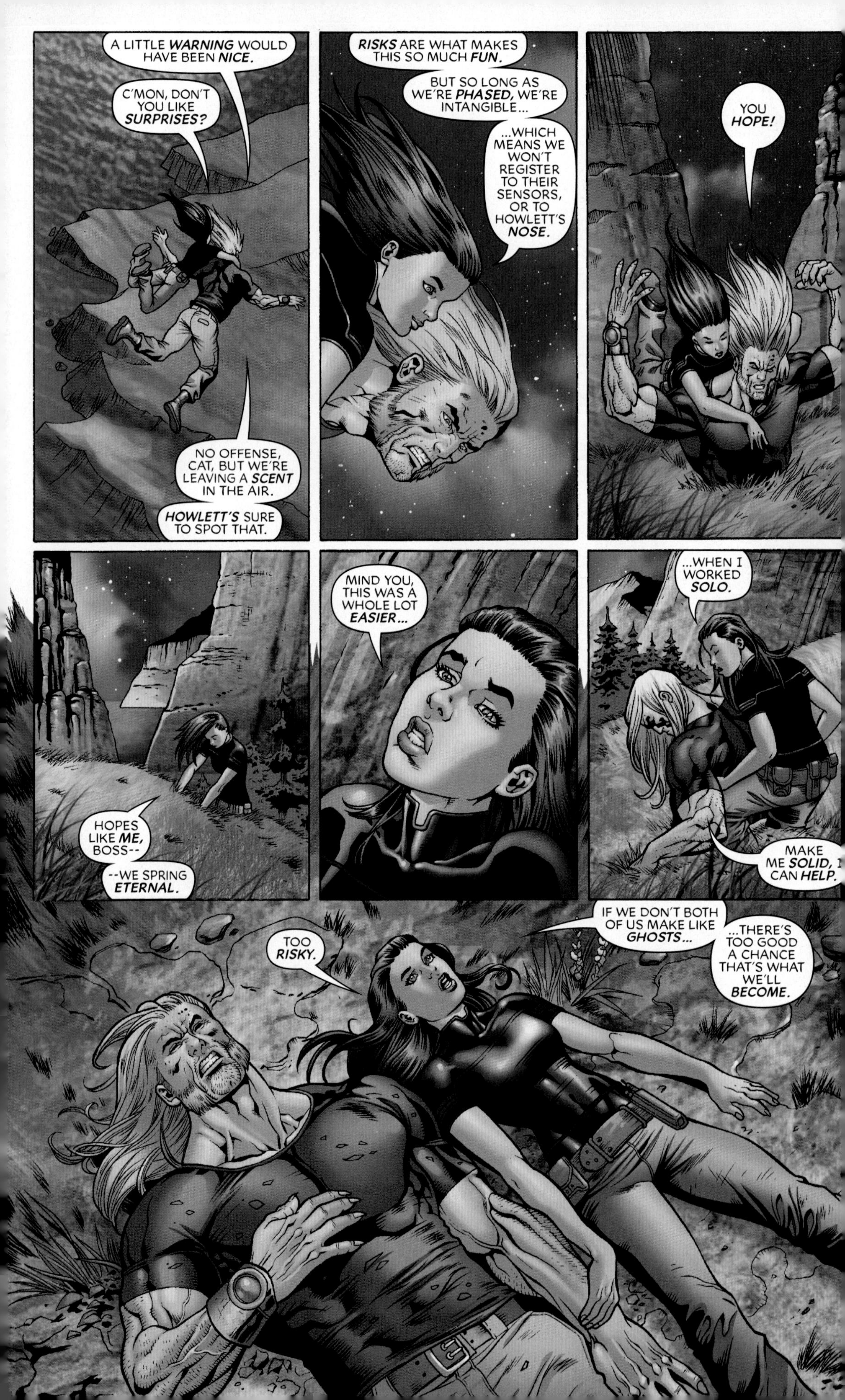

A LITTLE WARNING WOULD HAVE BEEN NICE.
C'MON, DON'T YOU LIKE SURPRISES?
NO OFFENSE, CAT, BUT WE'RE LEAVING A SCENT IN THE AIR.
HOWLETT'S SURE TO SPOT THAT.
RISKS ARE WHAT MAKES THIS SO MUCH FUN.
BUT SO LONG AS WE'RE PHASED, WE'RE INTANGIBLE...
...WHICH MEANS WE WON'T REGISTER TO THEIR SENSORS, OR TO HOWLETT'S NOSE.
YOU HOPE!
HOPES LIKE ME, BOSS--
--WE SPRING ETERNAL.
MIND YOU, THIS WAS A WHOLE LOT EASIER...
...WHEN I WORKED SOLO.
MAKE ME SOLID, I CAN HELP.
TOO RISKY.
IF WE DON'T BOTH OF US MAKE LIKE GHOSTS...
...THERE'S TOO GOOD A CHANCE THAT'S WHAT WE'LL BECOME.

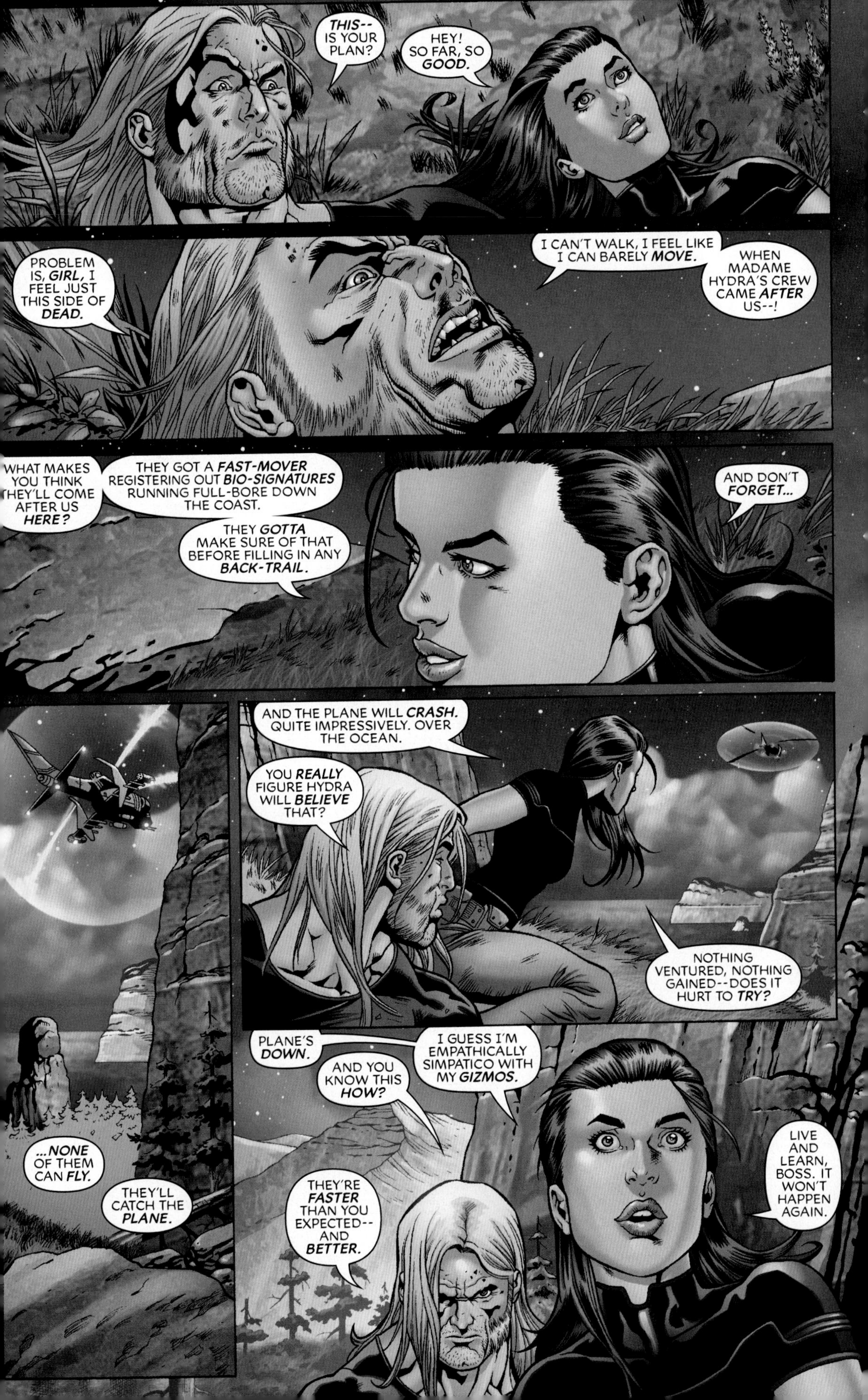

THIS-- IS YOUR PLAN?
HEY! SO FAR, SO GOOD.
PROBLEM IS, GIRL, I FEEL JUST THIS SIDE OF DEAD.
I CAN'T WALK, I FEEL LIKE I CAN BARELY MOVE.
WHEN MADAME HYDRA'S CREW CAME AFTER US--!
WHAT MAKES YOU THINK THEY'LL COME AFTER US HERE?
THEY GOT A FAST-MOVER REGISTERING OUT BIO-SIGNATURES RUNNING FULL-BORE DOWN THE COAST.
THEY GOTTA MAKE SURE OF THAT BEFORE FILLING IN ANY BACK-TRAIL.
AND DON'T FORGET...
...NONE OF THEM CAN FLY.
THEY'LL CATCH THE PLANE.
AND THE PLANE WILL CRASH. QUITE IMPRESSIVELY. OVER THE OCEAN.
YOU REALLY FIGURE HYDRA WILL BELIEVE THAT?
NOTHING VENTURED, NOTHING GAINED--DOES IT HURT TO TRY?
PLANE'S DOWN.
AND YOU KNOW THIS HOW?
I GUESS I'M EMPATHICALLY SIMPATICO WITH MY GIZMOS.
THEY'RE FASTER THAN YOU EXPECTED-- AND BETTER.
LIVE AND LEARN, BOSS. IT WON'T HAPPEN AGAIN.

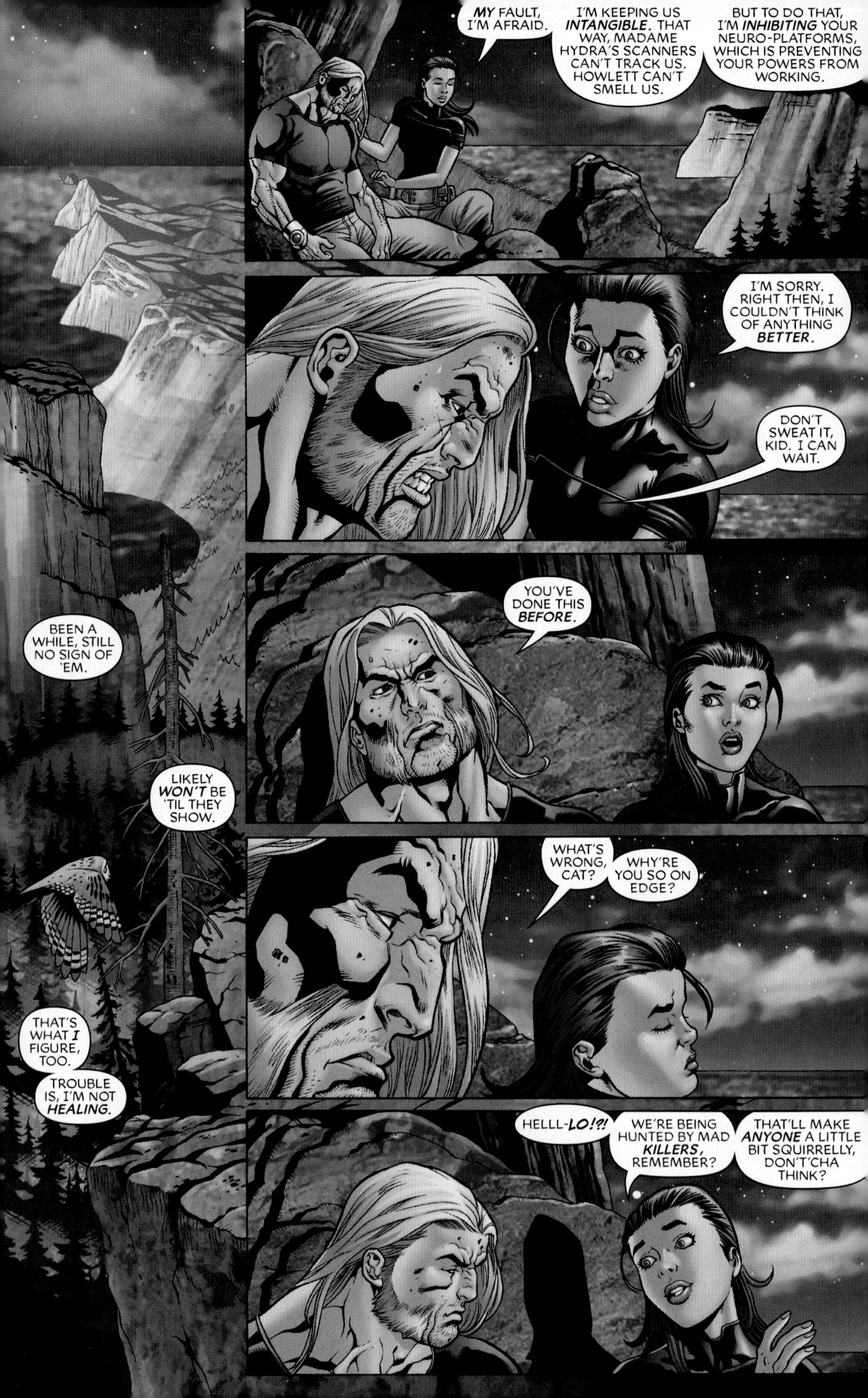
MY FAULT, I'M AFRAID.
I'M KEEPING US INTANGIBLE. THAT WAY, MADAME HYDRA'S SCANNERS CAN'T TRACK US. HOWLETT CAN'T SMELL US.
BUT TO DO THAT, I'M INHIBITING YOUR NEURO-PLATFORMS, WHICH IS PREVENTING YOUR POWERS FROM WORKING.
I'M SORRY. RIGHT THEN, I COULDN'T THINK OF ANYTHING BETTER.
DON'T SWEAT IT, KID. I CAN WAIT.
BEEN A WHILE, STILL NO SIGN OF 'EM.
YOU'VE DONE THIS BEFORE.
LIKELY WON'T BE 'TIL THEY SHOW.
WHAT'S WRONG, CAT?
WHY'RE YOU SO ON EDGE?
THAT'S WHAT I FIGURE, TOO.
TROUBLE IS, I'M NOT HEALING.
HELLL-LO!?!
WE'RE BEING HUNTED BY MAD KILLERS, REMEMBER?
THAT'LL MAKE ANYONE A LITTLE BIT SQUIRRELLY, DON'T'CHA THINK?

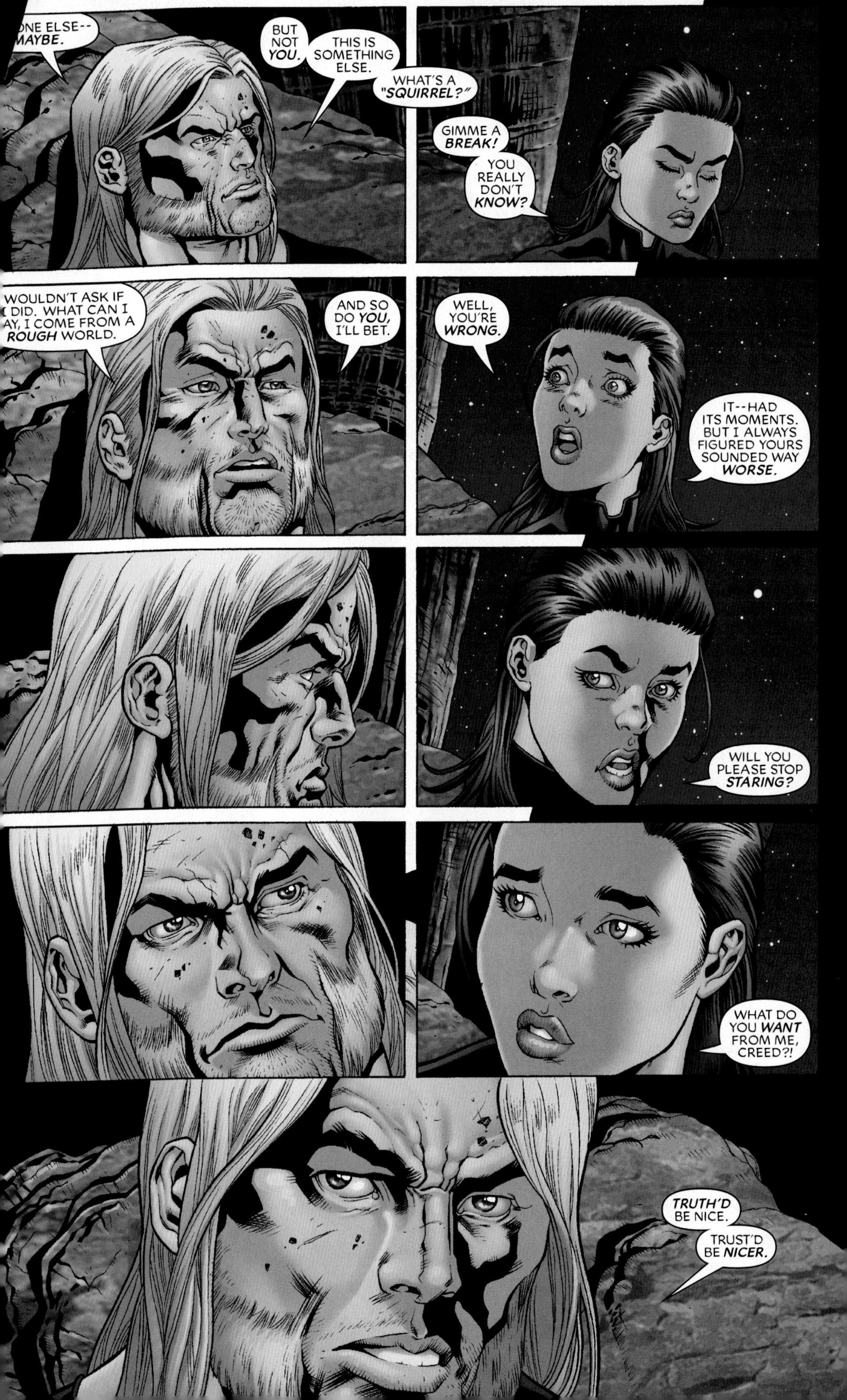
ONE ELSE--
MAYBE.
BUT NOT YOU.
THIS IS SOMETHING ELSE.
WHAT'S A "SQUIRREL?"
GIMME A BREAK!
YOU REALLY DON'T KNOW?
WOULDN'T ASK IF I DID. WHAT CAN I SAY, I COME FROM A ROUGH WORLD.
AND SO DO YOU, I'LL BET.
WELL, YOU'RE WRONG.
IT--HAD ITS MOMENTS. BUT I ALWAYS FIGURED YOURS SOUNDED WAY WORSE.
WILL YOU PLEASE STOP STARING?
WHAT DO YOU WANT FROM ME, CREED?!
TRUTH'D BE NICE.
TRUST'D BE NICER.

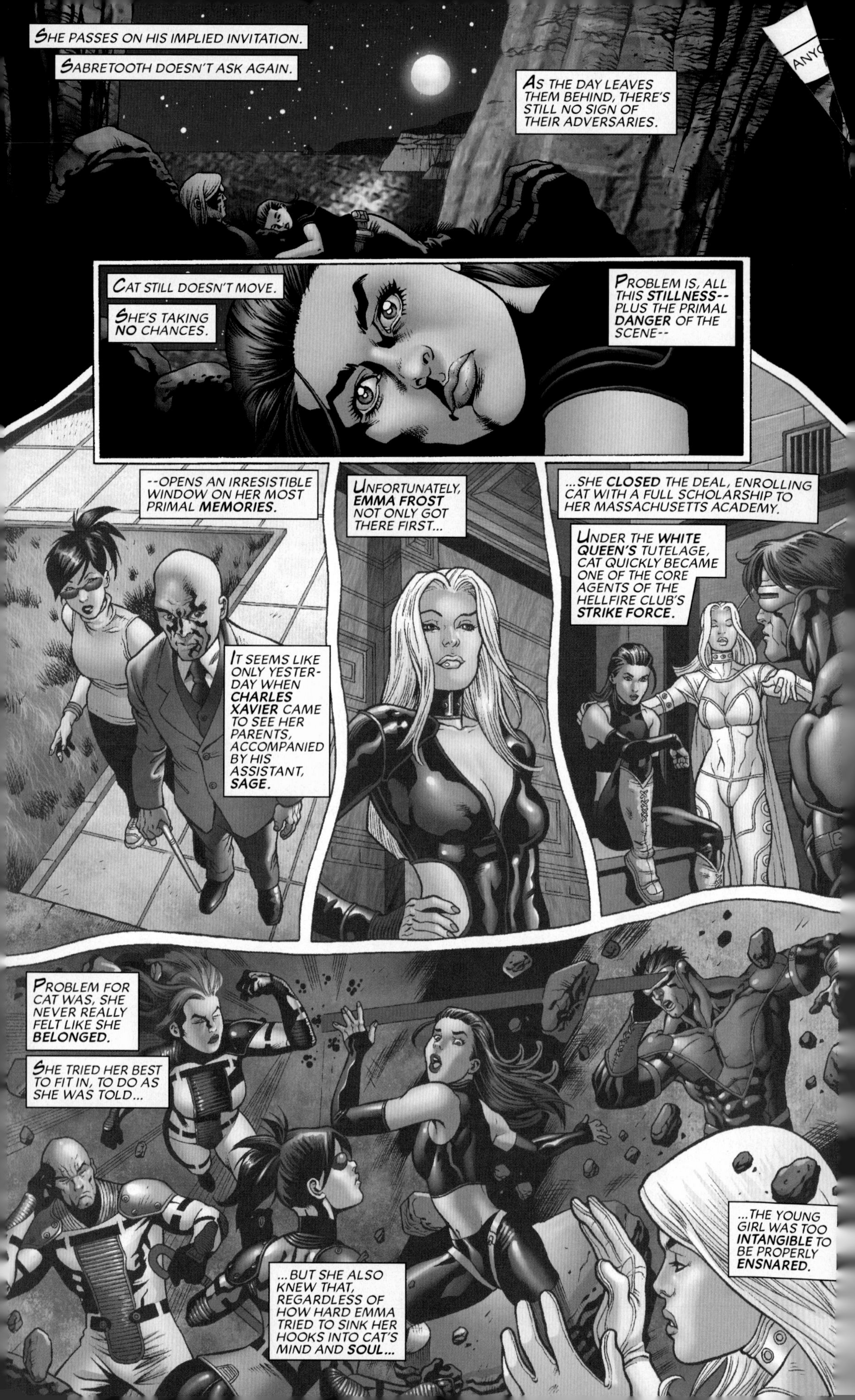
SHE PASSES ON HIS IMPLIED INVITATION.
SABRETOOTH DOESN'T ASK AGAIN.
AS THE DAY LEAVES THEM BEHIND, THERE'S STILL NO SIGN OF THEIR ADVERSARIES.
CAT STILL DOESN'T MOVE.
SHE'S TAKING NO CHANCES.
PROBLEM IS, ALL THIS STILLNESS-- PLUS THE PRIMAL DANGER OF THE SCENE--
--OPENS AN IRRESISTIBLE WINDOW ON HER MOST PRIMAL MEMORIES.
IT SEEMS LIKE ONLY YESTER-DAY WHEN CHARLES XAVIER CAME TO SEE HER PARENTS, ACCOMPANIED BY HIS ASSISTANT, SAGE.
UNFORTUNATELY, EMMA FROST NOT ONLY GOT THERE FIRST...
...SHE CLOSED THE DEAL, ENROLLING CAT WITH A FULL SCHOLARSHIP TO HER MASSACHUSETTS ACADEMY.
UNDER THE WHITE QUEEN'S TUTELAGE, CAT QUICKLY BECAME ONE OF THE CORE AGENTS OF THE HELLFIRE CLUB'S STRIKE FORCE.
PROBLEM FOR CAT WAS, SHE NEVER REALLY FELT LIKE SHE BELONGED.
SHE TRIED HER BEST TO FIT IN, TO DO AS SHE WAS TOLD...
...BUT SHE ALSO KNEW THAT, REGARDLESS OF HOW HARD EMMA TRIED TO SINK HER HOOKS INTO CAT'S MIND AND SOUL...
...THE YOUNG GIRL WAS TOO INTANGIBLE TO BE PROPERLY ENSNARED.

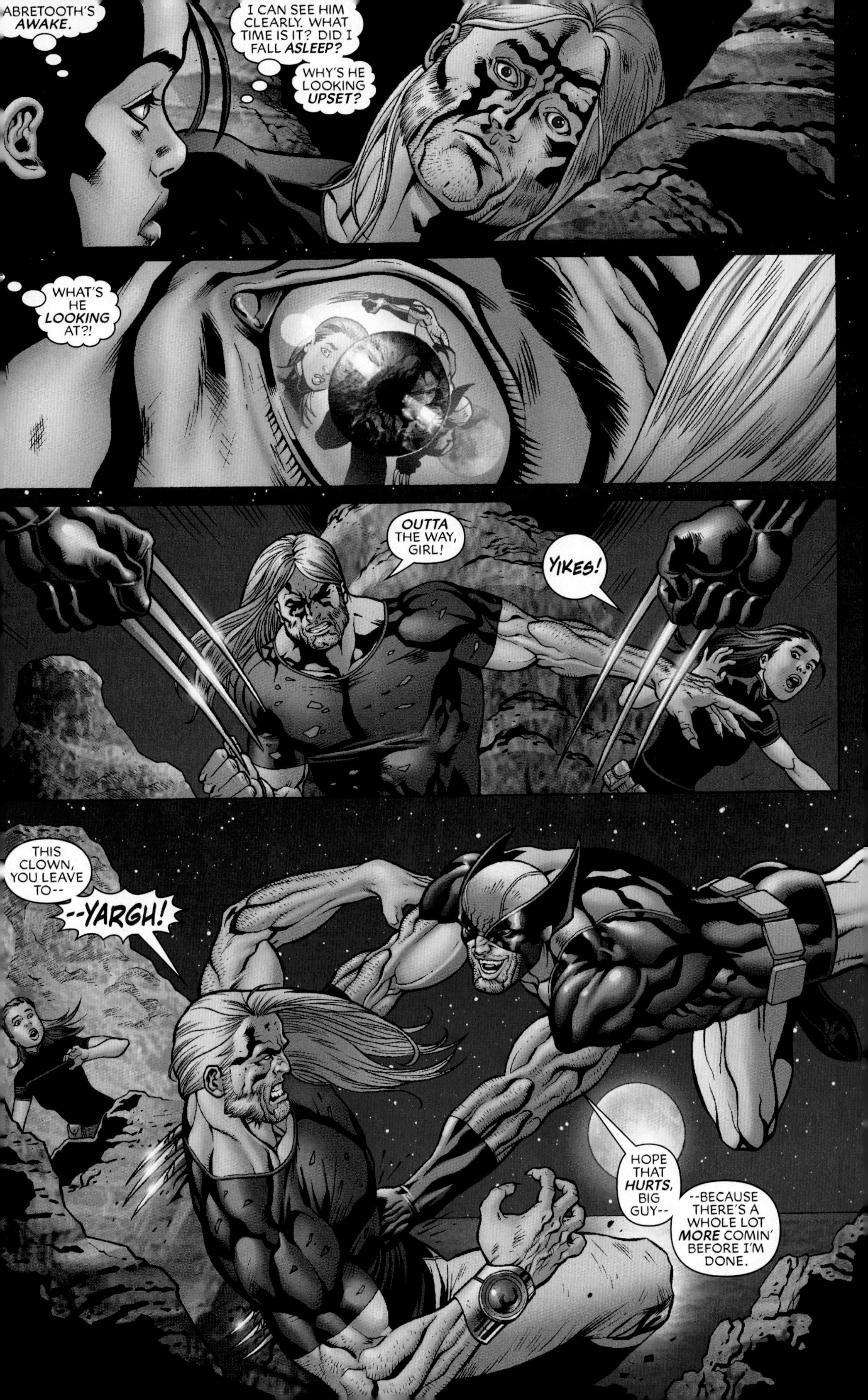
ABRETOOTH'S AWAKE.
I CAN SEE HIM CLEARLY. WHAT TIME IS IT? DID I FALL ASLEEP?
WHY'S HE LOOKING UPSET?
WHAT'S HE LOOKING AT?!
OUTTA THE WAY, GIRL!
YIKES!
THIS CLOWN, YOU LEAVE TO--
--YARGH!
HOPE THAT HURTS, BIG GUY--
--BECAUSE THERE'S A WHOLE LOT MORE COMIN' BEFORE I'M DONE.

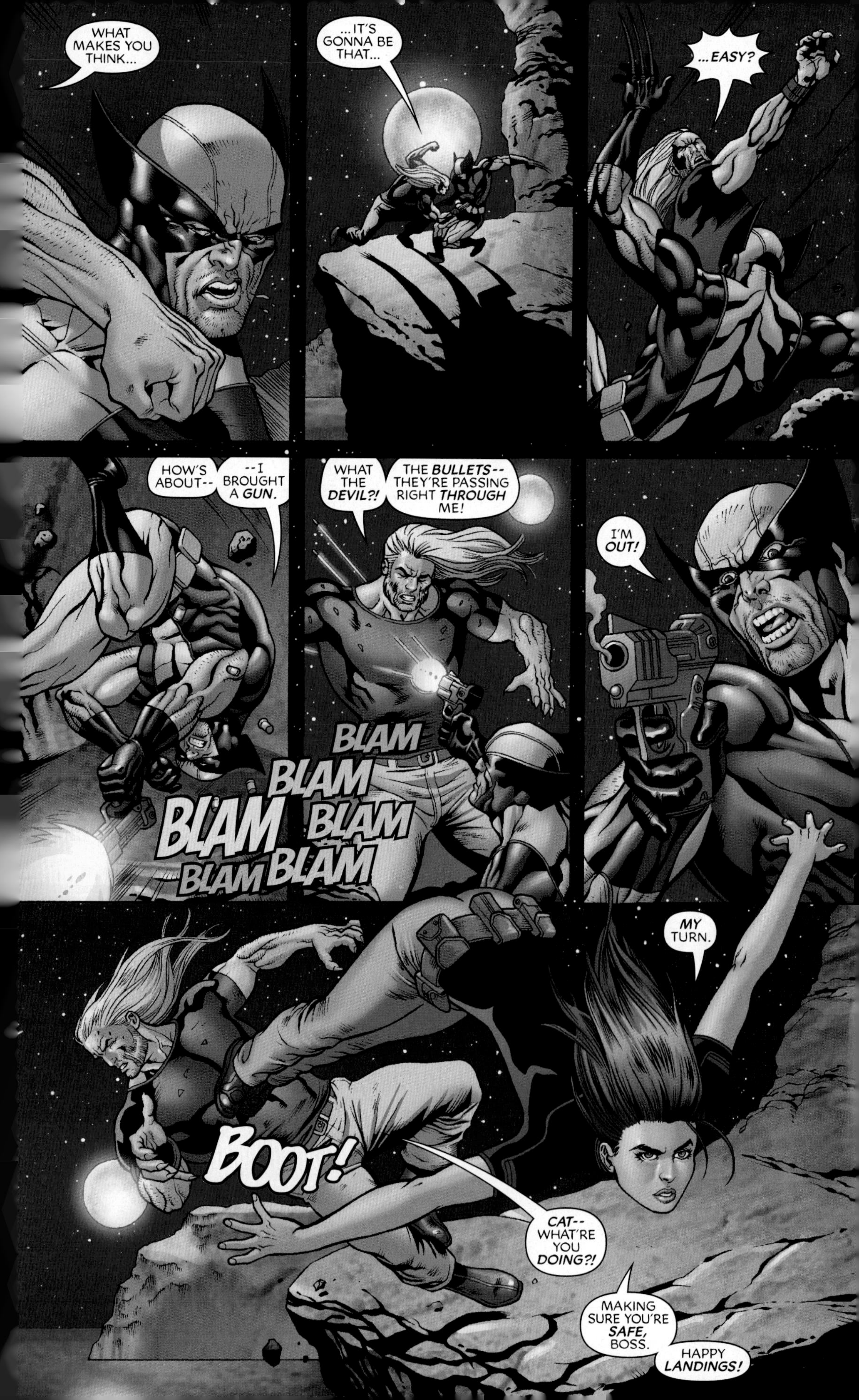

WHAT MAKES YOU THINK...
...IT'S GONNA BE THAT...
...EASY?
HOW'S ABOUT--
--I BROUGHT A GUN.
WHAT THE DEVIL?!
THE BULLETS-- THEY'RE PASSING RIGHT THROUGH ME!
BLAM
BLAM
BLAM BLAM
BLAM BLAM
I'M OUT!
MY TURN.
BOOT!
CAT-- WHAT'RE YOU DOING?!
MAKING SURE YOU'RE SAFE, BOSS.
HAPPY LANDINGS!

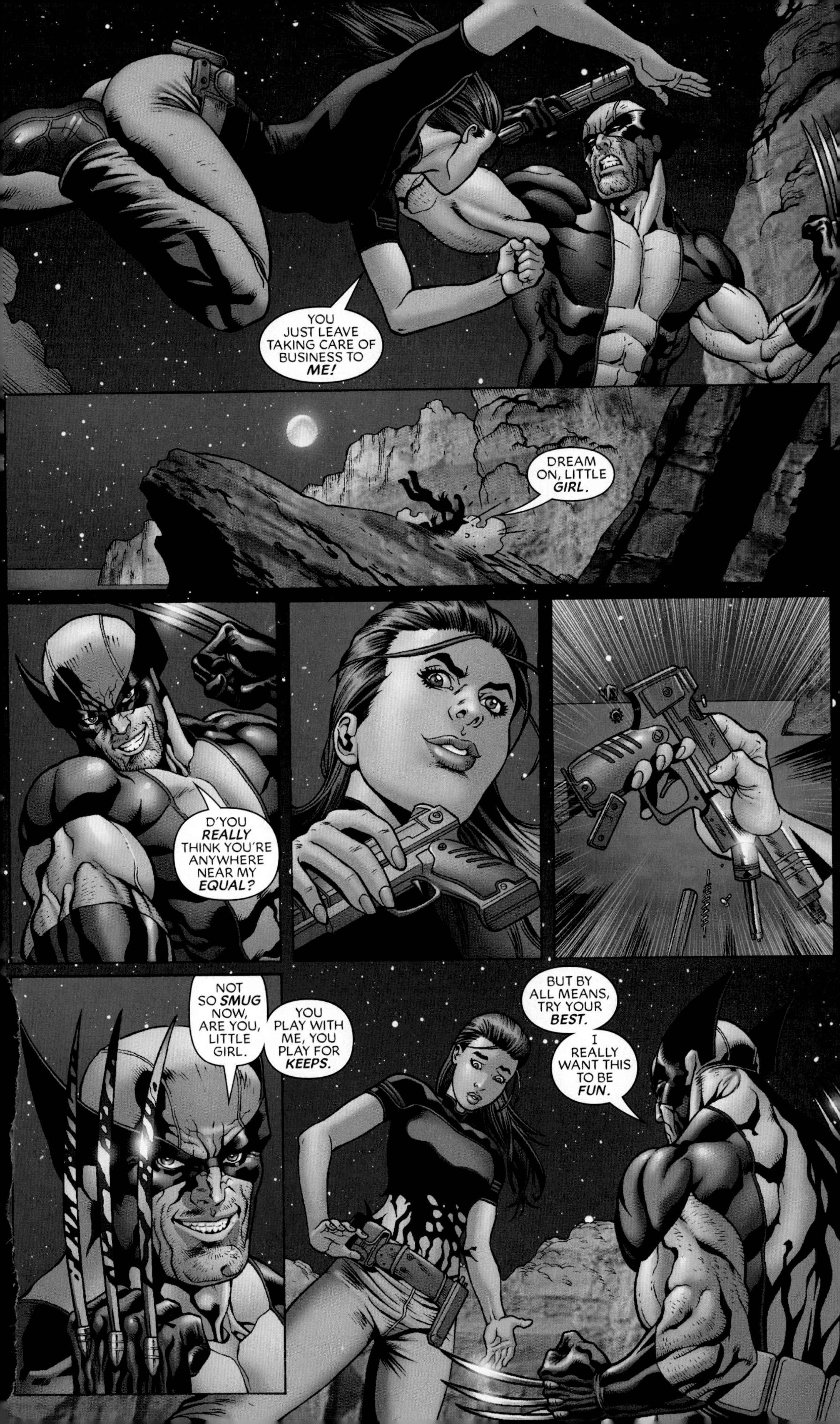
YOU JUST LEAVE TAKING CARE OF BUSINESS TO ME!
DREAM ON, LITTLE GIRL.
D'YOU REALLY THINK YOU'RE ANYWHERE NEAR MY EQUAL?
NOT SO SMUG NOW, ARE YOU, LITTLE GIRL.
YOU PLAY WITH ME, YOU PLAY FOR KEEPS.
BUT BY ALL MEANS, TRY YOUR BEST.
I REALLY WANT THIS TO BE FUN.

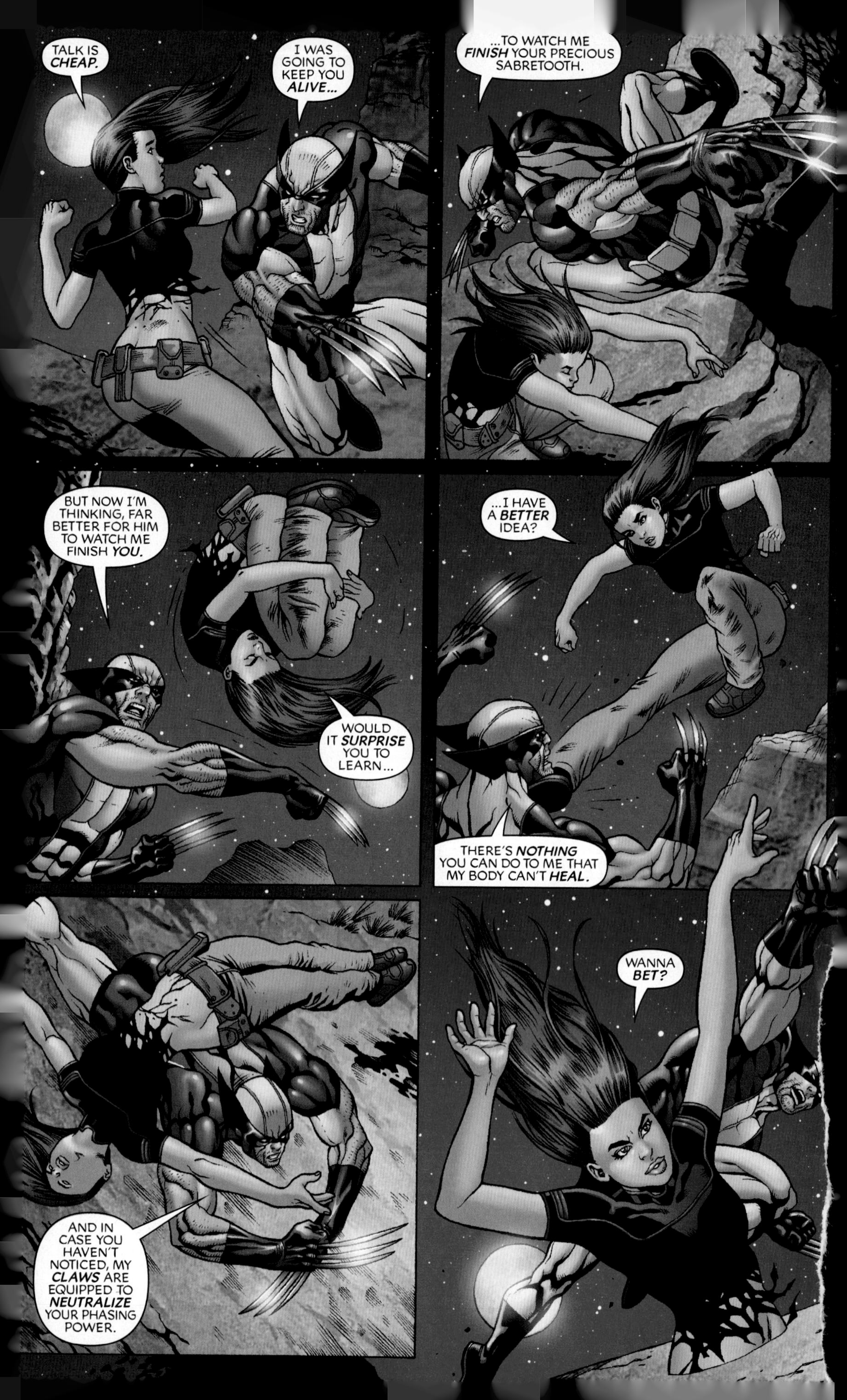
TALK IS CHEAP.
I WAS GOING TO KEEP YOU ALIVE...
...TO WATCH ME FINISH YOUR PRECIOUS SABRETOOTH.
BUT NOW I'M THINKING, FAR BETTER FOR HIM TO WATCH ME FINISH YOU.
WOULD IT SURPRISE YOU TO LEARN...
...I HAVE A BETTER IDEA?
THERE'S NOTHING YOU CAN DO TO ME THAT MY BODY CAN'T HEAL.
AND IN CASE YOU HAVEN'T NOTICED, MY CLAWS ARE EQUIPPED TO NEUTRALIZE YOUR PHASING POWER.
WANNA BET?

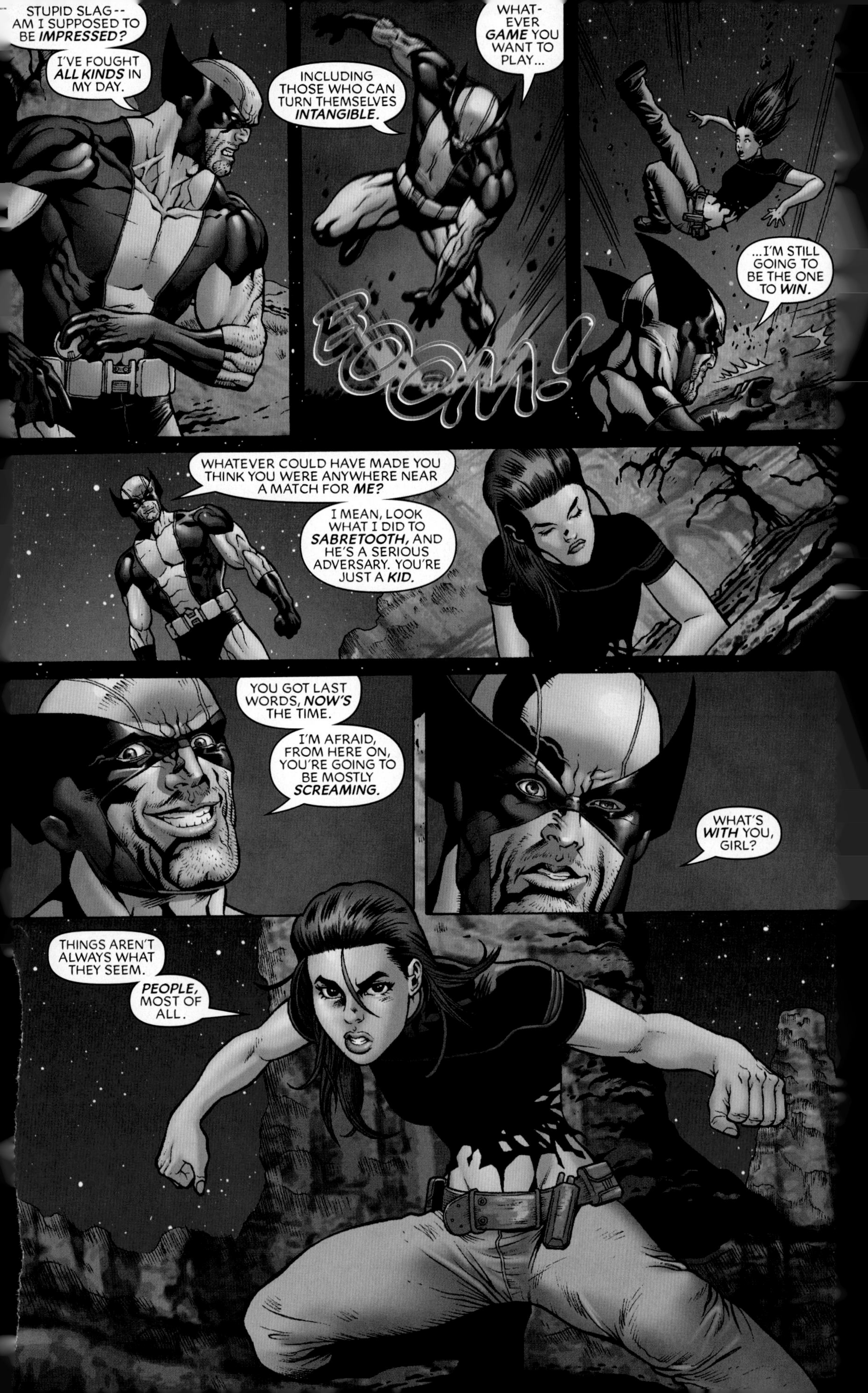
STUPID SLAG-- AM I SUPPOSED TO BE IMPRESSED?
I'VE FOUGHT ALL KINDS IN MY DAY.
INCLUDING THOSE WHO CAN TURN THEMSELVES INTANGIBLE.
WHAT-EVER GAME YOU WANT TO PLAY...
BOOOM!
...I'M STILL GOING TO BE THE ONE TO WIN.
WHATEVER COULD HAVE MADE YOU THINK YOU WERE ANYWHERE NEAR A MATCH FOR ME?
I MEAN, LOOK WHAT I DID TO SABRETOOTH, AND HE'S A SERIOUS ADVERSARY. YOU'RE JUST A KID.
YOU GOT LAST WORDS, NOW'S THE TIME.
I'M AFRAID, FROM HERE ON, YOU'RE GOING TO BE MOSTLY SCREAMING.
WHAT'S WITH YOU, GIRL?
THINGS AREN'T ALWAYS WHAT THEY SEEM.
PEOPLE, MOST OF ALL.

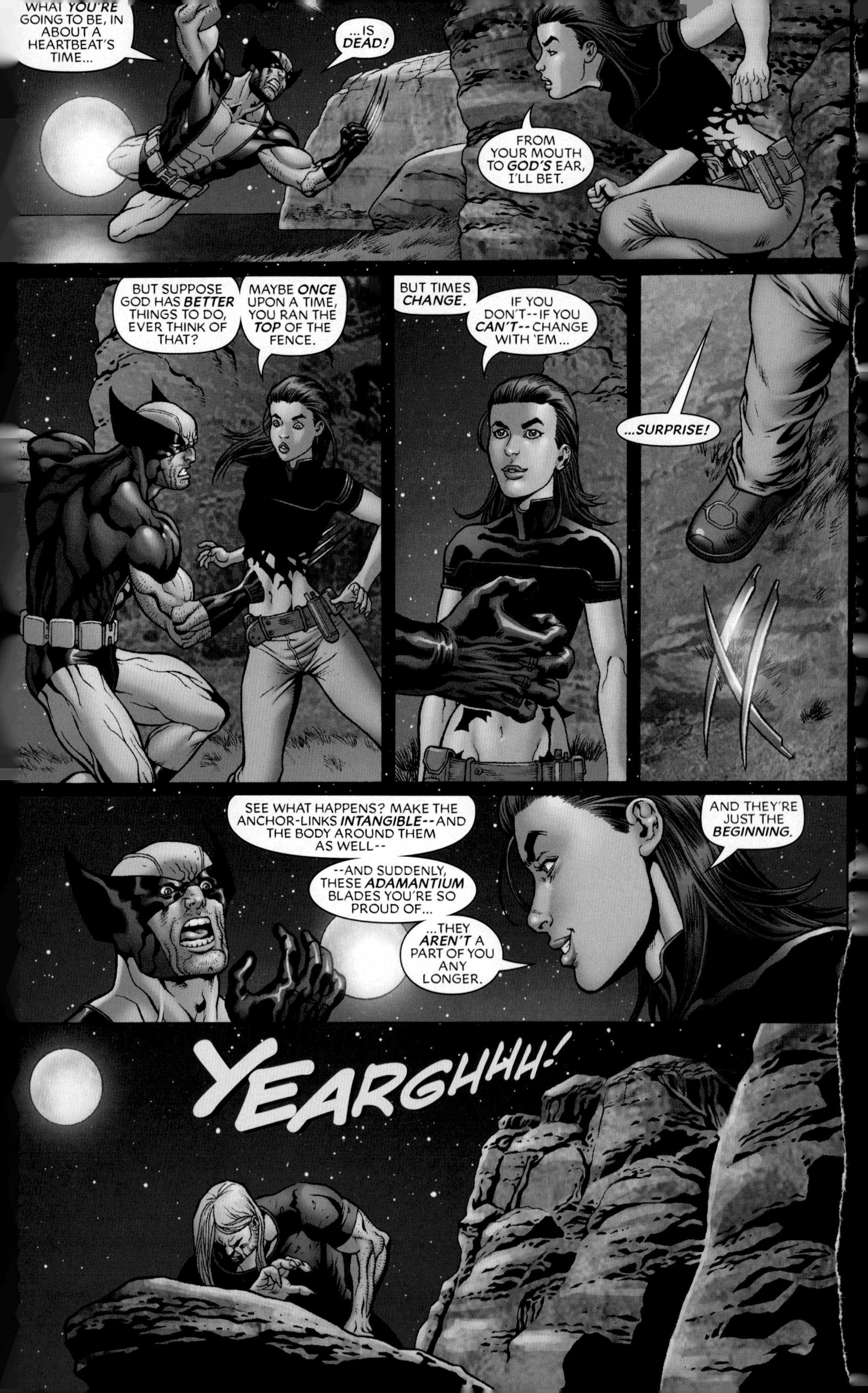
WHAT YOU'RE GOING TO BE, IN ABOUT A HEARTBEAT'S TIME...
...IS DEAD!
FROM YOUR MOUTH TO GOD'S EAR, I'LL BET.
BUT SUPPOSE GOD HAS BETTER THINGS TO DO, EVER THINK OF THAT?
MAYBE ONCE UPON A TIME, YOU RAN THE TOP OF THE FENCE.
BUT TIMES CHANGE.
IF YOU DON'T--IF YOU CAN'T--CHANGE WITH 'EM...
...SURPRISE!
SEE WHAT HAPPENS? MAKE THE ANCHOR-LINKS INTANGIBLE--AND THE BODY AROUND THEM AS WELL--
--AND SUDDENLY, THESE ADAMANTIUM BLADES YOU'RE SO PROUD OF...
...THEY AREN'T A PART OF YOU ANY LONGER.
AND THEY'RE JUST THE BEGINNING.
YEARGHHH!

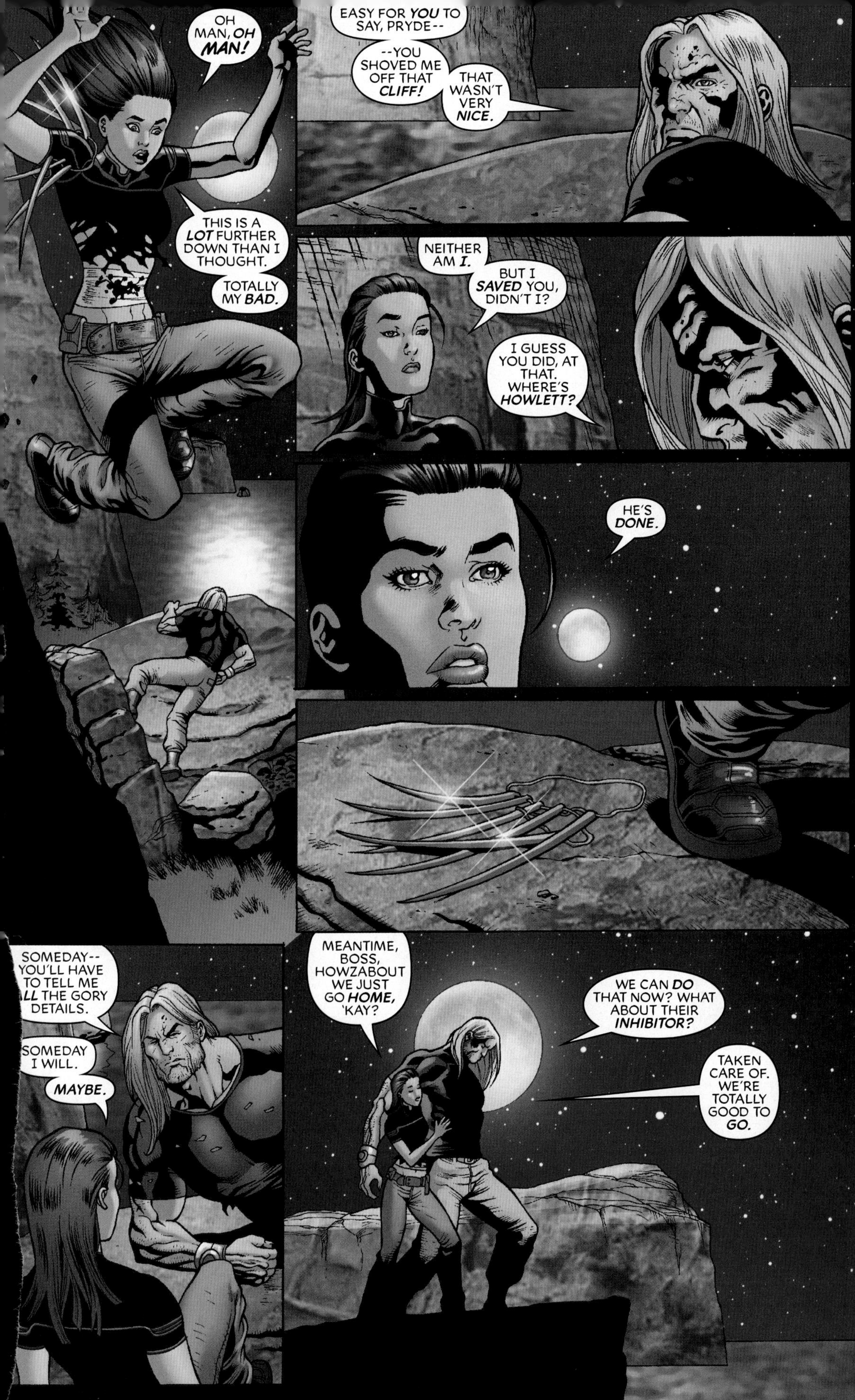
OH MAN, OH MAN!
THIS IS A LOT FURTHER DOWN THAN I THOUGHT.
TOTALLY MY BAD.
EASY FOR YOU TO SAY, PRYDE--
--YOU SHOVED ME OFF THAT CLIFF!
THAT WASN'T VERY NICE.
NEITHER AM I.
BUT I SAVED YOU, DIDN'T I?
I GUESS YOU DID, AT THAT. WHERE'S HOWLETT?
HE'S DONE.
SOMEDAY-- YOU'LL HAVE TO TELL ME ALL THE GORY DETAILS.
SOMEDAY I WILL.
MAYBE.
MEANTIME, BOSS, HOWZABOUT WE JUST GO HOME, 'KAY?
WE CAN DO THAT NOW? WHAT ABOUT THEIR INHIBITOR?
TAKEN CARE OF. WE'RE TOTALLY GOOD TO GO.

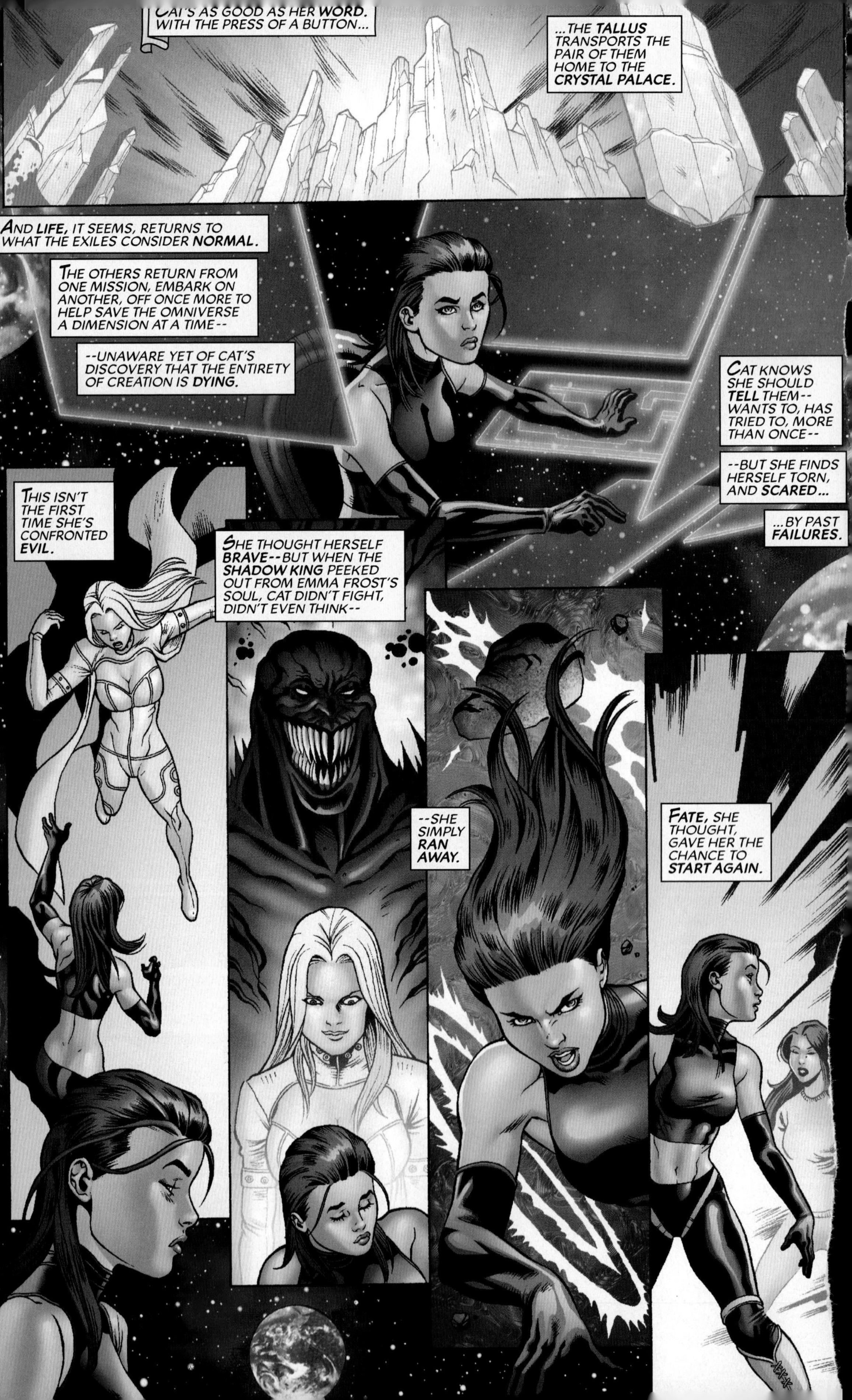
CAT'S AS GOOD AS HER WORD. WITH THE PRESS OF A BUTTON...
...THE TALLUS TRANSPORTS THE PAIR OF THEM HOME TO THE CRYSTAL PALACE.
AND LIFE, IT SEEMS, RETURNS TO WHAT THE EXILES CONSIDER NORMAL.
THE OTHERS RETURN FROM ONE MISSION, EMBARK ON ANOTHER, OFF ONCE MORE TO HELP SAVE THE OMNIVERSE A DIMENSION AT A TIME--
--UNAWARE YET OF CAT'S DISCOVERY THAT THE ENTIRETY OF CREATION IS DYING.
CAT KNOWS SHE SHOULD TELL THEM--WANTS TO, HAS TRIED TO, MORE THAN ONCE--
--BUT SHE FINDS HERSELF TORN, AND SCARED...
...BY PAST FAILURES.
THIS ISN'T THE FIRST TIME SHE'S CONFRONTED EVIL.
SHE THOUGHT HERSELF BRAVE--BUT WHEN THE SHADOW KING PEEKED OUT FROM EMMA FROST'S SOUL, CAT DIDN'T FIGHT, DIDN'T EVEN THINK--
--SHE SIMPLY RAN AWAY.
FATE, SHE THOUGHT, GAVE HER THE CHANCE TO START AGAIN.

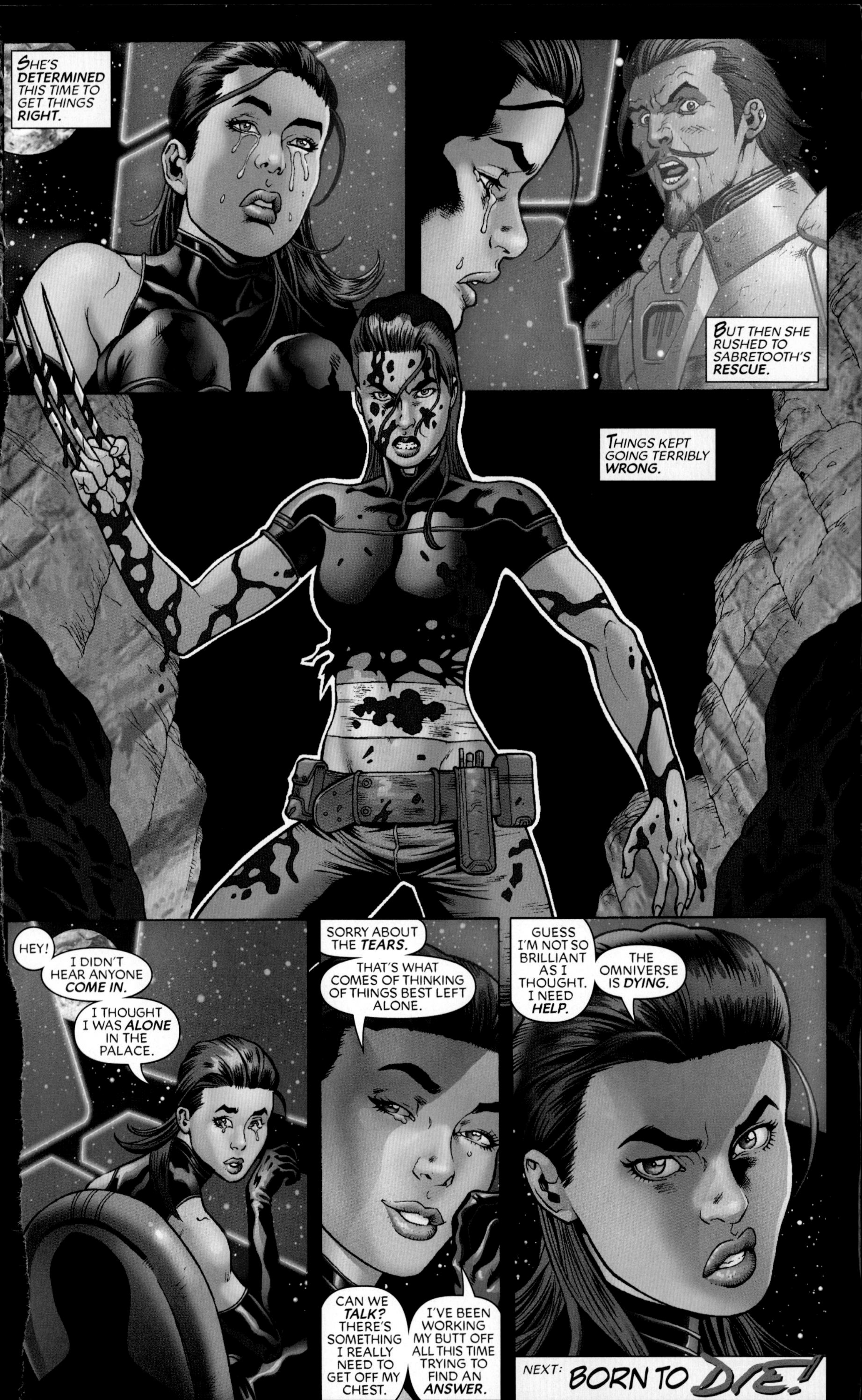
SHE'S DETERMINED THIS TIME TO GET THINGS RIGHT.
BUT THEN SHE RUSHED TO SABRETOOTH'S RESCUE.
THINGS KEPT GOING TERRIBLY WRONG.
HEY!
I DIDN'T HEAR ANYONE COME IN.
I THOUGHT I WAS ALONE IN THE PALACE.
SORRY ABOUT THE TEARS.
THAT'S WHAT COMES OF THINKING OF THINGS BEST LEFT ALONE.
CAN WE TALK? THERE'S SOMETHING I REALLY NEED TO GET OFF MY CHEST.
I'VE BEEN WORKING MY BUTT OFF ALL THIS TIME TRYING TO FIND AN ANSWER.
GUESS I'M NOT SO BRILLIANT AS I THOUGHT. I NEED HELP.
THE OMNIVERSE IS DYING.
NEXT: BORN TO DIE!